CIVILIZING CHENGDU

Harvard East Asian Monographs, 186

Civilizing Chengdu

Chinese Urban Reform, 1895–1937

Kristin Stapleton

Published by the Harvard University Asia Center
and distributed by Harvard University Press
Cambridge (Massachusetts) and London, 2000

Printed in the United States of America

The Harvard University Asia Center publishes a monograph series and, in coordination with the Fairbank Center for East Asian Research, the Korea Institute, the Reischauer Institute of Japanese Studies, and other faculties and institutes, administers research projects designed to further scholarly understanding of China, Japan, Vietnam, Korea, and other Asian countries. The Center also sponsors projects addressing multidisciplinary and regional issues in Asia.

Library of Congress Cataloging-in-Publication Data
Stapleton, Kristin Eileen.
   Civilizing Chengdu : Chinese urban reform, 1895–1937 / Kristin Stapleton.
     p. cm. -- (Harvard East Asian monographs ; 186)
   Includes bibliographic references and index.
   ISBN 0-674-00246-6 (alk. paper)
   1. Urbanization--China--Chengdu. 2. City planning--China--Chengdu. 3. China--History--20th century. I. Title: Chinese urban reform, 1895-1937. II. Title. III. Series.
HT147.C48 S76 2000
307.1'216'095138—dc21

HT147
.C48
S76
2000

99-059751

Index by the author

⊗ Printed on acid-free paper

Last figure below indicates year of this printing
10 09 08 07 06 05 04 03 02 01 00

An earlier version of Chapter 7 appeared as "Yang Sen in Chengdu: Urban Planning in the Interior," in Joseph W. Esherick, ed., *Remaking the Chinese City: Modernity and National Identity, 1900–1950* (Honolulu: University of Hawaii Press, 1999), 90–104.

To Jiang Mengbi 姜夢弼 (1919–)

and the memory of Li Jieren 李劼人 (1891–1962)

ACKNOWLEDGMENTS

The research on which this book is based was supported by the Committee on Scholarly Communication with China, the Harvard University History Department, the NCR Foundation, the University of Kentucky Research Foundation, and the National Endowment for the Humanities. For their invaluable assistance, I would like to thank the archivists at the First and Second Historical Archives and the Sichuan Provincial Archives and Chengdu Municipal Archives in the People's Republic of China, as well as at the Academia Sinica and Academia Historica in Taiwan and the United Church Archives in Toronto.

Many teachers and friends have commented on this project over the years. I am particularly grateful to Philip A. Kuhn, Mary Backus Rankin, William C. Kirby, Jerome Chen, David Strand, Joseph W. Esherick, Christopher Reed, Judy Wyman, Di Wang, Nancy Park, Tom Stapleton, Lee McIsaac, Mingzheng Shi, Andrea McElderry, and my colleagues in the Department of History of the University of Kentucky. Dick Gilbreath of the University of Kentucky Cartography Lab designed the maps. Gregory Epp helped see the project through in many ways.

This book is dedicated to two natives of Chengdu—a novelist whose fiction is itself a tribute to the city and the friend who did more than anyone else to acquaint me with its history.

K.S.

CONTENTS

Reference Matter

MAPS AND FIGURES

CIVILIZING CHENGDU

INTRODUCTION

Between 1895 and 1937, the management of cities emerged as one of the Chinese state's chief challenges in the minds of many officials and other political activists. Due in part to the influence of European ideas and colonial cities in East Asia, the city as a distinctive political and social entity attracted unprecedented attention from Chinese political theorists. Drawing on Western models as well as established Chinese institutions, urban reformers sought to remake Chinese cities by promoting a new type of orderly and productive urban community in population centers that before had been treated mainly as hubs for trade and seats of central government. Proponents of this new order borrowed the Japanese concept of *bunmei* ("civilization"; Chinese: *wenming*) to characterize the new values they wished to instill. *Wenming* evoked Japan's success in establishing itself as a world power by selected borrowing of ideas and institutions from Western Europe and the United States. It implied not a rejection of China's own great and ancient civilization but a desire to re-energize that civilization by infusing it with innovative institutions and ideals. Among the institutions and ideals that seemed to have propelled first the West and then Japan to economic wealth and international power were those dedicated to promoting public health, public safety, trade, and civic pride. Through *wenming*, reformers sought to strengthen China by increasing the capacity of the state to harness the energies of the populace for the sake of the nation.

In one form or another, the struggle to imbue cities with *wenming* lasted some forty years before the urban-oriented political agenda of the late Qing and early Republican periods gave way to the "problem of the countryside" that preoccupied political activists as diverse as Mao Zedong and the conservative agrarian reformer Liang Shuming. Not until the era of Deng Xiaoping in the 1980s did Chinese cities again achieve the prominence in Chinese politics that they had enjoyed from 1895 to 1937. This study investigates the history of urban planning and administration during modern China's first age of city-centered politics. Once the city had been identified as an important arena for social and institutional change, those charged with urban governance faced the challenge of transforming the city. I examine how successive administrators responded to this challenge.

My focus is the provincial capital of Sichuan, Chengdu. Under the Qing, provincial capitals had no city administration. Rather, they were home to a bewildering and varied array of governments. Depending on the capital, a governor-general, a governor, a prefect, a circuit intendant, and one or more county magistrates, not to mention military, educational, and judicial officials, could be responsible for various overlapping jurisdictions, both geographical and topical, within the city. Most, including Chengdu, were also the chief cultural and commercial centers of their region and attracted a large population of merchants and the cultural elite. The central government left urban affairs largely to the local officials, and maintenance of public order was their chief if not only concern. Large-scale, systematic programs for civic improvement were rare before 1895. Even after 1895, cities were not immediately seen as distinct or particularly important arenas for social change, and no special importance was attached to city administration except insofar as the provincial capitals served as convenient showcases in which to begin implementation of new policies provincewide. As this study of Chengdu illustrates, despite policy reversals and setbacks, four decades of efforts to promote *wenming* transformed the city in many ways. Perhaps the greatest change was the acceptance of the idea of city administration itself. Rather than studying the national- and provincial-level officials who authorized reform, however, I seek to explain this transformation by examining the motives and actions of the second-tier officials who implemented specific programs and of the people of the city to whom the new policies were applied. The tensions between and among these protagonists of the reform movement illustrate the complexity of the process and the practical difficulties of implementing reforms.

The city of Chengdu lies over 1,000 miles west of Shanghai and about 800 miles from Canton. Despite its distance from centers of foreign influence in China, the city's political prominence as the capital of Sichuan province ensured that urban innovations elsewhere in China and around the world quickly became known to Chengdu activists. Yet the city's reformers developed their plans in an environment relatively free from overt imperialist pressure, which allowed them room to experiment and to build new urban institutions that incorporated existing features of the local administration. Chengdu administrators were innovative in some ways, but their visions of the appearance and organization of a modern, civilized city were strongly influenced by ideas that were simultaneously transforming cities throughout the world. Insofar as reform in other cities in China's interior was shaped by these same ideas and by the same legacies from the Qing administrative system and late imperial social patterns, Chengdu's experience with urban reform is generally representative of that in cities distant from the coast and the capital. In some ways, however, reform in Chengdu was influenced by the city's particular circumstances.

The book is organized around two important urban reform programs in the fifty years before the establishment of the People's Republic of China: the New Policies of the late Qing period (initiated in 1901) and the city administration movement of the 1920s. The latter was in many ways a revival of the late Qing reforms, but with a more explicitly urban focus.

During the first wave of reform in the late Qing, the most important model of urban administration was Tokyo. The Japanese reforms of the Meiji period had long attracted the attention of those Chinese who believed that their own political and economic systems had to change to respond effectively to the challenges of imperialism. When the foreign powers forced the Qing court to accept a reform program after the defeat of the Boxer uprising in 1901, thousands of Chinese traveled to Tokyo to learn how the Japanese had become powerful enough to defeat their Chinese neighbors in the war of 1894–95 and to threaten Russia in northeast Asia. The New Policies reforms launched in the final decade of Qing rule reflected the concern about national strength. Because of the widespread belief that the power of a nation depended on the attainment of particular attributes of modern "civilization," such as urban sanitation, a disciplined, martial citizenry, and modern armaments, the New Policies included a wide range of administrative and civic reforms. Most leading reformers did not consider the New Policies strictly urban in emphasis; they were not, for example, intended to change the relationship between city and countryside within the Chinese political system. A striking result of the way the reforms were implemented, however, was the remarkable transformation that occurred in many of China's provincial capitals, including Chengdu. Because the provincial cities were seen as models for other administrative units to emulate, money and energy were poured into these cities to make the reform program a success. Even after the money ran out and revolution dissipated the energy behind the reforms, the provincial cities were left with new institutions and ways of thinking that set them apart from their hinterlands in significant ways.

After an introductory chapter that describes Chengdu and its administrative traditions at the end of the nineteenth century, the book examines the origins and nature of the New Policies reform movement and introduces the men who were instrumental in bringing it to Chengdu. Among these, Zhou Shanpei (1875–1958) was the most important. The son of a Qing county magistrate, Zhou joined the wave of young Chinese who went to Japan to study its success. While serving six Sichuan governors-general in Chengdu between 1902 and 1912, Zhou Shanpei established a police force, helped reform the city's welfare system, bringing it firmly within the purview of the state, took charge of promoting industry in Chengdu, and contributed to the redesign of the city's public spaces. His career in the first ten years of the twentieth century shows that the ill-fated Qing dynasty could still command the services, if not the unquestioning loyalty, of talented and energetic civil administrators.

The new police system, described in Chapter 3, was the key to the New Policies because it was intended to create the disciplined subjects needed by the modern state. However, the new institution achieved some but not all of the aims of its supporters. Although Chengdu's force seems to have been relatively free of the corruption that had, from the point of view of officials, hobbled the system it replaced, the new constables by no means shared their superiors' enthusiasm for disciplining the populace. Nevertheless, Chengdu's police reform was judged a success by many, and it set a pattern for police organization in the city throughout the subsequent Republican period.

Chapter 4 provides a detailed look at the impact of the New Policies on Chengdu's social and physical structure and demonstrates that significant changes occurred in several areas. The state, for example, took greater responsibility for social welfare, in the interest of increasing the economic productivity of city residents and "cleaning up" the streets. Zhou Shanpei and other officials began to coordinate economic development projects in the city, such as the new electric lighting plant and telephone system. In the course of these activities, they altered the appearance of the city, erecting new buildings and paving some streets. They also introduced to Chengdu features associated with modern cities in Japan and the West, such as public parks, shopping arcades, and public theaters. In Chengdu, however, the primary focus of the New Policies remained firmly on institutional and social reform rather than on physical changes in the city. Zhou Shanpei also tried to transform the place of women in public life by encouraging theaters to set aside sections for women and creating a plan to upgrade Chengdu's squalid and illicit red-light district into an elegant "licensed zone" à la Tokyo. It was here that Zhou met the most ardent opposition from Chengdu's elite; they scuttled his plans to allow women to share theaters with men and protested vehemently against the idea that the state should legitimize prostitution. Usually, however, Zhou was successful in rallying elite support for his plans; he was a skillful politician who used his close connections with influential residents to good advantage. A case in point is the new chamber of commerce, which cooperated with him in promoting his development plans.

Because of Zhou Shanpei's skill, many of his reform projects were firmly established by the time the next major element of the New Policies reforms was introduced in Chengdu (Chapter 5). By the turn of the century, many Chinese had come to believe that China could be strong only if its people became citizens: full participants in the political processes that determined national priorities and local government. By 1906 they had persuaded the Qing court to allow local assemblies to be formed and to play a part in public affairs. When provincial, county, and city assemblies gathered in Chengdu beginning in 1909 and began to look for matters in which to involve themselves, they left Zhou Shanpei's initiatives pretty much alone. Given the relative maturity of institutions like the police in Chengdu, the assemblies would have found it difficult to insert themselves into their management, even if the state had been willing to give them a role. As it was, the provincial government tried to limit the assemblies to a subordinate, advisory position. The government was successful, on the whole, with the county and city councils in Chengdu, although outside the capital such councils were often quite active. The provincial assembly, for its part, challenged the government over the provincewide issue of the ownership of railroads planned to link Sichuan to eastern China. The tremendous uproar in Chengdu when the Qing government announced in 1911 that it planned to grant the rights to railroad construction and management to foreigners in exchange for a loan eventually brought Qing rule to an end. Chapter 5 concludes with a discussion of the 1911 Revolution in Chengdu, with particular reference to the role played by the police force and other New Policies institutions and ideas.

The fall of the Qing marks a sharp turning point in Chengdu's history. The political fragmentation of the Republican period lessened the significance of Chengdu's status as a provincial capital. The near constant warfare that plagued Sichuan between 1911 and 1935 cut off Chengdu from its hinterland and from much of the rest of the country at times. Chapters 6 and 7 explore how the city evolved and managed itself in the absence of the familiar authority of a powerful governor-general and in the midst of civil war that brought it under the control of a succession of militarists concerned chiefly with fending off rivals. Chapter 6 shows that some Qing institutions, including the police force, survived this period but began a slow decline as the funds that had supported them were diverted to Sichuan's expanding armies. The local assemblies disbanded and reconvened several times but never exerted much authority over local affairs. More influential were two groups who together filled the administrative vacuum created by the indifference of Chengdu's militarist leaders toward civic affairs: the "gowned brothers" and the prominent men known as the Five Elders and Seven Sages.

"Gowned brother" was the name given in Chengdu to a member of the network of underground brotherhood organizations, or secret societies, that had spread across Sichuan in the late Qing. These groups had played a visible and crucial role in the revolutionary events of 1911, and for a short time their leaders became public heroes, lauded in Chengdu's press and by the new government. The secret societies were soon banned once again but continued to play an important role in Chengdu. A large percentage of men joined brotherhoods, and their leaders became powerful forces in the community, adjudicating disputes and controlling markets. Wealthy families were careful to maintain good relations with them, since there was no effective state security apparatus to protect them from kidnappings and other threats. The Five Elders and Seven Sages occupied a very different position in Chengdu society. They were Chengdu's most prominent scholars, degree holders from the old Qing system and prestigious teachers. Even the militarists felt obliged to accord them respect. Because of their leverage and moral training, the Elders and Sages believed they had a responsibility to speak for the community when the militarists trampled too viciously on local interests. In efforts to mediate for the city, they sometimes joined with foreign missionaries, who also exerted a degree of power over the militarists. The YMCA, in particular, attempted to persuade Chengdu's militarists to support its projects for benefiting the city.

The YMCA was partly responsible for bringing to Chengdu the city administration movement, the second great wave of reform and the topic of Chapter 7. This movement developed as an offshoot of a worldwide interest in urban reform that in the early twentieth century produced settlement houses in the United States, the Garden City movement in England, and a range of other innovations in urban design and administration. Chinese students who encountered these innovations while abroad brought them back to China, set up programs in urban administration at colleges in Beijing and Shanghai, and founded professional associations to promote a new ideal of the modern city. Where the Qing New Policies had envisioned a disciplined community in service to the modernizing state, this new movement emphasized scientific rationality in planning, sometimes even in defiance of nationalist feeling, although usually the two were judged to be congruous. Unlike the New Policies reforms, the city administration movement, which saw the problems of cities as different from those of rural areas, focused specifically on urban reform. In Chengdu, in contrast to the New Policies focus on institutional development, this second wave of reform emphasized strengthening the infrastructure and recasting the form of the city. In the 1920s, plans were drawn up for every part of the modern city, each by an appropriate specialist. The planners went to work with special vigor in Shanghai, but they attracted supporters in other major cities in China also.

Their champion in Chengdu was Yang Sen (1884–1977), the military leader who fought his way into possession of the city in 1923, only to be driven out again a year and a half later. In that brief period, however, Chengdu was "modernized" with a vengeance. Yang Sen, a veteran of Sichuan's civil wars, hoped to build a reputation as an administrator and to this end seized on and promoted the philosophy and projects of the city administration movement. Yang was particularly infatuated with modern transportation systems and had many of Chengdu's neighborhoods torn up to widen and pave the streets. Yang Sen also supported a range of infrastructural and social initiatives proposed by the YMCA leadership and other adherents of the city administration movement. Unlike Zhou Shanpei, however, he was not an astute politician, and his approach alienated many and hindered accomplishment of his aims. Had not some of Yang's reforms been quietly revived in gentler form with the help of the Elders and Sages after he left Chengdu, his influence on the city might have been fleeting indeed. The Elders did what they could to remove the iconoclastic "scientific" and "rational" flavor from the projects of the 1920s, and with their intervention, the city administration movement in Chengdu ultimately led to a revival of the late Qing style of urban reform, which persisted into the 1930s.

The book concludes with a chapter reflecting on the changes in the administration of Chengdu between 1895 and 1937, when it became a center for refugees escaping the Japanese occupation of eastern China. Over these years, Chengdu had a rich history of urban reform. In the Qing period, it had been counted as one of the most "progressive" cities in the empire. Relative decline had set in thereafter, but the reforms of the 1920s introduced many of the infrastructural innovations that were transforming coastal Chinese cities. The ambitions of the city's urban architects of the Republican period were thwarted, however, by a combination of local resistance, political instability, and lack of funds. To them, the new prominence of Sichuan as the center of resistance to the Japanese afforded another chance to advance their projects to redesign and develop the city, but the governmental and academic refugees from the east who poured into the city in the late 1930s had little interest in these schemes. To the easterners, Chengdu was a temporary haven from the ravages of war, frustrating yet charming in its bucolic backwardness and conservatism. Laying claim to parts of the city that had been remade by prewar urban authorities, outsiders made them even more jarringly foreign to the natives. Chengdu's wartime experience did much to erase the legacy of its earlier urban reformers. Nevertheless, Chengdu's appearance, culture, and administration changed fundamentally between 1895 and 1937, and in the new urban era of the 1980s it is possible to see shades of the urban reform activism that began at the end of the Qing.

The New Policies thus left a lasting legacy to China's provincial capitals, where the reforms were implemented with the greatest energy. In Chengdu, Zhou Shanpei successfully established new institutions with the help of a supportive reform community. He was a politically adept practitioner of traditional Chinese statecraft, working within the system to bring about innovation for the traditional aim of strengthening and maintaining the state. His accomplishments were overtaken by the unrest of the revolution, and reform languished. Eventually, however, Zhou's work provided a foundation for later reforms begun by the warlord Yang Sen and continued by professional city planners in a milieu in which city administration had become an important activity in its own right and was connected to an international movement. By then, change and tumult had created a topsy-turvy situation in which the reform era of 1901–11 was viewed with conservative nostalgia by those in Chengdu who sought a model for contemporary governance. In the history of reform in Chengdu, we can see how officials and residents of Chinese cities came to believe in city administration and grappled with the question of how it should and could be accomplished.

I LATE IMPERIAL CHENGDU, PROVINCIAL CITY

Shengcheng—Provincial City—is the name commonly used in the late nineteenth century for the walled enclave that occupied portions of Huayang and Chengdu counties in western Sichuan. The name points to the most significant fact about the city in the era when the Qing bureaucratic system still flourished. Within its walls of earth and brick stood the clusters of official buildings—the yamen—that housed Sichuan province's highest officials. The rigorously educated and experienced men who governed from the yamen of the provincial city were appointed by the emperor in Beijing, who charged them with keeping the peace, collecting taxes, and elevating the morals of inhabitants of the province. From the earliest construction of a walled city on this site, which at the latest was in 310 B.C.E.,[1] up to the end of the nineteenth century, Chengdu's rulers generally saw it not as an important economic and social unit in itself but as a command post from which to govern a broader territory. This task had never been as complicated and demanding as it was in the last decades of the Qing dynasty, when officials in their Chengdu headquarters claimed authority over a province that was home to some fifty million people.[2]

For the majority of the inhabitants of Chengdu, who numbered more than 300,000 at the end of the Qing dynasty,[3] one might sup-

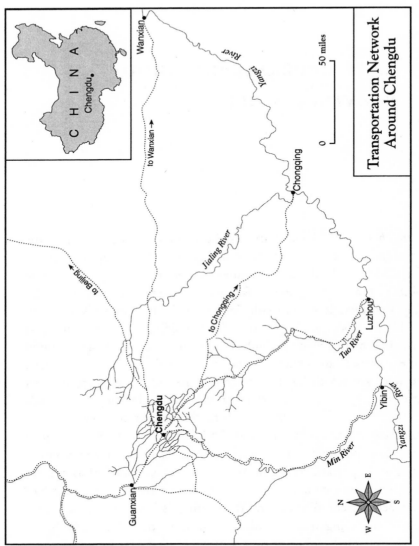

Map 1. Chengdu's geographical setting. Redrawn from Hubbard 1923.

pose that the city's status as administrative center was secondary to the daily pleasures and trials of living in a Chinese city. Chengdu shared certain characteristics with many other Chinese cities at the time and, indeed, with many nonindustrial cities across the world. At the same time, Chengdu's distinctive history and geographic setting (see Map 1), at the center of a rich agricultural region on the western frontier of the waning Qing empire, made life there different from that in other provincial capitals. Still, there is no doubt that the residents of Chengdu were quite conscious of the high administrative status of their city—it affected their lives in too many ways for them not to have been.

Premodern Chinese city, prosperous juncture between settled farmland and Tibetan highland, provincial city—all these identities contributed to Chengdu's urban character and conditioned the lives of its inhabitants in the late nineteenth century. The reformers whose projects form the subject of this book were well aware of the physical, political, economic, and social structures of early twentieth-century Chengdu. The inspiration behind their efforts to "civilize" the city, as many of them thought of their work, lay largely outside Chengdu— in other parts of China or the world or even in other eras of history, as we shall see. Nevertheless, because they tried to implement their visions in Chengdu, they were forced to face up to the "flesh and stone" of Chengdu, as it had developed over the centuries.[4] And so must we, if we are to understand their actions and the consequences. Some aspects of Chengdu's earlier history are considered in more detail in subsequent chapters. This one aims to impart a sense of the city and its administrative traditions, as they existed at the end of the nineteenth century.

Chengdu as a Premodern Chinese City

Like the great majority of Chinese cities before the modern era, Chengdu was surrounded and divided by walls (see Map 2).[5] The main city wall was roughly rectangular, tilted slightly off the north–south axis favored by ancient city-planning guidelines in China.[6]

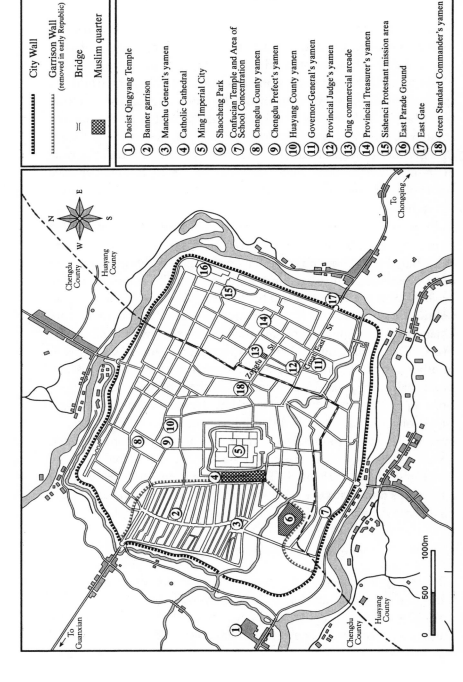

	City Wall
	Garrison Wall (removed in early Republic)
)(	Bridge
▨	Muslim quarter

① Daoist Qingyang Temple
② Banner garrison
③ Manchu General's yamen
④ Catholic Cathedral
⑤ Ming Imperial City
⑥ Shaocheng Park
⑦ Confucian Temple and Area of School Concentration
⑧ Chengdu County yamen
⑨ Chengdu Prefect's yamen
⑩ Huayang County yamen
⑪ Governor-General's yamen
⑫ Provincial Judge's yamen
⑬ Qing commercial arcade
⑭ Provincial Treasurer's yamen
⑮ Sishenci Protestant mission area
⑯ East Parade Ground
⑰ East Gate
⑱ Green Standard Commander's yamen

Map 2. Chengdu in the late Qing. Redrawn from a map in Tō-A dōbunkai 1917.

Thirty to forty feet high and about eight miles long, the city wall consisted of an outer face of stone and brick and an inner face, composed primarily of large bricks, forty feet inside the outer face. In between the two, packed earth made up the bulk of the wall. On top of the earth, large stone slabs gave the wall a smooth upper surface[7] (see Fig. 1.1 for a section of the city wall and a gate). As they rose above the rivers that circled the city like a moat, Chengdu's walls appeared quite formidable. When the heavy rains fell in the summer months, however, the thinner inside face was susceptible to collapse and required frequent maintenance.[8]

As imposing as they may have been visually, Chengdu's walls rarely stood as an unyielding barrier between the worlds outside and inside the four massive gates. Many people lived in the suburbs outside the East and North Gates; hundreds of porters and tons of produce passed through the walls every day, under the gaze of the soldiers assigned to open and close the gates at designated hours and the officials who collected taxes on goods brought into the city. The walls around Chinese cities can be deceptive in their apparently sharp-edged bounding of urban and rural.[9] Figure 1.2 shows some of the thickly settled area outside the North Gate, and Figure 1.3 shows agricultural plots within the walls at the northeast corner of the city.

Foreigners who visited the city early in the twentieth century loved Chengdu's walls for the recreation they afforded.[10] As can be seen in Figure 1.1, stone staircases inside the city led to the top, where a promenade offered views of the surrounding countryside, and even the first peaks of the Tibetan highlands to the west, when the day was clear. Looking inward, one could see all the way across town. As in other Chinese cities, Chengdu's "skyline" was very low and very regular; few buildings exceeded two—or even one and a half—stories. Trees planted in internal courtyards rose above the gray-tiled roofs. In the most densely populated parts of Chengdu in the eastern section, building lots were commonly narrow and deep. Living quarters occupied the rear of each lot, farthest from the street. At the other end, shop fronts or workshops separated by brick fire walls crowded each other along streets rarely wider than twenty feet. Most

Fig. 1.1 A pedestrian walk ran atop the broad city wall of Chengdu. One of the stairways leading up from inside the city can be seen near the gate. (The United Church of Canada / Victoria University Archives, Toronto: catalog no. 98.083P/26.)

construction was of wood and plaster, with some buildings of baked mud and some of sturdier brick. In wealthier areas, such as the northeastern part of town, families could spread out a little more. There, the *gongguan* style of residence (a walled compound with an elaborate gate) prevailed (Fig. 1.4). Inside, space was divided to form the traditional *siheyuan*, or four-sided courtyard residence, with one-story buildings dedicated to various functions surrounding a series of square courtyards with a garden, perhaps, in the rear or along the side.[11] Some *gongguan*-like structures were home to many families, who each rented a part of one of the buildings surrounding the court-yards. Such residences were called *zayuan*, or mixed courts.[12]

The walls surrounding these compounds, which stretched the lengths of the streets in parts of the city, made these areas lonely at night—the narrow stone streets between the long rows of residences were illuminated only by the feeble light of vegetable-oil lanterns

Fig. 1.2 The North Gate of Chengdu seen from outside the city wall. (The United Church of Canada / Victoria University Archives, Toronto: catalog no. 98.083P/24N.)

Fig. 1.3 A 1934 aerial photograph of Chengdu, looking southeast, shows the city's northeast corner. A branch of the Min River flows around each side of the city. The city wall runs along the bend of the river. The East Parade Ground is at the top of the photograph just within the wall. (The United Church of Canada / Victoria University Archives, Toronto: catalog no. 98.083P/11.)

Fig. 1.4 A view of Sishengci Street shows the elegant gateways of the *gongguan* residences that were common in more well-to-do sections of Chengdu. Those seen here were occupied by foreign missionaries. Notations on the back of the photo indicate that the low wall just left of center is the entrance to a public toilet. (The United Church of Canada / Victoria University Archives, Toronto: catalog no. 98.083P/21.)

hanging at the gates to compounds. The livelier business areas of Chengdu had night markets, where merchants set out their wares along streets lined with lanterns.[13] But travel about the city at night was not encouraged. After dark, watchmen who lived in small huts at intersections closed off many streets with tall wooden barriers. Those who wished to pass had to justify their movements and possibly pay a small fee.[14]

Other structures common to Chinese cities up until the establishment of the People's Republic in 1949 were scattered throughout Chengdu: memorial arches that spanned the wider streets, massive temples dedicated to the Buddha and other gods, drum and bell towers, guildhalls, pawnshops and Shanxi banks, teahouses, inns, and public baths.[15] Not all the area within the walls was built up, however; patches of land dedicated to vegetable gardens provided a break in the otherwise largely uniform expanse of tile roofs and treetops.[16] Tall trees grew on temple grounds, most notably in the large Buddhist monastery called the Wenshu (Mañjuśrī in Sanskrit) Academy inside the North Gate. Chengdu residents with leisure time often headed to the temples. The Daoist temple compounds southwest of the city wall and the nearby temples dedicated to the Tang poet Du Fu and to Zhuge Liang, military strategist of the Three Kingdoms period, offered outdoor teahouses with bamboo chairs. Outside the East Gate, close to the docks where boats bound downriver toward Chongqing moored, stood the Thunder God temple, and adjacent to it the River-Watching Pavilion rose above a profusion of bamboo and Xue Tao's Well, where another Tang poet was said to have obtained the water she used to manufacture fine paper.[17]

Chengdu's social organization, like its layout and buildings, shared many characteristics with that of other Chinese cities in the late Qing era. The rich aspired to and often succeeded in building extended, multigenerational households inside their expansive compounds. Their household servants—gatemen, watchmen, cooks, men to carry sedan chairs about town—lived in side buildings. Well-off families also purchased slave girls and concubines from brokers who bought or kidnapped the daughters of poorer families in the city and surrounding countryside.[18] Merchants who could not afford a courtyard house lived with their families in quarters in back of their shops, often with several young apprentices who did the household chores as well as much of the shop work. Less prosperous merchants and artisans rented rooms and sold their merchandise from street stalls or door to door. Many inexpensive articles of daily use, including prepared food, were produced by women and children to be hawked about the city by men. Women of families of moderate or better means generally stayed off the streets or traveled through them in enclosed sedan chairs, except on special occasions, such as festival days. On the sixteenth of the first lunar month, women and men alike strolled along the top of the city walls in a customary quest for good health in the coming year.[19]

Groups larger than families coalesced for a number of purposes. Most of Chengdu's five hundred blocks[20] had at least one local association headed by a director, appointed annually from among the prominent men in the neighborhood. This neighborhood head supervised the collection of fees from each family to support an annual celebration to honor the local spirits through feasting, Daoist ceremonies, shadow-puppet shows, and fireworks. Small shrines to neighborhood deities (*tudimiao*) stood on many streets.[21]

Nominally, at least, most of Chengdu's families were also tied together in the *baojia*, or mutual supervision system, as were all other Chinese communities during the Qing. Missionaries living in Chengdu at the time called this the *tithing system*, because of its resemblance to the frankpledge institution of premodern England.[22] As in England, ten neighboring households were supposed to be grouped together as a unit (a *tithe* in English terminology, a *pai* in the Chinese) and held mutually responsible for overseeing the conduct of all families in the unit. Ten family units in the Chinese system were joined together in a *jia*, and ten *jia* in a *bao*. Ideally, from the standpoint of officials who designed and tried to implement the *baojia* system uniformly across China's cities, towns, and villages, any misconduct or dispute within a multifamily unit was to be reported to the *pai* head, chosen from among the heads of member-households, who would either settle the matter or report it to his superiors, the *jia* and *bao* heads. The *bao* head, who was also a household head, was to serve as the link between the thousand families in his unit and officialdom, reporting any problems in the community to the agents of the formal administration.[23]

Throughout the Qing period, the *baojia* system was an administrative ideal, dear to the hearts of political theorists if not to most of the people who were supposed to be enmeshed in it.[24] The enthusiasm of local officials for implementing the system, however, depended largely on the priorities of their superiors and local social conditions. The extent to which the system actually existed and functioned in Chengdu in the late nineteenth century is discussed in more detail below. Here I note only that the city's population was hardly the rational, orderly collection of disciplined, patriarchal families that the *baojia* ideal seemingly required. The gap in social status between wealthy households and poorer ones would have made the task of "mutual supervision" complicated, to say the least. Moreover, as in other Chinese cities, many of the people who passed through Chengdu's streets were not settled permanently in households, but were transient laborers or beggars. Thousands of men in Chengdu worked as porters and chair bearers, living in huts or small inns and barely earning enough to feed themselves from day to day.[25] Many of them covered long-distance routes that frequently took them out of the city (Fig. 1.5). Beggars were a common sight on Chengdu's streets during the day (Fig. 1.6). At night, they slept under bridges or in one of the dreary "chicken-feather inns" (*jimaodian*) outside the city wall. A foreign traveler recalled seeing hundreds of beggars outside the East Gate as he approached it in 1883, "and it was with difficulty that we pushed our way through the mass of rags and dirt which held the bridge, which spans the stream flowing southwards under the eastern wall."[26] Joshua Vale of the China Inland Mission estimated the beggar population of Chengdu at 15,000 in 1906.[27] Most of them were men. Women who had no place within an economically secure family were more likely to become prostitutes in the brothels concentrated near the eastern wall north of the East Gate. The well-regulated family may have been the anchor of the Qing political and ideological system, but harsh economic conditions ensured that many of Chengdu's inhabitants bobbed about in rocky waters.

Chengdu was home to several types of associations established by men for various purposes and common to most Chinese cities, such as commercial and trade organizations. Prominent among them were native-place associations set up by merchants and officials from other parts of China. Some of these built elaborate guildhalls in Chengdu, equipped with stages for hosting performances of Sichuan's colorful variety of Chinese opera.[28] Associations of craftsmen of all kinds—from masons and carpenters to actors—met in guildhalls or teahouses to settle disputes and set standards and policies for their trades. Like neighborhood and native-place associations, the craft guilds taxed their members to hold annual fairs in honor of their patron gods.

Fig. 1.5 Chair bearers pose with their sedan chairs while transporting missionaries to Chengdu from Chongqing in 1933. (The United Church of Canada / Victoria University Archives, Toronto: catalog no. 98.083P/4.)

Some special festivals belonged to the city as a whole. The popular opera *Mulian Saves His Mother* attracted huge crowds when it was performed every year in a temple outside the North Gate. Three times a year the parade of the city gods wound its way through many streets inside and outside the walls.[29] Once a year, on the eighth day of the fourth lunar month, various small animals purchased for the occasion were given a taste of freedom during the Buddhist festival for releasing life (*fangshenghui*), held beneath the River-Watching Pavilion east of the city walls. The longest running public event was the annual flower festival, said to have first been held during the Tang dynasty. For a month every spring, thousands of people headed every day to the Daoist Qingyang Monastery west of the city walls, where lively entertainments and tempting foods created a favorable environment for merchants selling all manner of agricultural and craft products.[30] Chengdu's winters are not terribly harsh, but they are cold and damp, and it is not hard to imagine the joy with which men and women welcomed the spring at the flower festival. Comparing his experience of the festival to the more regulated pattern of

Fig. 1.6 A few of the beggars who thronged the streets of Qing Chengdu. (The United Church of Canada/Victoria University Archives, Toronto: catalog no. 98.083P/7.)

life in the city at other times, the scholar and writer Guo Moruo (1892–1978) wrote that "it was as if China had become three thousand years younger."[31]

Particularities of Chengdu's History and Geography

As much as it shared with other Chinese cities in physical appearance and social organization at the end of the imperial era, Chengdu was quite distinct in significant ways. Tucked away at the far western edge of Han-dominated territory and isolated from much of the rest of China by rugged mountain ranges, Chengdu was nevertheless not a typical "frontier town."[32] The great agricultural wealth that sustained the city had done so for more than two thousand years, and Chengdu's identity as a cultural and administrative center predated that of a great many eastern Chinese cities.

Chengdu's wealth came from the soil and from water. In the early spring of every year, just before the flower festival got under way, the circuit intendant who oversaw administration in western Sichuan traveled forty miles west of the city to the foothills of the Tibetan plateau and worshipped in a temple dedicated to Second Gentleman (Erlang), the son of Li Bing, who completed his father's great Dujiangyan waterworks on the Min River at Guanxian in the third century B.C.E. Then, the intendant presided over the opening of Dujiangyan's main channel, which was always closed for repairs during the time of low water in the winter. As soon as the temporary dams were breached, he got into his sedan chair, and the bearers raced him back to Chengdu, trying to beat the water.[33]

The farmland along their route is among the most productive in the world. Chengdu sits near the middle of the Chengdu plain, some 2,000 square miles of thick soil carried down the Min and deposited in the basin of what was probably once an inland sea. Li Bing and his son and the laborers they supervised made it possible to irrigate this great expanse of soil by creating a series of dams and channels to divide the Min and send it fanning out over the countryside around Chengdu in innumerable streams and canals, which join up again south and east of the city and then continue south to the Yangzi River. Within the pocket formed by the high mountains to the west of the plain and the lower chains on the other sides, the area around Chengdu is often overcast. Chengdu dogs, the saying goes, bark with surprise when they catch a glimpse of the sun. Nevertheless, the weather is fairly mild all year around, and nineteenth-century farmers could grow two cycles of crops each year in this "Granary of Heaven"—often rice in the summer and then wheat or vegetables in the winter.[34]

Impressive as it was and is, the Dujiangyan water control system did not always work. Even if the channels and dikes were given the careful maintenance they required, flooding was still a threat on the Chengdu plain, although droughts were quite rare in this part of Sichuan.[35] Branches of the Min circled the walls of Chengdu city and one rivulet was allowed inside the walls through a water gate on the west and back out on the east. When heavy rains hit the city, however, this small river often could not carry the water away fast enough, and sections of the town became submerged. At such times, typhoid and cholera devastated the population. A French doctor resident in the city in 1903 witnessed a typhoid epidemic that killed 30,000 people in the city in a month, according to official accounts he was given.[36]

Despite the frequent flooding and outbreaks of disease, however, the fertile Chengdu plain had a very long history as a center of Chinese settlement. "The road to Shu is difficult," wrote the Tang dynasty poet Li Bo, referring to the Chengdu plain by its traditional name, but the wealth to be found there made the trip worthwhile to many an immigrant and certainly to the representatives of successive Chinese states. And, as in other regions of China in the imperial era, aspects of the rich history of the Chengdu plain were publicly flaunted. Monuments to the achievements and tragedies of the local past abounded, written into gazetteers and poetry and carved as images in the temples to heroes such as Liu Bei, the third-century C.E. founder of the Shu-Han dynasty, and his adviser Zhuge Liang or on memorial arches to more obscure but equally virtuous chaste widows and filial sons. Chengdu's history as an imperial city was honored in intangible and tangible ways. It was common knowledge that one of Chengdu's nicknames, Hibiscus City (Rongcheng), had its origin in the Later Shu period, when in 950 C.E. one of the emperors of that short-lived dynasty had those plants cultivated along the top of an outer wall of his imperial capital.[37] At the end of the fourteenth century, the Ming founder Zhu Yuanzhang permanently altered the city's layout by ordering a grand imperial palace built in the middle of Chengdu for his eleventh son, upon whom he bestowed the title Prince of Shu. In Ming times the city was full of royal residences, as successive Princes of Shu built palaces for their offspring.[38]

All that was lost for a time in the second half of the seventeenth century, when Chengdu ceased being a city at all, except in memory and the history books. Zhang Xianzhong, who led a successful uprising against Ming rule in Sichuan, chose Chengdu as the headquarters from which to build his empire. Instead of enriching Sichuan, though, he devastated it, perhaps to encourage his troops to fight on to other parts of China. Unable to repel the advancing Manchu troops of the new Qing dynasty, Zhang reduced Chengdu to rubble in 1647 and killed or drove out most of its inhabitants. Sichuan's population dropped from some 3.1 million in the late Ming to a mere 80,000 in the first years of the Qing era.[39] According to local legend, Zhang paused in his murderous rampage long enough to write down a justification for his actions and have his complaint inscribed on a stone: "Heaven produced the ten thousand beings to nourish humanity; humans have not shown even a single virtue in response. Kill, kill, kill, kill, kill, kill, kill." In the late Qing period, this "Seven Kill" stela was kept in the yamen of the Chengdu county magistrate, carefully guarded. Symbol of Chengdu's saddest days, it was credited with evil powers.[40]

Ambitious and expansionary, the early Qing emperors encouraged the repopulation of Sichuan and sent governors to rebuild Chengdu.[41] The city walls, reconstructed in the early 1660s, enclosed an area slightly larger than that of the Ming city. Immigrants streamed into Sichuan from the eastern provinces, attracted by the rich farmland and Qing promises of tax exemptions. The provincial population surpassed Ming levels by the middle of the eighteenth century and kept growing at a rapid rate. Although the eastern parts of the province were greatly affected by the White Lotus uprisings of the late eighteenth century, the Chengdu plain was not, and it also escaped the devastation visited on much of eastern and central China by the fighting between Qing and Taiping forces in the mid-nineteenth century. Sichuan once again became one of China's wealthiest provinces, producing rice, salt, sugar, silk, and cotton. As Sichuan's economy expanded, Chengdu flourished along with it. As a sign, perhaps, of Chengdu's revitalization, a provincial official had hibiscus planted once more along the wall in 1784.[42]

Despite Chengdu's agricultural wealth, commerce was limited by problems of transportation. It generally took twelve days for porters to walk the 200 miles between Chengdu and Chongqing and fourteen days from Chengdu to Wanxian, further east along the Yangzi, about 275 miles from Chengdu. The trip to Chongqing by river was considerably quicker, but only when the water level allowed it in the summer. Then, getting to the prosperous Jiangnan area, center of much of the domestic and foreign trade, required a trip through the Yangzi River gorges on Sichuan's eastern border, a very risky venture until well into the twentieth century. Salt, rice, medicinal goods from Tibet, and opium did make it through in large quantities in the late nineteenth century, but the merchants who enriched themselves in those trades based themselves in Chongqing and other cities of southeastern Sichuan.[43]

"A Sichuan resident will rarely acknowledge that he belongs to the Province," observed a missionary early in the twentieth century, pointing to one legacy of Sichuan's immigrant history.[44] A local analyst of Chengdu's early twentieth-century population left this description of the inhabitants' origins:

> One-fourth were originally from Hunan and Hubei.
> Three-twentieths were originally from Yunnan and Guizhou.
> One-tenth were originally from Jiangxi.
> One-tenth were originally from Shaanxi.
> One-tenth were originally from Jiangsu and Zhejiang.
> One-tenth were originally from Guangdong and Guangxi.
> One-twentieth were originally from Shandong and Henan.
> One-twentieth were originally from Anhui.
> One-twentieth were originally from Fujian, Gansu, and Shanxi.[45]

Many of the families who moved to Sichuan maintained ties to their old communities, teaching their children the languages of their home regions, returning to participate in rituals to honor ancestors, and bringing in brides from their old villages.[46] As it grew into a large city, Chengdu became much more of a melting pot than did Sichuanese villages, however, and most of its inhabitants spoke a common Sichuanese variant of Mandarin. Provincial origin does not seem to have been an important factor in the makeup of Chengdu's neighborhoods, although it probably played a role in business and marriage ties.

There was, however, a distinct Muslim enclave within the city, located to the west of the Ming imperial city, with nine mosques by the late Qing.[47] According to a census taken in 1909, 2,615 Muslims lived in the city, many employed as butchers, tanners, and restaurateurs.[48] A foreign traveler who passed through Chengdu in the first decade of the twentieth century and took an interest in the Muslim population noted that some had recently arrived from Gansu province, "but the oldsters cherish the memory of their Turkish origin. Though they point with pride to pedigrees of forty generations on Chinese soil, they proudly say they are not Chinese; however little may be the Turcoman blood in their veins, yet they look back to that distant strain, and disclaim local nationality."[49] Chengdu's proximity to Tibet made it a center of commerce between the farming communities of the plain and the hunters and herders of the mountains and grasslands, a trade in which the Muslims took an interest. Tibetans and other peoples of the highlands west of Sichuan visited the city during the winter months, although few remained in the city year-round.

Chengdu as a Provincial City

Chengdu's status as a provincial capital was evident in many ways in the late nineteenth century. The pattern of traffic on the streets announced it. So many high officials traveled into and out of the spacious yamen that pedestrians in the busiest parts of town often had to dodge out of the way of corteges of retainers, who bore placards announcing the identities and virtues of their masters and shouted to clear the path for the sedan chairs or ponies that followed. Much of the area within the walls was occupied by government offices and military parade grounds. And the entire western section of town, one-fifth of the walled area, was divided off from the rest to form the Banner garrison, home to some 20,000 Manchu and Mongol soldiers and civilians in the late Qing (see Map 2).

Shortly after the dynasty established control over the Chinese heartland, the Qing government began to assign soldiers from each of the Eight Banners, the units into which the Manchu people and some of their Mongol and Han allies were organized, to strategic places throughout the empire. Among these key spots were most of the provincial capitals. When it was built at the end of the Kangxi period in 1718, Chengdu's Banner garrison was a concrete symbol of the military superiority that had allowed the Qing rulers to conquer the Chinese heartland and extend their realm throughout the southwest and into Tibet. Chengdu's detachment of 1,600 soldiers set up an orderly camp under the command of a Manchu general in the western part of town, cutting it off from the Han city with another wall. The streets in the garrison were called *hutong*, as were those in the Banner section of Beijing, and, in contrast to the square-block layout that prevailed in the main city, they extended like veins on a leaf from a main north-south artery. At the northwestern end, the garrison controlled the West Gate of the main city wall. At the south end, the Manchu general presided over garrison affairs from a large yamen next to the river that flowed through the entire city. The walls of his yamen were painted with colorful images of deified military heroes, and a large flowering plum tree said to date from the Kangxi era graced the inner courtyard in the late Qing.[50]

Most of the members of the Banner garrison and their families relied on stipends of rice collected from the fifteen counties of Chengdu prefecture, which covered the whole of the Chengdu plain. The garrison was also endowed with land east of Chengdu, which had once served as pasture for Banner horses but had very early been rented to Han farmers. As in other provincial capitals, however, the stipends grew less and less adequate to support the garrison population. By the late nineteenth century, many of the Manchu and Mongol residents of Chengdu were impoverished, and few were able to raise large families. Given the absence of new immigrants and the limits on the growth of the Manchu community, the population density of the garrison area, called the Shaocheng (younger city) by Chengdu residents, was much lower than that of the other areas of the city, even with the several thousand Han merchants and servants who lived within the garrison walls.

Foreigners who visited the garrison in the late Qing were unanimous in their scorn for the inhabitants: "parasites battening on Government pay," the British geographer/official Alexander Hosie called them in an account of his visit in 1883. "Much of the land in this quarter, which is thickly wooded, is devoted to gardens, but I should question whether these slip-shod, down-at-heel, lazy-looking Tartars possessed the energy to grow sufficient vegetables to supplement their government rice."[51] Less obsessed than Hosie with questions of productivity, the French doctor Aimé-François Legendre nevertheless could not help but imagine the martial ancestors of the garrison inhabitants writhing in their graves as they contemplated the devotion their descendants lavished on their pet songbirds.[52] In truth, although they still received military training, it had been some time since the soldiers of the Banner garrison had seen any action. During the eighteenth century, they fought the Miao and Tibetans and White Lotus sectarians many times. After 1813, however, they seldom were offered a chance to lay down their lives for the dynasty. One of the few occasions Banner troops left the garrison was in the 1870s, when a hundred soldiers were selected to move with their families from Chengdu to the Hangzhou garrison to rebuild it after the devastating Taiping occupation of that city.[53] The Chengdu Banner community itself was spared the wrath of the Taipings, but not the corrosive degradation that resulted from the decline of the Banners as a significant political institution and effective military force. Some of Chengdu's Manchu and Mongol inhabitants left the garrison and found success in other occupations—one became the city's most famous caterer of banquets in the last years of the dynasty, specializing in "complete Manchu and Han dinners" for official entertainments with as many as a thousand guests.[54] Most of the Bannermen, however, remained in the Shaocheng, struggling to make ends meet and enjoying what pleasures they could.

Thus, by the beginning of the twentieth century, the Banner garrison of Chengdu had come to symbolize the decline of the Manchus, at least to the foreigners who walked its quiet streets lined with dilapidated walls and crumbling houses. Nevertheless, the vigor of the Qing imperial bureaucracy was still evident in other parts of Chengdu. New government buildings stood grandly on the site of the old Ming imperial palace in the center of town (Fig. 1.7). Instead of royalty, however, they housed several key institutions of civil rule, including the rows of cubicles for the triennial civil service examinations, a granary, and a mint. The other centers of provincial authority, the yamen of the governor-general and his subordinates, occupied the eastern and northern parts of town and, in many cases, lent their names to the streets on which they were located (see Map 2).[55]

Sichuan's administration was unusual because the governor-

Fig. 1.7 This photograph of a courtyard in the Chengdu Imperial City compound was taken November 27, 1911, the day that an independent Sichuan government was declared (see Chapter 5). (The United Church of Canada / Victoria University Archives, Toronto: catalog no. 98.083P/22.)

general's jurisdiction was limited to one province, and he concurrently assumed the functions of provincial governor, taking charge of both civil and military affairs in the province. Technically, the Manchu general was his equal, but that official's authority was limited for the most part to matters concerning the Banner garrison.[56] After the governor-general, whose yamen occupied a prominent spot in the middle of the business district, the important provincial officials included the treasurer and judge in the civil bureaucracy and the military commander for the Army of the Green Standard. Led by the provincial commander of the Green Standard forces, a group of military officials supervised the Han soldiers stationed in small garrisons in the city and throughout the province. Among the lower-ranking civil officials were a number of specialized personnel, such as the commissioners with responsibility for education and the taxes on salt and tea, and a hierarchy of regional officials, including the intendant for the western Sichuan circuit, the Chengdu prefect, and two county magistrates. Like other provincial capitals, Chengdu had no civil administration of its own but was divided between two counties—Chengdu and Huayang in this case—each of which extended far beyond the city walls. The two county magistrates, whose yamen were inside the provincial city, were primarily responsible for public affairs in their sector of the city, as well as in the many towns and villages in the surrounding area.[57] Thousands of Chengdu's inhabitants were employed in the service of the officials based there: clerks, guards, chair bearers, and the various functionaries who assisted the officials in their work.[58]

As the headquarters of so many powerful officials, provincial cities attracted large numbers of the cultural elite, as well as lowlier bureaucratic servants and hangers-on. Unlike the provincial capitals of the eastern coastal area around the Yangzi delta, Chengdu in the nineteenth century had no real rivals in the form of thriving commercial cities that could support a rich urban culture. The only Sichuan city that approached Chengdu in size was Chongqing. Designated a treaty port in 1891, Chongqing's commerce developed rapidly in the last years of the dynasty, and its population may have exceeded Chengdu's before the turn of the century.[59] But Chongqing's unpleasantly hot climate, difficult, precipitous hills, and cramped location at the juncture of two rivers made it less attractive as an urban base for wealthy Sichuan landlords. They probably regarded Chongqing as a grubby place, dominated by pragmatic merchants in the salt and rice trades. Chengdu, on the other hand, was clearly the center of gentry life in the province. Even its main industry, the weaving of silk brocade on elaborate looms, contributed to the elegant feel of the place. A foreigner familiar with frenetic Canton and Chongqing expressed astonishment at the relaxed, stately pace of life in Chengdu.[60]

Like administrative cities throughout the world, Chengdu benefited from being the headquarters of officials who controlled a sizable treasury and the elite who enjoyed hobnobbing with them. Government buildings in the city were far from opulent and actually seemed quite run-down to the foreigners who visited at the end of the Qing, but public and private money was spent on construction in Chengdu that was not available for similar projects in other Sichuan cities. Perhaps most important, Chengdu was the site of the most famous schools in southwestern China. The Jinjiang Academy, founded in

1704, occupied a large compound next to the stately Confucian temple in the southern part of town. Scholars from around the province could petition to live at the academy, supported by stipends and prize money from the monthly exams.[61] In 1874 Sichuan's education commissioner, Zhang Zhidong, built up the Zunjing (Respect the Classics) Academy, funded by a surcharge on the land tax, to train promising scholars.[62] Chengdu and Huayang counties also maintained official academies, and well-known scholars of the Classics tutored many more young men in private schools of their own.

Another of Chengdu's advantages over other cities in Sichuan was its position in the networks of official communications. More than a thousand official documents passed into and out of the governor-general's yamen every day in the late Qing, as Sichuan's 140-some county magistrates reported on business and the provincial government kept in touch with the emperor and court. The governor-general maintained three squads of messengers to carry memorials to Beijing, and the Manchu general had couriers of his own.[63] They traveled a well-worn route out of the city along the Great North Road leading through the mountain passes toward Xi'an and on to the capital. Officials traveling the 1,600 miles between Chengdu and Beijing were granted eighty days for the trip, although couriers with urgent business could do the distance in as few as twenty days.[64] Official funds paid for the upkeep of horses at hundreds of post stations so that messengers could change mounts frequently. The northern route continued to be the most important pathway for official communication up to the end of the dynasty, but by the late nineteenth century technological change had created new traffic flows to and from Chengdu. The introduction of steamships on the lower Yangzi and, eventually, a rail line between Hankou and Beijing made braving the trip downriver through the Yangzi gorges more worthwhile. Scholars traveling from Chengdu to Beijing for the civil service exams began to prefer the overland route due east to Wanxian, just above the gorges, or the Min river route south to the Yangzi at Yibin. In the mid-1880s, telegraph lines connected Chengdu to Beijing, dramatically reducing the time required for news from the Qing court to reach the interior.[65]

The provincial government tried to keep a firm grip on the sensitive political information at its disposal. That was one reason the Qing government strongly resisted pressure from foreigners to allow consulates in Chengdu, which it did successfully until the beginning of the twentieth century. Nevertheless, political gossip and intrigue spilled through the streets of the provincial city, gaining momentum in the many teahouses, wine shops, and opium dens, where men whiled away much of their time. In the more upscale establishments, wealthy landowners and merchants might sip expensive tea from Jingdezhen cups while discussing the latest edicts in the *Capital Gazette (Dibao)*, carried to Chengdu and then reissued by several authorized shops.[66] Humbler folk—tradesmen and small merchants, clerks and chair bearers—pulled their bamboo stools together to talk about the news of the day or listen to fortune-tellers and storytellers, perhaps while having their heads shaved and ears cleaned out, in unadorned rooms open to the street. Tenant-farmers, come to the city to deliver rice to their landlords, spent a few hours in the teahouses before heading back to their villages to share anecdotes and news with their neighbors.[67] To the novelist Li Jieren, Chengdu's wealth, lively culture, and political significance made the city powerfully attractive to those Sichuanese who, restless or ambitious, longed to be part of a wider world.[68]

Governing Chengdu in the Late Qing

How was an administrative city like Chengdu administered in the late Qing period? Despite the steady stream of memorials and edicts that flowed back and forth between the city and Beijing, the central government seldom took notice of Chengdu's mundane problems, although it might deal harshly with any governor-general who failed to prevent a serious disturbance. The Qing court set the general guidelines for the maintenance of law and order in the city in the form of a criminal code to be enforced uniformly throughout the empire and a set of administrative regulations specifying the number and duties of civil and military personnel stationed in the provincial capital. Imperial institutions also contributed significantly to the development of the status system that existed in Chengdu in the late nineteenth century. Most important, the privileges and prestige granted those who successfully navigated the civil service examination system set such degree holders and their families on a plane far above the great majority of Chengdu residents. Holders of provincial- and national-level degrees were particularly favored, enjoying frequent social contact with the lofty officials who governed Chengdu.

If Chengdu was not controlled directly by Beijing, its administration nevertheless resembled that of Beijing in the extent to which it was dominated by officials.[69] In some Chinese commercial cities, such as Shanghai, Hankou, and Chongqing, merchant guilds and native-place associations had assertively taken over many of the tasks of urban government in the course of the nineteenth century.[70] But in most provincial capitals the weight of Qing officialdom still bore down heavily on the community, compressing and limiting the initiative of all other social groups. The merchants of Canton had begun challenging Qing authority in some ways,[71] but Chengdu was still quite obedient, for many reasons. In the scale of Chinese urban history, most of Chengdu's inhabitants were recent immigrants. The wealthy landlords of western Sichuan had made their fortunes on the plain and set up households in Chengdu in the heyday of Qing power; they had not been forced to build strong, autonomous lineage organizations in order to survive on a disorderly frontier, as so many families in southern China had done. Instead, they poured their money into more land and into education for their sons, in the hopes that the latter would join the ranks of the officials, or at least be able to share in the cultural delights of elite Chengdu. Likewise, Chengdu's merchants depended on officialdom as their honored, best customers. Many of the native-place associations in Chengdu were dominated by sojourning officials, rather than merchants.[72] Of all the merchant organizations, noted a foreign observer, the silk merchants' guild was the most "tyrannical."[73] But its tyranny was directed toward the small-scale weavers who supplied the silk shops, rather than the officials and gentry who purchased their products. The merchants could afford to be demanding of the weavers, because in their line of work they were able to develop close personal and financial relationships with officials.

And so Chengdu was an officials' town, but the officials were not of the town or particularly attached to it. Governors-general came and went, although not as frequently as their subordinates. From 1850 to 1911, six governors-general served more than three years each in the position, including one whose tenure lasted over nine years.[74] The magistrates of Chengdu and Huayang counties, on the other hand, rarely remained in office more than two years. Perhaps they preferred it that way; a posting to one of the two "premier counties" was desirable because of its prestige and the opportunities it afforded for becoming well acquainted with bureaucratic heavyweights, but the demands of the job were onerous. Not only did these magistrates have to work under the constant gaze of the governor-general, but they were also saddled with the burdensome and costly responsibility of entertaining a steady stream of visiting dignitaries.[75]

Given the large number of ambitious officials stationed in the city, one might think that competition to control public resources would have been intense, with frequent clashes between officials with overlapping jurisdictions. Qing political institutions ensured, however, that within the formal administration in Chengdu there was overwhelming pressure toward low-key, minimalist teamwork in the name of the governor-general. Before the twentieth century, the Qing bureaucratic system did not reward officials for urban activism, except in the imperial capital and perhaps a few cities with sufficient charms to attract imperial visits. Sichuan's governors-general built their reputations at court by their management of issues that had relatively little to do with Chengdu itself. Most important to them in the late Qing was the regularity with which the county magistrates in their jurisdiction delivered the proceeds of the land tax to the provincial treasury, which forwarded a substantial portion to Beijing. Also important was their ability to prevent or exterminate organized resistance to government agents or harassment of foreigners, a problem that loomed very large in the last decades of the nineteenth century. At a time when Li Hongzhang, Zhang Zhidong, and other governors-general in areas of the middle and lower Yangzi and along the coast were gaining imperial approval to begin experiments in industrial manufacturing, Sichuan's governors-general were primarily engaged in putting down uprisings and keeping a wary eye on affairs in Tibet.

Lower-level officials in Chengdu owed their employment largely to the governor-general, and their hopes for the future depended on his opinion of them. Although they were assigned to service in Sichuan by the court in Beijing, the governor-general evaluated them and recommended them for honors and promotions.[76] Thus, the administrative priorities of the top provincial bureaucrat were generally shared by his formally appointed subordinates. And, compared to maintaining order in the city, all other issues of urban administration were minor concerns in nineteenth-century Sichuan. That is not to say that governors-general frowned on all schemes to improve the city's appearance and infrastructure or to better the welfare of the people. On the contrary, they often encouraged the weak community groups that did exist to handle many routine city affairs, donating funds at their disposal and bestowing official seals of approval—perhaps a sample of their calligraphy on a congratulatory plaque—when privately organized philanthropies collected money to care for orphans or refurbish a dilapidated temple, for example.[77] The maintenance of public order, however, was by far the most fundamental activity of the formal administration of Chengdu before the twentieth century, and the prefect and county magistrates cooperated closely with the governor-general to achieve it.

To keep the peace in Chengdu, Qing officials adopted several strategies. State ideology grounded in the Confucian Classics and the traditions of imperial rule laid the primary responsibility for preventing deviant behavior on the family. County magistrates, or "father-and-mother officials," frequently called on the patriarchs in their communities to educate and restrain their sons and younger brothers—it was assumed and usually the case that no urging was needed for parents and parents-in-law to keep daughters in line. But, even without such exhortation from magistrates, the notion that unorthodox public behavior, which was rather comprehensively and sharply defined, reflected badly on a family and should be corrected by family elders was ingrained in much of Chengdu's population. It was the moral underpinning of many of the stories from the classical literature and traditional romances recounted by storytellers in the teahouses and conveyed in the puppet shows that children loved. Certainly, stories that reflected other points of view circulated as well. One of the primary concerns of officials, however, was to stamp out ideas threatening to what they considered the natural moral order of modest behavior and obedient respect for elders and officials. Popular culture and public performances received close government scrutiny, although some late Qing officials in Chengdu were rumored to enjoy "debauched" performances in private.

The *baojia* system, described briefly above, was meant by officials to extend the self-regulation of the family to larger units, the neighborhood and community. In this, however, late Qing administrators were far from successful. In some commercial Chinese cities in the nineteenth century, *baojia* had evolved into a system of "careerist headmen," who were responsible to officials for reporting on crime and local disturbances in neighborhoods throughout the city, but whose work depended not at all on hierarchical groupings of families.[78] Like the administrators of these cities, officials in Chengdu continued to maintain the fiction that the population was divided into functioning *baojia* groupings, and the names of the various *bao* were preserved in the local gazetteer.[79] There is no sign that such groupings had any administrative substance, however. And, as a provincial city, nineteenth-century Chengdu relied less on neighborhood headmen than on soldiers and yamen functionaries for policing. Each city neighborhood had a headman, who organized the festivals to the local deities and kept an eye on neighborhood affairs, but the careerist type of *bao* constable, who made a living assisting the magistrates on issues of local security, was found for the most part in the suburbs and villages outside the city.[80]

Ten military battalions occupied barracks around Chengdu's parade grounds and the yamen of the Green Standard commander, each with four hundred or so soldiers on the books. Some of the troops were charged with guarding the four city gates and sending patrols throughout the city, particularly during the tense "winter defense" (*dongfang*) period, when poverty hit hardest and criminal activities increased.[81] Other street patrols were organized by the two county magistrates, who had large staffs of "runners" to carry out policing and judicial duties, such as serving summonses and arresting suspected offenders. In the 1880s, Sichuan's magistrates were ordered to monitor the movements of foreigners in their territories and take responsibility for their safety;[82] the result was reported by Alexander Hosie in an account of his 1883 visit to Chengdu: "We had no sooner settled down in a comfortless inn than the underlings of the various officials came to prey upon us. They came laden with offers of assistance; they departed each with a handful of cash, satisfied that they had done their duty. We saw none of them again—the key to peace and quietude was cheap at the price."[83] The necessity of tipping runners charged with protecting travelers and maintaining order in the city points to one of the long-standing tensions in the Chinese system of local administration. Qing administrative codes actually mandated and stipulated payment from official funds only for a small percentage of the clerks and runners who carried out the tasks of government. Most of the men who served on the staffs of Chengdu's officials were not paid from the taxes remitted to the provincial treasurer; they shared in the division of the "customary fees" that every person who had dealings with officials was routinely obliged to pay.[84] Not surprisingly, given their need to be entrepreneurial in order to support themselves, runners had very bad reputations in Chengdu and throughout China, according to elite writers, who saw them as corrupt parasites who fed off the misfortunes of the people and colluded with local bullies.[85]

Zhou Xun, who was Huayang county's last Qing magistrate, believed that the soldiers and runners who patrolled Chengdu's streets were very susceptible to corruption. He recalled one incident involving a soldier named Zhao assigned to the North Gate military patrol in the 1890s who had made himself leader of a gang of gamblers and ruffians. His misbehavior came to light when a young bodyguard of the governor-general led a raid on Zhao's gambling den and the soldier stabbed him. Zhao's superior tried to protect himself, claiming to have ousted Zhao from the army well before the incident in question, but the Chengdu county magistrate, an unusually resourceful official, had already personally led runners to Zhao's residence in the middle of the night in order to secure his patrol lantern and badge as proof that he had not been dismissed.[86]

Whenever Qing officials perceived the predatory behavior of soldiers and runners as being out of control, or when other threats to local order arose, there was generally a movement for the revival of the *baojia* system. That indeed occurred in many parts of China in the years during and following the Taiping uprising. In the wealthy Jiangnan area, the impetus for *baojia* revival seems to have been due to a great extent to the activism of men who were not officials. New *baojia* bureaus were set up in Jiangnan cities and staffed by members of the local elite under the supervision of officials.[87] In Chengdu, a Provincial-City Baojia Bureau (Shengcheng baojiaju) was established some time in the 1870s,[88] but, unlike its eastern counterparts, it appears to have been completely dominated by civil officials, not local elites. And, despite the name, the bureau concentrated primarily on patrolling the city, rather than organizing the populace into mutual-supervision groups. An expectant official with the rank of circuit intendant supervised four chief deputies, who held the rank of county magistrate. Each was assigned to an office with responsibility for maintaining order in a fourth of the city, including the adjacent suburbs, and assisted by several deputies who were also expectant officials. The deputies led nightly patrols of hired constables (*juding* or *juyong*), whom Zhou Xun considered relatively free from evil influence.[89] He did, however, recall one case in which a bureau chief (*zongban*) became infatuated with the daughter of a merchant and regularly took advantage of his authority to inspect household registers in order to look the woman over. The merchant got his revenge, however. While the bureau chief was inspecting the shop's residents, the merchant had a servant put a bundle of the family's clothing in the chief's sedan chair and then reported that items from his shop had been missing each time there was an inspection. Enraged that there was a thief in his entourage, the chief had everyone searched. When the package was discovered, the merchant threatened to go to the governor-general, and the mortified chief was forced to settle the matter to the merchant's satisfaction.[90]

With such an array of soldiers, runners, and *baojia* constables, Chengdu's system for enforcing order was quite complicated. Zhou Xun's tale of soldier Zhao suggests that it was not completely free of internal conflict.[91] Nevertheless, the terror that the governor-general could bring to bear on anyone who attracted his ire ensured that conflicts rarely got so far out of hand that they were made public. The punishments that governors-general and even county magistrates were authorized to impose on miscreants were indeed terrible.[92] Qing officials, and many of their subjects, believed in the deterrent effect of heavy and public punishment. Convicted criminals might be paraded through the streets and put on display in front of yamen for days, their heads locked inside heavy wooden collars, their crimes advertised in large characters. Compared to European cities, a foreigner observed, violent actions were quite rare among the people of Chengdu.[93] Officials, however, could use violence almost casually. Zhou Xun tells an admiring story about one Chengdu prefect who, earlier in his career as magistrate of Luzhou, had seen an elderly woman walking along the street cursing loudly. He ordered his attendants to give her a beating, then and there, but stopped them when he noticed a well-dressed young woman watching from a shop front. Calling on them to release the old woman, he had them beat the younger one severely. Afterwards, when Zhou Xun asked him why he had acted as he had, the official told him that the old woman only needed a good fright in order for her to mend her ways, whereas the younger one was clearly a streetwalker who had disobeyed his order for such people to leave the city. Asked how he knew she was a prostitute, the official ticked off his reasons: her clothing and ornaments were too fine for a woman who was clearly from a poor family, the shop she was standing in appeared to be an opium den and she was probably there to solicit customers, and no upright young woman would be so eager to watch a public beating.[94] In matters concerning the maintenance of public order among the urban poor, legal procedures specified in the Qing Code could often be safely ignored by officials.

Chengdu residents had their own ways of dealing with oppressive officials. They corrupted the runners and soldiers who were supposed to be the government's loyal servants, buying them off to prevent official inquiries.[95] Bumbling officials might be manipulated. The unhappy *baojia* bureau chief who lusted after the merchant's daughter was outwitted on another occasion as well, according to Zhou Xun. When the Xianfeng emperor's widow died in 1881, the bureau chief ordered his constables to strictly enforce the law forbidding any man to shave the front part of his head during the mourning period of a hundred days. A group of men who had not obeyed the directive to remain unshaven surrounded the constables sent to arrest them and shaved off the constables' hair. The latter "consulted together and decided they could do nothing but abandon their uniforms and run away. All those who heard the story spat out their rice" in their amusement.[96]

Chengdu people also protected themselves by clinging to customs and conventions. Living with a justice system that operated more to enforce rules deemed useful by the state than to protect the personal interests and liberties of the people, many Chinese found conventions to be very useful.[97] The state ideology itself paid homage to the ways of the past, and local traditions were celebrated by the scholars who delighted in compiling detailed histories and ethnographies of their hometowns. Thus, the argument that "things have never been done that way here" could be quite potent, enabling one to rally sympathetic support from neighbors and even strangers on the street, if need be, in order to prevent some unusual and possibly threatening action. In telling his story of the shorn constables, Zhou Xun noted that one reason Chengdu people were so glad to see the *baojia* bureau chief outwitted, and made heroes out of the impromptu barbers, was because the chief had tried to enforce a law that other officials had customarily ignored.

The people who were most conscious of and fascinated by the power of custom to set limits on the behavior of all Chengdu residents, official and commoner alike, were the foreigners living there at the end of the Qing era, who found themselves frustrated but also bound by the conventions that governed city life. When the first group of Protestant missionaries to settle permanently in the city arrived in 1881, they quickly decided to adopt Chinese dress to try to minimize the jeering they encountered on the streets (Fig. 3.5, p. 102, shows that the practice continued in some measure until at least 1897). Forty years after the Protestants' arrival, one of the early missionaries tried to re-create the city's atmosphere before the turn of the century for the benefit of his younger colleagues:

Social life in Chengdu in those days was very circumspect. For example, when the ladies of the [British China Inland Mission] came to call on the [recently arrived] Canadians, the gentlemen of the new party gallantly stepped forward in the open court to shake hands, when with a look almost of terror the single young lady exclaimed, "Oh! Not here, why the Chinese (a few chair coolies were standing near), the Chinese might see us. Wait until we get indoors." . . . Foreign ladies rarely left the compounds, except in closely-curtained sedan chairs. One young lady, now a senior missionary, ventured to walk from Sishengci [location of the Canadian mission in the northeast corner of the city] to Shaanxijie [where the American Methodist mission stood just south of the Imperial City] to a union Chinese meeting, with the pastor of the church, and was nearly sent home for her imprudence. Another young lady almost lost face in the community because she rode through the streets with the upper front curtain raised.[98]

Anxious to avoid giving their enemies any excuse to attack them for their "barbarous" behavior, missionaries thus felt obliged to enforce local standards of public conduct within their own communities.

Just as custom imposed strict limits on the lives of those women who needed social respectability, so conventions of architectural style and beliefs about property rights strongly influenced Chengdu's appearance. Such conventions clearly hampered the missionaries' attempts to establish themselves physically in Chengdu. In 1893, the Canadian Methodist Episcopal Mission bought a piece of property from a local priest and started building a foreign-style house there before the compound's outer walls had been raised, causing crowds to gather on the site and discuss the possible evil influences of the unusual building on the local atmosphere. The missionaries judged the people of Chengdu to be firm believers in *fengshui*—the traditional principles of layout and construction that were thought to ensure a healthy flow of *qi,* or vital energy, through a neighborhood or house.[99] Even if a deep commitment to *fengshui* was not widespread, however, innovations in building design were quite rare in most Chinese cities in the Qing[100] and could easily be condemned as a breach of customary standards. In the case of the Canadian venture of 1893, community reaction was decidedly negative. When a construction shed collapsed and killed a man (a thief trying to make off with firewood, according to the missionaries), the neighbors destroyed the place. Complaints to the officials brought the foreigners recompense for the lost materials, but they were informed that "the people objected to a priest disposing of temple property" and were forced to find another location for their church. Two years later the Canadians built a house during a spell of unusually dry weather, and local concerns again became an issue:

When no rain fell the people began to wonder if this new house was too high, or too wide, or too deep and disturbing the fengshui. . . . One day half a dozen big red visiting cards were sent in. The gateman announced that the Street-Officials would like to interview the Mushi (pastor). What a solemn group they made, as they stood at different angles, and compared the height of the house with surrounding objects. It was an anxious moment. Fortunately our neighbors had a fire wall, and from the level of the ground they looked to be about equal in height. One old veteran cocked up his eye and said, "Pretty high, eh?" Another stepped back, cocked up his eye, and said, "The house and the wall are *chabuduo*" (not much different,—a phrase constantly used by Chinese, and is an indication of their willingness to be satisfied with things though not quite right). The situation was saved. *Chabuduo* clinched the verdict. A cup of tea and a present of a couple of strings of cash sent the august delegation away in high spirits to inform the neighbors that the house was *chabuduo*.[101]

The foreigners' frustration with Chengdu's customary and negotiable style of urban regulation is quite visible in this account. Local headmen did feel empowered to look into unusual phenomena on behalf of the neighborhood and could seem quite nosy to people with a different understanding of the rights of private property holders. Although no reference was made by the "street-officials"[102] to the formal legal system, it was clear to the Canadians that neighborhood opinion mattered, as it had in the case of the temple property they had been forced to give up. Officials could not be counted on to ignore it in favor of abstract legal principles, and the foreigners themselves dreaded antagonizing their neighbors and thereby inviting mob retribution.

Chengdu in the late Qing era was thus a city of well-established customs, dominated by high provincial officials who had little interest in urban affairs, as long as it remained an orderly headquarters for their provincial administrations. To keep it orderly, they exhorted the heads of households to practice right conduct and require it of their families. When that failed to prevent offenses against the criminal code or standards of public behavior, the magistrates relied on runners and soldiers to pursue malefactors and bring them to the yamen for trial. Harsh punishment usually followed, if the offender did not have connections to powerful underworld figures or prominent families who could intervene to intimidate or buy off the servants of the law. In their role as guardians of the people and property of Chengdu, the Qing bureaucrats stationed there seldom had lofty ambitions, leaving most matters of social welfare in the hands of wealthy members of the community. Given the position of the provincial city in the Qing political system prior to the twentieth century, there was little room for any alternative vision of urban administration to arise or take root in Chengdu. That would change, however, in the new century, with the launching of the New Policies and their enthusiastic and creative implementation across the country.

2 NATION BUILDING AND THE CITY, 1895–1911

For ten years, between 1901 and 1911, the Qing political system was tweaked and nudged, pushed and pulled about, by an extensive and contradictory series of reforms collectively known as the New Policies (*xinzheng*).[1] Before this, some provincial officials had promoted a policy of "self-strengthening" through improvements in the manufacture of weapons and in transportation. This the court could tolerate, but it resisted wholesale administrative reorganization of the weakening empire, successfully frustrating attempts to introduce such changes in the late nineteenth century.[2] Many at the court opposed political surgery that they knew would be disruptive and probably suspected could be fatal to the venerable and vulnerable imperial order, or at least to the dynasty itself. The disaster of the occupation of Beijing by foreign armies in the course of the Boxer uprising in 1900, however, convinced the Empress Dowager and her circle of advisers that there was no choice but to redesign the empire, acceding to some of the demands of the foreign powers and accepting some of the proposals offered by increasingly nationalistic Chinese officials and scholars. In January 1901, therefore, an imperial edict called for all high-level Qing officials to submit detailed plans for the reform of the institutions of government.[3] After that, although they often tried, cautious courtiers and anxious provincial bureaucrats were no longer able to suppress the reformist energies that galvanized many of their colleagues and compatriots, transformed an array of social institutions, and paved the way for political revolution in 1911.

The New Policies defy simple characterization.[4] They were not issued as a coherent program but evolved over the years between 1901 and 1911 as officials with different visions of how to remake the empire gained influence within the national government and various provincial administrations. By 1911, the New Policies had come to touch on almost every aspect of the Qing political system. They were motivated to a large extent, however, by the single overriding goal of national strength. The "death of the country" (*wangguo*), which would be "sliced up like a melon" (*guafen*), phrases on the lips of many politically engaged Chinese in the years between 1895 and 1911, was the frightful alternative to national strengthening in the age of the imperialistic nation-state. In order to secure national survival against the encroaching European and Pacific powers, analysts inside and outside the Qing government were convinced that China needed a strong, centralized state, capable of fielding a respectable army and commanding the active loyalty and obedience of the inhabitants of its territory.[5] The New Policies had, therefore, two major emphases: institutional reform to increase the capacity of the state and constitutional reform to change the relationship between the state and a new citizenry.

The story of the attempts of the Qing and subsequent Chinese regimes to build a modern nation on the foundation of an empire in decline has been told many times, and in many ways. Earlier narratives often portrayed the New Policies as empty and cynical gestures on the part of a Qing court desperate to stave off the attacks of its critics but determined not to submit to anything but superficial change.[6] Subsequently, however, historians have argued that whatever the intentions of the Empress Dowager, the New Policies affected the Chinese polity in important and wide-ranging ways. These studies show that the late Qing reforms deserve serious re-evaluation, and not only from the perspective of how they impeded or promoted the development of a modern Chinese state. As Prasenjit Duara has pointed out, the implementation of the New Policies changed Chinese community dynamics in fundamental ways, "creating immense tensions in rural society."[7] Their impact in provincial cities such as Chengdu was different but just as profound. Whereas in rural areas, according to Duara,[8] the tax increases and incomplete bureaucratization of the New Policies era caused "state involution" and the disintegration of long-standing community institutions, in cities like Chengdu new state institutions were introduced fairly smoothly and achieved many of the goals reformers set for them. This did not occur without social tension, but, as the next few chapters make clear, many aspects of the New Policies found widespread acceptance in urban communities.[9] One reason for relatively greater acceptance of the reforms in urban areas was that provincial authorities subsidized their implementation in cities, whereas rural areas were saddled with the burden of paying for them. As implemented in Chengdu, some of the New Policies helped bring about the collapse of Qing rule, but many also set standards for urban administration that lasted long after the dynasty's demise.

This chapter briefly surveys the crises of the late nineteenth century that gave rise to the New Policies, with particular attention to events in Chengdu during that period, and then explores the place of China's cities in the plans of some of the key architects and promoters of the reforms. The powerful provincial officials who set the guidelines for the New Policies did not consider cities as uniquely important targets for reformist action. Rather, they thought of Qing administration as a vast fabric that spread across the land, and they hoped that the New Policies would link capital and province, city and village, in a more tightly woven whole. Their conception of reform, therefore, was broad. Nevertheless, their strategies for implementing reform often privileged provincial capitals, as the sites for model institutions. And many of the men recruited to carry out the reforms found the challenge of creating modern cities particularly compelling and worthy of exceptional effort. Such was the case with Chengdu's outstanding New Policies reformer, Zhou Shanpei.

The Background of the New Policies: Imperialism and Internal Unrest

The ideas and impulses that contributed to the New Policies can be traced back well before 1895.[10] Nevertheless, the events of that year convinced many Chinese of the need for reform. The weakness of the Qing government was driven home dramatically early that year as the Qing government was forced to sue for peace in the disastrous war with Japan that had begun in Korea the previous summer. News of China's humiliating defeat and the government's acceptance of Japan's harsh terms in April 1895 traveled quickly to Chengdu. The writer Han Suyin's uncle, seven years old at the time, recalled that his own uncle had read the news in the *Capital Gazette* at the yamen of one of the magistrates and returned to the family compound "screaming and waving his arms: 'They have beaten us, they have beaten us. The Japanese devils have beaten us.'" Han Suyin's great-grandfather, who had had a distinguished military career in the Qing suppression of the Nian and Hui uprisings of the 1860s and 1870s, ordered the entire family to wear mourning clothes when he heard of China's humiliation.[11]

The elites were not alone in their angry reaction to the loss to Japan. Foreign missionaries in Chengdu believed that it increased local hostility toward them and contributed to another event in 1895 that, like the Japanese ambush of the Chinese fleet off the coast of Shandong, signaled the grave crisis facing the Qing. One month after the Treaty of Shimonoseki was signed to end the Sino-Japanese war, crowds destroyed all mission properties in Chengdu, and the thirty-one foreigners resident in the city were forced to flee for their lives to the Huayang magistrate's yamen. All but two French Catholic priests left for Chongqing ten days later, to return gradually after the Qing government agreed to recompense them generously for their losses and punish the officials whom the foreigners considered responsible for the attacks.[12]

The motivations of those who attacked the missions in Chengdu in May 1895 were interpreted in different ways. Whether many of

Chengdu's residents were concerned with the fate of a Chinese "nation" is impossible to say. It is clear, however, that local residents were uneasy about the actions of the highly visible foreigners in their communities. Many missionaries believed that the general and long-standing suspicion of them had been exacerbated intentionally by xenophobic officials, who the month before had tolerated the public display of the corpse of a woman who died while being treated by a Canadian doctor. Officials, the foreigners claimed, had also done nothing to counter widespread rumors that the missionaries kidnapped children in order to use their body parts for medicine. The actual incident, according to all accounts, started when people celebrating a rather rowdy annual holiday on the East Parade Ground near the Canadian compound saw a Canadian carrying a child into the compound.[13] People massed at the compound gates—menacingly, according to the foreigners inside, who fired rifles over the heads of the crowd. Rather than running away, however, the crowd beat the gate down and destroyed the buildings inside, while the Canadians fled. Safe in the magistrate's yamen the next day, the foreigners were confronted with a boy whom people had delivered to the Baojia Bureau office, saying they had discovered him in a box under the floorboards of the missionaries' house, mute and with black powder in his nostrils and mouth. That day, the missionaries claim, the head of the Baojia Bureau posted a proclamation telling people to be calm; the foreigners had abducted a child, but all was now under control. The missionaries attributed the subsequent destruction of all other mission properties in Chengdu, and many elsewhere in Sichuan, to this proclamation and the alleged refusal of officials to send guards to protect the properties. The Chengdu prefect, some claimed, actually encouraged the people to destroy the Catholic church, while warning them against injuring the foreigners physically.[14] Later, in an official complaint to the Qing government, the U.S. minister to China added another facet to the foreigners' indictment. Unwilling, perhaps, to believe that hatred of missionaries was widespread and genuine, he adduced an economic motivation: the people had destroyed the churches in order to get employment rebuilding them.[15]

The official Chinese account of the trial of the twenty-some people arrested in the aftermath of the incidents in Chengdu and elsewhere also downplays the role of antiforeign sentiment among the people. The Chengdu prefect reported that six people identified as the ringleaders in Chengdu had heard the story of the kidnapping and taken advantage of the anger of the crowd, inciting it to attack foreign properties so that they could loot them.[16] Contrary to the assertions of the British minister in Beijing, officials in Sichuan denied that inflammatory proclamations had been posted or that the story of the kidnapping had been spread by telegram, causing unrest in other areas. Nevertheless, in the face of foreign pressure, the Sichuan governor-general was dismissed and ordered "never to be employed again" and the head of the Baojia Bureau was removed from his post.[17] The incoming governor-general requested imperial permission to execute the six "ringleaders"; and two other suspects died in jail during the course of the trial and settlement.[18] The *North China Herald* in Shanghai reported that the executions of thirteen of those arrested in Chengdu that summer were accompanied by public protests that shook the city so badly that shops were closed for three days.[19] The French bishop in Chengdu negotiated reparations of more than half a million dollars for the loss of church property in Chengdu, and the French minister in Beijing took advantage of the events to press the Qing court to grant his country economic concessions in Yunnan, the province south of Sichuan that bordered French Indochina.[20]

Costly diplomatic disasters such as the antiforeign attacks in Chengdu and the defeat by Japan produced, in Jerome Ch'en's words, "a sense of panic" throughout China.[21] Attacks on missionaries increased foreign belligerence, and the war demonstrated that China could not hope to defend itself against foreign aggression. The Japanese destruction of China's navy demolished the hope that the Qing "self-strengthening" efforts to acquire the technological trappings of powerful nations would suffice to turn it into one. For twenty years before 1895, China's provincial officials had been busy buying warships, building arsenals, and training troops, only to see their labors come to naught in the space of a few months. The events of 1895 opened the way for more radical solutions to the problem of China's weakness. Li Hongzhang, leading proponent of the technological approach to national strength, became a target of ridicule.[22] And in Beijing that year, candidates gathered for the imperial examinations showed their anger and impatience with the ineffectual Qing self-strengthening efforts by signing petitions pleading for comprehensive reform and by founding a "Society to Study Strength" funded by prominent officials to discuss among themselves what should be done.[23]

Japan's surprisingly rapid rise to international prestige led these men and others to take a closer look at Japan's nation-building experience since the Meiji Restoration of 1868, as well as the histories of the Western powers that the Meiji leaders had taken as models. For this, they turned to the writings of Huang Zunxian and Wang Tao, who had lived for long periods in the East Asian cities that had been most strongly influenced by European ideas—Tokyo, Hong Kong, Singapore, and Shanghai. Huang, Wang, and several other widely read essayists of the 1890s argued that Europe and Japan were powerful not so much because of their guns but because of their social institutions, which served to focus the energies of the people on national goals.[24] Over the next few years, many activists came to share the conviction of Kang Youwei, one of the leaders of the 1895 examination candidates, that what China needed was substantial institutional reorganization in order to achieve what he considered to be the source of Western strength: "the capacity for united will and collective action across the barrier between the ruler and the ruled."[25] In Hunan province in 1897, reformers supported by Governor-General Zhang Zhidong and Governor Chen Baozhen established a School for Current Affairs, headed by Kang Youwei's close associate Liang Qichao, to train talented youth to contribute to China's institutional overhaul. Huang Zunxian, China's top expert on the Meiji reforms, served in the provincial government and encouraged the Hunanese to make their province into "China's Satsuma and Chōshū," the domains that had produced many Meiji leaders. He also created new government bureaus in the capital, Changsha, based on the administrative system he had closely observed in Tokyo.[26]

For a brief time in 1898, it appeared that the activists gathered in Hunan might see their programs put in place on a national scale, when the Guangxu emperor took up the cause of systemic reform. That summer the emperor issued a stream of edicts demanding changes to the educational system and bureaucracy and encouraging military reorganization and greater state involvement in economic development. Several of the Hunan reformers, as well as Kang Youwei himself, were given positions in the central government. The experiments of 1898 ended abruptly and tragically, however. For reasons that are still debated, the Empress Dowager and her supporters turned against the reform program and carried out a coup that took the government out of the hands of the Guangxu emperor. Six of the newly elevated reformers of the "Hundred Days" of 1898 were executed, Kang Youwei and Liang Qichao escaped into exile, and Zhang Zhidong was instructed to shut down the new institutions set up in Hunan.[27]

In Chengdu, the failure of the 1898 reform program was felt deeply in some quarters, although the reform measures themselves had little impact on Sichuan. The governor-general appointed to office in the aftermath of the disturbances of 1895 had been dismissed in 1897, and his permanent replacement did not arrive in Chengdu until after the Empress Dowager's coup.[28] The Sichuan government, therefore, had lacked a strong leader. Before provincial officials had been obliged to respond seriously to the startling edicts of 1898, they were rescinded. Nevertheless, some prominent scholars in Chengdu had been closely involved in the 1898 reform program. Among them were several members of the first class to enter the Zunjing Academy established by Zhang Zhidong in Chengdu in 1875. As students at the academy, Liao Ping and Song Yuren had become interested in "New Text" interpretations of the Confucian tradition that could be used to buttress arguments for radical institutional reform. In the 1880s Liao Ping wrote essays that strongly influenced Kang Youwei.[29] Their Zunjing Academy classmate Yang Rui served for a long time as a private secretary to Zhang Zhidong and later joined the circle of activists working in Beijing during the Hundred Days of 1898. Song Yuren, who had earned the highest civil degree in 1886 and was in

Europe on an official mission during the war with Japan, returned to Sichuan in 1896 with an appointment to oversee commercial affairs in Chongqing and "brought the sparks of the institutional reform movement" to his home province.[30] In 1898 he moved to Chengdu to become the director of the Zunjing Academy. There he founded the city's first journal, modeled on one set up in Changsha. The paper, the *Sichuan Study Gazette (Shuxuebao)*, supported the reform movement, offering news about it and explaining its goals. Some two thousand copies of each issue circulated throughout the province and other areas of China.[31]

The new journal, and the Chengdu study group associated with it, did not survive the coup.[32] Far more bitter for the scholars in Song Yuren's coterie than the loss of their paper, however, were the deaths of Yang Rui and Liu Guangdi, the two Sichuan officials among the "six martyrs" hastily executed in the fall of 1898.[33] Yang and Liu had been important figures among the Sichuan elite, who made much of the relatively small number of men from the province who attained high office in Beijing. Sichuan men who traveled to Beijing became acquainted with such colleagues at the Sichuan Native-Place Association (Sichuan huiguan), and earlier in 1898 Yang Rui and Liu Guangdi had helped set up the Sichuan Study Society (Shuxuehui) with ties to Song Yuren's group in Chengdu.[34] The executions so outraged one promising young Sichuanese scholar, Xu Zixiu, who figures prominently later in this book, that he abandoned all plans for an official career and devoted himself entirely to teaching. One of his students recalled that even before the fall of the Qing Xu told his classes in Chengdu that the dynasty had forfeited the Mandate of Heaven when it executed the six martyrs.[35] The events of the late 1890s thus helped create a reform constituency in Chengdu but also severely damaged the prestige of the ruling dynasty in the eyes of many of the members of this group.

During the year after the failure of the 1898 reform movement, the Boxer uprising gained momentum on the north China plain. Unlike the unrest in Chengdu a few years earlier, the antiforeign and anti-Christian activities of the Boxer groups could not easily be contained, leading some Qing officials to abandon attempts to suppress them in favor of a strategy of using them against the foreigners. In 1900, this strategy backfired when the Boxer siege of the foreign legations in Beijing resulted in the foreign military occupation of that city and the port city of Tianjin to the east. This time, the foreigners were not satisfied with reparations for lost property and punishment of xenophobic officials; they stepped up their demands for fundamental institutional reforms that would enable the Chinese government to control the countryside and guarantee the safety of missionaries and converts.

The shock of being driven from Beijing seems to have convinced the Empress Dowager that there was no choice but to announce her support for substantive reform of the imperial system. While in exile in Xi'an she issued the edict that Douglas Reynolds has likened to the Meiji Charter Oath of 1868.[36] Rather than welcoming back the exiled Kang Youwei and Liang Qichao and their party to join in the remaking of the empire, however, she put the reform program in the hands of men who, in her view, were more reliable—well-seasoned servants of the Qing state occupying key positions in the provincial administrations. Many of the New Policies that they proposed were heavily indebted to the work of the group that had coalesced in Hunan in 1897. Because of the 1898 purge, however, the men chosen to implement the New Policies had to navigate through highly politicized waters. For those from Sichuan, the fate of Yang Rui and Liu Guangdi was a powerful reminder of the danger of bold action in the service of defensive rulers who could be both arbitrary and merciless. At the same time, the reformers faced challenges from other quarters, including revolutionaries convinced by the events of the last few years of the nineteenth century and the humiliating Boxer settlement of 1901 that China could never be strong as long as it was ruled by the Qing.[37]

The Place of Cities in the Theory of the Late Qing Reforms

The New Policies were not meant as a program of urban reform. Cities, as discrete social entities, hardly figured in the reform currents of the late Qing period. In Europe, architectural theorists and utopian writers had been devising radically new plans for the ideal city since the sixteenth century.[38] By contrast, as Arthur Wright has pointed out, throughout China's imperial age "city theory" occupied a "relatively insignificant place . . . in the literary tradition."[39] Whereas one can see in the early nineteenth century the beginning of a strong urban preoccupation among European social thinkers, as "more and more writers began to address themselves to specifically urban phenomena—to the problems posed and the possibilities offered by city growth,"[40] no such urban orientation was yet visible in Chinese political theorizing. In Japan, the 1890s saw a growing concern with "social problems" (*shakai mondai*), many of which were linked to the rapid development of cities.[41] In China, however, the modern factories built by the self-strengtheners had not changed the cities to the extent that industrialization had altered those of nineteenth-century Europe and Japan, where they had created shocking new forms of class struggle and attracted vast populations of "rootless" young laborers. Chinese cities certainly changed in significant ways over the course of the Qing dynasty, but these changes, if they were observed at all, were not seen as fundamental challenges to old ways of thinking about cities. Although William Rowe points to "the beginning of self-conscious class differentiation" in Hankou in the 1870s and the rapid intensification of that phenomenon in the 1890s,[42] it had not yet seeped so far into the consciousness of the Chinese advocates of political reform that they recognized any specifically urban social problems as deserving of special attention. That would come only in the second decade of the twentieth century.[43]

Kang Youwei articulated the views of many when he argued that the Qing government's problems were due primarily to an imbalance in the distribution of authority among the various levels of the polity. He did not argue that county magistrates were handicapped by the inclusion in their large jurisdictions of both urban and rural sectors requiring significantly different sorts of administration. Rather, officials at all levels suffered, as did the people, from the restrictive political controls imposed by the central government out of fear of insubordination and rebellion. The result was "administrative impotency," to borrow Kung-chuan Hsiao's summary of Kang's argument.[44] Administrators needed new tools to do their jobs better. Among these Kang counted "practical" education in place of the old-style literary scholarship oriented toward the civil service examinations, a new division of responsibilities for different types of administration among specialized officials at each level of the state, and, most important, greatly expanded popular participation in political deliberations, which would allow administrators to act in harmony with the people whose public affairs they administered. Popular participation in government could more effectively ensure good administration than could cumbersome top-down control mechanisms. It could also help stamp out the corrupt practices that flourished in a secretive political system, in which officials treated governmental authority as their own private property.[45] And, as Liang Qichao eloquently argued in many essays, broader participation in government could serve to make the people more public-spirited and unify them behind national goals, which was the key to national strength.[46] Not one of the new administrative tools Kang identified had anything characteristically urban about it—every element of the institutional and constitutional reform he and Liang advocated was to be implemented at the proper scale at every level of the polity.

Kang Youwei's later writings, completed while he was in exile, clarify his attitude toward cities and illustrate the widespread tendency of late Qing theorists to think of the polity as an undifferentiated whole, stressing neither regional nor urban/rural differences. Kang's utopian work *One World* (*Datongshu*) foresaw the development of advanced industry across China, as well as all other parts of the world.[47] But, unlike in Europe, industrialization would occur in China without producing serious urban social problems. Kang did not believe that it would be necessary to create different types of administrative structures for use in urban and rural areas, because the organization of the human populations of these areas would be essentially the same. In Kung-chuan Hsiao's description, Kang

forecast that as people . . . would live either in public buildings devoted to various enterprises (agriculture, industry, transportation, development) or in public institutions (schools, hospitals, homes for the young or aged), there would be "practically no private houses" nor "people living scattered in villages." As population concentrations would be basically agricultural (i.e. rural) or industrial (i.e. urban), centering respectively around extensive farms or large factories, the divisions for local self-government would be made not on a territorial but on a functional basis. Each farm or factory would constitute a unit of local self-government, the director of the farm or factory would be the head of local government, and all inhabitants working in the unit would take part in making decisions. Each farm or factory would have its own educational and welfare institutions . . . in addition to bureaus of public works and economic affairs. Each local self-governing unit was to be a self-sufficing integral community, operating on thoroughly democratic principles.[48]

The idea of organizing government around functional rather than territorial units may owe something to traditional *baojia* theory, which would have been quite familiar to Kang from his training in Chinese history and government. The more novel part of this conception of China's future human geography is Kang's vision of collectivized agriculture, which would in effect urbanize the countryside. There was no place in either the industrial or the agricultural units of Kang's imagined China, however, for the sort of urban problems that worried contemporary Europeans. Even Kang's less utopian colleague Liang Qichao discounted the likelihood that the industrialization of China would produce the extremes of wealth and poverty and the resulting social tensions that characterized European cities. Chinese society, Liang argued, "unlike Western society, was largely composed of middle-class families and hence was not an economically polarized one."[49] Industrialization and any accompanying urbanization did not threaten to change that fundamental social condition quickly.

The provincial officials who did the most to define the general outlines of the New Policies shared Kang Youwei's and Liang Qichao's concern about China's lack of national unity but not their enthusiasm for the direct involvement in government of those outside the bureaucracy. Zhang Zhidong, according to Daniel Bays, saw the solution to China's fragmented polity as "vigorous action from the throne, supported unanimously by leading officials and the entire bureaucratic elite," and believed that the "central government could command the united support of the nation by correct policies, correctly implemented."[50] The great majority of reform proposals sponsored by Qing officials envisioned strengthening the state through the creation of new nationwide institutional networks that the central government could use to train and discipline its subjects, as well as to make use of their labor. Zhang Zhidong and his close colleague Liu Kunyi were the among the first to try to set the tone for the New Policies era; they submitted long and detailed memorials to the court shortly after the call went out for new ideas. Zhang's own approach to reform emphasized education, which he hoped to see redesigned so that it would produce men of talent and virtue to lead the bureaucracy, technically skilled specialists to develop Chinese industry and agriculture, and loyal officers to command modern military forces. As governor-general, he had already established new agricultural, industrial, and military schools in Wuchang, the capital of Hubei province and the location of his yamen.[51] In the fall of 1901, the court adopted many of his recommendations, changing the content of the civil examinations, abolishing the military examination system, and drawing up a plan for an unprecedentedly comprehensive national network of schools, to be linked hierarchically from counties to the provincial capitals.[52]

Although Zhang Zhidong may have been the "foremost spokesman for a comprehensive reform movement" in 1901,[53] his position as a New Policies leader was overshadowed rather quickly by the activism of another high provincial official, Yuan Shikai. Yuan, who had gained the confidence of the Empress Dowager and was also well regarded by the representatives of the foreign powers in China, was appointed governor-general of Zhili, the province that surrounded the imperial capital, in 1901. According to an epigram that made the rounds of elite society in the late Qing, "Zhang Zhidong is learned but lacks [administrative] skills (*youxue wushu*); Yuan Shikai lacks learning but has plenty of [governing] skills (*wuxue youshu*)."[54] From 1901 to his fall from power in 1908, Yuan energetically carried out administrative reform in Zhili province and Beijing, creating a number of new institutions that the court cited as models for other governors-general to emulate. As we shall see in the case of Sichuan, provincial authorities were not compelled to follow Yuan's lead in devising ways to achieve the overall reform goals of the dynasty.[55] It was not until the promulgation of new administrative codes beginning in 1906 that the central government seriously attempted to standardize and control the implementation of the New Policies across the country.[56] Nevertheless, Yuan's activities in Zhili were publicized in his new *Beiyang Gazette* (*Beiyang guanbao*) and influenced reformers across the country.[57]

Whereas Zhang Zhidong focused on education, Yuan Shikai gave priority to security. Zhili was the political heart of the empire, as well as a center of Boxer activity and alarmingly vulnerable to foreign invasion. The New Army that Yuan built in the first decade of the twentieth century has long been considered the most significant accomplishment of his late Qing career.[58] It is also one of the few New Policies institutions that was not conceived as a network extending evenly across China. The top commanders of the Army of the Green Standard, which the New Army was to replace, were usually headquartered in the provincial cities, but their troops were distributed in small units throughout the provinces, where they assisted officials in such tasks as "the transport of bullion, grain, prisoners, and mail" and could be called on for police duty when the staffs of county magistrates were unable to handle a local disturbance. Such a decentralized constabulary was difficult to rally for wider military actions.[59] The New Army, in contrast, was to be a unified, well-trained fighting force capable of handling foreign threats. A higher degree of centralization was, therefore, imperative. Yuan Shikai had another compelling reason to concentrate his New Army around his base in Tianjin—the foreign armies that had been occupying the city since 1900 to protect the foreign-controlled concessions there refused to hand the city over to Yuan until he convinced them that he could keep the peace in that part of Zhili province.[60]

To compensate for the consolidation of the military, Yuan planned a network of police forces responsible for maintaining order in localities throughout Zhili. The idea of establishing a new type of police had been promoted enthusiastically in the 1890s by Huang

Zunxian, who considered the Japanese police to be among the most successful of the Meiji reforms.[61] Noriko Kamachi, Huang's biographer, believes that Huang saw in police forces a solution to the longstanding problem of predatory yamen runners. Professional, well-trained, adequately compensated constables would carry out the law enforcement and security functions that had previously been the responsibility of undisciplined, uncontrollable runners and ineffectual *baojia* leaders.[62] In Changsha in 1897, Huang directed much of his effort toward setting up a new police bureau, which was to be closely supervised by a committee of officials and local elites. In an analysis of the 1897 Hunan reforms, Lin Nengshi finds Huang's attempts to involve local elites in police work the most interesting part of his plan and links it to the growing sentiment in favor of local self-government. The police bureau was to be centered in Changsha and tied to a reformed and centralized provincewide militia system under the command of the director of the provincial police bureau, a position reserved for a high-ranking official.[63] After the coup of 1898, Zhang Zhidong renamed the Changsha police bureau the "Baojia Bureau," but maintained its organization. When the New Policies era began, he established a similar force in Wuchang.[64]

Yuan Shikai was familiar with Huang's Changsha experiment, but may have come to appreciate the institution of the police more from encountering it in the two north China cities occupied by the foreigners in 1900, Beijing and Tianjin. There, the Japanese and other foreigners had recruited officers and constables from among the Chinese residents to staff "pacify-the-people" offices (*anmin gongsuo*).[65] Even before the foreigners had withdrawn from Tianjin, Yuan set up a police force of 500 former soldiers in Baoding, his temporary capital. In the fall of 1902, he took this force with him to Tianjin, where he combined it with the force employed by the foreigners, and "made Tianjin the heart of his police reform program."[66] This program included police academies, workhouses for petty criminals and vagrants, and a model prison. Like the new school system, the police program was to be extended to the province at large.[67]

Along with the educational and police systems, the third great institutional network of the New Policies era was the hierarchy of local councils and higher-level assemblies mandated in local self-government regulations issued beginning in 1907. Roger Thompson's history of this reform movement discusses the range of opinions about what sort of constitutional arrangements were most appropriate for China, highlighting in particular the different approaches of Yuan Shikai and Zhao Erxun. For Zhao, effective political reform would "bring rural elites into new structures of power that reached to Beijing."[68] Yuan Shikai and the Japanese-trained legal scholars he employed, on the other hand, went beyond the sort of administrative reorganization favored by Zhao to politicize the Zhili elite, encouraging them to think of themselves as citizens with an important role in the realm of "local self-government" (*difang zizhi*).[69] After allowing provincial officials to experiment with these new political forms for a number of years, officials in Beijing adopted much of Yuan's model in regulations setting forth procedures for the election of councils in county seats, towns, and townships.[70] Other regulations guided the elections of provincial assemblies, which brought representatives from each county to the provincial capitals, and a National Assembly, which met for the first time in Beijing in 1910.[71]

In addition to these three institutional networks and the New Army, the New Policies included many other types of reform: a new legal code was drawn up, the cultivation and consumption of opium was banned, some attempts were made to rationalize local finance, restrictions on certain interactions between Manchu and Han subjects were abolished, and plans were laid to encourage the development of China's economy. Foreigners—many of whom had thought of China as the "sick man of Asia," mired in the stagnant swamps of Confucian conservatism—were astonished at the energy of the reformist government. Some, to be sure, viewed the New Policies with cynicism, claiming that they amounted to little more than piles of paper regulations and new ways of "squeezing" the people.[72] Those who believed this were quite wrong, however. Although they were not designed for precisely that end, the implementation of the New Policies created a new type of city in many of the provincial capitals and changed the position of cities in the geography of Chinese politics.

The Place of Provincial Cities in the Implementation of the New Policies

It is ironic, given the great concern of officials like Yuan Shikai and Zhao Erxun to control the countryside in the aftermath of the Boxer uprising, that the New Policies ended up doing so much to distance the provincial capitals from their hinterlands. That had certainly not been their intent. And yet, as David Buck notes in his study of Shandong's capital, Ji'nan, "the atrophy of the lower centers of political power and the increasing importance of Ji'nan as the center of political power . . . is a major strand of the city's history" after the advent of the New Policies era.[73] Roger Thompson, in his work on the constitutionalist aspects of the late Qing reforms, argues that it was because of the way the New Policies were implemented that the era marks the beginning of "the building of a wall between rural and urban China."[74] The foundations of this wall, Thompson believes, were laid by the inexperienced young men who gained important positions in Beijing after returning with degrees from universities in Japan and Europe. The returned students lacked an understanding of the delicate balance of interests and authority that existed in Chinese communities among leaders of functionally specific groups such as merchants, militiamen, and educators—a phenomenon that Thompson calls "local corporatism." They based their self-government regulations on foreign models that took the individual citizen as the basic unit, with no role for mediating corporate groups. The result was disruptive factionalism that burst the corporatist restraints of the old system.[75] Regulations for local assembly elections that favored elites based in market towns and county seats exacerbated the factional struggle and left the rural elite shut out of the political realm much more completely than it had ever been before.[76]

Thompson's observations on the politics of the local assemblies are perceptive and convincing. Long before the court approved the creation of local assemblies, however, the implementation of earlier New Policies projects had begun to open up a wide gap between the cities, especially provincial capitals, and rural areas.[77] Virtually all the New

Policies were implemented first in the provincial capitals. Money and attention were lavished on these cities by officials who were deeply committed to them and found allies among urban elites outside the formal bureaucracy. The extension of the new institutions to prefectural and county seats, market towns, and villages was much more difficult in many ways, and few of the New Policies leaders took the trouble to pay much attention to it, until ordered to do so by the court beginning in 1908.[78] Even those who did, including most prominently Yuan Shikai, had limited success. According to Stephen MacKinnon, Yuan's efforts to extend the new educational system across Zhili were effective, achieving a "remarkably even distribution of primary schools throughout the province." He does admit, however, that the "curriculum in the new schools varied a great deal, although not by design."[79] Yuan's police reforms were welcomed enthusiastically in some parts of Zhili, but Yuan hardly built the new police forces into a tightly integrated and disciplined network. His "administration's contribution to local police reform was indirect and technical, limited for the most part to setting standards and training leaders in central police academies."[80] Magistrates who had little interest in police reform were able to ignore it, for the most part. MacKinnon concludes that the Zhili police program was characterized by "rapid proliferation, but also semiautonomous and irregular development."[81]

The decision to make the provincial capitals the showcases for the New Policies is understandable in terms of late Qing governance. The pattern of taking a provincial capital as the base for a wide range of reform projects that were intended eventually to be extended down through all levels of provincial administration is visible in the 1897 Hunan reforms designed by Huang Zunxian. Provincial cities were, after all, the seats of government of those who controlled the resources and political authority necessary to make significant changes in the Qing system. Governors-general, who had to hold audiences with sundry subordinate officials and communicate regularly with the court, spent most of their time in their yamen in their capitals. Likewise, their advisers stayed close by them, ready to handle the miscellaneous duties thrown their way. It was, therefore, only natural for the experimentation of the early years of the reform effort to be concentrated in these cities. To encourage greater cooperation from the residents in support of the reforms, or perhaps to justify their own preoccupation with the capital cities, the governors-general often referred to these cities as *shoushan zhi qu*, an expression that conveyed the idea of a model zone, a central site that set the standards for more peripheral areas.[82] Outside these model zones, responsibility for funding the new institutions was assigned to communities themselves. Governors-general exhorted the "gentry and scholars" (*shenshi*) throughout the realm to take up the New Policies cause.

Historians of the New Policies have cited the self-interested conservatism of elites based in the countryside to explain their uneven implementation. Zhang Zhidong, Daniel Bays observes, believed that the early difficulty he encountered in expanding his school system beyond Wuchang lay in the unwillingness of members of Hubei's elite to commit funds to schools that they doubted would adequately prepare their sons to pass the civil service examinations. To expand the reform in education, Zhang lobbied to abolish the examination system and tie prospects for social advancement more closely to the new school system.[83] In the case of school reform, this strategy seems to have been successful. The abolition of the examination system did indeed stimulate strong interest in the new schools. Even so, the most immediate result was a flood of students toward the provincial and prefectural capitals, where the most prestigious and best-funded schools attracted hundreds of student-boarders from the countryside. In Sichuan, for example, the sole high school (*gaodeng xuetang*) was located in Chengdu, as was the normal school, which sent its graduates to staff most of the elementary schools across the province. Other specialized schools that guaranteed their graduates respectable employment, such as the military and police academies and the railroad engineering school, were also built in the provincial capital, and most of the province's law schools could be found there.[84] The old examination system, with its uniform and limited curriculum, had allowed for a tutorial style of education in which prominent scholars traveled to the households of their wealthy patrons. Under the New Policies, the content of instruction was expanded, and education became a matter of geographically fixed institutions, many of which clustered in the provincial cities.[85]

Joseph Esherick, in his study of Hunan and Hubei, points out that, outside the provincial capitals, the New Policies were undertaken most seriously in prefectural seats, not in wealthier commercial cities without important administrative status. "Thus," he argues, "though the practitioners of educational or police reforms were often young men with Westernized educations, the areas where they could institute their reforms most effectively were established centers of gentry influence. New blood was being pumped into established channels of gentry power."[86] Esherick calls these young men "the urban reformist elite," the heirs to a long process of "alienation" of China's elite "from the affairs of the countryside," which had accelerated during the commercial revolution of the late Ming and early Qing. Urban culture and the promise of commercial profits brought landlords into the cities, and banditry and the "insecurity of the countryside in the late nineteenth century" turned the trend toward urban residence into a flight to the cities. And, whereas the politically active elite of previous generations had considered disorder in the countryside to be the most significant issue it faced, Esherick argues that foreign aggression had taken the place of internal unrest at the top of the political agenda by the beginning of the twentieth century. This also drew people to urban activism, since "the imperialist threat at the turn of the century manifested itself in the urban centers and had to be confronted there."[87] As Esherick explains, the imperialist threat to the urban reformist elite was more than a military one; it also comprised commercial warfare. With the many controversies over concessions of mineral resources and railroads, people throughout China were becoming more aware of the concept of economic exploitation on an international scale—or, in contemporary terms, the danger that foreigners would take away China's power to make profits (liquan).[88]

Esherick's argument that New Policies activists focused their efforts in cities because it was there that their influence was greatest and that the battle against imperialism was to be waged is quite convincing. But he neglects another factor, which I believe is particularly relevant to the history of the New Policies in Chengdu and which is likely to have been generally significant: the influence of Tokyo and foreign-dominated Shanghai as models of clean, well-ordered, "civilized" communities, which appealed strongly to the social and aesthetic sensibilities of officials who were quite conservative, politically and culturally. Just as today's immaculate, prosperous Singapore fascinates a new generation of Chinese elites who happen to be Communists, so Tokyo and Shanghai spurred the imaginations and creative energies of a group of young Confucian administrators in the age of the New Policies.

Zhou Shanpei: Chengdu's Confucian Technocrat

One young administrator who was particularly important in remaking Chengdu was Zhou Shanpei (Fig. 2.1). When Zhou was a boy in Sichuan in the 1880s, Shanghai and Tokyo stood on the faraway periphery of China's cultural landscape, at least as viewed from the perspective of a young would-be official. Zhou's ancestral native place was actually fairly near Shanghai; his grandfather had traveled to Guizhou from his home in Zhejiang to work on the staffs of various officials, and his father, Zhou Zhen, did the same in Sichuan, before becoming an official there himself. The Zhou men were "Shaoxing secretaries," some of the many natives of that prefecture who made their livings by serving as legal and administrative experts in yamen throughout China.[89] For them, the pivot of the universe was still Beijing, with subsidiary axes at the provincial cities and lesser administrative seats. That is where they received degrees, were received in audience, and vied for appointment to the posts that could bring them fame, respectability, official perquisites, and an assured income. Zhou Zhen had done very well for himself. His skill as a private secretary led one governor-general to assign him the huge task of auditing Sichuan's provincial treasury.[90] In 1890, when his son Shanpei was sixteen, Zhou Zhen moved from Chengdu to Yingshan in north-central Sichuan, as the new county magistrate. Within a year, however, he died, and Zhou Shanpei and his mother and siblings returned to Chengdu to live.[91]

Fig. 2.1 Zhou Shanpei. Family
photo courtesy of Anne Chou.

Zhou Zhen intended his sons to be officials, and he devoted much attention to their education. One of Sichuan's foremost poets and literary scholars, Zhao Xi, was invited to serve as tutor to the young Zhou boys. Zhao and Zhou Zhen had Shanpei spend half of each day studying the Classics and the other half developing the analytical and writing skills that would allow him to be an effective administrator inside a Qing yamen. This training proved useful early in his life, Zhou Shanpei recalled in an interview more than sixty years later. Shortly after his widowed mother had moved the family back to Chengdu, clerks in the county yamen at Yingshan pestered the family to repay 800 ounces of silver that they claimed Zhou Zhen had borrowed from the county treasury before he died. Zhou Shanpei submitted a petition to the provincial treasurer, asking that the case be investigated, but got no response. Desperate, he staked out the yamen of the treasurer and waylaid the latter when he was escorting some guests out the gate. The treasurer looked at his petition and then inquired who had written it for him. When Zhou Shanpei claimed authorship, the skeptical treasurer demanded that he recite it from memory. His successful recitation so impressed the official that he ordered the debt problem resolved immediately.[92]

While Zhou Shanpei was steeping himself in the arcana of the Qing legal code and mastering the vocabulary and calligraphy necessary for the correct composition of Qing official documents, other young people were beginning to discover the new cultural world of the colonial cities and rapidly growing treaty ports. Huang Zunxian first visited Hong Kong in 1870 and came away impressed with its municipal government, as did Kang Youwei several years later.[93] Their early interest in unfamiliar urban institutions was unusual, however. Wang Jiajian notes that one of the first Chinese accounts of the foreign settlements in Shanghai, published in 1876, dwelt at some length on the constables employed to patrol the streets, describing their uniforms and policing techniques. Even though the author discussed their use of a telegraph system to communicate with the head office, he nevertheless concluded finally that Shanghai's foreign-controlled police were "no different from runners." Wang argues that such early descriptions of Shanghai did little to attract attention to this new type of municipal police.[94] Curiosity about Shanghai and its organization and evolving urban style began to grow in the 1890s, however, as a new literature set in Shanghai emerged.

Late Qing literature blossomed with the development of new printing technology and new commercial wealth.[95] Shanghai novels, such as *Sing-song Girls of Shanghai* (*Haishanghua liezhuan*, 1892–94), emphasized the worldly and sensual allure of the city and featured characters modeled on Shanghai's prominent men and beautiful courtesans. The International Settlement's colonial status, which insulated its Chinese residents from Qing efforts to enforce cultural standards, allowed for a certain exuberant experimentalism.[96] The young intellectuals arriving in Shanghai around the turn of the century to take advantage of its new schools participated in this "moment of fascination and excitement."[97] Shanghai's growing ranks of "petty urbanites"—merchants, shop clerks, office workers, and students—created a "demand for romantic stories composed with comparative sophistication and dealing with the common denominator of metropolitan life."[98] The authors of some of the Shanghai novels were inspired by the depictions of city life in the great European urban novels of Dickens, Balzac, and Hugo, which were becoming available in the Chinese translations of Lin Shu. As social criticism, however, the novels are more akin to earlier Chinese literature, such as *The Scholars* (*Rulin waishi*), which ridiculed the hypocrisy and venality of officials and their hangers-on. Class conflict is not central to the plots of the late Qing urban novels, nor are they infused with the nostalgic sense of the passing of an old social order, as are some Japanese novels of the period, which portray a Tokyo changed almost beyond recognition with streetcars, electric lights, and public parks.[99]

Perry Link has argued that to most Chinese visitors at the end of the nineteenth century, Shanghai was a spectacle, "almost as extra-terrestrial as extraterritorial."

Western cultural institutions in general were labeled with the characters *wen-ming*, the modern compound invented in Japan to translate "civiliza-tion." By investigating the by-ways of Shanghai one could savor impressions of *wen-ming* clothing fashions, a *wen-ming* marriage, or *wen-ming* theatre. The spirit was voyeuristic rather than practical; to the bulk of those who had any experience with it, Shanghai and its reformist ferment appeared as little more than an interesting experiment.[100]

By the New Policies era, however, those who hoped to influence the Qing reform movement were beginning to take the idea of *wenming* very seriously. As this passage from Link suggests, *wenming* was an elastic concept, and it was not the exotic cultural products of Shang-hai that impressed the New Policies reformers most. The *wenming* that they saw and admired in Shanghai's International Settlement, and even more clearly in Tokyo, was an orderly and productive urban community.

Zhou Shanpei, like Huang Zunxian and Kang Youwei before him, appreciated how International Shanghai, Hong Kong, and Tokyo *worked.* Where visionary theorists such as Liang Qichao conceived of the modern city as a "center of light," from which to carry out their "mission to illuminate and awaken the Chinese people,"[101] many of the New Policies activists inside the bureaucracy had a different atti-tude toward the phenomenon. For them, Tokyo in particular was worthy of attention because it set a new standard for what committed and honored servants of the state could achieve in enriching a com-munity and endowing it with the beauty of orderliness. Schooled in the pragmatic statecraft tradition of the imperial official, Zhou and others like him could not help but be impressed by the ambition and accomplishments of administrators in these cities.[102] The well-run city itself became their emblem of statecraft skill, and the *wenming* of the Tokyo-style city was something a skillful official could create. Yes, the people of China should be "illuminated," but the "civilized" population to be produced as a result of the New Policies reforms would not be so different from what Chinese officials had long endeavored to cultivate: hard-working, orderly communities respectful of the leadership of the wise men who lived among them—but above them—to maintain their harmony, elevate their morals, and rally them against internal and external threats.

At the same time that they set new standards for good administration, well-run cities were the most striking hallmark of advanced nations, which the masters of Hong Kong and the International Settlement were and Japan was obviously fast becoming. Thus, the fact that young Chinese officials in the New Policies era concentrated their efforts in the provincial cities does not indicate that they lacked a broader vision for China. Reflecting on the nationalism of Jin Bangping, Yuan Shikai's Tokyo-educated chief adviser on issues of self-government, Roger Thompson notes that his "ambition would not have been contained by Tianjin's walls even if they had been still standing."[103] As an official based in Tianjin, he worked for China's future. Nevertheless, even Jin's attempts to extend the institutions of self-government across Zhili, which involved bringing students to Tianjin to study at a self-government school, contributed to the allure of the urban *wenming* that was so significant in the late Qing cultural environment.

Zhou Shanpei's interest in Tokyo and its new institutions was first stimulated in Changsha, when he joined the staff of Hunan's educational commissioner at the height of the 1897 reform effort there. He was in his early twenties and had experienced some frustration in pursuit of success in the examinations in 1894 and 1897; twice he had been listed as a *fubang*, a consolation prize for a performance that had not quite merited the *juren* degree that opened the way to a career in the regular bureaucracy.[104] Nevertheless, his talents and possibly a word from his tutor Zhao Xi won him a position in Hunan. In 1898, the educational commissioner recommended him for a special examination planned for that year in Beijing, and he traveled to the capital. One of his students recalled Zhou telling him in 1933 that he had been very close to Liu Guangdi in Beijing in 1898 and had actually warned Liu to flee on the fateful day of the Empress Dowager's coup. When Liu refused to go and faced execution several days later, according to this story, Zhou paid off the guards to allow him to approach Liu, who, in grand martyr tradition, rebuffed Zhou's attempt to pass him a tranquilizer.[105] Zhou's son, however, states that his father was in Shanghai when the executions took place, preparing to accompany Huang Zunxian to his new post as China's minister to Japan.[106] In a memoir Zhou Shanpei wrote about his relationship with Liang Qichao, he portrays himself as maintaining a firm distance from the political events of 1898; while living in Changsha in 1897, he says, he never once visited Liang at the School for Current Affairs, because he had "always shied away from hustle and bustle."[107] Whether he was forced to flee there because of his connections to the reformers, as some accounts have it, or went on his own to "investigate things," as he states himself, Zhou's first visit to Tokyo was in 1899.

Tokyo in 1899 had already experienced thirty years of transformation. The city had become, in the words of Edward Seidensticker, "the political center of the modern country, leading the way into Civilization and Enlightenment."[108] For thirty years the Meiji statesmen had carefully been studying the institutions and cultures of Europe and the United States and selecting what they considered the best aspects, with their own modifications, for implementation in their showcase city.[109] Skyscrapers, horse trolleys, rickshaws, newspapers, city councils, police, hotels, electricity, postal service—all of these were shining examples of Japan's rising position in the world. By 1900, urbanization was occurring so rapidly that it alarmed some observers, who decried what they saw as the degradation of wholesome agrarian values.[110]

Judging from Zhou Shanpei's subsequent obsession with molding Chengdu into a Chinese Tokyo, he was little influenced by the antiurbanism of the Japanese agrarian thinkers. His connections in Japan were formed through Liang Qichao, who introduced Zhou to his circle of elite "friends of China." According to Marius Jansen, late Meiji elites did not want their country linked in the eyes of Europeans to an Asia that was seen as backward. Therefore, they were hesitant about establishing strong ties to China. On the other hand, they feared that a weak China would invite further European imperialism, which could threaten Japan. Many also believed they had a responsibility to help China overcome its problems, because of what they considered to be Japan's past debts to Chinese civilization. Their response to this dilemma was to celebrate their relationships with the Western powers openly, while quietly encouraging a diverse group of Japanese activists to build friendships with and extend aid to Chinese interested in strengthening their country in cooperation with Japan.[111] The Japanese friends and acquaintances Zhou Shanpei made during the four months of his first visit included such prominent statesmen as Ōkuma Shigenobu and Inukai Tsuyoshi.[112] With such friends as these, Zhou would have been afforded ample opportunity to see Tokyo at its most orderly and productive.

In the fall of 1899, Zhou Shanpei returned to Chengdu, where he organized an English-language class for himself and others at the home of a Protestant missionary. At the same time, he recruited Nakajima Saishi, a Japanese supporter of China's nation-building efforts, to teach Japanese in a rented compound in Chengdu. This Japanese-language school lasted only a few months, but caused a splash with its exotic subject and its student uniform of narrow-sleeved jackets and leather boots. The missionary who had hosted Zhou's English classes, and who lived next door to the Japanese school, believed that it had disbanded because Zhou and the students "came under suspicion" during the Boxer uprising. Nakajima, however, is said to have blamed expensive tuition for the failure of the school.[113] After the school closed, Zhou Shanpei led a group of twenty students to Japan. This was the first group sponsored by the Sichuan administration to join what was fast becoming a flood of students heading to Tokyo.[114] After a few months, Zhou returned once more to Sichuan, to teach for a short time at a school in southern Sichuan set up by his former tutor, Zhao Xi. In 1902, when he was twenty-six, his bureaucratic career gained new life. The New Policies era had begun, and all ambitious governors-general were seeking experts to assist them to build the new institutions called for by imperial edict. Zhou was hired by Cen Chunxuan, newly appointed governor-general, to help provide Sichuan with modern police.

From 1902 to 1911, as an adviser and then as an official, Zhou Shanpei was involved in many New Policies projects. After helping to found the Chengdu police in 1902–3, he followed Cen Chunxuan when the latter was transferred to Guangdong. There, he became Cen's chief secretary and took responsibility for training officers for the New Army brigades Cen commanded. He also traveled once more to Japan and went to Hong Kong twice to converse with Liang Qichao.[115] In 1905, Zhou Shanpei was awarded the official rank of circuit intendant, on Cen's recommendation, and he petitioned the Board of Civil Appointments for assignment as an expectant official in Sichuan. According to his son, Zhou's decision to return to Sichuan was made for reasons of filiality: his mother wanted to return to Chengdu to show her acquaintances there how successful her son had become.[116] If so, she was a proud woman between 1905 and 1912, for her son worked for five governors-general, winning rapid promotion to the highest levels of provincial government (Fig. 2.2).

From 1905 to 1912, the New Policies transformed Chengdu in remarkable ways. Zhou Shanpei was not the only person responsible for this transformation; some of his colleagues were also activists, and there were people outside the bureaucracy with plans for improving Chengdu. When local historians sum up the New Policies era in Chengdu, however, they often use a shorthand reference to five programs that Zhou either initiated or had a hand in developing: the four *chang* and one *cha*. The four *chang* are the creation of a licensed zone for prostitutes (*changji*), a workhouse for beggars (*qigai gongchang*), a new theater at which a "reformed" Sichuan opera was to be sung (*chang*), and Chengdu's first commercial arcade to encourage local enterprises (*quanyechang*). The one *cha* is the police (*jingcha*).

Zhou Shanpei's interests and activities were not confined to Chengdu and its immediate environs. As Sichuan's intendant for

Fig. 2.2 Acting Governor-General Zhao Erfeng (front row, second from right) with provincial officials and foreign diplomats in Chengdu in 1907. On Zhao's right is the Chengdu Manchu general. Zhou Shanpei is in the back row, third from right. (The United Church of Canada/Victoria University Archives, Toronto: catalog no. 98.083P/126.)

economic development between 1908 and 1911, he devoted some time to economic issues that affected a much larger area than Chengdu. Most notably, he was an active participant in a project to establish a shipping company on the upper Yangzi. He also supported efforts to improve the quality of Sichuanese silk products and presided over a conference of dike managers from the Chengdu Plain that attempted to devise new ways of handling disputes over water rights.[117] But, above all, Zhou is remembered for what he accomplished in Chengdu. His greatest enthusiasm was devoted to remaking that city, although, as a servant of the Qing state, he never would have called himself a municipal reformer. His greatest inspiration was Tokyo, but since he considered his actions in Chengdu fully consistent with the goals of the Chinese bureaucratic and moral tradition, he would have rejected the titles of "Westernizer" and "modernizer" as well. As we examine the history of his four *chang* and other projects in Chapter 4, we will see that not all inhabitants of the city accepted all components of his vision of a civilized Chengdu; some indeed considered certain parts of his agenda too alien. But first we must inspect the tool that made it possible for him to attack those social and cultural phenomena that displeased him—the *cha* that sustained the four *chang*—the new police.

3   THE KEY TO URBAN REFORM:
THE NEW POLICE

Chengdu's new police system was conceived in the fall of 1902. Throughout the previous months, the Chengdu plain had been rocked by a series of attacks on Christian communities, wealthy landlords, and government offices. It was rumored that Boxers who had fled northeastern China the year before had regrouped in Sichuan and joined with local sectarian groups to harass their enemies, foreigners and native Christians, whom they considered responsible for a drought that had driven up the price of rice in western Sichuan. One charismatic leader, a sixteen-year-old known as "Goddess-of-Mercy" Liao (Liao Guanyin), led thousands of supporters in battles against troops sent to destroy her Red Lantern Society (Hongdenghui), based just north of Chengdu.[1] For several months, the provincial forces were thwarted, and the rebellion spread. On September 15, disaster struck the administration of Governor-General Kuijun; several dozen sectarians forced their way into the provincial capital through the South Gate, armed themselves with knives at an ironmonger's shop, and took command of the street running along the front of the governor-general's yamen.[2] The seventy-five-year-old provincial judge, who happened to be leaving the yamen just as it came under attack, got out of his sedan chair and directed his bodyguards and the yamen soldiers as they killed or captured most of the rebels.[3]

Kuijun had already been criticized for his inability to deal with the uprisings. A few months earlier, two censors had complained to the throne that Kuijun was failing to supervise and discipline corrupt subordinates and had allowed the provincial army to deteriorate. He was also accused of letting his interest in Buddhism interfere with the performance of his official duties: he meditated when he should have been holding audiences with his officials and hesitated to mete out the death penalty. Before executions, he abstained from eating meat and chanted sutras.[4]

To save Sichuan from the harmful effects of such soft and ineffectual leadership, the governor of Shanxi, Cen Chunxuan, had been ordered to Chengdu in August, even before the events of September 15 occurred, with instructions to restore order. He arrived and took over from Kuijun within two weeks of the Chengdu incident. Over the next few months, Cen sent teams of crack troops he had brought with him from Shanxi to the major centers of unrest on the Chengdu plain. Hundreds of people were killed, and dozens were brought back to Chengdu for execution outside the North Gate.[5] In a memorial, Cen reported that although he believed that "Goddess-of-Mercy" Liao had been a puppet in the hands of rebel leaders, given her notoriety he felt obligated to behead her, in order to "pacify the people's hearts."[6] She died in Chengdu in January 1903, just as the city's first class of police officers began their training.

Securing public order was the overwhelming priority of the provincial government during Cen Chunxuan's eight months in Sichuan.[7] It was accomplished, more or less, by regular military forces dispatched from their barracks in Chengdu and other garrison towns. Cen, however, also aimed to revive the militia system (*tuanlian*) associated with *baojia* organization, in the hope that a strong local militia would enable magistrates and the local elites who worked with them to maintain control without having to summon soldiers from outside the community. In his justification of the militia reforms, it is possible to see Cen's recognition of the need for imperial bureaucrats to gain the close cooperation of local elites: he declared that the work of the Provincial Baojia Bureau (Tuanlian baojia zongju) in Chengdu had been ineffective in the past because it was dominated by officials, who had tolerated its steady decay. The reorganized bureau would be managed by officials with the active participation of local elites, who had a greater stake, presumably, in making it effective over the long haul. Cen directed the staff of the bureau to consult the regulations of Huang Zunxian's policing organization in Hunan, as well as those of European and Japanese police systems, as they drew up plans for the reform of Sichuan's security forces. As in Hunan, the provincial capital was given its own separate force. Instead of paraprofessional militia forces, composed of local men called together for regular patrols only during the winter months and as needed at other times of the year, Chengdu's streets and markets would be supervised continuously and permanently by a professional police force.[8]

Much about the form and activities of Chengdu's first professional police force had precedents in the city and in other parts of China. As I argue in Chapter 2, the late nineteenth-century Chengdu Baojia Bureau was *baojia* in name only: its directors were bureaucrats, and the forces they commanded were paid professionals, even though they were very minimally trained. Certain military units in Chengdu specialized in police work, although military policing was nowhere near as comprehensive in Chengdu during the Qing as it was in Beijing. (The large Beijing Constabulary occupied itself entirely with policing that city and had long exercised a degree of control over the streets and population that exceeded levels attained by police forces in most large cities of the world, prior to the invention of advanced electronic surveillance and communications technology.)[9]

But the police reform in Chengdu during the New Policies era was a significant undertaking, nonetheless. Initiated by Qing officials in the crisis year of 1902 as part of a wide-ranging effort to gain control over an unruly province, Chengdu's police force was heavily subsidized by the provincial treasury, to the point that within a few years twelve hundred closely disciplined officers and constables patrolled the city streets in regular shifts, both night and day. Because of this greater effort in Chengdu, state authority became much more visible and effective, as well as more predictable, there than it was in the rest of the province. The successful construction of this new instrument of state control fired the ambition of its creators. Zhou Shanpei, in particular, attempted to use the police institution and its budget and prestige to mold Chengdu into the Tokyo-inspired city he wished to see it become. By so doing, he put the management of Chengdu near the top of the agenda of the provincial administration, a place it had never occupied in the late imperial era. The servants of the state became unprecedentedly energetic regulators of city life in Chengdu, ushering in a new age of activist urban planning and management.

The next chapter examines the regulatory projects of Zhou Shanpei and his colleagues in Chengdu. Before we turn to that subject, though, it is useful to take a close look at the Chengdu police force that helped make them possible, and to explore its organization and institutional style and assess its reception among the people of Chengdu. Zhou Shanpei was firmly grounded in Qing statecraft and incorporated certain Chinese administrative practices—most importantly, aspects of *baojia* organization—into the foreign police model that had impressed him as he saw it realized in Tokyo. The available evidence, while mixed, suggests that his innovative institution-building was welcomed by a broad swath of urban residents in the years before 1911.

The Chengdu Force: Officers and Constables

Chengdu's police force was the second that Cen Chunxuan had founded. While serving as governor of Shanxi in 1901 and 1902, he established a force in its capital, Taiyuan, although the court had not yet instructed governors to do so.[10] Like Yuan Shikai, another favorite of the Empress Dowager, Cen Chunxuan had the confidence and energy to act with considerable initiative. And, like Yuan and all other successful late Qing provincial leaders, Cen was constantly on the lookout for knowledgeable and talented administrators for his personal staff. In Chengdu, he appointed an expectant circuit intendant to head the new police bureau as was customary for provincial-level bureaus, but he assigned Zhou Shanpei the job of drafting regulations for the police and training personnel. Zhou had no official rank at the time, but his father's connections in the provincial administration, his own ties to Chengdu's elite via his tutor Zhao Xi, and his experience in Japan garnered him a recommendation to Cen as a promising young administrator.[11]

Zhou Shanpei's plan for the Sichuan police foresaw the incremental establishment of professional forces in administrative seats, market towns, and villages throughout the province and the gradual replacement of the old *baojia* and militia systems.[12] Until 1908, however, the reformers in the provincial administration concentrated their efforts almost entirely on the Chengdu force, which was to be a model for all lower jurisdictions. To ensure that the Chengdu police would be an outstanding example, Cen Chunxuan gave the reformers a sizable budget in support of their work. In addition to the 25,000 taels that had been the entire annual budget of the Baojia Bureau in Chengdu, the city's new police bureaucracy was granted more than 150,000 taels from various provincial sources to pay for salaries, uniforms, and equipment.[13] This generous funding undermined the value of the Chengdu force as a model for country magistrates, however—no other administrative jurisdiction in Sichuan could tap the resources of the provincial treasury as it set up a police force.[14]

For its headquarters, the Police Bureau appropriated the building in the north-central part of the city that had housed the Baojia Bureau. To organize police work geographically, Chengdu was divided into six precincts: four corresponding to the cardinal directions, a central precinct, and an Outer East precinct outside the East Gate along the road to Chongqing. Each of these was divided into six or eight subprecincts, for a total of forty. The South, North, and West precincts had subprecincts outside the city walls, and the Outer East precinct included one subprecinct assigned the task of policing boat traffic on the river. The Banner garrison was not subject to the authority of the Chengdu force, but in 1906 a separate Banner police force was established for it. Offices and barracks were set up in each precinct and subprecinct (see Fig. 3.1) in temples and a few other "public buildings" (*gongsuo*), including several guildhalls and sites

Fig. 3.1 A police subprecinct office in Chengdu. This building was constructed to be a police station; other such offices occupied temples, guildhalls, and other "public" buildings throughout the city. (*Sichuan Chengdu disanci shangye quangonghui diaochabiao* 1908.)

owned by philanthropic societies.[15] Plans were drawn up to assign constables to posts at street intersections or to regular beats mapped out by bureau officials.[16]

To train the Chengdu police, the bureau established a police academy (*jingwu xuetang*) for officers and a training camp for constables (*xunjing yubeiying*). Zhou Shanpei compiled textbooks and led classes at the academy, and military officers taught the ordinary recruits to march and handle weapons at the training camp. Officers and constables alike listened to lectures on "police philosophy" (*jingcha zhuyi*), which included the history of police in China and the West and discussions of the role of the police in society.[17] The most important document in the training regimen of police personnel was the *Regulations of the Sichuan Provincial Police Bureau*, drafted by Zhou, based in part on Japanese police regulations, and approved by Cen Chunxuan and the Qing court's Board of State Affairs (Zhengwuchu).[18] From among its detailed regulations, it is possible to piece together a picture of the sort of police force Zhou Shanpei envisioned.

The force would operate in a highly systematized, bureaucratic way. The regulations set forth strict rules for the recruitment of personnel, who had to come from "upright" families. Literacy was required of all officers and constables, to enable them to fill out the myriad forms the bureau devised to allow it to monitor police activities. Constables would carry record books in which all incidents encountered on duty were to be noted. Sergeants assigned to subprecinct offices to supervise the forty-some constables attached to each were responsible for five different types of forms, covering daily arrest records as well as shift rotations, transfers, assignments, and evaluations of the performance of constables. Officers at the precinct and subprecinct levels had even more paperwork to complete in Zhou Shanpei's plan.

Zhou Shanpei's conception of the professional style to be cultivated by the Chengdu police was clearly influenced by a concern that the new constables not be identified with abusive yamen runners and *baojia* constables of the past.[19] Over and over the regulations forbade constables to enter the houses of city residents, even those suspected of criminal activities, without a warrant from officials of the Police Bureau. Constables were forbidden to extort money from those who reported crimes, and the penalty for violating this rule was mutilation of an ear, a form of shameful branding. The constables were to employ their nightsticks only on armed and dangerous suspects, and all use of nightsticks had to be reported by the subprecinct office to the bureau. The constables' uniforms prominently displayed the name of the subprecinct office to which a constable was attached, as well as his own badge number. The regulations, which were publicized and distributed as a pamphlet, encouraged city residents to report abuses by constables to the bureau.[20]

The rules of conduct required the constable, while on duty, to wear his uniform; to refrain from laughing; to speak politely to residents with complaints; to walk in a dignified way, barring exceptional circumstances that required haste; and to coil his queue around his head and to shave his forehead every seven days. In addition, constables were to refrain from carrying or wearing any object not specifically mentioned in the regulations on dress; from joining a crowd at an entertainment unless there to supervise it; from using an umbrella, smoking, eating, drinking, or buying things while on duty; and from entering a teahouse, opium den, theater, or other "improper place" unless ordered to inspect it.[21] A constable, unlike a yamen runner, was to be dignified.

The lifestyle awaiting a recruit was as restricted as that of a military boot camp. Constables lived in police barracks at each subprecinct office, took their meals in the barracks at specified times, and slept according to a schedule drawn up by the officer in charge. The regulations limited leaves to two days per month, and only for those with urgent business. The police would be more than urban soldiers, however. In a memorial to the throne on the establishment of the police, Cen Chunxuan described his vision of the broad role police should play in society: "Above, they should provide support in the many affairs of government; below, they should serve as models of correct behavior for the people."[22] Such a description might just as well have applied to the ideal county magistrate of the Qing.

In training and appearance, then, the new police were to resemble disciplined soldiers. Yet, in their relations with the people, they were to be considerate and helpful, as well as stern and correct. Their social role was to act as the local embodiment of the morality of the dynastic state; they were not so much servants of the people as county magistrates of the street, protecting the common people while inspiring them to live upright lives. In Zhou Shanpei's formulation, the New Policies police reform can thus be considered an attempt to bring what Qing bureaucrats thought of as the moral force of the state closer to the people, via a "radical expansion of local officialdom," as David Strand has described it.[23] The reform sought to replace the yamen runners, never perceived in theory as much more than the amoral and unwieldy tools of officials—certainly no one ever thought of them as models for the people—with professional, caring guardians of proper conduct, not father-and-mother officials, exactly, but elder-brother officials, perhaps.[24]

To encourage the constables to fulfill this role of moral exemplar, the plan required that they be paid regularly and adequately, so they would not feel pressured to prey on the people. It also held open the possibility of merit-based advancement through the ranks, which yamen runners had been denied for the most part, since they—and their sons and grandsons—were forbidden to take the civil service examinations. Constables with excellent evaluations could hope to be promoted to sergeant, and especially worthy sergeants could be chosen as subprecinct officers. Officers who amassed a certain number of service awards during a tour of duty could be promoted into another branch of the provincial administration, to civil service positions such as acting county magistrates or to positions in command of military units.[25] Even while serving in the Chengdu force, officers had some of the traditional responsibilities of the county magistrate; a judicial officer assigned to each precinct was granted the authority to hold hearings in minor criminal cases and disputes and could impose a range of punishments, including beatings, fines, and compulsory labor, on those found guilty in the police court.[26]

Zhou Shanpei thus hoped to build a large, disciplined corps of professional police who would approach their paternalistic duties with high morale and personal commitment. Several factors, however, prevented the Chengdu force from quickly achieving these goals. The project was dealt a blow when the court transferred Cen Chunxuan within a month after the first constables began patrolling the streets on April 27, 1903. Zhou Shanpei accompanied Cen to his new post in Guangzhou, where Cen had him train officers for Guangdong's New Army. Xiliang, Cen's successor in Chengdu, was less interested in police reform and allowed the new force to drift along without much direction over the next two years.[27] Even after Zhou returned to Chengdu and was appointed director of the Police Bureau by Xiliang late in 1905, however, the force continued to suffer to some extent from a problem that plagued local civil administration in China throughout the late imperial era: the lack of effective cooperation between elitist officials and their lowly underlings.

Diana Lary has observed that in the Qing military the social gap between officers and the men they commanded was not great. A military career was not prestigious, and officers and soldiers shared more experiences, expectations, and tastes with each other than the officers did with civil officials, prosperous merchants, and scholarly gentlemen. That changed in the Republican period, Lary notes, in part because of the establishment of modern military schools that did confer prestige on their graduates and thus attracted the sons of elite families.[28] Chengdu's late Qing police force, at least in regard to the relations between officers and men, resembled the Republican armies more than it did those of the late Qing, except that the social gap between officer and constable was even wider. This gap was partly a result of the great contrast in the backgrounds and expectations of the officer and constable recruits. It was also, however, written into the regulations that guided the force's development, as a result of Zhou Shanpei's fear that the new police would be equated with old yamen runners. For officers, Zhou's new institution offered some room to establish their reputations as capable and enthusiastic civil servants; for constables, that was rarely the case. In managing the constables, the police bureau emphasized obedience and reacted harshly at the first sign of failure in this regard.

Officers for the Chengdu force had to be either non-native civil officials posted to Sichuan for service or military officers, who could be Sichuan natives. Candidates for training at the Police Academy were recruited by examination, and most of the applicants were low-ranking expectant officials waiting for assignment. The first few years of the twentieth century had seen a remarkable growth in the practice of rank-purchasing and consequently in the number of expectant officials in Chengdu. Men who had bought the status of *jiansheng* (student at the Imperial Academy) then made an appropriately large contribution to some official fund-raising effort—for naval defense or disaster relief, for example—and were rewarded by the financially strapped court with a minor expectant rank in a provincial adminis-tration. By 1910, Sichuan was so oversupplied with expectants that officials were organizing charitable funds to support fellow-provincials stuck in Chengdu without employment.[29] In 1911 the gov-ernor-general offered to pay the traveling expenses of any low-level expectant willing to return to his native province.[30]

For a man such as Lu Guangzhong, who arrived in Sichuan in 1902 with the low rank of county jail warden (*dianshi*), service as a police officer may have been attractive not only for the salary—a subprecinct official received forty silver dollars a month, a substantial sum (constables were paid five dollars per month, plus food)—but also as a way to improve his chances of getting a post in the bureaucracy. A provincial rule stipulated that each expectant official assigned to Sichuan had to serve for at least one year as a "deputy" (*weiyuan*) in a government agency before he could be evaluated for appointment to a "real" bureaucratic position (*shique*).[31] Jobs assigned to deputies included managing tax-collection agencies, investigating legal cases, overseeing the compilation of local histories, and staffing *baojia* bureaus.[32] The Police Bureau created new opportunities for entrée into bureaucratic service after 1902; both precinct and subprecinct chiefs qualified as *weiyuan*.

On the other hand, many of these young men may have found police work a genuinely attractive career choice on its own merits. Like the New Army, the Police Bureau was undoubtedly seen as an institution with a bright future. In itself, it may not have been at the heart of the concept of "civilization" (*wenming*) but, given the importance of police reform in Japan's modern history, it was central to *weixin*, which might be translated as "modernizing reform," the goal of many a young, Japanese-educated patriot in the early twentieth century. At least fifteen young men from Sichuan had traveled to Japan to study police work by 1910.[33] Even some of those who went to Japan to study the most popular subjects—law and administration—advised the provincial leadership on their return that establishing modern schools and training a modern police force were essential first steps in the process of creating constitutional government.[34] The uniform for police officers specified in the Chengdu regulations included Western-style insignia and leather boots, articles which advertised to at least a part of the community that their wearers were men of the future, progressive builders of a new, strong China. The uniforms of constables also incorporated Western features (Fig. 3.2). Governor-General Xiliang, who was rather conservative in some ways, is reported to have criticized the police uniforms on his arrival in Chengdu as "too foreign."[35]

Fig. 3.2 The northern gate of Sishengci Street, Chengdu. Residents pose with missionary L. L. Allan and a constable (center). At left is one of the lampposts erected by the police bureau. Notations made on the back of the photo indicate that the policeman "is smaller than average," that "this street crowd are better dressers than the average," and that the mission had paved the street. Dated 1908. (The United Church of Canada / Victoria University Archives, Toronto: catalog no. 98.083P/20.)

Police work offered some more traditional sources of satisfaction, as well. A 1912 drawing of a police subprecinct officer holding a hearing (Fig. 3.3) is strikingly similar to the familiar image of a county magistrate presiding at court. The plaintiffs are kneeling in front of the officer's desk, on which are placed neatly folded petitions and the various implements needed for writing judgments. Attentive constables flank the officer, who sits on a dais above the litigants. Although this drawing represents the Chengdu police in the first year of the Republic, it is quite likely that the subprecinct offices were intended from the beginning to look like the audience halls of county magistrates. Barely visible in a 1908 photograph of one such office in Chengdu (Fig. 3.1) is a dais like the one in the 1912 drawing.[36] That the plaintiffs in the drawing kneel before the police offi-

Fig. 3.3 Drawing of police court in session. (*Tongsu huabao*, July 1, 1912.)

cer suggests strongly that these men carried out their jobs enveloped in the authoritarian aura of the "father-and-mother" official, which must have been pleasing to many of the ambitious, young, expectant officials.

Demands on police officers were heavy. Evaluations of their work preserved in the imperial archives in Beijing show that they were expected to supervise their subordinates closely, go out on patrol often, and attend bureau meetings regularly. One line in a long satirical verse called "The Present State of Officialdom" published in a Chengdu guidebook advises: "For a cushy job, work in the bursary (*zhiyingju*); for a tough time, be a police officer."[37] Zhou Shanpei apparently believed that many of the students he had trained a few years earlier had proven themselves unfit by 1906. That year as bureau director he fired 32 of the hundred-some officers for a variety of reasons, such as exhibiting general incompetence, mishandling important cases, exceeding authority, indulging in corrupt behavior, consorting with prostitutes, and failing to properly discipline subordinates.[38] Some cases of misconduct among officers and their punishment received notice in the local papers, the *Sichuan Official Gazette* (*Sichuan guanbao*) and the *Chengdu Daily* (*Chengdu ribao*).[39]

For those who impressed Zhou Shanpei and subsequent heads of the Police Bureau, however, the rewards of a job as a police officer could be great. Many found real job security on the Chengdu force and became valued specialists in police work. Twenty-two officers served at least five of the first six years after the force was founded.[40] Others left the Chengdu force only because they had been invited to organize police forces in other parts of Sichuan.[41] The career of Lu Guangzhong, for example, shows the heights to which a Chengdu police officer could aspire. Lu was a member of the first class of the Police Academy and served for five years in subprecinct and precinct offices in Chengdu. In 1907 he earned the top spot in a general evaluation of all the officers in the city, winning a promotion in official rank but retaining his job as head of the South precinct. He continued to make regular financial donations to official causes until eventually he acquired the rank of magistrate of an independent department (*zhili zhou*). In 1909 he was appointed magistrate of Qiongzhou, southwest of Chengdu, by Zhao Erxun, Xiliang's successor as governor-general. By 1911, he had returned to Chengdu as a top official in the Police Bureau and concurrent head of the constable training school.[42]

Unlike Lu Guangzhong, who found a ladder of success in the police academy, the constables whose training he undertook had relatively little hope of advancement, despite Zhou Shanpei's determination to expand the civil service to embrace them. Their backgrounds were too different from those of the officers to allow them to move into the new world of ambitious civic reform being created by such men as Zhou Shanpei. Nevertheless, perhaps precisely because they did not share the activist spirit of their superiors, the new constables seem to have acquired a rather positive reputation among many in the Chengdu community, as we shall see when we examine the public's reaction to the force.

Late in 1902, 1,800 constables were recruited from the towns and villages surrounding the city and from the ranks of local units of the Army of the Green Standard, which was being disbanded in favor of the New Army.[43] Although the regulations required that they be literate, many could not read or write. A demand made in 1910 by the new superintendent of police that constables start following the regulations on keeping written records of their work reveals that they had not been doing so. Noting that, despite their illiteracy, many of the more experienced constables were excellent workers, he permitted them to ask literate colleagues for help with the reports. At the same time, however, he required them to acquire writing skills and warned that they would be fired if they could not write their own reports within three months.[44]

As this warning and Zhou Shanpei's 1906 purge of officers suggest, bureau officials were free to fire police personnel as they wished. There was no grievance process. They also had wide latitude to discipline officers and constables. The modes of discipline were quite different for officers and constables, however. Officers who had collected many demerits were fined, if the offenses were minor, or stripped of official rank and dismissed, if their offenses were serious. Constables received corporal punishment. In one case publicized in the *Sichuan Official Gazette* in 1906, two subprecinct officers were removed from their positions for failing to investigate a murder case but retained on the bureau staff, where, it was announced, they would face "arduous assignments" (*kuchai*). The police sergeant in that subprecinct and his assistant were given "one thousand strokes with a stick" and paraded in wooden collars around the bureau headquarters.[45]

The harshness of the punishments meted out to sergeants and constables is a sign of the lack of trust police reformers accorded their commoner underlings. Although the Western-style system of beat patrolling adopted in Chengdu in 1903 required that considerable authority be placed in the hands of individual patrolmen, New Policies officials never developed a high enough opinion of the constables to encourage in them a sense of being independent and impartial agents of the law. Police authorities still tended to regard them as tools for limited purposes, not as autonomous actors. Their sphere of action was restricted, for the most part, to the public areas of the city occupied by the common folk. Stories in the local newspapers about interaction between Chengdu residents and the police organization tend to involve people who were not part of the elite: small merchants, peddlers, chair bearers, prostitutes. Wealthier residents shunned contact with constables, as is suggested in two news snippets that appeared in the *Chengdu Daily*:

December 19, 1904: On the eleventh day of this month [December 17 according to the solar calendar], in the residence of the Chen family of Zitong Bridge, a constable was caught in the reception room. The constable was wearing his uniform. He was tied up and sent to the Bureau. We understand he was attempting to seduce a maid.

December 20, 1904: Several days ago Constable Ling Yuanzhang saw a man enter the Chen family residence at Zitong Bridge in a hurried manner and thought he looked suspicious. The constable then followed him into the courtyard. The inhabitants of the Chen compound tied him up and sent him to the precinct office, which forwarded him to the bureau. The constable was carrying a lantern and his nightstick, and certainly had no ulterior motives. But he is a new recruit and did not know the section of the regulations that states that without a warrant from the Bureau police may not enter people's homes. He has been punished and fired.

Police Bureau authorities, whose presence seems evident in the second report, were anxious to reassure the city's rich and powerful that constables would not be allowed to interfere with them in their own homes without explicit instructions from the bureau. They also wished, though, to defend the force against accusations of corrupt behavior; hence they tried to squelch speculation about "ulterior motives." Ling's constable colleagues, on the other hand, might have derived a different lesson from this incident: since mistakes committed in the course of zealous policing met with strict punishment, the wiser course was to be only as active as necessary to avoid censure from officers.

Many of Chengdu's constables seem to have tested the limits of passive policing between 1903 and 1911. During quarterly evaluations, their officers were rarely taken to task because constables were found to be exceeding their authority or mistreating civilians, although many of the officers themselves were criticized for this reason. Constables were more likely to disregard regulations on proper conduct. They stood at their posts in bare feet or failed to wear their uniforms correctly. They slept while on duty or left their barracks without permission, sometimes even disappearing entirely. They were caught patronizing teahouses and opium dens. At least once officers were punished for failing to prevent constables from bringing a prostitute into their barracks.[46] There appear to have been some conscientious constables, however: three of the forty subprecinct officers on the 1911 roster had entered the force as constables.[47] It is unlikely that they had achieved promotion without having racked up a good number of merit points in their days as constables.

As bureau director, Zhou Shanpei aimed to improve the force by attracting literate candidates for the post of constable. In 1907 he founded the constable training school to replace the training camp and thus sever the connection between the police and the army. This school recruited students on a regular basis, apparently from among the residents of Chengdu. The editors of the *Sichuan Official Gazette* reported that people they designated "middle class" (*zhongdeng shehui*) made up almost a majority of the applicants to the second class. The editors saw this as a sign that the people of Chengdu were becoming more progressive in their thinking. Being a constable, they implied, was beginning to be considered a respectable career.[48] In 1909 applicants to the fourth class of the constable school took a two-part written examination. For the first part, they had to compose a 200-character essay on the topic of "teamwork" and, for the second, an essay discussing the following statement: "Those who are willing to ask questions of others will do well; those who rely on themselves will remain inferior." Fifty people wrote acceptable essays and gained admittance to the school.[49] Constables who joined the Chengdu

force after 1908 thus may have been better educated than earlier recruits, although, judging from the topics of the essay questions, the
bureau was still concerned that they subject themselves to organizational control, even as it hoped they would take more initiative in
carrying out their duties. In 1911, however, police authorities were still
criticizing constables for their tendency to avoid involvement in alter-
cations on the streets.[50]

An incident involving the recruits at the constable school and
middle school students in Chengdu in the fall of 1908 points to the
dilemma facing police administrators. On the one hand, they wished
to build a force of professional constables they could use to enforce a
new order in Chengdu's public life, but, on the other, they had to operate in an environment in which an influential sector of the public
considered such men to be akin to the base and bullying yamen runners. That fall, schools in Chengdu held the city's third field day.
Representatives from the constable training school performed a
military-style drill during ceremonies before the competitions began
and then entered some of the events. During the hurdles race, an al-
tercation broke out between a constable trainee and a runner representing the elite Chengdu prefectural middle school, who accused the
trainee of knocking him down during the race. The fight became serious when the constable trainees began to use their bayonets,
brought for use during the opening ceremony, to stave off the on-
rushing middle school students. The middle school students managed to wrest away fifty of the weapons and turn them against the
constable trainees before the melee was quelled by the guards of very
angry officials.

Over the next few days, many students in Chengdu walked out of
classes to protest the fact that the constable trainees had participated
in the event at all. Letters sent to the provincial government by leaders of the educational community, who mediated the dispute, blamed
the constable trainees for resorting to violence.[51] The students' objections to even sharing a field with the constable trainees, however,
suggest that a degree of class consciousness was at work. The constable students, who were joining the force at a time when officials were
striving to make it attractive to educated young men, may have per-

ceived and taken offense at the superciliousness of students representing Chengdu's elite middle schools. Guo Moruo, in his memoirs of his student days in Chengdu during the last years of the Qing, reflected on the elitism that prevented him from considering enrollment in any but what he called the "proper track" (*zhengdao*) schools—general or normal schools that emphasized the humanities and sciences, rather than the "side track" (*pangdao*) professional and technical schools.[52] By establishing such institutions as military and police schools and linking them to advancement in the bureaucracy, the New Policies reforms were beginning to challenge entrenched thinking about occupational and professional hierarchies, and it is not surprising that tensions resulted. According to the novelist Li Jieren, who probably attended the field day, the fight seriously damaged relations between the police force and students in Chengdu for a time.[53] It may have convinced some provincial officials that the unassuming, phlegmatic constables of the past had their good points. At least they did not offend the elite community.

Although Zhou Shanpei had concluded during his year at the head of the Police Bureau in 1906–7 that the force was not doing a satisfactory job of regulating the community, he seems to have been aware of the difficulties that stood in the way of a more assertive force. His attempt to attract better-educated constables via the constable school was launched in conjunction with another initiative designed to anchor the force more firmly in the community. Zhou's plan to cultivate street headmen as liaisons between the police and city neighborhoods reflected the influence of traditional Chinese political theory. As such, it was probably welcomed more warmly in much of the community than the attempts of subsequent police authorities to goad the constables to more forceful action.

Police Commissioners and Street Headmen

The original regulations Zhou Shanpei drafted for the Chengdu police included a provision for the appointment of two "police commissioners" (*juzheng*) at each subprecinct office. This was most likely a carryover from Huang Zunxian's plans for Hunan, with which Zhou was familiar from his service in Changsha in 1897. As noted in Chapter 2, Huang had wanted the elite community of Changsha to share in the work of his new police bureau and recommended that committees of local notables serve in the police administration. Zhou Shanpei's plan stipulated that two local men "chosen by the people" would serve as liaisons between subprecinct officers and the residents of the subprecinct. The regulations, however, do not spell out their duties. Information on the identities and activities of the commissioners in the early years of the force is sparse. Several subprecinct officers were disciplined for abuses in nominating commissioners, but the nature of the abuses is not described in the records of the bureau.[54] Perhaps local residents complained about the selection process, or bureau officials decided that some of the commissioners proposed by subprecinct officers were unqualified for the job. The selection process for commissioners was probably not well regulated. In 1908, a man identifying himself as a member of Chengdu's educational community petitioned the bureau, requesting that it "follow the example of Western elections of councilors and have commissioners and street headmen (*jiezheng*) elected by ballot." The bureau responded favorably to the proposal, and the editors of the *Sichuan Official Gazette* chimed in with their support, but subsequent issues of the paper make no further mention of the plan. Nor does the suggestion appear in police documents from that period.[55]

The "street headmen" mentioned in this petition represent a major modification of the police institution, initiated by Zhou Shanpei in 1906 shortly after he became director of the bureau. Zhou intended that street headmen represent the people and work with the police as liaisons to their neighborhoods. Whereas there were only two police commissioners per subprecinct, which contained on average close to 9,000 residents, enough street headmen were appointed (379 according to a census in 1909) to make the ratio approximately one per 800 residents.[56] If, on the Hunan model, the police commissioners were local elites brought in primarily to advise the police authorities and help them raise money when needed, street headmen were intended to be more like *baojia* leaders, as these existed in Chinese political theory. Headmen—volunteer community leaders—would help the police by providing information on the neighborhood and by explaining police regulations to other residents. Through their liaison with police officers, they would in theory help their neighborhoods, both by making the police more effective and by bringing abusive police behavior to the attention of the bureau.

In a memoir written in the 1950s, Zhou Shanpei recalled his attempt to reinvent *baojia* and attach that system firmly to his professional police:

> In the past, Chengdu had only had *xiangyue* and *dibao*, and, because such men had to kneel before officials and carry out errands for them, no good people were willing to take on these jobs. . . . When I was in charge of the Police Bureau, I had each street publicly nominate (*gongtui*) one street headman. The regulations stated that they could confer with officials while seated and were only to help the police carry out business; they would not be used for any other sort of errand. After this, gentlemen (*shen*) and merchants were also willing to come forward and serve as street headmen.[57]

Zhou Shanpei, it would appear, was satisfied with his efforts to recruit men who could be depended on to act in concert with officials as they formed a mediating layer between the police force and the neighborhoods. Unfortunately, the nature of the relationship between the headmen and the police, on the one hand, and the headmen and their neighbors, on the other, is not at all clear from the historical records that survive. As community mediators, the street headmen show up much more frequently in newspaper accounts of the subsequent Republican era (1912–49).[58] Perhaps street headmen became more active as the decline of the police force after 1911 allowed them to take a greater role in local affairs. However, newspaper coverage of local affairs was much more extensive in the Republican period, as well as less focused on the actions of the formal administration, and that may be enough to explain the greater coverage of street headmen and their doings.

There is some evidence that police commissioners and street headmen played a role in tax collection in their neighborhoods. In 1905 the police force began assessing a tax on shops and residences to support police activities. Other special taxes, on such businesses as teahouses and theaters, were added later. Revised police regulations submitted to the Interior Ministry by one of Zhou Shanpei's successors as head of the Police Bureau in 1909 included a provision to award a bonus each quarter to police commissioners who helped collect these taxes. Street headmen were not mentioned in this regard, however.[59] This may be further evidence of a distinction between the duties of police commissioners and street headmen, with the latter more closely involved in day-to-day neighborhood life and the former working more directly with the bureau on such vital issues as funding. In 1911 a commissioner was awarded a congratulatory plaque with the words "public-spirited" in the calligraphy of the superintendent of police, in honor of his efforts to repair roads in a poor part of town.[60]

Police commissioners and street headmen sometimes joined together to claim the status of community representatives on petitions presented to officials, even on matters that were not clearly linked to police work. In the winter of 1909–10, for example, a police commissioner and several street headmen from the North Six subprecinct submitted a petition to the provincial administration regarding the operation of an elementary school. Their signatures headed the list of petitioners and were followed by those of people calling themselves "directors" (*shoushi*), most likely the heads of neighborhood associations that put on annual street fairs.[61] To some extent, then, the commissioners and headmen used the positions and official seals conferred on them by the Police Bureau to bolster broader claims to authority that extended outside the police system. Headmen may also have been granted the dignity of a small office. According to a guidebook to Chengdu published in the last years of the Qing, an "office for reasoned speech" (*jiangli gongsuo*) was set up on each street in 1906.[62] The timing, which coincides with the appointment of the street headmen, is suggestive, but nothing else is yet known about the design of these sites and how they were used.

Although it is impossible to say how the street headmen fulfilled their duties and juggled their roles as police informants, mediators, public ombudsmen, and possibly tax collectors, Li Jieren gives us a fictional picture of such a person in *The Great Wave*, his long novel of the Chengdu of his youth in the years before the 1911 Revolution.

Li's street headman is a good-natured and respectable person of not particularly elite status who is expected by his neighbors—who often engage him in friendly chats—merely to know what is going on in the city.[63] In contrast to the authoritarian street militia chiefs who populate Li's stories about Chengdu in the 1920s,[64] this headman's role in his neighborhood is quite limited. He is his neighbors' peephole into the omnipresent but remote world of officialdom and the machinery of the state.

Policing the Streets

Although we lack a clear understanding of the extent of the cooperation between street headmen and police personnel, we can begin to evaluate the impact of police reform on public life in Chengdu. Chengdu's constables may not have been the stalwart models of rectitude that Zhou Shanpei had envisioned in 1903, but their very presence in large numbers in the streets at all hours of the night and day was enough to contribute to the orderly urban atmosphere that he hoped to create in Chengdu. Bureau officials celebrated the achievements of the force in thwarting pickpockets and thieves and capturing fleeing servant girls for return to their owners. The force developed procedures for controlling crowds that were regularly implemented on festival days and other special occasions. Officers worked with the county magistrates and their runner-detectives to ferret out serious criminal activity. The police subprecinct offices became the most frequented points of contact between the Qing official world and Chengdu residents.

The police patrolled streets from which trash had been removed by street cleaners the bureau hired as part of its permanent staff. On the orders of the bureau, 2,000 oil lamps were set out on lampposts throughout the city (see Fig. 3.2), and they illuminated (quite faintly) the sanitized streets at night. When Zhou Shanpei became director in 1906, he also rid the streets of what he considered human debris—unemployed vagrants and beggars of all ages. These he hoped to enlighten, as well, in several workhouses he set up under the control of the bureau to teach the rewards of productive labor. Thus, the police force began its work as one of several key elements of the New Policies ordering of urban life. As Zhou was no doubt aware, the success of the police reform was essential for winning public approval of many of his other urban reform initiatives.

The most enthusiastic accounts of the activities of the police force in Chengdu's streets came from the pens of European and American missionaries, who were delighted by the new police system. Joshua Vale of the British China Inland Mission, a resident of western Sichuan since the early 1890s, declared in an early report that "the streets are quieter, cleaner, and freer from disputes and obstructions; and thieving is much reduced owing to the police patrol at night."[65] One of his colleagues remarked on the skill of a constable in mediating an incident that occurred early in the history of the force:

One of our missionaries was riding through a busy street, and the chair-bearers, who are often very rough, encountered a beggar, somehow got entangled with him, and broke his staff. A gentleman, passing by, suggested a "few cash" as compensation for the loss, but, before any arrangement could be considered, a policeman was on the spot, and quickly managed the business, to the satisfaction of the beggar and the offenders.[66]

Li Jieren also noted a sharp decrease in the frequency of teahouse brawls after the inauguration of the force.[67]

The deterrent effect of the new force was called into play whenever there were large public gatherings, such as at marketplaces or the many periodic temple fairs and guild festivals. Christian missionaries were especially interested in the crowd control practices of the force at the last provincial civil service examination held in 1903 in the Imperial City in the center of Chengdu. To attract a literate audience to their teachings, the missionaries had stationed themselves near the entrance to the examination grounds (Fig. 3.4) to distribute free tracts to the examinees (Fig. 3.5 shows them similarly engaged six years earlier). From that vantage point they observed the following scene:

The great area immediately in front of the main entrance was nearly filled with soldiers, policemen, officials and deputies; their duty being to preserve order. . . . Nothing happened other than what one would expect, when a few

Fig. 3.4 A group of Qing government officials stands before the entrance to the examination hall in Chengdu during the triennial examinations of 1897. (The United Church of Canada/Victoria University Archives, Toronto: catalog no. 98.083P/19.)

hundred students, and a few hundred coolies, men carrying boards, boys carrying vegetables or delicacies, and a mob of men trying to drive a drove of hogs,—all met in a narrow space. Our new police are an excellent institution. They stood in their places, armed with very light strips of bamboo, which they wielded vigorously and with good effect, whenever the mob of enterprising coolies encroached too far.[68]

Like the lines of constables in front of the examination grounds, stationary and patrolling constables throughout the city were supposed to be a visible reminder to city residents of the line between acceptable and unacceptable public behavior. When the Guangxu emperor and the Empress Dowager died in 1908, the police superintendent ordered constables to enforce the ban on jewelry and colorful clothes. They instructed the constables not to threaten and forcibly tear off

Fig. 3.5 Foreign missionaries and Chinese assistants stand ready to distribute religious books at the triennial examinations in 1897. (The United Church of Canada/Victoria University Archives, Toronto: catalog no. 98.083P/12.)

such articles, but rather to "calmly and politely admonish" the "foolish rustics" who arrived in the city from afar unaware of the rule.[69]

When it could not deter crime, the police force investigated it. According to the bureau's own records, reported to the central government as part of its officer evaluation procedures, thefts were the most common type of criminal case handled by the police, followed by kidnappings, gambling, counterfeiting, and trafficking in restricted goods such as guns. Murder cases were reported very rarely, at most twice a year. The total number of criminal trials held in the six police courts was not large for a city of over 300,000. Based on reports to Beijing, it would seem that on average a total of some fifty cases per year were heard in all six police courts combined.[70] Zhou Shanpei publicized police records for a three-month period in 1906 in the *Sichuan Official Gazette*, and, judging from this report, police were frequently asked to track down runaway wives, servant girls, and apprentices, who were generally accused of theft as well.[71]

In the early years of the force, beat constables could be assigned in an ad hoc way to investigate particular crimes, as in this 1905 case, reported in the *Chengdu Daily*:

The Police Bureau has ordered all inns in the city to have patrons store their valuables at the desk, in order to prevent thefts. A Muslim merchant named Ajie from Xinjiang was staying at the Chunli Inn in the neighborhood of the Imperial City [the Muslim quarter], with eleven bars of gold in his possession. . . . Nine of these were stolen from his room. He reported the theft to the police, and we understand that the precinct officer has sent constables out in the four directions to make a secret investigation.

The next day the paper reported that suspects had been arrested in Meizhou, some eighty miles southwest of Chengdu, and that the magistrate there was sending yamen runners to accompany the police as they transported the culprits back to the capital.[72] The special status of the Chengdu force as the capital police allowed them wide latitude in pursuing cases outside their own precincts. In 1906 several Chengdu police officers were sent on special assignment to Nanbu county, east of Chengdu, to capture the leaders of an uprising in which Revolutionary Alliance (Tongmenghui) activists had been involved.[73] In 1910, in response to instructions from the Interior Ministry in Beijing, the Police Bureau announced its intention to establish a permanent detective staff within the bureau and instructed all precinct officers to recommend outstanding constables for training as detectives.[74]

Even before the detective squad had been set up, however, police officers were credited with uncovering a serious plot: the 1908 Su Zilin case. According to reports by the police and other provincial authorities, Su Zilin was the leader of an underground sect. In 1908, he declared himself the "Firmiana King" (*wuhuawang*)[75] and rallied his disciples for an attack on government offices, as well as churches and other foreign buildings, in Chengdu. The day before the planned uprising, the Chengdu police got wind of it. Officers led a band of constables to a teahouse outside the North Gate, where they arrested

Su Zilin and some of his comrades. Others were arrested in an inn inside the city walls. The officers who led the investigation were the same ones who had successfully tracked down the rebels in Nanbu county. Among them was the highly decorated Lu Guangzhong.[76]

A case from the previous year—the Birthday Plot—that was similar in some respects to the Su Zilin case nevertheless shows that the Chengdu police force did not monopolize all aspects of policing in the city. In 1907, a group of young men who had joined the Revolutionary Alliance while studying in Japan planned to assassinate provincial officials when they gathered to commemorate the birthday of the Empress Dowager. One revolutionary constructed six bombs, which were brought into the city in a sedan chair hired by a teenage accomplice. Information about the plot leaked, however, and several of the conspirators were captured when a curfew was imposed on the city and the inns where the conspirators had been staying were searched.[77] In this case, the plot was thwarted by the Chengdu prefect and the Chengdu and Huayang magistrates, who used their own staffs to arrest the revolutionaries, according to a report to the throne from acting Governor-General Zhao Erfeng.[78]

The case of the Birthday Plot demonstrates that the staffs of local officials were still active in Chengdu, despite the establishment of a new police force. The Chengdu and Huayang magistrates still needed numerous runners to extend their authority throughout their respective counties. The police system did not begin to replace the old runner system in the towns and villages of the two counties until 1909, when a particularly enthusiastic Chengdu county magistrate began to promote police reform vigorously with the encouragement of provincial authorities. That year, the Chengdu magistrate announced that he had fired over half his clerks and runners and had given the rest special identification markers, so that people could not pretend to be his employees. The Huayang magistrate also reported the dismissal of 100 staff members that year.[79]

Although many runners still worked for the county yamen in the city in the early years of the Chengdu police force, there is no evidence of conflict between runners and the new constables. Apparently the Police Bureau successfully laid claim to responsibility for routine matters of public order within Chengdu as soon as the force was able to begin its patrols. Nevertheless, the complicated policing system that had existed before the New Policies reforms involved many different actors, and not all of these could be replaced immediately. Yamen runners continued to have a role in Chengdu, as did a variety of other security personnel, as this story from the *Chengdu Daily* illustrates:

On the twelfth of this month, some soldiers and militiamen from Tuzhumiao in Huayang county were escorting an important criminal, Li Shutang, to the city [for trial]. They entered the city in the evening and spent the night at Dai Rongsheng's inn on Xishuncheng Street. After the fourth watch, the criminal took advantage of the fact that his guards were asleep and climbed out of the room. Central Six subprecinct officers Sun and Xiong led constables in a search for him. They captured him at dawn on the thirteenth in Guzhongshi Street.[80]

Clearly the Police Bureau publicized this story to draw attention to the vigilance of the police, in comparison to the negligence of runners, militiamen, and soldiers. The case reveals, however, that as of the end of 1904, prisoners being transported to the county yamen were not handed over to the police when they arrived in the city. The multiplicity of agents authorized to deal with detainees must have caused some confusion.

In the case of the Birthday Plot, the identities of the conspirators may have had something to do with the minimal police role in its suppression. The conspirators were all educated, well-connected youth, and police were not the tool of choice when officials had to deal with crime within Chengdu's elite community. Degree holders and men with official rank were considered to be subject to the guidance of the provincial educational official and others in the provincial administration. People with degrees and official ranks did not appear in police courts, even when they had violated police regulations such as those forbidding gambling. In 1910 a man who had earlier been stripped of his official rank and ordered to return to his native county for a gambling incident was caught gambling once more in Chengdu. The superintendent of police reported this directly to the governor-general, who ordered the Chengdu prefect to try the man.[81] In contrast, an ordinary city resident would have had a quick trial and harsh punishment at the police precinct. When dealing with offenders in the military, the police authorities asked military officials for assistance. In 1910 a drunken officer of the city garrison and some of his friends mistook a private residence for a brothel. When the neighbors tried to persuade them to leave, the officer arrested one of them and took him to military headquarters. After complaints were made to the police, the bureau asked the garrison command to join it in impeaching the officer.[82]

For the most part, cases involving people with official status, be it a military or civil degree or official rank, were quickly passed by the police to the appropriate provincial official. During Zhou Shanpei's term as director, the bureau did take on a few high-profile cases involving well-connected defendants, including a Chengdu county yamen clerk accused of secret society activities and adultery, a degree holder accused of meddling in legal cases, an alleged local thug who was the nephew of a *baojia* leader in the southern suburbs, a brawling chair bearer employed by Zhao Erfeng, and the head of the Zhaojue monastery, who was accused of bringing his lover into the temple.[83] Zhou, who publicized all these incidents in the local papers, apparently wanted the police to establish a record of dealing uniformly with city residents of all types. When he supervised the police collection of census data in 1906, he made a big show of sending investigators first to the residence of the provincial treasurer. According to Zhou's own account, the treasurer angrily refused to supply the information requested, haughtily replying that "this family does not harbor prostitutes, nor do gamblers congregate here." Zhou, however, had the backing of Governor-General Xiliang, who ordered the treasurer to report to the precinct station personally to fill out the census forms.[84]

Zhou Shanpei's zeal in projecting the authority of the police force over the entire community made him unpopular within official circles and was probably a central reason behind his transfer out of the Police Bureau after only a year and a half as director. In 1907, new administrative regulations promulgated by the central government created three new provincial positions: educational superintendent (*ti-*

xueshi), police superintendent (*xunjingdao*), and superintendent for economic development (*quanyedao*). Zhou was appointed to the last position, where, as we shall see in Chapter 4, he continued to try to transform Chengdu. Instead of Zhou, the prefect of Chengdu, Gao Zengjue, was promoted to be the first police superintendent. Although Gao was also an active promoter of the police system, he did not attempt to increase its authority relative to Chengdu's elite community. His efforts were devoted primarily to extending the police institution to other parts of Sichuan.[85]

Local Reaction to the Force

Zhou Shanpei's bold attempts to subject his fellow officials to police regulation may have been intended to win popular respect for his police project by cultivating an aura of impartial authority around it. Zhou clearly cared what the residents of Chengdu thought of the police. In 1906 he sent police officials to each of the precinct stations twice a month to deliver lectures to the public explaining the duties of the force and why they were necessary. Zhou himself gave the first lecture at the Central precinct, and a transcript of his speech was published in the *Chengdu Daily*. "If we do not deny freedom to certain types of people and certain types of actions," Zhou explained, "then there will be no way to protect the freedom of all types of people and actions. Therefore, we must restrict certain types of people and certain types of actions." His list of the nine types of people and actions that required police regulation included Daoist priests, prostitutes, rubbish collectors, and fortune-tellers.[86] The crowd's reaction to this line of reasoning was not recorded in the paper.

Certain other features of the Police Bureau program seem likely to have won it more supporters than did the lecture series. Like the Japanese police forces Zhou had observed, the Chengdu police force carried out a range of public services in addition to its policing responsibilities. Most significantly for Chengdu, the police force fought fires. Evaluations of officers between 1903 and 1908 show that the police responded to fires between three and seven times every month.[87] Prior to the establishment of the force, firefighting had been an ad hoc affair of neighborhood bucket brigades fetching water from large cisterns located along the streets. When fires threatened to spread, yamen runners arrived to pull down nearby houses and create a firebreak. The police originally adopted the same tactics, but in 1905 the Bureau ordered the Chengdu arsenal to manufacture several dozen simple pumps, and special fire brigades within the police force trained with them regularly.[88] In 1906 Zhou Shanpei had a 40-foot watchtower constructed at bureau headquarters, complete with a fire bell. When a fire was spotted, the watchmen rang the bell according to a code that indicated the location of the fire to the brigades.[89] In 1910 Gao Zengjue expanded the number of firefighters to eighty, with an additional forty trainees, and built two more watchtowers in different parts of the city. He claimed that it took no longer than five minutes for the upgraded force to reach any fire in the city.[90]

Given the frequency of fires in Chengdu, the new police force had plenty of opportunities to advertise itself. According to a missionary report, the police response to a terrible flood in the city in 1907 also marked it as a vigorous and effective agency. The police "systematically distributed biscuits to the families in the flooded areas, and ordered those in dangerous places to move at once. . . . Many women and children were carried on men's backs, but in some parts the police were obliged to make rafts, with which they rescued a goodly number."[91] Almost every officer on the force received merit points for flood relief efforts in the quarterly report from the fall of 1907.

Fire and flood, like crime, did not affect everyone equally. The richest were already fairly well protected from urban hazards, since many of them lived in the northern part of town, in walled compounds guarded by gatemen. Those who benefited most from the disaster-response capabilities of the police were the merchants who crowded into the wooden shops of the fire-prone neighborhoods inside the East Gate, the lowest part of the city where the floodwaters collected in 1907. Theft was also more common in the busy mercantile quarters than it was in more out-of-the-way residential areas. The *Chengdu Daily* contains many paid advertisements from merchants along the Great East Street thanking officers for tracking down wayward apprentices and stolen merchandise.

Nevertheless, Chengdu's merchants took a stand against the Police Bureau in 1905 following an announcement that the police intended to begin collecting taxes of between 500 and 1,000 copper cash per month from all shops and residences to help defray operating costs. Prior to the imposition of this property tax (*fangjuan*), the Police Bureau's budget had been drawn entirely from provincial funds. Cen Chunxuan had justified this as follows, in a 1903 proclamation concerning the police:

Since the police are responsible for protecting the people, the people, therefore, have the responsibility of paying for the police. This is a principle common to all nations, East and West. . . . However, in the beginning, the people cannot provide much support, and the benefits that will result from the establishment of the police are not readily apparent. If we were to require them to pay, resentment would be unrestrained.[92]

So, for the first few years the Chengdu force was paid for by the people of Sichuan in general. The decision to shift the burden to property holders in Chengdu in February 1905 was not welcomed there. Resentment was unrestrained; merchants refused to pay and shuttered their shops in protest. Missionary accounts report that the government dealt harshly with strike leaders. They also state, however, that the Police Bureau immediately issued a proclamation declaring that the merchants had misunderstood its intentions: the tax was only to be imposed for four months. Complaints quickly quieted down after this.[93] Sometime afterward, however, the bureau began imposing a similar levy, renamed a "lamp-oil tax" (*dengyoujuan*), possibly to remind city dwellers of one of the uses to which it would be put. It may have taken Zhou Shanpei's re-energizing of the police in 1906 to convince the merchants that the force was worth paying for.[94] With the exception of the student unrest in the wake of the 1908 field day, there is no record of any organized protest concerning the funding or actions of the Qing-era police force in Chengdu subsequent to the 1905 strike.

Constables and officers of the Chengdu force gradually gained the trust of many in the community, who began to turn to them frequently to mediate disputes that broke out on the streets. The *Chengdu Daily*, a government-funded paper that got its start in 1904, reported on many such incidents in the years before 1911. Typically, a dispute between a shopowner and a customer would escalate to the point that blows were exchanged or property damaged. A crowd would gather, and someone would summon a constable. Occasionally there are reports of bystanders compelling combatants to take their cases to the subprecinct station. Judging from Li Jieren's fiction, Chengdu people had long been accustomed to loud, public arguments, staged theatrically in front of an audience/jury in a teahouse or marketplace. After the establishment of police stations, such public disputes were often held there, perhaps in part because the police regulations promulgated in 1903 prohibited dispute-resolution (*ping-li*) in teahouses.[95]

In many respects, then, the Chengdu police force found acceptance within large sectors of the community and built a reputation for self-discipline and public service that the yamen staffs had long lacked. Nevertheless, many of the people of Chengdu, according to Guo Moruo, hated Zhou Shanpei himself with a passion and would have liked nothing better than to "eat his body and sleep on his hide."[96] The Communist general Chen Yi, who was a child in Chengdu during the late Qing, recalled that when he misbehaved, his relatives would say, "Baldy Zhou is going to come take you away."[97] Zhou's fearsome reputation was not due to his creation of the new police force. Many appreciated the benefits associated with the police, such as effective firefighting and reduced theft, and few in Chengdu had to bear much of the expense. Rather, Zhou was disliked because of his zeal for reforming public behavior in the city. He used the police force to carry out part of his civilizing mission, as we will see in the next chapter, but few blamed the constables for implementing what so clearly was their boss's own plan for the city.

4 THE WINDS OF PROGRESS:
THE LATE QING URBAN
REFORM AGENDA

Throughout the fall of 1906, Zhou Shanpei made use of the reputation and authority that he had attained through his effective management of the Chengdu police force to extend his activism to other areas of Chengdu life. Unlike the next wave of reformers, he and his collaborators had no overarching plan for the economic and physical development of the city, but they did have an overriding goal: public orderliness and industriousness, especially among the masses of the poor. National strength was to be achieved through creation of a well-regulated society; minor physical changes in the city were sometimes necessary for—but secondary to—the social and institutional changes. In the drive to create an orderly and productive city, Zhou expanded the duties of the police force and the regulatory reach of the Police Bureau to involve it in such matters as sanitation, medicine, prostitution, and vagrancy. As superintendent for economic development after 1907, Zhou directed his efforts to a wider range of commercial matters, including guild reform and the promotion of industry and a new business culture.

In the course of implementing these and other projects, Zhou Shanpei and his colleagues never developed a clear vision of what they hoped Chengdu would become as a result of their labors. As I suggest in Chapter 2, Zhou seems to have been trying to equal the achievements of the Meiji activists, who had turned Tokyo into a technologically sophisticated, "world-class" city. Zhou's interest in establishing a licensed quarter for prostitution in Chengdu testifies to his admiration of Tokyo. The fact that Japanese writers disturbed by the Meiji transformation of their city considered the Yoshiwara district the "decayed" center of the old "Edo culture" is, I think, merely ironic. To Zhou Shanpei, the Yoshiwara as it existed in 1900 was an example of a well-policed and businesslike urban space, not a melancholy reminder of the costs of the advent of modern industrial civilization.[1]

Like many other late Qing intellectuals, Zhou Shanpei often used a vague expression to characterize his intentions in Chengdu: he claimed that he was acting to "civilize its customs" (*kai fengqi*). Literally, the Chinese phrase suggests an opening of the atmosphere, as if to let in fresh air. As used by many late Qing elites, it meant to be civilized, to be open to the "winds of progress." The nature of this hoped-for civilization was largely taken for granted by many activists in Chengdu in the New Policies period. Meiji Japan's success in building a strong economy and military demonstrated sufficiently to officials such as Zhou Shanpei that its path of state-directed development was progressive and civilized. Others, however, could rally around a call to "civilize customs" and understand by it a more traditional appeal for moral revitalization. Zhou Shanpei himself saw no inherent contradiction in these two interpretations of the nature of "civilization." Zhou's achievements in Chengdu owe much to his ability to act decisively while avoiding explicit discussion of his visions of the future of the city and province. This allowed him to attract support both from cultural conservatives within Chengdu's elite community—who saw in him the brilliant student of one of Sichuan's most outstanding scholar-officials, determined to carry on the best traditions of Confucian statecraft—and from more radical men who hoped to see Chengdu join the new world of industrialized cities and aggressive nation-states.

In the last years of the Qing, Zhou Shanpei fostered and made use of a strong reform community within Chengdu that, for a while, united in support of many New Policies initiatives. Between 1906 and 1909, he was the de facto leader of this group. In the course of four active years, Zhou used his prominent position in the provincial government to draw on the skills, energies, and financial resources of the gentry and merchant elite in Chengdu. The projects he and his allies launched set a pattern for the management of Chengdu that remained influential well after the fall of the Qing. Zhou's dominion over the city began to falter in 1909, however, when the central government's constitutional reforms produced "self-government" assemblies that quickly positioned themselves as rivals to provincial bureaucrats. The complex local politics of constitutionalism and revolution, which abruptly ended the New Policies era in Chengdu, are the subject of the next chapter. Here we take a closer look at the late Qing reform community in Chengdu and the patterns of city administration set during the years when it rallied around Zhou Shanpei and his attempts to open the city to the "winds of progress" as he understood them.

Chengdu's Reform Community

Chengdu's late Qing reform community was itself largely a product of the New Policies reforms. Chengdu had seen relatively little of the elite public activism characteristic of the Jiangnan region in the late nineteenth century. Before 1901, a small number of Chengdu scholars, most notably Song Yuren, had joined in the national political debate launched in 1895 by Kang Youwei and his comrades in the wake of China's military defeat by Japan. But their efforts to "bring civilization in" (*shuru wenming*), in the words of the manifesto of the *Sichuan Study Journal*,[2] had withered in the wake of the Empress Dowager's 1898 coup. The launching of the New Policies reforms gave these scholars and their protégés a new justification for political activism and new institutions through which to work—the schools and public associations created as part of the reforms. Between 1901 and 1911, Chengdu saw the formation of a chamber of commerce, a railroad company, and associations for education, agriculture, opium suppression, and reform of Sichuan opera.[3] Almost all the leaders of these institutions were degree holders close to Song Yuren and Zhou Shanpei.[4] Many of them had experience in Japan.

Xu Zixiu (1862–1936) was the most prominent of these leaders. An accomplished scholar, Xu Zixiu was so disgusted at the 1898 executions of the six martyrs in Beijing that he abandoned all thought of seeking office in the Qing government. Instead, he began to study Western political theory and to devote himself to improving education in Sichuan. In 1901 the governor-general invited him to select students to study in Japan, and he organized a school, the Dongwen (Japanese) Academy, to prepare students for study abroad. Two years later he traveled to Japan himself to investigate the education system there. That year he also helped found the Huayang Academy, the first of many new schools in Chengdu to adopt the organization and curriculum specified for schools in the New Policies. He was an enthusiastic supporter of the Sichuan–Hankou Railroad company, established in 1905, and was instrumental in convincing the Chengdu elite to accept the government's plan to fund the railroad through a surtax on the land tax, for which landowners would receive shares in the railroad company. He advised the provincial government to send students to Belgium in 1904 to study railroad construction and mining. He was the first principal of the provincial normal school and director of two new provincial bodies, the Educational Association (Jiaoyu zonghui) and the Agricultural Association (Nonghui).[5] The events of 1898 had turned Xu Zixiu against the Manchus, but he remained deeply committed to the elitist ideology that sustained the imperial system. Thus, he was an ideal ally for Zhou Shanpei and other provincial officials, who wanted to achieve economic development and a more tightly regulated urban society through an expansion of the meritocratic and authoritarian bureaucracy.

During the second, constitutionalist, phase of the New Policies, a new type of extra-bureaucratic leadership emerged in Chengdu to launch an open challenge to the provincial administration. Like Xu Zixiu, though, most of the prominent men in Chengdu in the early years of the New Policies accepted Zhou Shanpei's state-centered approach to reform. A few stand out as unusual, nonetheless. These include a small number of Tongmenghui revolutionaries, who were antagonistic to the imperial system and thus resistant to co-optation by officials like Zhou Shanpei. Six of these very young men were arrested in 1907, after the failure of the Birthday Plot to assassinate provincial officials (see Chapter 3). Zhou Shanpei later claimed that he had helped persuade his superiors to be lenient with the culprits, who came from well-connected families.[6] Other Tongmenghui members taught or studied at some of the new schools in Chengdu, but they were unable to build up much of a following.[7] Some, like Yang Shukan, a future governor of Sichuan, left Chengdu for Chongqing, a more favorable site for underground activities.

One of the most exceptional figures in late Qing Chengdu was a revolutionary of another sort. Fu Qiaocun, author of the *Comprehensive Guide to Chengdu* (*Chengdu tonglan*), assumed the innovative role of public cultural critic of the Chengdu community at large. Fu, the son of a provincial degree holder, grew up in the city. In his youth, he was a prolific writer on a broad array of topics, including Qing military history and international commerce. In 1898, while in his mid-twenties, he became a student at the Zunjing Academy and contributed articles to Song Yuren's reformist journal. Up to this point, his career was fairly similar to that of Xu Zixiu. Unlike Xu, however, Fu Qiaocun refused to settle into a customary life of elite teaching and conferring with high-level officials and instead chose to become a newspaperman and an advocate of "popular enlightenment." In 1900 he established his own publishing company, which produced detailed maps of the city, and in 1901 he began issuing the *Enlightenment Colloquial News* (*Qimeng tongsu bao*), a paper directed at the multitudes of semi-literate city residents. In 1909 he added a pictorial newspaper to his other publications.[8] To encourage newspaper reading among Chengdu residents, he opened two public reading rooms and stocked them with Beijing and Shanghai periodicals, in addition to his own. During a trip to Japan in 1903, he bought color printing equipment and a movie projector.[9] Fu used all these media to introduce Chengdu to the new cultural values associated with the late Qing reform movements, including popular literacy, civic consciousness, industriousness, and better hygiene and opposition to footbinding and opium smoking.

Fu Qiaocun's attention to popular literacy and his desire to persuade large numbers of ordinary city residents of the benefits of the new cultural currents constituted an unusual approach to reform in Chengdu. In eastern China, the late Qing "popular enlightenment" movement attracted considerable support and produced such prominent activists as Chen Duxiu, who later founded the Chinese Communist party. Some advocates of newspapers for the masses even went so far as to state that the nation could be saved only by ordinary farmers, artisans, merchants, and soldiers; the traditional educated class was too set in its ways to reform China.[10] In eastern China, where the growth of commercial wealth had long been transforming notions of social hierarchy, such views were still relatively rare; in Chengdu, they had even less of an audience. Fu Qiaocun's attempts to mobilize a broader reform constituency were not widely emulated until after the 1911 Revolution. Christian missionary accounts suggest that he had to turn to the foreign community for help in funding his newspapers.[11] Fu's contacts with missionaries, his willingness to open his reading room to a wide range of Chengdu people, and his enthusiasm for novel commercial ventures (such as a company that built and rented rickshaws, which at the time were considered an innovative and enlightened form of transportation) made him seem eccentric to status-conscious Chengdu literati and cut him off from elite circles.[12]

However isolated Fu Qiaocun was from the elite core of the reform movement in Chengdu, the New Policies benefited from the favorable publicity accorded them in his newspapers. In relatively simple language, cartoons, and illustrations of current events, Fu tried to convince his readers of the value of many of the cultural changes that Zhou Shanpei and Xu Zixiu sought through top-down institutional reform. Of all the Chengdu activists, Fu Qiaocun most fully shared Zhou Shanpei's enthusiasm for the leading roles of the city in creating a new civilization and of the police in effecting urban reform. Zhou Shanpei, in turn, helped Fu Qiaocun with a number of his city-boosting projects. Despite the fact that neither official documents written by Zhou nor his memoirs mention an association with Fu Qiaocun, Zhou undoubtedly provided much of the data on city institutions and commercial establishments that Fu included in his *Comprehensive Guide to Chengdu*, published in eight volumes from 1909 to 1910. A true monument to Fu Qiaocun's engrossment in Chengdu's affairs, the *Comprehensive Guide* surveys the city's history, population, administrative and cultural institutions, customs, and commerce. Under headings such as "The Temperament and Customs of Chengdu People" and "Things That Need to Be Prohibited or Reformed in Chengdu," Fu Qiaocun affirmed his hometown's potential to develop a new civic culture, even as he pointed out the obstacles that needed to be overcome: complacent merchants lacking the spirit of enterprise, lazy officials addicted to opium, superstitious women who invite fortune-tellers into their homes, literati who form factions and flatter officials.[13] In different ways, both Fu Qiaocun and Zhou Shanpei sought to put the transformation of the city at the top of the political agenda.

Chengdu's Receptivity to Change

Chengdu's reform community, as small and elitist as it was, operated amid considerable public sentiment in favor of institutional and cultural change. Fu Qiaocun's publicity efforts may have contributed to this sentiment, but there were more important sources for the enthusiasm for the New Policies in Chengdu. Above all, there were the new schools. As many historians have pointed out, the abolition of the civil service examinations and the creation of an extensive public school system provided a critical impetus for New Policies activism. By abolishing the civil service examinations and linking official recruitment to the school system in 1905, the Qing court created new educational communities almost overnight. By 1907 Sichuan had close to 8,000 public and private schools, with more than 240,000 students, following the new national curriculum, more than any other province. The schools exposed young people to knowledge of the outside world, as well as anti-imperialist sentiment, brought back to Sichuan by hundreds of scholarship students returned from Japan to teach in them.[14] Chinese classical education was not neglected, but, in addition to memorizing Confucian texts, students at the new middle and high schools heard lectures on such subjects as comparative government and world history. Among the books published by the official provincial press in Chengdu by 1908, many intended as textbooks, were studies of the legal systems of various countries, as well as a tract called "Hygiene to Promote Self-strengthening" ("Ziqiang weishengxue").[15] One British traveler in Chengdu in 1908 visited the provincial high school and commented that "the students are cramming Western subjects in a way to cause intellectual dyspepsia." She also noted that classes were observed by large numbers of curious spectators at the open windows.[16] The new schools thus served to advertise the reform program itself, as well as to promote the ideas on which the New Policies were based.

Contemporary Japanese education and the New Policies curriculum modeled on it gave a prominent place to science and technology, the better to develop the skills necessary for rapid industrialization. Many young Chinese men took a keen interest in such subjects, hoping to "save the nation through industry" (*shiye jiuguo*). In Sichuan, however, despite the popularity of the machine shop exhibit set up in 1910 by YMCA secretaries,[17] there was as yet no ready market for advanced technological skills in the private sector. During the New Policies era, the institutions of the state were expanding far more rapidly than was the economy, and the prestige of a government job was still high. For many in Chengdu, the New Policies reforms were welcomed because they promised employment. In the early decades of the twentieth century, the city was home to large numbers of educated men who hungered for respectable, steady jobs, particularly those that held out the possibility for advancement into officialdom. Hundreds of graduates of the new schools found their way into the police forces and the New Army, which recruited engineers and surveyors as well as field officers. Provincial officials with influence over employment decisions, such as Zhou Shanpei, could use patronage to garner substantial political support for their New Policies programs.[18]

The significance of elite employment as a factor in the reception of the New Policies in Sichuan is illustrated by a dispute over the staffing of the offices of public attorneys and the law courts. In 1911, after Zhou Shanpei had been elevated to the position of provincial judge, one of his first acts was to reject as unqualified 800 students enrolled in a short-term training program to staff the new courts. The disappointment led one spurned candidate to commit suicide by jumping into a well, prompting a demonstration against Zhou for cruelty.[19]

Behind this case lay tension between New Policies activists in Chengdu and elites from other parts of Sichuan. By the fall of 1910, the Qing court was trying to spread the New Policies institutional reforms beyond provincial capitals to county seats. The students in the training program for legal aides had been recommended for it, under a quota system, by magistrates from all the counties in the province. Earlier, such representational recruiting had not been the rule. Because of this, Chengdu elites and men with close connections to the city benefited most from the new employment opportunities in the first years of reform.[20] In the summer and fall of 1910, Sichuan's constitutionalist paper, *Shubao*, took up the question of the legal training program. The Chengdu-based editors were outraged that men who had merely sat through a two-month training course were permitted to take the legal examination alongside those who had degrees from law and administration schools in Chengdu. They compared such short-term courses to "starting to bind the feet while getting into the wedding sedan chair." After the results were posted, the paper also accused the presiding examiners of favoritism.[21] Zhou Shanpei's disbanding of the training program was in part, then, a response to pressure from Chengdu elites who argued for the need to maintain high standards for new personnel. The rejected candidates, though, might easily have interpreted the action as unwillingness on the part of the Chengdu elite community to share the employment wealth with their brethren from the provincial hinterland. The jobs created by the New Policies reforms had a strong appeal across the province, but Chengdu elites were best positioned to take advantage of such new opportunities.

The expansion of the state cost money, of course, in addition to providing elite employment. In a study of late Qing Sichuan, S. A. M. Adshead argues that Chengdu-based landholders grew increasingly anxious watching their profits sacrificed to the advantage of Chongqing merchants in the years before 1911. But, as Adshead suggests, concern over the costs of New Policies programs among Chengdu's elite was concentrated on the issue of control of the Sichuan–Hankou Railroad company, which, as mentioned above, was financed by requiring landholders to purchase stock in proportion to the land taxes they paid.[22] The elite leadership of the railroad company was based in Chengdu and did indeed react strongly when the government nationalized the railroad in 1911. Other sorts of economic protests were common in late Qing Sichuan, but for the most part they were staged by small farmers and tenants in outlying counties who were most threatened by tax increases.[23] After the 1905 merchants' strike over new police taxes discussed in Chapter 3, there were only a few brief strikes in Chengdu before 1911.

It is clear that Zhou Shanpei and other provincial officials tried to give the impression that their initiatives in Chengdu "paid for themselves" by improving administration and eliminating corruption. One example is Cen Chunxuan's announcement, cited in Chapter 3, that the people of Chengdu would be required to pay for the new police force only after it had proven its worth. The provincial administration also experimented with an official lottery, which appears to have been popular.[24] Another strategy adopted was to tax commercial establishments that required special police supervision and regulation. Because such establishments as pawnshops, teahouses, inns, and theaters were vulnerable to official criticism for a tendency to undermine social order, the Police Bureau claimed the authority to regulate them. In the process of drawing up regulations for these businesses, the bureau negotiated specific fees to support many New Policies programs.

Zhou Shanpei's treatment of the pawnshop guild is a good example of his use of the authority of the Police Bureau both to strengthen the government's control over commercial matters and to raise money for other projects. He proposed new pawnshop regulations in a petition to Governor-General Xiliang, noting that "those who carry on this occupation exploit the people, and thieves rely on them to fence

stolen goods, . . . yamen underlings and soldiers protect the perpe-
trators in return for customary fees (*lougui*)." His regulations would
have limited the interest rate pawnshops could set and imposed a tax
equivalent to the illegal customary fees, in exchange for police protection of the shops from further demands by officials or their servants. Zhou intended the pawnshop tax to support the workhouses
the Police Bureau was building for the poor (see below), but after his
new regulations were announced in the newspapers, the director of a
school in the city petitioned the Police Bureau to inform it that the
provincial education commissioner had planned to tax pawnshops to
support Chengdu's new schools. The Police Bureau replied that it
had no knowledge of the education commissioner's plan, but if it had
been approved by the governor-general, then the bureau would consult with the commissioner and work out a compromise.[25] By 1911,
the Police Bureau was collecting taxes on teahouses and inns, as well
as on pawnshops and opera performances. In at least one case, Police
Superintendent Gao Zengjue negotiated with the new Chamber of
Commerce to secure funding for a New Policies project. In 1910 he
induced the chamber to approve a tax, to support a female reformatory (*jiliangsuo*), to be levied on all real estate transactions.[26]

In addition to the vulnerable guilds and merchants, the other attractive target for money-hungry New Policies reformers was Buddhist institutions. As with so many other aspects of the New Policies,
the attack on the resources of Buddhist temples demonstrates the
convenient overlap between certain strains of Chinese bureaucratic
practice and the new sort of "civilization" being promoted by admir-
ers of the Meiji reforms. Zhou Shanpei was one of a long line of
Chinese statecraft thinkers who saw popular religion as a challenge to
the dominance of official ideology and the accumulation of wealth in
Buddhist temples as a threat not only to the economy but also to the
authority of the civil administration. He used his position in the Police Bureau to assail belief in fortune-tellers and shamans and to extort money from Buddhist clergy. In what was probably the most
sensational police case in Chengdu in the New Policies era, Zhou
claimed to have uncovered evidence that the abbot of the ancient

Zhaojue Monastery outside Chengdu's North Gate had married and fathered a son. The abbot was publicly beaten and ordered to leave the priesthood. As an added penalty, the temple was required to make large contributions to fund New Policies projects and turn over six-tenths of its landholdings to the government.[27] Later, when he was superintendent for economic development, Zhou commandeered a temple in Guanxian near the Dujiangyan waterworks and turned it over to an institute for the study of silk production. A foreign observer reported a good deal of consternation in the Guanxian community over Zhou's harsh treatment of popular religious institutions, but no organized opposition to his exactions.[28]

Zhou Shanpei's antagonism toward the Buddhists and other local religious communities contrasts with his interest in the foreign Protestants in Chengdu. As early as 1899, he had turned to them to learn about the world outside China, organizing English classes in the home of a missionary. To men like O. L. Kilborn, who practiced medicine and promoted Protestantism in the city between 1892 and 1920, the period right around the turn of the century was the turning point of their careers. Suddenly, they were in demand as teachers to the elite, and their chapels were crowded. After a decade of overt hostility, it must have seemed as if a heavy cloud had lifted. Reflecting ruefully on this twenty years later, Kilborn observed that many who flocked to the churches in the years immediately following the suppression of the Boxers in eastern China did so because they "wished to share the increased prestige of the foreigner, rather than the blessings of the Christian experience."[29] As newly powerful institutions, Christian churches attracted interest from people who had private scores to settle, as well as those who, like Zhou Shanpei, wanted to learn the secrets of Western power. Kilborn's observation calls attention to the tension that the presence of foreigners and their institutions created in Sichuan throughout the late Qing period. The existence of this tension raises the complicated issue of the "foreignness" of the New Policies themselves and the extent to which Zhou Shanpei's projects were tainted by the circumstances of their inception. Did many in Chengdu, in other words, think of the reform pro-

gram as a bitter pill forced on the Chinese by the armies of imperialistic foreign powers even as they looted and pillaged the sacred spaces
of the dynastic capital? Zhou Shanpei's ability to establish the
Chengdu police as an effective institution, despite what Xiliang considered their "foreign-looking uniforms," suggests not, but clearly
more needs to be said on this subject if we are to understand the basis
of local support for the New Policies.

There are few signs in the historical record that people in
Chengdu considered the New Policies to be inappropriate for the city
because they were too "foreign."[30] Of course, in addition to the ordinary difficulties associated with attempts to evaluate popular opinion
in Qing China, the search for evidence of this sort is complicated by
another circumstance. Since the New Policies were announced by
imperial edict and officially supported by provincial authorities, public criticism might be interpreted as rebellion and was therefore dangerous. There are other possible explanations for the silence of the
sources, however. As Judith Wyman has pointed out, the very meaning of "foreignness" was somewhat hazy in late Qing Sichuan, where
people of European descent were rare and yet Catholic communities
thrived.[31] Chengdu's residents had no International Settlement to
teach them to identify foreign architecture and urban institutions.
Although Chongqing became a treaty port in 1891, its foreign enclave
never developed the distinctive treaty-port ambiance of Hankou and
the coastal cities. Whether or not the imperialist pressure and foreign
ideas that produced the New Policies were closely associated with the
reform measures themselves by people in China's far southwest is an
open question, to which my provisional answer is no.

The New Policies era certainly must have been regarded as a time
of great change by most people in Chengdu, but officials like Zhou
Shanpei often played down the novelty and exoticism of what they
were doing. Already in 1898, Song Yuren had supplied what became
the official line by insisting in his *Sichuan Study Journal* that institutional reformers might learn something from the Western countries
but should by no means be slavishly devoted to all things Western.[32]
When provincial officials patronized the initiatives of Protestant

missionaries in the New Policies era—visiting the grand new hospital the Canadians built in 1905, for example, and the YMCA's mechanical exhibits in 1910—their congratulatory speeches emphasized the usefulness of such projects in accomplishing the traditional statecraft goals of bringing order to the community and improving the livelihood of the people. Xu Zixiu delivered an address in which he "dwelt upon the broad character of the YMCA, which belongs not to any one nation or people. Its cosmopolitanism, he said, enables one to detect one's own faults and to appreciate and emulate the best in others."[33] However, Zhao Erxun's 1910 order to parents in the city to stop sewing red crosses on their children's clothing as talismans against the missionaries suggests that many Chengdu residents continued to consider the foreigners strange and intimidating, no matter what they thought of the new buildings.[34]

The New Policies era in Chengdu was thus a time of tension as well as enthusiasm. Nevertheless, the attractions of the New Policies program—the connection to intellectual currents in the broader world, the new jobs, the promise of a more orderly society—were sufficiently varied to appeal to a wide range of Chengdu people. And the provincial authorities were careful to distribute the financial costs of the Chengdu projects so as to minimize discontent. Finally, as we shall see more clearly below, some of the principal targets of Zhou Shanpei's activism were groups and activities long considered by Chengdu elites to be socially and morally suspect. All these factors contributed to Zhou's ability to use the new police and the other New Policies institutions to change Chengdu in significant ways. Of the four *chang* popularly identified as Zhou Shanpei's primary contributions to Chengdu's New Policies, the beggar workhouses (*qigai gongchang*) and regulation of prostitution (*chang*) were justified as necessary to bring order to the city. The police bureaucracy, therefore, took charge of these programs, as well as others related to public health and conduct. The two remaining *chang*, the reform of opera and the "industry-promotion arcade" (*quanyechang*), were intended to elevate Chengdu's popular and merchant cultures. In such matters, Zhou enlisted the energies of the Chengdu reform community through the new Chamber of Commerce and other associations.

The Police Program: Beggars, Prostitutes, and Public Health

Early in 1903, Chengdu's streets were swept clean of accumulated debris and illuminated at night by 2,000 oil lamps set on posts, in order to provide a fit space for the inauguration of the new police force. The success of the police force, in turn, made possible a more thoroughgoing attack on other sorts of disorder and gloom that, to the minds of Zhou Shanpei and his supporters, stood in the way of the progress of civilization in Chengdu. One of the most serious of these was the problem of beggars.

Joshua Vale of the China Inland Mission undertook a study of beggars in Chengdu in the first years of the twentieth century and estimated that the city held some 15,000 beggars (see Fig. 1.6, p. 23). He pointed to the economic insecurity of the vast numbers of farmers and laborers in Sichuan as a primary reason for the abundance of beggars. Floods, droughts, and illness quickly wiped out the savings of small farmers and craftsmen. "I have known, too," Vale continued,

many cases of coolies who have become beggars within a week or ten days. Suppose an official or merchant engages fifty coolies from Wanxian to Chengdu, a distance which takes fourteen days to cover. The coolie, when he starts out on the journey, receives a certain percentage of his pay for expenses en route; he leaves a portion of this, possibly, to support his family, or, as is more frequently the case, to pay off old debts incurred during the days he has been waiting to be hired. If all goes well he will have a small balance to draw on his arrival at the capital. This, with "wine money" given by his employer, will enable him to get back to his home by boat or wait until he gets another engagement in some other direction. But, if he becomes footsore or gets a chill by the way, he has to hire a substitute to carry his load, so that, by the time he has arrived at his destination he has used up all his money and probably drawn something of his "return money" from the head man. Having settled with his employer and "head man," no one is responsible for him to see that he gets back to his home, and after a few days in a strange city the innkeeper will not allow him to stay in his inn; he has also pawned his last garment, and within a week he is on the street with a bowl and a pair of chop-sticks, using the piteous cry of *shanren laoye, guoba shengfan*: "benevolent sirs, crusts of rice, or surplus rice," or some such cry, too often heard from these unhappy creatures, who swarm in the large cities of China.[35]

Chengdu's beggars had a loose organization of their own, according to Vale and other foreign observers. "A king, who is recognized by the local magistrates, rules over the beggars, and is responsible to the authorities for their good behavior. This man can often be seen standing on a bridge outside the great East Gate, and levying a tax upon his followers as they go out of the city." The beggar king's duties did not extend so far as to see his subjects buried upon their deaths, however. Dead bodies were a common sight in some parts of town in winter, often remaining in place for several days. Eventually, charitable societies hired men to remove them to paupers' graves.[36]

Such was the state of things for Chengdu's most destitute residents before Zhou Shanpei effected what Vale termed a "revolution" by extending police control over all Chengdu residents who had no means of support other than begging. The Police Bureau under Zhou built "beggar workhouses" outside the South and East gates to take in healthy adults, an orphanage for destitute youths, a sanitarium for elderly people without families, and a hospital for injured and sick workers. Police were ordered to send anyone caught begging on the streets to the appropriate institution. Within a few months, according to Governor-General Xiliang's report to Beijing, 1,500 beggars from the streets of Chengdu had been rounded up and sent to the two workhouses. The new orphanage inside the eastern wall became home to 500 youths shortly after it opened early in 1907. The sanitarium and charity hospital, both located outside the North Gate, accommodated 100 and 300 inmates, respectively.[37] If Xiliang's reports are to be trusted, over 2,000 Chengdu residents became wards of the Police Bureau in 1906 and 1907.

What happened to those among Chengdu's estimated 15,000 beggars who did not find themselves transported to workhouses? Many fled the city. Fu Qiaocun's *Comprehensive Guide to Chengdu* congratulates the Police Bureau for ridding Chengdu's streets and markets of beggars, but notes that travelers outside the city could still expect to be pestered by the destitute who congregated in large groups along the busiest roads.[38] The failure of Zhou Shanpei and other provincial officials to address the problem of the migration of beggars to the outer, nonpoliced, suburbs of the city is evidence of their absorption in the city-management project they had begun with the creation of the police force.

The workhouses were intended to equip inmates with skills they could use to support themselves on their release. Inmates worked as labor crews for public construction projects, and some vocational training was provided. It is unclear how long an inmate could expect to be confined in a workhouse. In Xiliang's memorial on the workhouses, he states that inmates would be given 40 percent of the earnings from their labor and sent out to make their own living after three months. A recent history of the late Qing police reforms in Chengdu asserts, however, that the standard term was four years.[39] Many inmates tried to escape; police officers responsible for supervising the workhouses were given demerits when such attempts succeeded. In order to minimize the chances of success, workhouse authorities shaved off most of the hair on inmates' heads, leaving only a small patch as a marker.[40]

The orphanage provided vocational training, as well as instruction in reading and mathematics. Photos taken by Canadian missionaries show orphans making baskets (Fig. 4.1) and straw shoes (Fig. 4.2). Zhou Shanpei's penchant for using one New Policies initiative to advertise and promote other reform efforts is displayed clearly in the case of the orphanage marching band. He arranged for the orphanage to be provided with a music teacher and the instruments appropriate for a marching band. The band—known to the Western missionary community as "Zhou's Beggar Boys"—helped raise money for the orphanage by performing at funerals and on other occasions, particularly those associated with the broad reform movement, such as the athletic meets and industrial fairs (Fig. 4.3). The band performed at the opening ceremony for the Chengdu branch of the YMCA in 1910, when it was noted that its repertoire included such works as

Fig. 4.1 Boys at the beggar orphanage learn to make baskets from strips of bamboo. The orphanage and workhouses for adults established in 1906 and 1907 trained former beggars in new trades. (The United Church of Canada / Victoria University Archives, Toronto: catalog no. 98.083P/17.)

"Columbia" and "Marching Through Georgia."[41] Western music quickly became popular in Chengdu. The orphan trumpeters were in such great demand among the army units stationed in and around the city that some were enticed to run away from the orphanage, and Zhou Shanpei was obliged to request the governor-general to order military commanders to seek the approval of the orphanage administration before hiring bugle boys.[42]

In addition to clearing the streets of beggars, Zhou Shanpei used his police authority to change the way the state dealt with prostitution in the city by attempting to confine it to one neighborhood and subjecting it to police regulation and supervision. The site he chose for Chengdu's first "licensed zone," according to Fu Qiaocun's guidebook, had long been noted as a locus of "mean society" (*xialiu shehui*). Zhou renamed the site "Renovation Street" (Xinhua jie) and built a police station at the entrance, where regulations were posted.

Fig. 4.2 Boys make straw shoes at the orphanage. Orphans were also taught reading and arithmetic. Original caption reads "Beggar boys given an elementary education and taught trades at Chengtu City Temple." (The United Church of Canada/Victoria University Archives, Toronto: catalog no. 98.083P/16.)

Students, soldiers, and boys were forbidden to enter the area, and brothels were warned that any caught entertaining such customers would be punished. Police regulations justified the concentration of brothels in one part of town as necessary in order to extend police protection to prostitutes and customers alike, drive out the criminals who made their living by exploiting prostitutes, and bring order to a violent and wretched pocket of urban society.[43]

To begin the process of forcing all brothels to move to the new licensed zone, early in 1906 Zhou ordered police to affix plaques on houses throughout the city suspected of harboring prostitutes. The plaques declared that the inhabitants were "households under surveillance" (*jianshihu*). According to the regulations Zhou drafted for the police bureau in 1903, the police had the authority to identify the houses of "suspicious characters" and keep an especially close watch

Fig. 4.3 Zhou Shanpei's orphanage marching band arrayed in front of a temple. (The United Church of Canada/Victoria University Archives, Toronto: catalog no. 98.083P/15.)

on such sites. This was one of the many policing techniques Zhou had learned in Tokyo.[44] As bureau director, though, he applied it only to suspected houses of prostitution.

Of all Zhou's New Policies initiatives, his policies on prostitution stirred up by far the most controversy. Chengdu's elite community, otherwise united in the belief that tighter regulation of urban society was a necessary and urgent task, split over the question of labeling suspected prostitutes and creating a licensed zone. The debate was conducted, for the most part, within official and elite circles and via rumor—no signs of the controversy are apparent in official reports or in the local newspapers. The only publicly expressed opinion on the issue is that of Fu Qiaocun, and his statements on the topic are difficult to interpret. In the section entitled "Chengdu's Households Under Surveillance" in his guidebook, Fu noted that open and clandestine brothels had long been a feature of Chengdu life, and prostitutes had been known by a number of slang expressions. By calling them "households under surveillance," Fu wrote, Zhou Shanpei had given them an "elegant, civilized" new name (*wenming zhi meiming*). Fu might almost be suspected of satire, especially since he went on to express amazement that so many officials and literati in Chengdu supported and protected the "coarse, vulgar" courtesans (citing in particular a certain "Gold Butterfly") who flitted in and out of elite circles. But his subsequent list of those Chengdu prostitutes that he judged to be particularly "refined" suggests that he, like Zhou, did not object to prostitution per se.

Zhou's policy came under attack in two ways. First, complaints were lodged with the governor-general in regard to the "under surveillance" plaques. Zhou responded to these in a long memo to Zhao Erxun in 1908, in which he noted that approval of the 1903 police regulations, with their provisions to label suspect houses, had been sought and received from the central government and that the policy had been implemented with great care:

The harm resulting from prostitution was very serious and difficult to act against, and so I ordered the plaques to be put up, according to the regulation. Since I feared that some plaques might be mistakenly assigned . . . I ordered that two categories be created: open and secret. If a person claimed not to be a prostitute, we did not post a plaque, but assigned a constable to watch at all times and record any activities. The number of open prostitutes did not add up to one-third of such secret prostitutes. . . . After I left the bureau last year, it was said that some people were so angry and embarrassed because plaques were nailed to their houses that they committed suicide. The acting governor-general [Zhao Erxun's younger brother, Zhao Erfeng] ordered an investigation by [the two county magistrates], and they found that nothing like this had happened.[45]

The rumors that innocent women had been humiliated into committing suicide were apparently quite widespread in Chengdu in the summer of 1907. Although Zhou did not mention it in this memo, the Police Bureau issued a clarification of the police policy toward women suspected of being prostitutes—persons labeled "under surveillance" would be permitted to declare their innocence to street headmen and other "upright gentlemen." The plaques would then be removed, and they would be "treated in the same way as good people" (*zhao liangmin yilü kandai*). If, however, after making these pledges, they "dared to repeat their crimes," then they would be "imprisoned forever."[46] Not mentioned in Zhou's memo was the story that an enraged Chengdu resident had devised a plaque bearing the title "chief of the households under surveillance" (*zong jianshihu*)—"chief prostitute," in essence—and nailed it on Zhou's own residence.[47]

Two years after the establishment of the licensed zone, several natives of Sichuan serving in high positions in Beijing wrote a personal letter to Zhao Erxun, noting that they had recently been informed of the construction of a new street for brothels; they strongly objected to it. Although they admitted that prostitution had existed in Chengdu for some time, they emphasized that, unlike the situation in Shanghai or Chongqing, prostitution had never openly been considered an acceptable profession in Chengdu. By cleaning up the part of town in which prostitutes operated and chasing out the criminals who had controlled prostitution in the past, the Police Bureau was actually contributing to a decline in morality, according to these officials, because it was helping to make prostitution attractive to decent people. They scoffed at the police pledge to keep students, soldiers, and boys out of the area and predicted that the licensed zone would make visiting brothels fashionable, since it was protected by law. Chengdu, they concluded, could soon expect to be inundated with prostitutes and courtesans from Chongqing and Shanghai. They urged Zhao Erxun to turn the Renovation Street site into a vocational training center for women (*nügong xiyisuo*).[48]

This argument seems to have carried some weight with Zhao Erxun and with Zhou Shanpei's successor as police superintendent, Gao Zengjue. They did not reverse the policy of labeling brothels, but in 1909 they did set up a reformatory for prostitutes (*jiliangsuo*) along the lines of one established earlier in Beijing. The reformatory, like the workhouses and orphanage, provided some vocational training. Its regulations gave police officials the authority to send prostitutes under twenty to the facility against their will. Older prostitutes were to be encouraged to enter the reformatory voluntarily. Inmates were required to unbind their feet and forbidden to smoke opium. The reformatory staff had the power to arrange marriages for them, and Fu Qiaocun's guidebook mentioned several cases of well-known prostitutes who had "gone good" (*congliang*) after a stay at the reformatory.[49] The reformatory was still in operation in 1912 when Fu's pictorial, *Tongsu huabao*, covered the arrest of the courtesan He Yuqing. Fu reported that the men of Chengdu took a great interest in He's marital fate, and he suggested that the government raise money for the reformatory by holding a lottery for the right to marry her.[50] Fu Qiaocun's interest in the less fortunate among Chengdu's residents may have been more sincere than that of most educated men in the city, but, like Zhou Shanpei, Fu often expressed his concern through eagerness to charge the state with directing the course of their lives.

Despite the controversies, Zhou Shanpei's prostitution policies remained in place until the end of the Qing, although some brothels continued to resist relocation to the licensed zone. In 1909 there were 311 registered brothels (*changliaohu*) in Chengdu, of which five-sixths were in the north precinct, where Renovation Street was located; the rest were scattered throughout the other precincts.[51] That same year, however, Gao Zengjue's report to the Interior Ministry on the reformatory for prostitutes expressed confidence that the police would gradually put an end to the need for a licensed zone. After the reformatory was well established, he wrote, "the number of prostitutes with police-issued plaques permitting them to do business in the city will only be allowed to decline and not to increase, and eventually all will take up legitimate occupations (*cong zhengye*)."[52] Clearly that goal was not achieved.

Whereas the creation of the licensed zone and the workhouses appears to have been a consequence of Zhou Shanpei's own ideas of what Chengdu ought to become, he and subsequent police authorities were also called on to respond to New Policies initiatives launched by the central government. Many of these required that the new police substantially augment their knowledge of and control over urban neighborhoods. This is particularly true of the opium suppression policy adopted by the court in 1907 and the preparations for "self-government" elections in the following years. In both cases, the police took on the task of surveying the urban population and providing provincial authorities with detailed information on the professions and habits of the people.

In her history of the New Policies period, Meribeth Cameron argued that the opium suppression campaign was "the most successful of all the Manchu reforms."[53] It originated in the dispute between the Chinese and British governments over Britain's insistence that Indian opium be allowed into China as long as opium continued to be grown and marketed in China itself. To secure a British agreement to help halt opium imports, the Qing court agreed to ban domestic opium production and, through increasingly strict regulation, gradually outlaw consumption as well. In 1907 it ordered provincial authorities to find ways to limit sales of opium and register opium users. In Sichuan, an Opium Suppression Bureau (Jieyan zongju) was established to draft plans. The bureau ordered all but 26 opium shops in Chengdu to shut down; to these it gave licenses to act as the official outlets for the government's new opium monopoly. The bureau made the police responsible for identifying addicts and registering them so that they could be given permits to obtain and consume opium at the official shops.[54] The extent to which the police undertook this task is not clear from the historical record, although many police officers received merit points for their work in the campaign.[55] These may have been awarded primarily for the anti-opium raids that the police carried out beginning in mid-1910 to crack down on the private sale and consumption of opium. Police raids of clandestine opium dens received extensive coverage in local newspapers.

The work of registering opium smokers was not the first attempt by the Chengdu police to monitor the city's population. The 1903 police regulations assigned the Police Bureau responsibility for maintaining records on all households, updated by means of a regular census. The Baojia Bureau had done the same, in theory. Late in 1902, the Police Bureau posted new street signs throughout the city, indicating the police subprecinct to which each block belonged, and supervised the numbering of individual households and updating of the household registry plaques that each family posted. Information from the plaques, which included the ages, sex, and occupations of the inhabitants, was kept on file at both the subprecinct offices and the bureau headquarters.[56] In 1906 Zhou Shanpei had the police visit every household and fill out a registration form.[57]

The central government began to encourage Police Bureau efforts to keep even closer track of the population of Chengdu late in 1907. The committee charged with preparing for the establishment of a constitution asked provincial governors to compile reports on local customs for use in reforming the legal system and organizing elections. To this end, the court authorized the establishment of provincial investigative offices (*diaochachu*) and local statistics offices (*tongjichu*).[58] The Chengdu statistics office had a staff of six and was subordinate to the Police Bureau. With the assistance of police officers, it gathered data on the occupations of city residents, locations of commercial establishments, movement of population into and out of the city, births, deaths and their causes, and the size and meeting schedules of the "legally sanctioned associations" (*fading tuanti*) set up in the New Policies period. The statistics office compiled all these data into booklets, which were sent to the Interior Ministry twice a year.[59]

To what use was this detailed survey of Chengdu society put? Certainly it aided the police as they performed their other regulatory activities, such as identifying suspected prostitutes. After the 1909 census was conducted, the bureau focused its attention on other professions as well. Superintendent Gao Zengjue issued a set of regulations that gave the Police Bureau the right to license and supervise "employment brokers" (*daigu ren hu*)—or as the government-funded daily newspaper called them in its report, "so-called sellers of humans" (*suowei ren panzi*)—who arranged for the sale and purchase of women as maids and concubines. The rules were justified as necessary to decrease the number of lawsuits brought before the police courts involving the sale of kidnapped or allegedly kidnapped women.[60] Other targets of police attention were the private boarding houses (*jisushe*) that took in students who came from outside Chengdu to attend the many new private schools. Police regulations made it illegal for such houses to be operated by single women under fifty or by families with young women, unless the house was large enough to separate the women effectively from the lodgers. Owners were required to report to the local police subprecinct office every day at six P.M. and update the officers as to the identities and activities of their lodgers. The owners were to report any lodger who failed to return to the dormitory by the second watch.[61] Since similar rules existed for inns, it is unclear whether the police authorities were more concerned about the dangerous effects of urban attractions on the morality of the young students or the possibility that such establishments might become safe houses for illegal activities, such as plotting revolution.[62] As with other police regulations, there is little evidence to indicate how thoroughly these new measures were implemented. It is worth pointing out, however, that Tongmenghui activity in Chengdu ceased after the failed 1907 Birthday Plot and did not resume until the eruption of the Railroad Protection movement in 1911.[63]

In addition to matters concerning "preserving the peace" (*baoan*), as the Police Bureau described its involvement in most of the issues discussed above, the bureau recognized two other broad categories of police work: "reforming customs" (*zhengsu*), and "protecting health" (*weisheng*). Police authorities, from Zhou Shanpei on, generally satisfied the first responsibility by giving lectures and issuing proclamations urging the people to cease binding their daughters' feet, gambling, believing in "foolish superstitions," arguing in public, allowing their children to run about the streets in gangs, and dressing improperly. Some of these activities were specifically outlawed by police regulations, but, with the exception of gambling, police courts seem not to have prosecuted people for such activities. As I suggested in Chapter 3, police constables probably avoided intervening in such matters.

Police Bureau interest in public health began with Zhou Shanpei's attempt to reform public toilets, which in 1903 consisted of little more than long pits dug alongside the roads, tended by people who emptied the contents periodically to sell to farmers outside the city walls (and who also made house calls to collect night soil). During the 1903 clean-up to prepare for the launching of the police force, the Police Bureau supervised the construction of walls in front of the pits.[64] In 1906 Zhou Shanpei issued guidelines intended to set a construction standard for public toilets, requiring them to be shielded from the street and well ventilated and mandating their use by people who needed to relieve themselves while out in public.[65] Fu Qiaocun declared the toilet reform an unqualified success in his guidebook, but it is possible that he was not a frequent user of public toilets. A few years after the fall of the Qing, a commentator noted in a Chengdu police journal that there had been considerable opposition to and noncompliance with Zhou's toilet regulations. He attributed this, first, to a lack of "public morality" (*gongde xin*), and, second, to the bureau's failure to keep the toilets clean, "to the point that the feet of those who entered them would become stuck."[66]

In the summer of 1907, the Police Bureau initiated a program to license medical doctors. Six hundred medical practitioners sat for an examination, and 397 of these were given certificates stating that they had passed. Protestant missionaries who observed this procedure recorded the examination questions, which included one on the causes and treatment of malaria. According to their report, a successful candidate answered by citing classical texts and historical prescriptions, an approach that provided "ample evidence of the grossest ignorance of the very foundation principles of medical science."[67] Another exam was held a few years later, and this time successful candidates were awarded ratings; twenty-four were judged "superior," and forty merely "satisfactory." Fu Qiaocun published the names and ratings of this group in his guidebook.[68] Doctors who did not pass the examination were told to stop practicing medicine, but it is doubtful police were successful in preventing them from carrying on, since many doctors plied their craft from door to door. In 1909, however, one unlicensed city doctor was sued for malpractice, and Gao Zengjue heard the case personally. According to a newspaper story about the case, he asked the defendant several questions concerning the content of a famous medical text. When the defendant "appeared dazed and made no response," Gao rebuked him sharply and ordered him to reimburse the plaintiffs the amount he had charged them for his service, "as a warning to those quacks who mislead the people."[69] The relatively light penalty is a bit surprising, but Gao may have used the case primarily as publicity to prepare for a more concerted effort to extend the supervisory authority of the Police Bureau over the medical profession.

During the late Qing, the Police Bureau began a modest program to monitor the quality of the water in Chengdu's 2,824 public and private wells, in the name of public health.[70] Fu Qiaocun also credited it with moving slaughterhouses outside the city walls, forbidding the transport of diseased pork into the city, improving ventilation in inns, cleaning out the gutters along the sides of the streets, banning the cleaning of rice and clothing right next to wells, regulating the disposal of water from dye shops, and ordering the people to stop feeding pigs in the streets. Nevertheless, he urged the bureau to even greater efforts. The section on *weisheng* in his guidebook complained that most elite Chengdu residents considered the term to mean nothing more than eating refined food like swallows' nests and wearing wool clothing. Fu Qiaocun argued for a scientific understanding of the term and, by way of example, showed how one could calculate how much air entered and left the human body during an average day. His discussion of air quality stressed the interdependence of city dwellers who, rich and poor, shared the same resources. This interdependence justified firm action by the authorities to regulate public conduct. Fu ended his discussion in this section with a list of twelve health-related practices for families, including proper ventilation, clothes washing, spittoon use, and eating meals at set times.[71]

Although police regulation in the city did not extend as far as Fu Qiaocun would have liked, the Police Bureau under Zhou and his successors clearly had a broad conception of its responsibility to care for the people and ensure social order. When Zhou Shanpei was transferred in 1907 to head the Commercial Bureau (Shangwuju) and the Bureau for Industrial Development (Quangongju), he stepped up the level of the provincial administration's involvement in commerce in Chengdu, as well. For this task, he needed to work more closely with local elites. There is no question, however, that his achievements as director of police gave him substantial prestige within the elite community and thus made it easier for him to get its cooperation in a number of development schemes for the city.

State-Supervised Self-regulation: New Urban Bureaucracies and Associations

For the Qing government, one goal of the New Policies was to harness the energies of its educated subjects, who, from the point of view of the court, had become both increasingly active and dangerously alienated from the state in the decades before 1900. A new framework for involving elites in local affairs was devised: specialized "legal associations" (*fading tuanti* or *fatuan*) and matching governmental offices to supervise them. Several pairs of such new legal associations and bureaucratic units were formed in Chengdu soon after 1901. The education association headed by Xu Zixiu coordinated its efforts with a provincial education office; the Chamber of Commerce was linked to the Commercial Bureau, which Zhou Shanpei took over in 1907; and an "opera reform society" cooperated closely with both the Police Bureau and the Commercial Bureau. In the years before 1909, these paired institutions worked together quite harmoniously, on the surface at any rate, to balance the interests of the state and those of certain sectors of the community. In so doing, they achieved what Zhou Shanpei had intended the street headmen to do in conjunction with the police force—they made state power more effective by bringing key members of the community into closer relationships with officials, who had little difficulty dominating these relationships.

Chengdu's literati were quite accustomed to taking an active role in educational affairs. Nevertheless, the education association, in cooperation with the provincial educational commissioner, took on formal responsibility for certain matters in the New Policies years. Among its tasks was supervision of private schools, which had proliferated rapidly following the abolition of the examination system. In setting standards for such schools and evaluating the acceptability of certain teachers, the association always appealed to the provincial administration to validate its judgments. It tended, therefore, to be low-key and nonconfrontational in its role as lobbyist for the educational community at large. This accommodating approach rankled many in Chengdu's student community in 1908, when outrage over the field day melee ran high. Students who had gone on strike to protest the injuries inflicted on their classmates by the constable trainees were upset to hear education association leaders urge them to moderate their demands and return to school.[72] Meanwhile, the association conducted private negotiations with provincial officials to settle the matter quickly. Chengdu prefect Gao Zengjue's promotion to the position of provincial police superintendent was one of the measures the governor-general took to calm the furor; Gao was well liked within Chengdu's educational community.[73]

A year before the field day incident, Zhou Shanpei had been transferred from the Police Bureau to the Commercial Bureau. There, he developed as cooperative a relationship with Chengdu's Chamber of Commerce as the educational commissioner had built with the education association. The Chamber of Commerce had been established in response to an imperial edict in 1905, and its directors were appointed by the provincial administration. Governor-General Xiliang's speech at the chamber's first meeting expressed the hope that the organization would make it easier for officials and merchants to "unite their hearts" and dedicate their efforts to developing the great, untapped economic potential of the province, in order to compete against foreign products.[74] As this suggests, Xiliang's administrative vision embraced the province as a whole; he saw the Chengdu chamber as a useful tool in achieving provincial aims. The provincial Commercial Bureau, likewise, was instructed to promote commerce and industry throughout Sichuan.

The most notable achievement of the Commercial Bureau in its first few years of existence was the transformation of the annual flower festival, held on the grounds of the Daoist monastery southwest of the city walls, into a trade and industry-promotion fair (*shangye quangonghui*). The first was held in the spring of 1906. A missionary noted that many customary products such as flowers, baskets, birds, and wood crafts were still available in the second year of the reformed fair, but that each county had sent representatives from its industrial school to show off the products they had invented. These examples of the ingenuity of the people of Sichuan shared center stage with a small zoo, restaurants serving Western-style food, a model railroad, art collections, and an exhibit of Tibetan artifacts brought back by Zhao Erfeng from his campaign to shore up Qing authority west of Sichuan. "Possibly most interesting of all to the foreign visitor," the missionary continued, "was the wide carriage road and its conveyances from the south gate to the grounds at the southwest of the city. Here, side by side with old time foot passengers, barrows, sedan chairs, and ferries, ran up-to-date jinrickshas, drawn by reformed beggars, and well-built carriages, with coach and footman."[75] Xiliang's Commercial Bureau intended the fair as a stimulant for entrepreneurial energies across the province. With its exotic zoo, fancy restaurants, and delightfully novel transportation, however, the fair may have done more to augment Chengdu's long-established reputation as a center for luxury consumption and cultural spectacle.

As director of the Commercial Bureau and, beginning in late 1908, economic development superintendent for the province, Zhou Shanpei supported several projects intended to benefit the provincial economy. These included an embryonic steamship company to improve transportation on the upper Yangzi and a series of training centers to improve the quality of Sichuan silk so that it could be exported. Most of his time, however, was devoted to energizing the Chengdu merchant community and building a new infrastructure for the city. In a speech to the first students enrolled in a "commercial training institute" (*shangye jiangxisuo*) established in the city in 1910, Zhou urged them to embrace "competition" as their motto, for "competition is the source of progress." China should compete with foreign countries, Sichuan should compete with other provinces, Chengdu should compete with Chongqing, this shop should compete with that one.[76] The rhetorical emphasis on competition, however stirring it may have been to his audience, was undermined by the approach Zhou Shanpei took to economic development. Chongqing could not compete with Chengdu for his attention and funding, and he used his office to orchestrate collaborative merchant ventures to develop Chengdu.

Zhou Shanpei's management of the city's beggars, who had been a perennial source of annoyance to shopkeepers, must have garnered him some support among the merchant community. He also cultivated certain key allies. Among these the most active was the head of the bookstore guild, Fan Kongzhou. Fan opened a bookstore in Chengdu in 1884, and it became the local agent for the Commercial Press and other Shanghai publishers. In 1908 Zhou recommended his appointment as deputy head of the Chamber of Commerce and secured his assistance in convincing Chengdu's wealthiest merchants to finance and manage several large development projects, including a commercial arcade, an electric plant, and a large hotel. Fan persuaded a group of merchants to form the Chengdu Construction Company, Ltd., with himself as director. The company issued 40,000 *yuan* worth of stock to build the commercial arcade in the middle of town. The two-story building, completed in 1909, could accommodate 150 shops and was modeled on similar structures in Tianjin, Beijing, and Hankou. Zhou's Commercial Bureau issued regulations for commerce in the arcade: prices had to be posted openly and periodic inspections were carried out to ensure that merchants maintained the quality of their products and sold them at the posted prices. The company also raised 20,000 *yuan* to buy an electric generator in Shanghai so that the arcade could install electric lights, some of the first in Chengdu. Next door, another company headed by Fan Kongzhou built the Yuelai teahouse, which contained a 1,100-seat auditorium for opera performances and a deluxe hotel.[77] Through loans and exhortation, Zhou Shanpei also found merchant allies to assist him in schemes to pipe river water into Chengdu (Fig. 4.4), set up a telephone system, and organize several small factories in the city.[78]

Clearly Zhou Shanpei viewed being a catalyst for merchant cooperation as an important part of his role as superintendent for economic development. As a disciplinarian, however, he also did what he could to tighten the organization of merchant and trade guilds and turn the Chamber of Commerce into an instrument for regulating guild affairs. All guilds were told to register with the Commercial Bureau and submit their guild rules. If these rules included provisions of which Zhou did not approve, such as a requirement that all members contribute to the costs of worshipping the guild deity, he referred the matter to the Chamber of Commerce and asked it to draft appropriate rules.[79] In 1907, Zhou authorized the chamber to set up a

Fig. 4.4 Waterwheels drive pumps forming part of a new system to pipe river water into Chengdu. (The United Church of Canada/Victoria University Archives, Toronto: catalog no. 98.083P/13.)

"commercial mediation court" (*shangwu caipansuo*) to promote the chamber as the site for merchant self-regulation. In its four years of operation, this court, with judges chosen from among guild heads and other prominent merchants, heard hundreds of disputes. In each case, the judges sent a detailed summary of the case and their resolution of it to the provincial government.[80]

By 1909, Zhou Shanpei and the provincial government seem to have been well on the way to establishing a solid network of closely cooperating associations and government bureaus to support their increasingly ambitious regulation of city affairs. The men chosen to head the associations, impressed by the new urban order that Zhou had achieved with the police force, willingly cooperated with provincial officials to ensure that the spheres of education and commerce emulated the emerging orderliness of the streets. Nor was the realm of culture neglected. Zhou Shanpei's teacher, Zhao Xi, and other prominent scholars formed a society to reform Sichuan opera, just as Zhou's Police Bureau began enforcing its ban on lewd performances. This group met once a month to discuss its initiatives: monitoring performances in the city to make sure they adhered to the Police Bureau's decency standards and composing new plays to promote industriousness and nationalism and to combat superstition. They also helped Zhou Shanpei administer an examination for actors.[81]

The Urban Landscape

For all the changes that were occurring in Chengdu in the years before 1911, no thought was given to the overall spatial plan of the city. Zhou Shanpei certainly must be considered an urban reformer, but he understood the city as an established physical and social framework on which to add appropriate institutional and technical features to enable him to mold its people into a more orderly and productive whole. Unlike urban planners in Europe and the United States, he and his colleagues had no grand vision of the layout of the city as the expression of the values of a ruling house or nation. Within the Confucian canon that Zhou had studied so thoroughly as a boy, the *Rites of Zhou* contained such a vision, and it had influenced the design of imperial capitals and other administrative centers for 2,000 years.[82] Perhaps that fact in itself helps explain why New Policies activists, despite their urban preoccupations, were not given to drafting ambitious plans for redesigning the form of the Chinese city. Nevertheless, in mostly ad hoc ways, Chengdu's urban space did experience substantial physical transformation in the years before 1911.

One change in city form that was quite consciously planned was the opening of the city streets. When the police force began its patrols in 1903, most of the barriers that had blocked the intersections at night were removed. At the same time, workers were hired to keep the streets swept clear of debris, police regulations instructed shopkeepers to take down displays that jutted out from shop fronts, and public markets were built to accommodate the vegetable sellers who had lined some of the busiest streets. Along with the clearing of the streets, the Police Bureau tried to eliminate certain objectionable activities from the city, as well. Beginning in 1906, as we have seen, beggars were removed to workhouses outside the city walls. The police built a slaughterhouse just inside the city wall in 1909 and ordered Chengdu's Muslim butchers to stop slaughtering cattle in their own neighborhoods. At the same time, the city's tanneries were forced to relocate outside the walls.[83]

It is possible to see in these measures a new state interest in controlling urban space for a number of reasons: order, sanitation, and what might be called the "new urban look" of Tokyo. Fu Qiaocun's rickshaw venture and Zhou Shanpei's licensed quarter owed their existence largely to the power of Tokyo's image. There were also more local goads to innovation in urban construction projects. Christian missionaries, obliged in the previous decade to build as inconspicuously as possible, now dared to announce the grandeur of their missions architecturally. The Catholic church used the reparations money from the 1895 anti-Christian attacks to build a stone cathedral with a dramatic pillared façade northwest of the imperial city district. Other mission buildings were attached to the cathedral, completed in 1904. Altogether, the buildings covered 5,847 square meters.[84] The Methodist Episcopal Mission built a three-story hospital in 1905 using 800,000 bricks.[85] In 1903, the Canadians purchased a large plot of land south of the city walls and began drawing up plans for a mission college, which opened as the West China Union University in 1910 and, among other things, introduced Chengdu to the aesthetics of campus design.

Provincial authorities responded to the implicit challenge these large buildings and complexes presented, sometimes with unfortunate results. The high school, one of the first foreign-style buildings put up by the provincial government, was built in 1903 to accommodate up to 500 students. Two years later it had deteriorated to the point that it had to be completely torn down and rebuilt.[86] More often, though, the new buildings stood their ground. In 1906 the provincial government hired a German construction company to build a new arsenal outside the East Gate, to replace one built inside the city walls in the 1870s. This impressive building, which made use of steel girders to enclose a spacious factory floor, was still in use as a machine shop in the 1990s. The commercial arcade built in 1909 featured, in addition to electric lights, a huge clock fixed in a crown-like decorative element on top of its upper story.[87] Like the arsenal, which announced Sichuan's commitment to military preparedness, the commercial arcade and its associated hotel and theater were invested with symbolic significance. Commerce was now to be considered as important to civilization as literary studies.

Chengdu's elites accepted the elevation of commerce with enthusiasm, but they showed themselves to be divided once again over the question of the appropriate place of women in the city. Although some in the city called for the establishment of schools for girls or sent their daughters to the mission schools, others held fast to the belief that the only proper path in life for a woman was to accept the marriage her parents or masters arranged for her and then practice the womanly virtues of homemaking, venturing out of the house as little as possible. This vision clashed with Zhou Shanpei's plan to open the Yuelai theater balcony to female customers, in order that they might benefit from the moral instruction provided by the reformed operas and the theater might benefit from their patronage. The first theater built exclusively for opera performances in Chengdu opened in 1906, with Police Bureau permission to sell tickets to women. That permission was soon rescinded, however. Fu Qiaocun's explanation for this was that because "people considered women [in public] to be a strange thing, lots of incidents occurred."[88] Zhou Shanpei and Fan Kongzhou sought to avoid a similar problem when they built the Yuelai. It was designed to have two completely separate entrances, one for men that led to the main seating area, and one for women that led to a screened balcony. This, and the Police Bureau's assurances that extra constables would be assigned to the Central Precinct to keep constant watch on the theater, apparently satisfied enough of the critics to convince the governor-general to let the experiment go forward. The management of the Yuelai also ingratiated itself with the government by holding periodic benefit performances, donating the proceeds to various official causes such as famine relief.[89] The provincial government declined the request of another entrepreneur who wished to set up a theater exclusively for women in 1909, however. The police superintendent's response to the entrepreneur's petition announced that the existence of too many theaters for women would give them the mistaken idea that opera-watching was a proper way to occupy their time.[90]

If the Yuelai Theater represented a modest step toward legitimizing women's involvement in matters outside the home, the construction of the Shaocheng Park represented a giant leap toward the integration of the Manchu and Han sectors of the city. Throughout the New Policies years, administrators in the Banner garrison had been following the institutional developments in Chengdu and adopting many of them. In 1906, for example, several young Bannermen joined the sixth class of the Chengdu police academy and, upon graduation, set up a 200-man police force in the garrison area.[91] For the Banner community, however, the New Policies program began to appear increasingly threatening, because of growing sentiment among reformers that the Banners should be abolished and the dynastic rules that kept the Manchu and Han populations separate should be relaxed. An announcement in 1908 that Banner stipends would gradually be diminished and Bannermen encouraged to take up new professions caused an explosion in the Chengdu garrison. An angry crowd surrounded the entrance to the Manchu general's yamen, and some threw stones at the Banner officials who tried to reason with them. Governor-General Zhao Erxun, a Han Bannerman himself, rushed to the scene to give the crowd a tongue-lashing and arrest the ringleaders.[92] From that moment, the problem of providing the Bannermen with ways to support themselves acquired a new urgency. One result was Shaocheng Park.

The park was intended to provide a steady income to the Banner community by turning a large swath of the garrison into a central pleasure district. In addition to charging an entrance fee, the park administration rented space to teahouse and restaurant operators and built another theater for opera performances. As was the commercial arcade, Shaocheng Park was probably inspired by developments in Tianjin and Beijing. The opening of the park in the summer of 1910 was accompanied by the gradual opening of other parts of the garrison area to Han shopkeepers in an effort to stimulate the development of commerce and enable the residents to enrich themselves by renting property. In letters to his family in Beijing, the last commander of the Banner garrison reported with satisfaction on the new infusion of wealth into the garrison area, noting that some of its residents had proposed erecting a ceremonial arch to commemorate his virtuous administration. According to him, the park sold 3,200 tickets on its opening day, and a thousand men bought tickets to the opera performance, which, possibly because the theater lacked a balcony, women were not allowed to attend. He refused to attend the performances himself, fearing disorder among the crowd would cause "foreigners to mock us."[93]

The creation of new public spaces like the commercial arcade and Shaocheng Park occurred largely because of the interest of officials in promoting commerce. Officials also believed themselves to be fully justified in making already existing "public spaces" serve the ends of the New Policies program. Thus, temples were commandeered to house schools, the hospital for indigents, and police subprecinct stations. At least two police stations occupied parts of the compounds of native-place associations. In 1909, one of these asked that the station temporarily move out of the building to allow the association to put on its annual festival for the God of Wealth. The police superintendent rejected the proposal, noting that the station had been there for six years and had never before gotten in the way of the celebrations. Besides, he continued, although "people have the right to set up associations and societies," policing was an urgent public matter: the association should reflect on its priorities and care more for the public welfare.[94]

The expansion of the police institution across the city occurred with little new construction, because of the bureau's use of temples and other "public" buildings. Many other New Policies institutions did build up the area inside the city walls, however. The old Army of the Green Standard had maintained a number of shooting ranges in the city, and most of these disappeared in the years before 1911, as various new bureaus petitioned to build shops and houses on the land and rent them out to provide funds for schools and other projects. The government also forced private owners to sell it property for the construction of new official buildings.[95] So much construction went on in the city in the New Policies years that in 1910 land in some sectors cost more than ten times what it had cost in 1903.[96] New space was opened up in the imperial city, however, when the examination sheds were dismantled after 1905. That land was assigned to schools and the Commercial Bureau.[97]

Changes in city form, in short, tended to occur in conjunction with the institutional changes that Zhou Shanpei and his colleagues were promoting to strengthen the economy and make Chengdu orderly. Institutional change was at the heart of the New Policies from 1901 to 1911. Before 1909, however, provincial administrators controlled the course of this change fairly effectively in Chengdu. After 1909, political events presented them with powerful rivals: self-government advocates and revolutionaries.

5 SELF-GOVERNMENT
AND REVOLUTION

The years between 1903 and 1909 were very good for Zhou Shanpei and those residents of Chengdu who valued social order, public cleanliness, and ambitious state-sponsored economic ventures. Certainly, American and European visitors were impressed. A British traveler who visited the city in 1909 gave this account:

Chengdu is unquestionably the cleanest city in China, and probably is the most progressive and enlightened of any purely native city. The streets are broad and well kept, and the foreigner can walk anywhere without the slightest fear of molestation. At almost every street corner there is a policeman, and many of them have sentry-boxes. They are neatly dressed in a sort of European uniform, and are decidedly clean and civil. They wear a kind of small black sailor-hat, and the smarter ones wear black thread gloves of native manufacture and carry stout walking-sticks. Altogether, they are the best type of police we met. There are no beggars with their hideous whine and incomparable dirt. This is a magnificent triumph for the head magistrate, as a few years ago they numbered twenty thousand in Chengdu; but he was determined to put an end to the system, and has entirely succeeded. We met a large school of boys neatly dressed, and were told that these were the children of beggars, whom he had collected into a large school, where they are taught trades at the expense of the municipality.[1]

By 1909, it would seem, Zhou's activism had led foreign residents to represent him to visitors as the "head magistrate" of the "municipality" of Chengdu, despite his actual status as an official with provincewide responsibilities. Urban development, however, yielded to provincial politics in Zhou's last years in Chengdu. A little over two years after this assessment of his contributions to Chengdu was made, Zhou Shanpei was obliged to escape from angry crowds by hiding out in the orphanage, where he reportedly changed into women's clothes, departed the city over the wall, and fled for his life out of Sichuan.[2] He did not return to the province until after 1949.

Zhou Shanpei adamantly maintained that his humiliating departure from Chengdu in the fall of 1911 was due to the animosity of a small group of well-placed individuals who were jealous or resentful of him. The Qing government's decision some months earlier, taken without consulting the stockholders' association in Chengdu, to nationalize the Sichuan–Hankou Railroad and obtain foreign financing for it had resulted in an intense and complex political crisis. Zhou Shanpei was intimately involved in this crisis. Zhou's enemies— among whom he considered the most implacable to be the hundreds of candidates he had just rejected from the pool of potential law court staff—took advantage of the situation to spread vicious rumors about him, he insisted, and these rumors had completely misrepresented his actions and blackened his reputation. What this explanation downplays, though, is Zhou's status as a Qing official in a city that, over the two previous years, had become a center of the movement to introduce "local self-government" institutions across China. The constitutionalist movement of the last years of the Qing upset the carefully maintained harmony of interests between the provincial administration and provincial elites by demanding that the relationship between the state and the people be redefined. The railroad dispute was only the last, and most spectacular, in a series of conflicts involving the central government, provincial officials, and the leaders of the new provincial assembly over the division of responsibility for matters affecting Sichuan.

The political atmosphere in the city in 1910 and 1911 was electric, as the provincial assembly and the railroad stockholders' association tested the limits of the Qing commitment to constitutional reform. In one respect, however, Chengdu itself occupied the eye of the storm over how China should be governed. Because Zhou Shanpei and his colleagues had been so successful in building consensus among reform elites in support of the Chengdu police and the new style of urban administration, the governance of the provincial capital did not become a matter of serious contention in the tumultuous final years of the dynasty. The men elected to the provincial assembly and the many local councils throughout Sichuan spoke up loudly against official policies that they regarded as harmful to the nation and the province, but they endorsed and facilitated the state's increasingly strict regulation of life in Chengdu.

By destroying Qing legitimacy in Sichuan, the Railroad Protection movement destroyed Zhou Shanpei's career. As an urban administrator, however, Zhou Shanpei's proudest moment came during the citywide strike organized to protest the railroad nationalization decision, when "his" police and street headmen maintained order and discipline in the city. Twenty-seven years later he recalled with satisfaction that the British consul had visited him in September 1911 to tell him that no British city could have survived two weeks of a general strike without violence.[3] But by the end of that year, Zhou Shanpei had left Sichuan, and Chengdu's administration was in local hands. The urban order Zhou had done so much to create was briefly shattered and then restored relatively quickly. It would be more than ten years, however, before urban administration was once more a top priority of authorities in Chengdu.

Constitutionalism in Chengdu: Legal Reform

The late Qing constitutional movement, as Min Tu-ki has shown, attracted supporters in part because it addressed long-standing concerns among Chinese political theorists about the proper division of authority between the center and localities and the weaknesses of the centralized bureaucratic system. To many late Qing writers, and notably Zhou Shanpei's mentor Huang Zunxian, assemblies of local elites could manage most community affairs better than centrally appointed bureaucrats, because of their superior understanding of and devotion to their communities.[4] For other constitutional thinkers, however, the movement came to mean much more than a shift in the balance of administrative responsibility between the bureaucracy and local gentry. Liang Qichao, in his voluminous and influential writings from exile in the New Policies era, introduced the concept of popular participation in government as a right and duty of citizenship. Independent newspapers such as Shanghai's *Shibao* carried articles on democratic government and called for freedom of the press so that it could act as an independent monitor of the state.[5]

In Chengdu, the reform community's enthusiasm for the expansion of its own authority that the self-government bodies promised far exceeded its interest in the concept of civil liberties. As we shall see below, however, the occasional use by leaders of the provincial assembly of arguments about legal rights and limitations on state authority in their disputes with provincial bureaucrats altered the terms of political discourse in the city. Before we turn to these disputes, then, it will be helpful to examine local regulation in Chengdu in the New Policies era and how it was affected by late Qing legal reform.

As written, Zhou Shanpei's 1903 Chengdu police regulations showed the influence of the sort of constitutional thought that sought to define the authority of the state more sharply. Given Zhou's elitist political style, these features of his regulations are probably attributable to his reliance on late-Meiji Japanese police regulations as models. The 1903 document defined the authority of the Police Bureau in terms of "legislative," "executive," and "judicial" powers, and the limits on each of these types of powers were laid out in some detail. The Police Bureau was given the right to create rules concerning all matters of local security, although these rules were not to stand in the way of "the reasonable enjoyments or profits of the people"(*renmin yingyou heli zhi liyi*). Twenty-four sets of such rules appear in a section of the 1903 regulations. They are couched primarily as instructions to the police on how to deal with unacceptable behavior on the part of ordinary citizens, but they also served to define such behavior. For example, the "Regulations on Maintaining Order in Public Places" require those planning a special gathering in market areas or other public spaces in the city to notify the police in advance and secure a permit. The police are instructed to post a constable to special duty at the site and order him to prevent women from mingling in the crowd. The "Regulations on Markets" forbid people to feed pigs in the streets. "Census Regulations" explain what the police can and cannot do in order to secure population information.[6]

In a report to the throne on the 1903 regulations, Governor-General Cen Chunxuan claimed that local opinion had been consulted during the drafting of these rules.[7] Most of the rules dealt with issues, such as census-taking and gambling, that were among the traditional concerns of local magistrates. What is particularly noteworthy about this set of rules is that, unlike the usual particularistic, hortatory proclamations of officials, these are presented as if they constituted a systematic body of local ordinances. The police force was given the responsibility to publicize and enforce these rules, as well as the power to amend them, with the approval of the governor-general, as necessary to correspond to changes in the local situation and the "understanding of the people." New rules were not to be enforced before they had been publicized for ten days on bulletin boards located on each street. The 1903 rules themselves were published in a government gazette established that year, and constables were instructed to explain them to new arrivals to the city as they passed through the gates.[8]

The 1903 codification of local rules governing public and police conduct, as well as the creation of standard procedures by which these rules were to be amended and publicized, might have marked a turning point in the regulation of local society, if the rules had acquired some legitimacy independent of individual officials and if the procedures had been followed. Of course, the state—as represented by the governor-general—still claimed to be the ultimate arbiter of local regulation, with an obligation only to "consult with" community leaders. Nevertheless, the existence of a stable body of local ordinances, including limitations on police authority, might have encouraged a new way of thinking about law itself. The local police regulations might have come to seem like a durable codification of community customs and standards, subject to revision when community circumstances and sentiment demanded it.

In the years after 1903, however, provincial authorities and magistrates prevented any such development, continuing to issue orders and instructions on local matters, without reference to the 1903 regulations. In 1907, the Police Bureau, again led by Zhou Shanpei, produced another series of guidelines for public behavior that covered some of the same topics addressed in the 1903 regulations. The new regulations, however, took the form of directives rather than rules. Whereas the 1903 document had justified each rule as promoting public order, moral uplift, or sanitation, the 1907 list consisted of very specific and simply worded orders: "Do not argue in the streets." "Do not beat maidservants viciously." "Do not cheat foolish people by misrepresenting the goods you are selling."[9] The 1903 regulations never became the basis for a systematic set of local ordinances. Officials were too comfortable with a personal approach to local regulation. Indeed, Zhou Shanpei's own paternalistic style of administration undercut the explicit promise in the 1903 document that local regulation would be standardized and institutionalized.

About the same time that Zhou Shanpei was issuing his simplified and authoritarian police directives, the central government stepped up efforts to standardize the New Policies reforms in order to prepare for the adoption of a constitutional system of government. Before 1907, provincial administrators had been given great latitude in implementing the general New Policies edicts. Governors-general and governors did consult together and copy policies from each other, and they were obliged to send proposed regulations for New Policies institutions and reports on their activities to the central government for approval. In general, however, experimentation at the provincial level was encouraged in the early years of the reform era, even after central ministries had been established in areas of New Policies emphasis, such as commerce (1903), education (1905), and policing (1905).[10] The court's 1905 decision to move toward the adoption of a constitution, however, necessitated the overhaul of the country's system of laws. The legal scholar Shen Jiaben had been ordered to begin revising the Qing Code in 1902, but little was done, except in the area of commercial law, until after the decision to adopt a constitution.[11] Then, the court promulgated a revised criminal code and new law codes dealing with newspapers and the police. Shen's legal reform committee also designed a hierarchy of law courts that would take legal cases out of the hands of local magistrates. By the end of 1910, three levels of courts had been established in Chengdu: two "branch local courts" (*difang fenting*) for the two counties, one local court for all of Chengdu prefecture, and one higher-level court (the other higher-level court in the province was in Chongqing).[12]

Because late Qing judicial records for Chengdu do not survive, the effect of the new criminal, commercial, and newspaper codes on administration of the city is difficult to assess. The commercial code did legitimize Zhou Shanpei's efforts to gather information about Chengdu's merchant community, because it required individual firms to register with the Commercial Bureau so the bureau could compile business statistics to send to the Ministry of Commerce.[13] Zhou may have found this an effective tool in his dealings with city merchants. Fu Qiaocun's *Colloquial Daily News* (*Tongsu ribao*) was involved in what was probably the first application of the newspaper law in Chengdu. The details of the case suggest that, at least initially, the new law codes served the interests of officials. In 1911, when Fu was out of the province, the paper's chief editor and a sixteen-year-old reporter were sued for slander by a judge attached to the higher-level court. The reporter admitted in court to having heard gossip that the judge had ignored a procedural regulation and boasted in court of his close connections with officials and their relatives. Without checking the accuracy of this story, he wrote it up and submitted it for publication. The editor admitted to having published the news item without verifying it. Citing the danger that such rumors might undermine the credibility of the new judicial system, the Chengdu local court fined the editor and the reporter the maximum amount possible under the newspaper law's slander provisions: 200 *yuan* each. The court asked the police superintendent to investigate how the paper had come to hire such a young reporter, since the newspaper law specified that members of newspaper staffs be at least twenty years old.[14]

Of all the new legislation, the police law (*weijinglü*) had the most potential for changing the way the state operated in Chengdu. The law limited the jurisdictions of police courts and the types of punishments they could impose and, by so doing, challenged the authority of what had become the most powerful institutional regulator of Chengdu life.[15] Eight categories of misbehavior subject to police authority were outlined in the law: (1) political matters such as rumormongering and disturbing the conduct of official business, (2) matters of public safety such as the handling of dangerous substances or threats to the public posed by lunatics or crazed animals, (3) traffic regulations, (4) matters of communication such as the destruction of mail, (5) matters of public order such as misuse of public property and selling goods at higher than the official price (probably a reference to grain sales during famines), (6) matters of morality and customs such as vagrancy and unlicensed prostitution, (7) matters of health and sanitation, and (8) property matters such as the mistreatment of animals belonging to others. Any misconduct not falling into one of these categories was to be dealt with in the regular court system. In effect, the law removed civil cases such as marriage and property disputes and criminal cases such as fighting and petty theft out of the jurisdiction of police courts. Police courts had frequently settled such cases through mediation in the years before 1910. Newspaper accounts of incidents in which crowds of bystanders led antagonists to the nearest police station for settlement of their dispute suggest that police judicial officers had developed a reputation for effective resolution of neighborhood conflicts.[16]

The police law limited the punishments police courts could impose to fines of not more than fifteen *yuan* and jail terms of not more than fifteen days. Commercial establishments that violated police regulations could be shut down. The police courts were no longer allowed to beat offenders or make them wear heavy wooden collars, both common forms of punishment in Zhou Shanpei's era. In 1910, police officials in Chengdu reported that the police prison where Zhou Shanpei had required convicts to sit on display, braiding straw mats, had been transformed into a detention center for those awaiting trial, and police judges had been ordered not to use any form of corporal punishment.[17]

Despite their surface compliance with the requirements of the police law, provincial police authorities worried that it would compromise their ability to keep order. In 1909 Superintendent Gao Zengjue asked Zhao Erxun to seek clarification from the Interior Ministry of a provision in the police law that allowed officials to adapt it to local circumstances. He planned to revise Chengdu's existing police regulations to make up for the large gaps he saw in the police law and wanted to know what sort of punishments he could assign to various types of public misbehavior.[18] Gao's successor as head of police, Zhou Zhaoxiang, continued to prosecute cases in areas outside those specified in the police law. When complaints about this reached Zhao Erxun, he asked for an explanation. Zhou responded:

The police superintendent has a responsibility to oversee local affairs. The cultural level of the people is not high, and the composition of society is very complicated. We cannot simply make direct use of the methods of the West and Japan. At this time, when the judiciary has not yet become independent, the people still fear the heavy fees levied at the yamen of local officials and would rather take their suits to the police superintendent. The police superintendent has been accepting criminal and civil cases since the police were first established.[19]

The Police Bureau did not surrender its judicial authority to the new courts readily. When police officials wished to, however, they could also cite the new law to their own advantage. Zhou Shanpei's Commercial Bureau operated a program that gave small loans to city dwellers to set up street stalls or other modest commercial ventures. After the court system had been established, he induced a court official to ask the Police Bureau to continue what had apparently been the practice of sending constables to collect loan repayments from recalcitrant borrowers. The police superintendent refused, noting that legal experts had told him that the failure to make timely payments on the loans was not a criminal matter and should be dealt with by the courts in accordance with the commercial code. "It is not that the police seek to avoid a troublesome task," he continued, "it is a question of legal limits." Constables would be asked to remonstrate with those in their subprecinct who were in arrears, but they could do no more than this.[20] Read in conjunction with Zhou Zhaoxiang's insistence on pragmatic grounds that police courts still had a role to play in handling legal cases outside those specified in the police law, this apparently principled stand suggests that provincial officials found the new laws useful in their own bureaucratic rivalries. But that same tool could be used against them, as Zhou Zhaoxiang found in his dealings with the provincial assembly discussed below. In the early years of the new legal system, officials applied the laws to serve their own purposes. With the creation of representative councils, a wider range of elites laid claim to the laws for new ends.

Constitutionalism in Chengdu: Provincial Assembly and City Council

Sichuan's elite community welcomed the Qing court's 1909 call for the election of local councils and a provincial assembly. Officially sanctioned constitutional study societies were already active in many cities and towns, and enrollment in law schools had increased dramatically.[21] The prospect of participating in self-government institutions proved attractive even to police officers; the police authorities had to issue a general order forbidding officers to involve themselves in public associations, so that a clear distinction between the realm of officialdom and the realm of self-government would be maintained.[22]

Provincial authorities in Chengdu had a keen interest in controlling the boundary between "official government" and "self-government," because they hoped to fit the provincial assembly and local councils into the pattern already established with the Chamber of Commerce and the other "legal associations" discussed in Chapter 4. Self-government, in their view, was to function as a more formal manifestation of the customary mediation between central and local interests jointly practiced by provincial officials and elites. In his work with the Chamber of Commerce, Zhou Shanpei had shown that much could be accomplished when official bureaus guided select committees in carrying out well-defined public development projects like the commercial arcade. For a while, it seemed that the self-government bodies would operate in the same way.

Governor-General Zhao Erxun's speech on the occasion of the first meeting of the provincial assembly, in the fall of 1909, expressed his confidence in the ability of officials and assemblymen to work together harmoniously, despite the fact that "everyone" was predicting competition between them. Emphasizing the need for unity in a time of national crisis, Zhao called on officials and assemblymen alike to remember that the purpose behind the implementation of self-government was to make the nation stronger. All authority, he asserted, belonged to the nation; the bureaucracy and local representative bodies in themselves had no independent power. But the nation entrusted certain tasks to each, and each should do its utmost to serve the nation responsibly, without interfering improperly in the work of the other.[23]

This first meeting of the 104 representatives lasted a month and a half, and despite Zhao Erxun's appeal for unity in service to the nation, some friction between bureaucrats and assemblymen could not be avoided. At the closing ceremonies, Zhao Erxun warned delegates that they were taking too great an interest in "supervising administration" and not enough in "assisting administration." Pu Dianjun, the president of the assembly, promptly responded that the two could not be separated. If the people were denied the opportunity to examine and evaluate how officials made use of the funds the people were contributing to assist administration, then they would not be willing to provide this assistance.[24] In general, however, the session had proceeded fairly peacefully. Provincial officials presented the assembly with a number of proposals on such topics as raising money for the expansion of the police and school system, which the assembly criticized as too great a burden on the people. The assembly, in turn, proposed a number of measures to cut administrative expenses, to which the governor-general objected because they conflicted with regulations of the central government.[25] Neither side, however, took an uncompromising stand on any particular question.

Few of the issues considered by the assembly in its first year had much to do with the administration of Chengdu. This is not surprising. The assembly, after all, had a mandate to consider issues that affected the province as a whole. More important, implementation of the New Policies was proving much more troublesome and disruptive in areas outside the provincial capital than it had been in Chengdu, and that is where the assembly focused most of its attention. In the area of policing, for example, the effort to expand the police system to county seats and rural areas accelerated in 1908, as a result of urging by the central government. Whereas Chengdu's police force had been heavily subsidized by the provincial treasury and closely supervised by high-ranking officials, county officials had to find local funds to outfit the new forces and had to hire inexperienced young graduates of police academies to lead them. The assemblymen could hardly have been unaware of the growing resentment across Sichuan toward tax increases to support the police and schools and of the frequent clashes between county police officials and local elites.[26] In Chengdu, on the other hand, the authority of the police force was firmly established by 1909, and the assembly showed no inclination to interfere with the provincial Police Bureau's regulation of urban affairs.

Several of the provincial assembly's early proposals fit nicely with Zhou Shanpei's plans for Chengdu's economic and cultural development. Assemblymen called for the establishment of a provincial bank to stabilize the currency and free up capital for industrial development. They also urged the government to support the creation of a popular education society (*tongsu jiaoyushe*) in Chengdu, for the purpose, as the assembly explained it, of raising the cultural level of the people of Sichuan so that they would reject superstition and see the value of the New Policies. The society was to follow up on and expand the efforts of the opera reform group to cleanse popular culture of its "immoral" tendencies.[27]

The Chengdu-Huayang City Council (Cheng-Hua cheng yishihui), which met for the first time in 1910, lacked the visibility and prestige of the provincial assembly. The council was composed of 60 representatives elected from six city districts, three in Chengdu county and three in Huayang. These representatives chose fifteen of their number to serve as an executive council (*dongshihui*). Both the council itself and the executive body are rather shadowy organizations in the historical record. Unlike the provincial assembly, their activities received very little publicity in the local newspapers. Indeed, the identities of the council members themselves are quite obscure. Ten of the members of the larger council represented the Banner garrison, and the involvement of this group no doubt seriously compromised the cohesion of the body. The only council member mentioned in newspapers of the time was an "honorary" (*mingju*) member of the Executive Council, who had also served as the editor of the monthly provincial gazette. His name appeared in print when the editors of the official daily newspaper praised their colleague's dedication to self-government, which he had demonstrated by refusing the salary the council offered him for taking charge of its secretarial work.[28]

The city council's relative anonymity may have been due to its rather cozy relationship with provincial authorities. The council seems to have accepted the view that its role was to complement official government by carrying out public welfare projects that the bureaucracy authorized but did not have the means to undertake itself. Immediately after it was established, it was granted permission to raise "self-government funds" by taxing wine shops (which already paid a fee to the police) and long-distance porters.[29] Council members agreed to use some of the money to take over and expand the small loan agency that Zhou Shanpei's Commercial Bureau had been operating in the city.[30] Most of the other activities of the council were those that private philanthropic groups had long performed in the city—distributing rice, medicine, and padded clothing to the poor and burying unclaimed corpses. In tune with the spirit of the times, though, the council also arranged public lectures on self-government and established a newspaper reading room and three schools to teach basic literacy.[31]

Given enough time, the city council might have carved out more of a role for itself in city affairs. There is some evidence that it was interested in taking on a wider responsibility for local regulation; in 1911 it proposed a ban on rickshaws in the city. The governor-general, Zhao Erfeng, agreed to consider the idea, but only after the administration had recovered the money it had laid out to buy the rickshaws.[32] Given the common use of this sort of delaying tactic and the preoccupation of officials and elites with the political crisis of the last years of the Qing, the city council had no real chance to develop its own initiatives. Even if it had, however, the council showed no inclination to strengthen its relationship to the wider urban community, a useful step had it wished to increase its clout relative to powerful provincial institutions such as the Police Bureau. It was the Police Bureau, rather, that had direct ties to Chengdu's neighborhoods, through the street headmen, and the city council did nothing to change this.

The fact that the creation of the city council had no effect on the role of the street headmen is a strong indication that the provincial government succeeded in imposing the distinction between "official rule" and "self-government" in Chengdu and the subordinate role of the latter. The street headmen stood at the intersection of the police and the community, and their relationship to the city council could have been a matter for negotiation, had the council been concerned— or in a position—to make it so. The idea that the street headmen could represent the broad interests of the people in conjunction with the other self-government bodies had had a brief airing in 1908, when a Chengdu resident petitioned the Police Bureau asking that street headmen be formally elected, in order to promote constitutional government.[33] But the council did not follow up on the idea and attempt to create closer ties between itself and the headmen. Perhaps the powerful Police Bureau rejected all suggestions along these lines. The council members, however, may not have liked the idea themselves. The only proposition they sent to the provincial assembly for deliberation suggests that their primary concern was not to reach out to a broader constituency but to clarify their own status relative to the bureaucracy. The council asked the assembly to reform the terms of address used in communications between self-government bodies and government offices, which they objected to because they were the same as those for militia heads. As Roger Thompson notes, the council saw nothing wrong with the authoritarian style officials used when addressing old-style community leaders, such as militia heads. Self-government bodies, however, occupied an entirely different social realm, one more on a par with officials. The elitism evident in the council's reference to militia heads no doubt prevented members from thinking of street headmen as potential colleagues in the self-government cause.[34] Zhou Shanpei had attempted to induce "respectable people" to serve as street headmen, but council members may have persisted in equating them with lowly *baojia* personnel.

The tendency of the city council to see itself as a transcendent local leadership—a lofty body concerned with the welfare of the community but not integrated with it through representational political networks—continued long after the collapse of the Qing. As we shall see, street headmen in the Republican period continued to be associated with the police force, and city governments often acted as committees of experts, with little influence over the police or the broader community.

The Political Crisis of 1910–11

By the second annual meeting of the provincial assembly, in the fall of 1910, the orderly political climate provincial authorities had struggled so hard to maintain had seriously deteriorated. Rural unrest over New Policies taxation and census-taking had developed into open rebellion in several counties that year, and these developments had raised the level of tension in Chengdu.[35] Provincial assemblymen found conditions in rural areas worrisome, which increased their dissatisfaction with local officials and the central government. Just when provincial administrators most needed the cooperation of local elites to contain popular discontent, the provincial assembly began to adopt a political stance of open opposition toward officialdom. The second annual session of the assembly is notable for the number of outright attacks on and impeachments of officials, including the provincial police superintendent, Zhou Zhaoxiang. In the new atmosphere of open confrontation, parts of Chengdu's elite community rose up in opposition to two policies adopted by the Qing court in the winter of 1910–11 and the following spring: the decision to delay the formation of a national parliament and the nationalization of the Sichuan–Hankou Railroad. When the provincial government was unable to mollify the elites in the second instance, the basis for orderly rule was shattered, and a mass protest movement sprang up in a city that had long been a stronghold of Qing authority.

Rural unrest was not the only factor promoting political tension in Chengdu in 1910 and 1911. The constitutionalist movement drew strength from new cross-province ties. Chang P'eng-yüan has outlined the rapidly expanding propaganda efforts of the constitutional-ists, who traveled to Shanghai from all over the country in 1909 to plan a united strategy to increase the authority of self-government institutions. There were no Sichuan delegates to that first meeting, but assembly leader Pu Dianjun, who held the highest civil degree and had studied in Japan, was a close associate of the men who did meet, and he was involved in the petition movement for a national parliament. Another Sichuan activist who kept Chengdu elites in-formed about the increasingly rancorous relationship between the court and the constitutionalists was Deng Xiaoke, editor of the pro-vincial assembly's gazette, *Shubao* (Sichuan report).[36]

The very existence of *Shubao* changed the political atmosphere in Chengdu markedly. Before *Shubao* was founded in the fall of 1910, several local periodicals reported on affairs in Sichuan and promoted the New Policies. The most important of these, the *Sichuan guanbao* (Official gazette) and the *Chengdu ribao* (Daily), were set up in 1904 and subsidized by the government; their staffs were selected by the administration from among the corps of expectant officials. Official communications made up a substantial part of the content of these two periodicals, but they were by no means simple tools of provincial officials. Correspondents submitted news reports that often high-lighted problems in local administration, and both publications fre-quently carried editorials and news items originating in constitution-alist newspapers in eastern China, such as *Shenbao*, *Shibao*, and *Zhongwai ribao*.[37] Nevertheless, the editors of these two periodicals worked within the framework of official-elite cooperation; they might challenge the government to improve itself, but they would never suggest that it might be incapable of doing so without radical reform or criticize officials directly.

From its first issue, the approach of *Shubao* was different. Unlike other Sichuan periodicals, publisher Zhu Shan declared, *Shubao* would not avoid discussion of any political topic; no "authoritarian power" could restrain it. News of disputes between the provincial as-sembly and officials, which in the past had been limited to insiders or spread through the community as rumors, now appeared plainly in print. And *Shubao* upheld the point of view of the assembly leaders, in very strong language. The sixth issue, which appeared in November 1910, castigated the governor-general's refusal to allow the assembly to send investigators to government bureaus and schools to examine their organization and account books. "Even ordinary people and foreigners have the right to visit and inspect [schools and government offices], yet assembly members are denied the enjoyment of this right." Venal officials, the editors concluded, must be trying to cover up mismanagement and corruption.[38] For provincial administrators, who were unaccustomed to justifying their own positions in public, except with stock references to "benefiting the people" and "upholding morality," this sort of public attack must have been extremely vexing.

Shubao claimed to be the organ of the provincial assembly and to enjoy the support of all the "legal associations" in Chengdu. The name of Xu Zixiu, leader of the Educational Association, appears in a list of its backers in the first issue. Actually, however, the paper was controlled by a small group of articulate and radical constitutionalists, including Wu Yu, a legal scholar with Japanese training who served as its first editor. These men were very impatient with what they saw as the passivity of most Sichuan elites toward officials and the New Policies in general. Despite Xu Zixiu's nominal endorsement, the first issue contained a scathing attack on his Educational Association, which had just held its annual meeting. Only 60 of the 400-plus members had bothered to attend, and the meeting had adjourned within three hours without discussing any topic other than funding disputes and the animosity of officials and the people toward educational ventures. Compared to that of other provinces, the paper lamented, Sichuan's educational community appeared unable to provide the effective leadership the country desperately needed. In such outspoken terms, *Shubao* upset Chengdu politics both by publicly criticizing provincial officials and by challenging the accommodational political style that had prevailed among provincial elites for so long.

Police superintendent Zhou Zhaoxiang was one of the first officials in Sichuan to experience the newfound power of the press, when he was chased out of the province by *Shubao* in the spring of 1911. His troubles began the previous fall when the provincial assembly attacked him for exceeding the authority granted his office under the police law, a charge that prompted his memorandum to Zhao Erxun quoted above. The provincial assembly faulted him for ordering all pharmacies in the city to have an employee on duty at all times, in order to respond to medical emergencies, and then sending people around to the pharmacies in the middle of the night to test whether medicine would be available. The assembly viewed this as harassment. Even worse, Zhou had then pressured pharmacies to atone for violations of the order by donating funds for street repair, a form of punishment not authorized by the police law. These charges appeared in *Shubao*'s sixth issue.[39] In Zhou Zhaoxiang's impassioned defense of his actions to Zhao Erxun, he pointed out the inadequacy of the police law, cited Chengdu police precedent for his regulation of the pharmacies and his handling of the case, and claimed that the pharmacy guild had judged the penalty fair.[40] Apparently this satisfied his patron, Zhao Erxun. The matter dropped out of the official record.

Although in its case against Zhou Zhaoxiang the provincial assembly cited the police law and the limitations the law placed on state authority, this incident can best be understood in the context of the power struggle between assemblymen and provincial officials that developed in 1910, rather than as an indication that the provincial assembly had dedicated itself to upholding the legal rights of the citizens of Chengdu in general. Had Zhou Shanpei been the one to fine the pharmacies, just the sort of action he had often taken as head of the Police Bureau, assembly leaders, who were close to him, might very well have praised his "effective administration." The leaders of the assembly disliked Zhou Zhaoxiang, who lacked Zhou Shanpei's strong connections in the Chengdu community and tended to favor centralizing policies over official-elite condominium.[41] After Zhao Erxun left for a new post early in 1911, Zhou Zhaoxiang became more vulnerable. In April, he handed his enemies a golden opportunity when he closed down a newspaper for reporting the scandalous fact that he had hosted a banquet in a Western-style restaurant on a day set aside to mourn the death of the Empress Dowager. Once again, provincial assembly leaders used *Shubao* to attack Zhou Zhaoxiang, and again they accused him of exceeding his authority, this time by interfering in the operation of the newspaper and pressuring the private company that printed it to stop doing so.[42] Shortly after the story appeared in *Shubao*, Zhou Zhaoxiang left Sichuan to "study rural police reform" in Manchuria, where Zhao Erxun had been posted.[43]

Several facts about this case point to personal antagonism toward Zhou Zhaoxiang on the part of the *Shubao* editors and suggest that Zhou Shanpei may have been involved in Zhou Zhaoxiang's downfall. None of the names of the guests who attended Zhou Zhaoxiang's banquet, whose conduct might also have been considered disrespectful to the deceased Empress Dowager, was made public by *Shubao*. The banquet itself occurred on the grounds of the annual industrial fair, which Zhou Shanpei supervised, and the scandal broke in the pages of the industrial fair's daily newspaper, which Zhou Shanpei had established. The newspaper was printed by the Changfu publishing house, founded and managed by Fan Kongzhou, Zhou Shanpei's close associate in the Chamber of Commerce. Still, although Zhou Zhaoxiang's disgrace probably originated in the sort of personalized factional struggle that had long characterized elite politics in China, the publicity given his misbehavior in *Shubao* and the appeal to the new law codes showed the extent to which the old-style politics of private negotiation and compromise between officials and elites had come under attack.[44]

The selective nature of the provincial assembly's support for opposition to Qing authorities is demonstrated in another incident. In the winter of 1910–11, students in Chengdu rose to the challenge *Shubao* had issued when it criticized the passivity of elites in Sichuan. In this case, however, provincial assembly leaders hesitated to support the defiance of the administration. The students went on strike to protest the Qing court's rejection of a petition asking for the early opening of a national parliament. Leading constitutional activists across the empire had united to present a series of such petitions in the fall of 1910, and in November the Qing court ordered them to desist and leave Beijing. News of this blow to the constitutionalist movement spread rapidly across the country, and Chengdu students walked out of their classes in January. The provincial educational commissioner called the students together and reprimanded them, arguing that their actions weakened China and might lead to Japanese expansion into Manchuria. Irate students responded that it was the government that was inviting foreign conquest by delaying the adoption of a constitutional system. Teams of students paraded through the streets explaining their cause and criticizing government policy.[45] Governor-General Zhao Erxun, who had dealt with a similar protest movement two years earlier during the field day incident discussed in Chapter 3, again summoned the leaders of the educational community to his offices and ordered them to discipline the students. He also attempted to arrest the leader of the protest, who managed to escape from the city.[46] According to Guo Moruo, a middle-school student in Chengdu at the time, assembly leader Pu Dianjun himself joined in the effort to persuade the students to return to their classes, which they eventually did.[47] Although anxious to uphold their own status relative to officials, assembly leaders nevertheless remained uneasy about the possible dangers of broader and less restrained participation in the political debates of the day.

Shortly after the student strike, Zhao Erxun left Sichuan. The timing was good for Zhao Erxun personally; he avoided involvement in the tumultuous Railroad Protection movement of the spring and summer of 1911. For the Qing, however, it was unfortunate. Sichuan's community of officials lacked a strong leader who could deal decisively with the factionalism in the administration and the furious reaction of the provincial assembly and the railroad stockholders' association to the decision to nationalize the railroad. Zhou Shanpei's memoirs of the period leading up to and following the formation of the Railroad Protection Comrades Association (Baolu tongzhihui), headed by the leaders of the provincial assembly, show an increasingly united and passionate urban community confronting a waffling provincial administration, fatally divided into rival camps, alternately encouraging the association leaders to stick to their demands for a reversal of the nationalization policy and ordering them to submit to the imperial will.[48]

Sichuan's Railroad Protection movement transformed the political agenda in Chengdu; elite encouragement of urban development and interest in constitutional reform and self-government within the imperial system were overtaken and engulfed by a fervent and widespread enthusiasm for provincial autonomy in the name of nationalism.[49] The stockholders' association accused Sheng Xuanhuai, the minister chiefly responsible for the nationalization policy, of "selling out the nation" (*maiguo*) by taking the right to build the railroad away from the people of Sichuan and giving it to foreign capitalists. "Sichuan for the Sichuanese" was the rallying cry that united many of the discontented parties in the province and brought them into the railroad movement, until it grew beyond the capacity of its nominal leaders—and sympathetic officials such as Zhou Shanpei—to control. In the course of the summer of 1911, the New Policies era in Chengdu came to an end. The understanding that provincial officials and elites had shared regarding provincial priorities and their respective administrative roles crumbled and, given the widespread rebellion, could not be restored. The New Policies achievements on which Zhou Shanpei had built his reputation could no longer sustain it. By the fall of 1911, his identity as an outside official was all that mattered. Those who had benefited from his activism in Chengdu and remained supportive of him could do no more than help him escape from a hostile province.

Chengdu on Strike and Besieged

The crisis brought on by the Railroad Protection movement paralyzed provincial administration in Sichuan and contributed significantly to the collapse of Qing authority empirewide. Within the more limited context of Chengdu's local affairs, the history of the movement shows both the organizational skill of the movement leaders and the resiliency of the urban institutions created under the New Policies. The transfer of authority from Qing administrators to a new provincial regime, however, also led to the growth of military and secret-society influence in Chengdu, a new phenomenon that would become a prominent feature of Republican-era city politics, as we shall see in Chapter 6.

On June 17, 1911, an extraordinary meeting of representatives of Sichuan–Hankou Railroad stockholders was held in the company's headquarters in Chengdu. The meeting had been called four days earlier when company officials learned that the Qing government planned to take out a foreign loan in order to finance the construction of the trunk line between Hankou and Chengdu, control over which the government had just taken away from the privately managed railroad company. For stockholders—already upset over the news that they could expect to receive only government bonds, not cash, for their investment in the nationalized trunk line—the foreign loan was an outrage. Angry denunciations of the central government, and particularly Minister of Posts and Communications Sheng Xuanhuai, for selling out the national interest to foreigners, coupled with stirring appeals to resist the nationalization policy, brought tears to the eyes of the large audience in the hall. Witnesses claimed that the eight constables sent by the Police Bureau to keep an eye on the meeting joined in the weeping, calling out "We are also men of Sichuan; we also love our country."[50] Those attending the meeting agreed to form an association to organize the resistance and then set off as a body to the yamen of Wang Renwen, the provincial treasurer, who was serving as acting governor-general. Wang met with them and agreed to communicate to the central government the depth of the commitment of the people of Sichuan to build and control their own railroad.[51]

The march of the stockholders' representatives, including the leadership of the provincial assembly, over the quarter mile or so from company headquarters to the provincial treasurer's yamen was an unprecedented political act, as striking as *Shubao*'s public criticism of officials.[52] Men who usually traveled about the streets in private sedan chairs found themselves caught up in the exhilaration of collective public protest. The Railroad Protection Association built on the dramatic impact of this action by quickly organizing teams of speakers who spread out through Chengdu's streets in the next few weeks to rally all the city's residents, only a tiny minority of whom were stockholders, in support of their cause. The students who had recently tried, and largely failed, to stir up popular zeal for the early opening of the national parliament joined eagerly in this new campaign. Branches of the Railroad Protection movement sprang up at each school. On June 25, several thousand people gathered at the South Parade Ground for more emotional speeches to see off the men chosen by the association to take its case directly to Beijing. Three days later, the Railroad Protection Female Comrades Association had its inaugural meeting. Chengdu's merchants and Sichuan opera actors formed their own organizations as well, and there were reportedly more than twenty branches representing the city's Muslim community. Twelve-year-old Huang Jilu, future Nationalist party activist and director of the Historical Institute (Guoshiguan) in Taiwan, headed up the elementary school students' association and made an address at a meeting of the main association.[53] The birth of branch associations on many of Chengdu's streets was welcomed enthusiastically in the movement's newsletter, the *Report of the Sichuan Railroad Protection Comrades Association* (*Sichuan baolu tongzhihui baogao*), which appeared frequently after its inaugural issue on June 26. It gave glowing accounts of the patriotism of the branch associations, many of which pledged funds or land to support the railroad protection cause.[54]

The next stage in the movement came when thousands of students headed out of the city for their home counties, charged by the association with the task of carrying its message to their relatives and neighbors. Throughout July and August, county railroad protection associations formed, often organized by the leaders of the new schools, city assemblies, agricultural associations, and self-government study societies in the county seats. To association leaders in Chengdu, it seemed as if the central government would have no choice but to cancel the nationalization order, given the clear consensus of opinion in Sichuan, expressed through the New Policies institutions. The movement would succeed, the branch associations would dissolve, and politics would return to normal, except that now the leaders of the provincial assembly could expect to be taken more seriously by officials in Beijing.

In Beijing, however, the clarity of the protection movement's message was undermined by the support for the nationalization policy on the part of some prominent Sichuan natives serving the central government. Among these, to the great chagrin of the Chengdu activists, was Song Yuren, one of the early advocates of industrialization and institutional reform in Sichuan. Nationalization was necessary, these men argued, because the railroad served vital national interests and because the private railroad company had shown itself incapable of managing the huge project (it had lost much of the accumulated capital when the old-style banks it had invested in failed as a result of a financial panic in Shanghai in 1910). In 1911, six years after the company was granted the right to build the railroad, only a few miles of track had been laid.

On August 2, the new governor-general of Sichuan, Zhao Erxun's younger brother Zhao Erfeng, arrived in Chengdu from the west, where he had been quelling an uprising in Qing-dominated eastern Tibet. During the next three weeks, he attempted to mediate between the court and the Railroad Protection movement leaders in Chengdu. Beijing-based officials did not make this easy for him. Minister of Posts and Communications Sheng Xuanhuai submitted a memorial to the throne in which he called the protesters a mob of schoolboys intent on stirring up trouble, a characterization that naturally offended the activists. The central government persuaded the manager of the railroad company's eastern headquarters at Yichang in Hubei to leave the company's employ and work for the government railroad administration, bringing with him the company's account books. Company personnel in Chengdu felt betrayed. The protection movement was stymied. In response, association leaders called a citywide strike in Chengdu, to begin on August 24.[55]

All shops in Chengdu remained closed on the morning of August 24. Zhao Erfeng sent high-ranking officials out on the streets to urge merchants to open for business, and most responded by removing some of the boards that shuttered their shop fronts, but only while officials remained on the scene. The strike extended to students and workers, including the thousands of peddlers who fed the city and the porters who supplied it with water and carried away its human waste. Constables remained on duty, but the Railroad Protection Association called on all its branch organizations in Chengdu to help maintain order in the city. The strike was designed to convince Beijing of the unity and determination of the people of Sichuan, and therefore it had to be disciplined. No doubt for that reason, strike leaders showed some flexibility after a few days; peddlers reappeared in the streets, and porters resumed the tasks necessary to maintain the health of city residents.[56] At the same time, the people of Chengdu discovered a new way to indicate their seriousness, while making it very difficult for the government to label their actions as rebellion: they set up memorial tablets to the Guangxu emperor. Li Jieren writes that this new tactic was first adopted by shopowners who feared that soldiers would be sent to force them to open their stores. For protection, these merchants affixed tablets dedicated to the spirit of the Guangxu emperor to the front of their shops to indicate that the strike was an expression of loyalty to the former emperor, who had granted the people of Sichuan the right to build the railroad. Soon more and more of these tablets appeared throughout the city, many of them on arches spanning the streets. Townspeople rejoiced in the difficulties this presented to officials, who were forced to get out of their tall sedan chairs in order to pass under the low arches and yet, given the tense atmosphere in Chengdu, did not dare order their removal. According to Guo Moruo, the people of Chengdu believed that the reason the Manchu general took no part in the railroad controversy was because he was trapped in the Banner garrison by the memorial arches outside its gates and by his own disinclination to get out of his sedan chair and walk under them.[57]

The two weeks after the beginning of the strike represent a high point of official-elite cooperation in overseeing Chengdu's affairs. Neither side wanted disturbances in the city to complicate the railroad dispute, and officials met with protest movement leaders daily to exchange information and coordinate their activities. At least two public meetings were held during the strike to discuss security, and officials shared the stage with local leaders to encourage the populace to remain calm.[58] At another meeting Zhou Shanpei told street headmen that they bore chief responsibility for the difficult task of defusing tension in the streets. Ordinarily, he explained, the police stepped up to put an end to public arguments, but in a time of political crisis, their actions might be misconstrued and result in serious conflict. According to Zhou's memoirs, the headmen accepted his advice with gratitude.[59] Association leaders provided aid to city residents who suffered from the strike, and the Police Bureau agreed to temporarily waive the taxes that teahouses and theaters were obliged to pay.[60] All these actions served to keep the New Policies institutions, such as the police, out of the spotlight during the Railroad Protection movement. In Chengdu, therefore, a clear distinction was maintained between the New Policies and the railroad conflict.

When, after two weeks, the strike had failed to produce a conciliatory statement from Beijing, movement leaders began to discuss the merits of a provincewide tax revolt. Emotions in the city ran high, and unflattering caricatures of Sheng Xuanhuai and other Beijing officials appeared on broadsides passed out in the streets.[61] At the same time, the central government stepped up pressure on Zhao Erfeng to resolve the crisis and ordered the central railroad commissioner, Duanfang, to go to Chengdu and investigate Zhao's administration. On September 7, Zhao took the drastic step of summoning nine of the protest movement leaders, including the heads of the provincial assembly and the railroad stockholders' association, to his yamen and imprisoning them there. When the news leaked out, people gathered at the yamen entrance, holding aloft tablets dedicated to the Guangxu emperor and pleading for the release of the men. Zhao Erfeng's soldiers fired into the crowd, killing a number of people and injuring many. That night, soldiers occupied all the streets in the center of town and tore down all the memorial arches to the late emperor.[62]

The Chengdu massacre immediately galvanized the surrounding region. News of the event was quickly transmitted to activists outside the walls, most famously by "water telegrams": 200 small wooden boards inscribed with a brief explanation of the arrests and a call to arms, cast into the water east of the city for downriver sympathizers to find.[63] Within a few days, militias from nearby towns marched on the city to protest the massacre and demand the release of the prisoners. Zhao Erfeng's troops, battle-hardened from years of fighting in Tibet, chased them away, but more quickly gathered. Over the next few months, several "Comrades' Armies" (*tongzhijun*) coalesced, led by militia chiefs from across the Chengdu plain. Although these armies claimed solidarity with the Railroad Protection Association in Chengdu, they were also motivated by resentment of the costly New Policies institutions. Schools, police stations, and tax-collection agencies were ransacked all over Sichuan in the fall of 1911, as the Comrades' Armies fought with imperial troops for control of county seats.[64] Chengdu itself, gates closed and telegraph lines cut, stood isolated in a sea of rebellion.

The End of Qing Rule in Chengdu

Despite the chaos in the province, Zhao Erfeng held onto his office longer than many Qing governors did. When New Army units in Wuchang rebelled on October 10 and forced their commander, Li Yuanhong, to declare the independence of Hubei province, their action set off a wave of similar events across the country. In Sichuan, the troops Zhao Erfeng brought with him from the Tibetan campaign remained loyal to him, as did the old "provincial forces" (*xunfangjun*), which consisted primarily of recruits from Hunan and Hubei. With the exception of one unit of 230 soldiers that rebelled south of Chengdu and marched on Chongqing in the first week of November, Sichuan's New Army remained loyal to the Qing.[65] Nevertheless, the Comrades' Armies and local militias had some success in outlying parts of the province, and several rival governments were operating in various Sichuan cities as of mid-November. By that point, Zhao Erfeng had released the leaders of the Railroad Protection movement from captivity, after they agreed to work with him to restore order in the province. After all the contiguous provinces had rebelled against the Qing and it became obvious that appeals to Sichuan's militias to lay down their arms were having no effect, Chengdu elites persuaded Zhao Erfeng to resign his authority to the leaders of the provincial assembly, who declared Sichuan's independence on November 27. Pu Dianjun became governor, and the city was festooned with flags featuring the character "Han," surrounded by eighteen circles, representing China's eighteen provinces (Fig. 5.1). The authority of the Manchu government was no more.[66]

Zhao Erfeng's conditions for stepping down included his own resumption of the office of Tibetan border commissioner and an agreement by the new Sichuan government to continue funding his troops in Tibet. Sichuan leaders also agreed to protect the Banner community in Chengdu and to treat Manchus, Mongols, Muslims, and Han people as equals, despite the new "Han" flags. In the Shaocheng garrison area, soldiers and their families were nervous, nonetheless. Anti-Manchu sentiment ran high in some parts of the country, and the Banner communities in Jingzhou (Hubei), Hangzhou, and Xi'an had been attacked in the course of the revolution in those cities, with much loss of life.[67] In the case of Chengdu, however, disaster descended not on the impoverished Shaocheng, but on the wealthy merchants and gentry in the eastern and northern sectors of the city and on the fledgling provincial government itself. On December 8, less than two weeks after Pu Dianjun's administration had formed, soldiers mutinied in the city, looted the provincial treasury and many of the prosperous shops and wealthy residences, and set fire to some of them.

The mutiny occurred just as Pu Dianjun was attempting to deal with the growing problem of idle soldiers in the city. In the days after the declaration of independence, soldiers had taken to roaming the streets, seeking amusement and getting into trouble. The provincial troops (*xunfangjun*) that had helped Zhao Erfeng to suppress the rebellions were recruits from other parts of China, and the uncertainty of their future in an independent Sichuan no doubt made them jumpy. Perhaps because of this, many of them swaggered aggressively about town, dressing and acting like warriors from the opera stage. City residents, particularly women, were terrified. A series of incidents involving undisciplined soldiers contributed to the sense of unease: two Sichuan opera actors were kidnapped by soldiers, a huge

Fig. 5.1 A flag of revolution was raised over Chengdu in November 1911. The character in the center stands for the Han people, and the eighteen circles represent the eighteen provinces of China at that time. (The United Church of Canada/Victoria University Archives, Toronto: catalog no. 98.083P/23.)

brawl in a brothel pitted New Army soldiers against soldiers from the provincial forces, and a newspaper office was ransacked after the editors criticized soldiers for wild behavior.[68] Pu Dianjun decided to solve the problem by calling all the provincial forces in Chengdu to a military review on the East Parade Ground, where each soldier would be registered and given orders and three months' pay. The soldiers did indeed gather, but when shots rang out on the outskirts of the formation, the ranks dissolved into chaos. Pu Dianjun and his officers ran for their lives, and the soldiers fanned out across the city and looted it, assisted by some of the bolder city residents.[69] By the end of the day, the commercial arcade, symbol of the New Policies civilizing effort, stood empty, all its windows shattered by the rebellious troops, all its merchandise carried away by crowds. Zhou Shanpei fled the city that night.[70]

Some degree of order, however, was quickly restored. Street militias formed for neighborhood self-protection. The leader of one of the more disciplined of the Comrades' Armies that had gathered in the outskirts of Chengdu brought his troops into the city, bivouacked them in the provincial assembly building, and organized street patrols. The highest-ranking Sichuan native in the New Army division headquartered to the north of the city, Yin Changheng, brought a detachment of troops into the city as well, and threatened to shoot anyone caught looting shops or homes. In addition to being a prominent military man in a time of crisis, Yin was married to the sister of the head of the Railroad Stockholders' Association. The day after the riot a delegation of local notables called on him to take up the office of military governor and form a new administration to replace Pu Dianjun's failed government.

Yin's vice-governor, Luo Lun, was also well connected, having served as vice-chairman of the provincial assembly. Luo Lun was instrumental in persuading the Banner garrison to disarm and surrender to the authority of the new provincial government, a difficult task given the fear of further rioting. Shortly after becoming vice-governor, Luo moved his family into a house in the Shaocheng, in order to reassure its residents that they would not be attacked. The government guaranteed members of the Banner garrison several months of rice stipends and gave them certificates of ownership of their property in the Shaocheng, as well as the right to sell it as they wished.[71]

Yin Changheng at first set up his government in the buildings of the Imperial City, since Zhao Erfeng still occupied the governor-general's yamen. In the days after the riot, however, signs that Zhao harbored hopes of regaining his authority surfaced; rumors linked him to the mutiny, and proclamations bearing his old title were discovered about town. Finally, Yin Changheng claimed to have intercepted an urgent message from Zhao to troops stationed in Tibet, ordering them to march on Chengdu. With this as evidence, Yin had his troops arrest Zhao Erfeng. A hasty public trial in front of the Imperial City ended with Zhao's execution, and Yin rode his horse down the Great East Street while displaying Zhao's severed head.[72] A week later, on January 1, 1912, Sun Yat-sen became provisional president of the Republic of China, and Sichuan's leaders quickly pledged allegiance to the new nation. The revolution had come to Chengdu, but what it meant for the city was not at all clear.

6 AFTER THE REVOLUTION: SOLDIERS, SAGES, AND GOWNED BROTHERS

The destruction of police stations, schools, and tax offices all over Sichuan in the fall of 1911 attests to the resentment of the New Policies programs throughout most of the province. In Chengdu, however, the schools survived, and no one took advantage of the December military mutiny to attack the police. The residents of Chengdu did not openly repudiate the changes that had occurred in the city over the previous ten years. The 1911 Revolution nevertheless had a tremendous impact on life in the city. By toppling the Qing, the revolutionaries released the city from the grip of the powerful provincial bureaucrats who had done all they could to turn Chengdu into a model of New Policies civilization. However, no effective government replaced the Qing bureaucracy. After the revolution, provincial regimes based in Chengdu sought in vain to command the authority that their predecessors had enjoyed.

New Policies institutions—the police force, the Chamber of Commerce, the self-government councils—continued to exist in Chengdu after the revolution, but changes in the political environment eroded their control over community affairs. The police force lost much of its funding and prestige. Street headmen and new urban militias assumed responsibility for many matters of local security that

the constables were unable to handle, despite periodic efforts by police administrators to revive the authority and reputation of the professional force. The Chamber of Commerce was no longer patronized by provincial officials and invited to contribute to Chengdu's
urban development; instead it was pressured to fund the armies of rival militarists. The self-government institutions, banned by Yuan
Shikai in 1914, reconvened after his death in 1916 only to discover that
interest in the old model of self-government had dwindled and that
few cared about their deliberations.

In the meantime, a new sort of institution emerged to play a key
role in the management of Chengdu: the semi-secret brotherhoods
known as the Gelaohui or Society of Elders and Brothers (described
in more detail below). Many of the city's male residents joined Gelaohui lodges in the years after the revolution, taking their places in a
loose network of "gowned brothers" (*paoge*) that extended across the
Chengdu plain and—at times and under certain circumstances—into
other parts of China. The weakness of formal state authority in Sichuan in the late nineteenth and early twentieth centuries allowed
these brotherhoods to grow rapidly. Even before 1911, public life in
many communities in Sichuan and neighboring provinces was
strongly influenced by brotherhood associations. With the fall of the
Qing, Chengdu itself was introduced to the ways of the gowned
brothers in dramatic fashion.

As Sichuan's civil wars intensified in the 1920s and provincial
politics became increasingly chaotic, the nature of the Gelaohui
evolved, and it took on new functions. At no time, however, did
Chengdu's gowned brothers see the city itself as an object for a special type of development. For them, the city offered opportunities for
organizing brotherhood activities on a grander scale than elsewhere,
but, other than that, it was not considered significantly different from
towns and villages across the Chengdu plain. This lack of distinction
between cities and villages as social forms recalls the attitudes of the
Qing provincial administration before the New Policies era. However, the Gelaohui had developed in areas where the state was weak;
an administrative center like pre-1911 Chengdu thus represented
enemy territory.

The Gelaohui occupation and appropriation of this enemy territory during the Republic was never complete, even though most of the militarists who claimed control of Chengdu and the merchants who accumulated wealth there found themselves obliged to make accommodations with the brotherhoods. Other public figures in the city who had relatively little to do with the gowned brothers, however, were able to carve out roles for themselves in city life in the early Republic. Key among these were two groups: the prominent scholars known as the "Five Elders and Seven Sages" (*wulao qixian*) and the activists associated with the foreign community in Chengdu, including the supporters of the YMCA. Unlike the gowned brothers, both groups consciously strove to shape Chengdu as a city, although in very different ways. The Elders and Sages, remnants of the elite reform community, dedicated themselves to upholding their vision of Chengdu as the cultural heart of western China. The YMCA, on the other hand, kept Chengdu connected to international currents in urban reform, even as the Gelaohui eclipsed the formal administration in controlling economic and neighborhood activities.

Chengdu in the Civil Wars: The Decay of Formal Administration

The influence of the Gelaohui, traditional elites, and foreign-aligned activists on city life after the revolution must be understood in the context of the power struggles that wracked Sichuan for more than a decade and weakened or diverted the formal administration of the city. The 1911 Revolution destroyed the imperial system that had channeled political ambitions and set the basic patterns in the relationships of bureaucracy to people and center to province and county. Revolutionary leaders believed that the destruction of this system would allow them to build a stronger nation on a new constitutional foundation, but in this they were frustrated. Too many political issues at the national and provincial level remained unresolved in the early years of the Republic. In Chengdu, one reason for the collapse of Pu Dianjun's provincial regime twelve days after it took power from the Qing was a dispute over whether men who were not native to the province would be allowed a role in Sichuan's public affairs. In the days after Zhao Erfeng's resignation, an association of non-Sichuanese residents of Chengdu—former and expectant officials, teachers, and merchants—formed to try to protect their interests in the newly hostile atmosphere.[1] Yin Changheng, it was said, had long chafed at having to serve under non-Sichuanese superiors, and other ambitious men doubtless felt the same.[2] Yin's decision to execute Zhao Erfeng in the wake of the December 8 mutiny may have been meant as a message to the men in Pu Dianjun's coterie, many of whom had close ties to Qing officials and other extra-provincials and wanted to see some of them remain in Sichuan. Whether or not Zhao's death was the catalyst, there was a substantial exodus of non-natives in the winter of 1911–12, including many officers in Chengdu's police force.[3] Between 1912 and 1937, almost all of Chengdu's prominent public figures and political leaders were native-born Sichuanese, or at least claimed to be.

Although Yin Changheng pledged Sichuan's loyalty to the Republic in January 1912, the constitutional disputes and power struggles arising from President Yuan Shikai's attempts to reassert central control produced open rebellion in parts of the province in 1913 and 1916. The weakness of the central government in the early Republican period also spurred the ambitions of many of Yin Changheng's colleagues, trained in the military academies set up as part of the New Policies. Even before Yuan Shikai's death in 1916, the leaders of Sichuan's various military units had begun to turn them into personal armies, which they used to expand their authority in regions of the province. Between 1917 and 1935, these armies engaged in hundreds of small- and large-scale wars, breaking the province up into occupation zones that grew and shrank and changed hands frequently.[4] In an era of such extreme political fragmentation and instability, no national or provincial project on the scale of the late Qing New Policies was possible.

These three decades of war affected Chengdu in innumerable ways.[5] Residents witnessed, and some participated in, terrible brutality in those years, particularly when military control over the city was contested.[6] Communal pride may have suffered and a certain defensiveness arisen from the fact that Chengdu no longer enjoyed the prestige and economic benefits of being the overwhelmingly dominant city in the province.[7] In the newly decentralized Sichuan, Chongqing was able to take full advantage of its key position in trading and communications networks. Although trade was considerably affected by the fighting, Chongqing's economy expanded much more rapidly than did Chengdu's. By the 1920s, its population had surpassed that of Chengdu. For a few years in that decade, the militarist Liu Xiang declared Chongqing to be the provincial capital.[8]

From the perspective of urban administration, one of the most significant consequences of the continuous warfare was the decline of complex urban institutions, particularly the police. Chengdu's police force, the key component in Zhou Shanpei's vision of urban civilization, deteriorated markedly as funds and personnel were diverted to the provincial warfare. The militarization of the province and the trajectory of police decay in Chengdu are both captured in the life story of Yang Wei, who at different times led rebellions and served as Chengdu's top police officer.

Yang Wei was born in 1887 into a wealthy family in the southern Sichuan county of Xuyong, one of the few places in the province where Sun Yat-sen's Revolutionary Alliance found a substantial following. While in his teens, he studied police administration in Japan and joined Sun Yat-sen's organization. In 1906 he participated in an uprising in central China and, when it was suppressed, found his way back to Sichuan. He was one of the conspirators in the plot to assassinate Sichuan's top officials as they gathered to commemorate the Empress Dowager's birthday in 1907. When the plot was discovered, Yang was captured and sentenced to life in prison. In the end, he spent four years there. With the fall of the Qing, the revolutionaries in Chengdu's jails regained their freedom.[9]

When Yang Wei was released from jail late in 1911, he impressed the young Guo Moruo as a hardened revolutionary, with long unkempt hair, a pale resolute face, and a deadly serious manner (see Fig. 6.1 for a photograph of Yang taken in prison at about the time he

Fig. 6.1 Yang Wei in prison in Chengdu, November
25, 1911. (The United Church of Canada/Victoria
University Archives, Toronto: catalog no. 98.083P/14.)

regained his freedom).[10] Because of Yang's Japanese training and ties
to the revolutionary leadership, Yin Changheng appointed him to reconstruct Chengdu's police force and use it to control the streets in
the wake of the military mutiny (Fig. 6.2 shows Yang in his police
superintendent's uniform). In addition to summoning the Chengdu
constables back to work in the days after the riot, Yang commanded
armed patrols, which he ordered to shoot suspected looters in the
streets. The heads of people caught looting or spreading rumors of a
Qing revival were displayed at busy intersections and in front of the

Fig. 6.2 Yang Wei as Chengdu's superintendent of police, March 1912. (The United Church of Canada/Victoria University Archives, Toronto: catalog no. 98.083P/15.)

commercial arcade. Yang's biographer credits him with imposing a "new revolutionary order" on the city.[11] Next, Yang revived the police institutions created by Zhou Shanpei, including the police academy and the workhouses, orphanage, and charity hospital. As a committed revolutionary, he also proclaimed the equality of men and women. Once again women were granted police permission to attend opera performances in the theaters opened during the New Policies era.[12] Guo Moruo reports that Yang was wildly popular among the people of Chengdu.[13]

In July 1912, Yin Changheng rode out of Chengdu at the head of an army, charged with a mission to bring Tibet under the control of the new Republic. During the transition from Yin's administration to that of Hu Jingyi, the acting military governor, Yang Wei apparently clashed with his superiors. Two days after Yin's grand parade launching his Tibetan campaign, newspapers reported that Yang Wei had resigned his job and left the city. Prompted by the loud outcry from the citizenry, Yin Changheng's own mother met with Yang Wei and pleaded with him to return, which he consented to do.[14] But his return was brief. Hu Jingyi, who had the support of Yuan Shikai, was soon appointed governor. Shortly thereafter, Yang Wei was summoned to Beijing, where Yuan threw him into jail. Yin Changheng, meanwhile, brought his armies back to Chengdu and threatened Hu Jingyi with war. Although Yin and Hu ultimately reached a settlement that sent Yin back to Tibet, the city had once more experienced the terror of impending battle.[15] It was to become a familiar sensation.

By 1914, Yang Wei had managed to win release from jail, with the help of prominent Sichuan natives serving in the capital, and was returned under guard to his native county.[16] He immediately began agitating against Yuan Shikai and in 1915 joined the anti-Yuan rebellion spearheaded by the powerful Yunnan forces of Cai E. In the spring of 1916, the governor of Sichuan declared the province's independence of Yuan's Republic, and Yang Wei entered Chengdu once more to patrol the streets, this time as commander of the first division of a new provincial army. When Yuan sent troops to retake the province, however, Yang Wei was forced from the city yet again.[17]

The anti-Yuan revolution and Yuan Shikai's death in the summer of 1916 encouraged the process of national and provincial political disintegration. For the next nineteen years, no central regime exercised much control over Sichuan, although many eastern militarists fanned the flames of Sichuan's civil wars by backing one side or another. Cai E, who won prestige as the leader of the anti-Yuan movement, marched into Chengdu and became Sichuan's governor in the fall of 1916. But his hold over the city lasted only a few days; he soon left to seek medical treatment in Japan, where he died. His departure precipitated a power struggle in Chengdu among various Sichuan commanders, troops loyal to Yuan's successors, and the Yunnan and Guizhou armies that Cai had brought with him. Twice in 1917, open warfare broke out in the city streets. Thousands of city residents were killed, many neighborhoods were doused with kerosene and put to the torch, and, in the second clash, a section of the Imperial City wall was blown up as troops from one army tried to force troops from another out of their stronghold in the center of Chengdu.[18]

Control of the city changed hands frequently in the next seven years. Between 1918 and 1920, Chengdu was occupied by the troops of Xiong Kewu, another former Revolutionary Alliance activist from southern Sichuan. Once again Yang Wei was appointed provincial chief of police, with direct responsibility for Chengdu's police force. Soon, however, Xiong felt a greater need for Yang's services as a military commander. Sichuan's armies were expanding rapidly. By 1919, formally designated units claimed 300,000 soldiers, up from 53,000 at the time of the 1911 Revolution.[19] In that year, Yang Wei left civil administration behind entirely and devoted most of the rest of his career to warfare and warlord politics. He was jailed again in 1927, this time by the left-wing Nationalist regime in Wuhan. After his release, Yang Wei retired to Chengdu, where he "closed his door, turned away all visitors, and chanted Buddhist and Daoist texts daily." He died of illness in Chengdu in 1928 at the age of 41.[20] At the time, Chengdu was in the third year of joint occupation by three separate armies.

Yang Wei's experience as head of the Chengdu police force in 1918 shows how irrelevant Zhou Shanpei's vision of the police institution as a disciplined, centralized, vigorous regulator of the urban community was to provincial authorities interested above all in defeating their military rivals. Trained in the same Japanese police methods that Zhou had studied only a few years earlier, Yang Wei shared his predecessor's conception of the role of the police. In 1912 he had been instrumental in ensuring that all the New Policies police programs survived Chengdu's transition from imperial to Republican city. Six years later, in proclamations published in the local newspapers, he professed himself shocked at the decline of the force. The constables lacked spirit and took their responsibilities lightly, and their superiors did nothing about it. Residents of the city had come to see the police as an affliction, he concluded. Yang called for a massive retraining effort and ordered officers to meet with the constables daily to discuss how to improve discipline and knowledge of police techniques. He also planned to revive the constable training institute, with students recruited from among graduates of middle schools. And he published a detailed guide, reminiscent of Zhou Shanpei's 1903 regulations, explaining how constables and the public should behave to show the proper respect toward each other.[21]

In 1918, Yang Wei purged the police force of many officers and constables that he judged to be corrupt or incompetent. He planned to hire and train replacements to bring the force back up to its previous strength, but left the Police Bureau before that could be accomplished. His successor, Zhang Qun, who later served as mayor of Shanghai, tried to continue Yang's rebuilding work,[22] but Zhang's term in office, too, lasted no more than a year. Throughout the 1910s and 1920s, at a time when Chengdu's population was growing, the force claimed some 600 constables, about half the number of the late Qing police.[23] As for finances, an official report published in 1920 asserted that, up through 1916, the Chengdu force had received 26,000 *yuan* per month from taxes on teahouse operators, theaters, and brothels, about the same budget as before the revolution.[24] No reliable information on police funding between 1916 and the 1930s is available, but a recent history of the force claims that in those years constables had to collect their own meager salaries by extorting money from households and businesses in their precincts and were regarded by the populace as little more than beggars.[25]

Another factor that contributed to the demoralization of the police was the presence of large numbers of undisciplined soldiers in the city. The soldiers threatened the image of the police as protectors of the urban community, an image that Zhou Shanpei and Yang Wei had assiduously cultivated. In 1912, shortly after Yang Wei ended his first stint as police chief, the provincial government complained that the laws prohibiting opium consumption were not being enforced in Chengdu, because soldiers stationed there had taken on the role of distributors, and police did not dare to intervene.[26] In 1914, the police chief issued a public notice that authorities other than the Police Bureau had no right to order constables around, clearly referring to military commanders.[27] During the street fighting in 1917, the rival armies refused to allow the police to put out the fires they set to impede the movements of their enemies. Retreating soldiers carried off women and forced any men they encountered to carry their equipment.[28]

Even in times of peace, the constables, who were not regularly equipped with guns until the mid-1930s, could not stand up to unruly soldiers without serious risk to their lives. Still, they sometimes tried, and the tension that prevailed between the police force and soldiers occupying the city after 1916 frequently produced outbreaks of violence. In the summer of 1922, for example, a police officer from one of the subprecinct offices outside the eastern wall of the city observed a soldier bathing himself in the river on a hot day. He approached the soldier and told him he was violating a police ordinance and beat him with a whip. More than 30 of the soldier's comrades later descended on the subprecinct office, tied up the officer and one of his subordinates, and took turns beating and kicking them. The constables attached to the subprecinct fled. The office was completely destroyed.[29]

Other urban institutions also suffered from the militarization of the province. The city assembly, disbanded in the Yuan Shikai era, was revived only in name after his death.[30] A new provincial assembly was elected and began meeting in Chengdu in 1918, but had difficulty gathering a quorum. Over the next few years, provincial assemblymen, as well as the editors of the many newspapers that had sprung up since 1911, could not avoid involvement in the militarists' political rivalries. With their ever-expanding armies, the militarists were able to amass land and tax most of the sources of wealth in the province, and they used that money to buy the support of civil and military talent.[31] Politicians, bureaucrats, and newspapers became identified with one or another provincial clique, leaving little room for them to serve as community spokesmen for the interests of the people of Chengdu or any other locality. Many of those who did try to maintain their independence of the militarists and speak out against their abuses, such as the journalist and novelist Li Jieren, were subject to arrest and other forms of harassment, if not assassination.[32]

In the early years of the Republic, the energies of Chengdu's Chamber of Commerce were almost completely absorbed in efforts to moderate the financial demands of the military and cope with the terrible instability of the currency. Beginning in 1912, the rapid expansion of armies led to the proliferation of military scrip (*junyong-piao*), which in turn led to the proliferation of disputes between merchants and soldiers over its value.[33] By the mid-1920s, each of Sichuan's important militarists controlled his own mint, producing a confusing array of coins that further complicated market transactions.[34] The *Citizen's Gazette* (*Guomin gongbao*), a local paper established right after the revolution by leaders of the Chamber of Commerce, published scores of articles and commentaries on the currency crisis between 1917 and 1935, when Sichuan's civil wars at last came to an end.

The Chamber of Commerce tried to act as a unified voice of protest in the case of currency problems, organizing meetings with each occupying militarist to discuss the issue. Before 1917, it also took a vocal stand against increased taxes. Fan Kongzhou, Zhou Shanpei's ally in the construction of the commercial arcade, was head of the chamber from 1913 to 1917 and confident enough of his prestige to speak out on behalf of Sichuan's merchants. In 1917, however, he was shot to death while traveling between Chengdu and Chongqing. It was widely believed in Chengdu that Liu Cunhou, one of the less diplomatic of the militarists, had tired of Fan's campaigns for a limit on the tax on salt and ordered his assassination.[35]

This blow to the prestige of the chamber was followed two years later by another, this time delivered by nationalistic students. In response to the May 4, 1919, demonstrations in Beijing against the transfer of German rights in Shandong to the Japanese, students in Chengdu held rallies and demanded a boycott of Japanese goods. The Chamber of Commerce failed to support the boycott, and in December 1919 angry students kidnapped the head of the chamber's general affairs committee and paraded him through the streets. A serious fight between merchants and students at chamber headquarters was averted only by the arrival of the civil governor, who chastised the merchants. As a result, the head of the chamber and his deputy resigned.[36] Caught between grasping militarists and militant nationalists, the faction-ridden Chamber of Commerce increasingly disappeared from public view. In the 1920s, it came to be dominated by a few merchants who used their wits and financial resources to reach secret deals with the commanders of each occupying army.[37]

Chengdu in the Civil Wars: Changes in City Form

As administrative and civic institutions in Chengdu deteriorated, the physical infrastructure of the city suffered as well, affected by a decline in both private and public investment. In a 1937 essay, Li Jieren assessed the prevailing mood of insecurity that limited housing and other city construction:

We modern Chengdu people were not so foolish. We knew that in a chaotic world no one could expect a long life, so it was useless to make a "Great Plan for a Hundred Years" (bainian daji). What we needed to do was just enjoy life as best we could. . . . So, from the last years of the Guangxu era [1875–1908] on, most of our houses were expected to last only twenty years or so. For roofs, the rule was to apply, on the thinnest of bases, one layer of modernized tiles. We were happy if there wasn't a big wind—which was sure to peel them off—or a thick snowfall—which would smash them. The annoying thing was when the cat's steps were particularly heavy; it was impossible to avoid periodically summoning the plasterer to patch up leaky spots.[38]

After a violent, but brief, coup in 1926, an observer reported that homeowners in the southern section of Chengdu had plastered their buildings with posters displaying such messages as "We dare not stand any more of the Republic's blessings," "Have been looted ten odd times," and "Everything has been robbed."[39]

One of the key symbols of the New Policies era, the commercial arcade, survived the street fighting in 1917, but was completely destroyed when it accidentally caught fire in December of that year. Its tenants immediately raised funds to have it reconstructed in its original form. The Yuelai Hotel next door, which had also burned, was not rebuilt, however. Instead, the Yuelai market, a replica of the commercial arcade, was built on the spot.[40] The decision to abandon the hotel is, perhaps, indicative of the changing nature of commerce in the city. Fan Kongzhou and Zhou Shanpei had intended the entire arcade/hotel complex to symbolize and support Chengdu's entrance into the world economy, and it was designed to accommodate merchants and visitors from afar. But warfare had cut Sichuan off from the rest of China and the world, and long-distance trade did not expand, except for the commerce in opium and guns through Chongqing.[41] After it helped spark the 1911 Revolution, the famous Sichuan–Hankou Railroad company faded away. Sun Yat-sen's provisional government turned over part of its capital to Revolutionary Alliance leaders from Sichuan, to equip a new Sichuan army for the Republic.[42] Over the next twenty years, disputes occasionally arose over what had happened to the rest of the money. None of it, at any rate, went into the railroad, and plans for it were eventually abandoned.

The reconstruction and expansion of the commercial arcade indicates that Chengdu's merchants were not completely bankrupted by the dislocations of the civil wars. Nevertheless, new merchant-sponsored construction was limited in the early years of the Republic. The three parts of town that experienced the greatest transformation in the period between 1911 and 1924 were the old Banner garrison area known as the Shaocheng, the space in the center of town known as the Imperial City, and the area outside the south wall that became West China Union University. The first two were transformed as a direct result of the revolution and civil wars; the latter developed because of increased missionary investment in the city, which the militarists welcomed.

By 1911, Shaocheng Park, discussed in Chapter 4, had already opened the garrison area to the wider city to some extent. After the revolution, the walls separating the Shaocheng from the rest of the city were demolished and Bannermen were awarded deeds to their property. Many quickly sold their land to Han Chinese.[43] The new residents included several famous military commanders of the early Republic, who bought large lots and built substantial mansions that served as both residences and headquarters.[44] The southern section of the Shaocheng, near the park (see Map 3), came to be one of the more desirable residential areas of Chengdu. It was said that, once the Yunnan and Guizhou troops had been run out of the province early in the 1920s, Sichuan's rival militarists reached a tacit agreement to spare one another's Chengdu residences during their own warfare.[45]

After 1911, the Imperial City at first housed the offices of the military governor of Sichuan (see Fig. 1.7, p. 31). In the summer of 1917, the fighting in the city was concentrated in this area, with great damage to the surrounding neighborhoods. Afterward, the new provincial authorities agreed to raze the Imperial City's side walls (see Map 3) and turn the area over to the public schools, many of which relocated to the Imperial City at this time. The provincial military headquarters was moved to the former Banner headquarters in the Shaocheng. This, Imperial City neighbors hoped, would prevent a recurrence of the type of standoff that had resulted in so much damage in 1917.[46]

While walls were going down inside the city, a new walled community was taking shape outside, to the south: West China Union University (see Map 3). West China Union University was, as its name suggests, a cooperative project financed by most of the Protestant mission societies in Chengdu, with a board of directors headquartered in Toronto. Beginning in 1905, promoters in Chengdu began raising money for a college and negotiated with the directors of several native-place associations to buy cemetery land south of the city. The university opened in 1910 with only a handful of students, but it grew slowly and steadily during the early Republican era. Its dental school, in particular, was famous. By 1914, a campus master plan had been devised, and buildings began to go up. Most of these, including the curious little clock tower that stood near the center of the cross-shaped campus, had English-style brick walls topped with Chinese-style curved roofs.[47] To one observer, West China Union

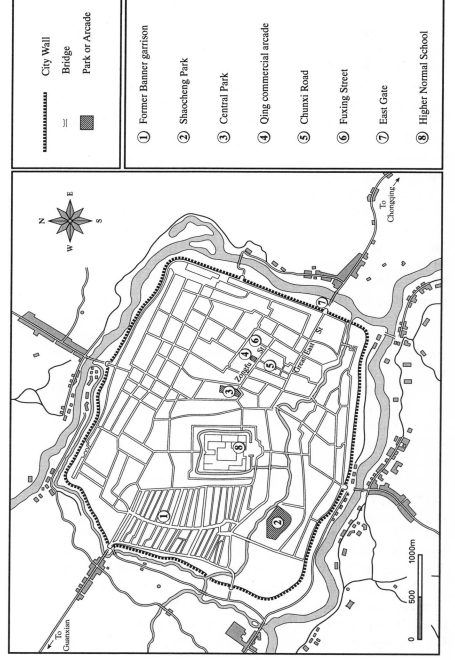

Legend

▮▮▮▮▮ City Wall

)(Bridge

▨ Park or Arcade

① Former Banner garrison

② Shaocheng Park

③ Central Park

④ Qing commercial arcade

⑤ Chunxi Road

⑥ Fuxing Street

⑦ East Gate

⑧ Higher Normal School

Map 3. Chengdu in the 1920s. Redrawn from a map in Tō-A dōbunkai 1917.

University and similar campuses in other parts of China stood out as "remarkably beautiful in an environment of squalor and stench, like so many medieval castles or cathedrals."[48] Sichuan's armies treated West China Union University as a neutral zone, and its campus served as a haven for the dependents of militarists during fighting in the area around Chengdu.

What did the ordinary citizens of Chengdu do during such times? Even those wealthy enough to have sturdy walled compounds of their own lived in fear. With the police authorities no longer able to manage the force and undisciplined soldiers roaming the streets, alarms were frequent between 1911 and 1937. In response, and with the encouragement of an impoverished administration, neighborhoods turned to self-defense. Street militias organized by neighborhoods helped transform Chengdu into a collection of insular communities in the Republican period.[49] In this transformation, the Gelaohui played an integral part.

Networks of Gowned Brothers

The Gelaohui did not originate in Chengdu. Like most Chinese secret societies, it is thought to have developed first among marginal groups in areas where Qing rule was weakest. The name first appeared in the historical record in the mid-nineteenth century, when Qing commanders fighting the Taiping armies noted the existence of groups with that name among their soldiers. Scholars have suggested that early Gelaohui lodges drew from at least two different sets of traditions: that of the White Lotus sects and that of the Guolu, a type of brotherhood association that flourished in parts of Sichuan in the eighteenth century. Early Gelaohui groups consisted of single men, particularly soldiers and disbanded soldiers, who did not have strong ties in settled communities. These young men formed lodges that exploited illicit economic opportunities, including salt and opium smuggling, gambling, prostitution, and banditry. They also created rituals and a secret language of gestures and other signals, so that travelers could identify themselves to and seek help from members of other lodges. Their moral code emphasized loyalty to the organization and mutual assistance among brothers, inspired in part by the great traditions of brotherhood in the stories of the Three Kingdoms period and in the novel *Water Margin*.[50]

By the late nineteenth century, with the decline of Qing control over the countryside, many Gelaohui lodges had become rooted in villages and towns on the Chengdu plain and had shed some of their aura of criminality. Well-off townsmen, including an occasional degree holder, joined Gelaohui lodges, even though they were banned by the Qing.[51] By 1900, lodges seem to have existed fairly openly in towns and villages throughout Sichuan. François Fleury, a French priest who lived in Sichuan in the late nineteenth century, said of the Gelaohui that "they have succeeded in getting into all the municipalities. Everywhere the leaders of the market towns are influential secret society members allowing them to take care of matters as they wish."[52]

The life of Liu Shiliang, author of a famous book on the Gelaohui tradition, illustrates this phenomenon. Liu Shiliang grew up in the 1890s in a village in Neijiang county, southeast of Chengdu near the salt-producing regions of Sichuan. Although poor, he was anxious to get an education and apprenticed himself to a literate fortune-teller. Mistreated by the other village boys for associating with this object of derision, he used his wits to counterattack and humiliate his opponents. His victories attracted the attention of the leader of the local Gelaohui lodge, a man of great stature in the village, who inducted him into the society and became his patron.[53] Liu Shiliang subsequently gained employment representing the interests of the Sichuan salt merchants in Chengdu and moved to the capital in the early years of the Republic. Exactly how his association with the village leadership, in the person of the Gelaohui chief, benefited Liu in his career is not clear, but it is evident that the Gelaohui lodge had become the authority in his native place.[54]

The history of the transformation of the typical Gelaohui group from a fraternity of marginal, desperate, young men to a territorially based association that extended membership to a large percentage of men in a community is not well understood, but the process was under way well before the fall of the Qing. In 1909, when Governor-

General Zhao Erxun asked the new provincial assembly to help him devise a plan to disband all secret bands (*huidang*), the assembly replied by noting that not all such associations in Sichuan were evil. Many assemblymen may have been closely connected to various Gelaohui groups in their native areas. Vice-chair Luo Lun's father, for example, was said to be a leader of a group of gowned brothers in northern Sichuan. Still, the transformation was not complete. The 1909 provincial assembly identified two types of associations: "filial and righteous societies" (*xiaoyihui*) and "river and lake societies" (*jianghuhui*). The former, which organized for community self-protection, arose in response to the latter, which preyed on villages, according to the assemblymen. Other reports from Sichuan around the time of the 1911 Revolution speak of two sorts of Gelaohui organizations active in the province: "clear water" (*qingshui*) and "muddy water" (*hunshui*). In contrast to the predatory muddy-water groups, the clear-water lodges are described as associations of upright men who act primarily as organizers of community self-defense efforts and regulators of local society—arbitrating local disputes and aiding members who meet with misfortune.[55]

There is evidence that Gelaohui groups existed in Chengdu during the early twentieth century, but the city does not seem to have been the base of any large or influential Gelaohui organizations until after the 1911 Revolution. Zhou Xun, the last Qing magistrate of Huayang county, believed that the majority of Gelaohui members in Chengdu before the revolution were affluent young thrill-seekers.[56] Li Jieren, who was a young student at the time, corroborates this view in one of his short stories, "Haorenjia" (Good guy), which describes the city after the breakdown of Pu Dianjun's provincial government in December 1911. Groups of young men dress up in theatrical garb, "elect" wealthy Chengdu residents to be the "helmsmen" of their Gelaohui lodges, parade them about the streets in decorated sedan chairs with banners emblazoned with the names of their lodges, and move into the residences of the helpless helmsmen, making free with their stores of food and opium—although not with their women, which would have been against the ethical code of the Gelaohui.[57] Whether these youthful Gelaohui enthusiasts were interested in anything other than entertaining themselves by emulating the dress and swagger of the heroes of *Water Margin* is open to question.

Accounts of the 1911 Revolution in Chengdu suggest the existence of a different sort of Gelaohui activity in the city at that time, involving a completely different set of people and contacts between lodges inside and outside the city. When, for example, a Revolutionary Alliance member wished to transport a supply of guns from within the city walls to militias in Chengdu's suburbs in the spring of 1911, he contacted Gelaohui figures via an intermediary, and they agreed to deliver the weapons.[58] Most Gelaohui activity in late Qing Chengdu was probably of this type—Gelaohui centers outside Chengdu were kept supplied with illicit goods and information about government projects by associates who resided in the city, including almost certainly some who worked in the yamen of the county magistrates and other officials.[59]

It was the events of the summer and fall of 1911 that brought the Gelaohui into Chengdu, and in spectacular style. Some leaders of the Railroad Protection movement encouraged Gelaohui organizations to ally with the stockholders' association in the fight against nationalization. The numerous Comrades' Armies that seemingly sprang up overnight in parts of Sichuan after the arrest of the leaders of the stockholders' assembly and the shooting of unarmed petitioners that summer were commanded by famous Gelaohui figures, several of them from the hilly areas to the west of Chengdu.[60] One organizer of the protection movement claimed that the propaganda teams set up by the movement's leaders contacted Gelaohui figures "on each street" in the city and got their support for the movement.[61] The Gelaohui-led troops besieging the city joined their comrades inside it after Zhao Erfeng abdicated.

Li Jieren's account of the carnival atmosphere in Chengdu's streets after the overthrow of Pu Dianjun's government suggests that many residents found Gelaohui ritual intensely exciting. Yin Changheng demonstrated his appreciation for the style and organizational principles of the Gelaohui by declaring his office the headquarters of the Great Han Lodge (Da Han gong). The new head of the Military

Affairs Bureau followed his chief's lead and declared the establishment of the Great Land (i.e., army) Lodge (Da lu gong) at army headquarters.[62] Soon, over 200 lodges had been organized in the city.[63] S. C. Yang, who acted as a liaison between the foreign community and the provincial government throughout the Republican era, notes:

On practically every street there was a "Gongkou" or Lodge of the Elder Brother Society which kept order for each street and prevented looting. Even Christians like Chen Weixin became "Paoge," or "Gowned Elder Brothers" or leaders in the secret societies, and opened "Gongkou" or "Matou," "harbors" or lodges, to protect the people, with the popular signs and symbols now quite familiar to the people.[64]

According to another observer, female Gelaohui lodges formed in Chengdu for the first time ever.[65]

The era of open celebration of the spirit of the Gelaohui was brief, however. A rival revolutionary government headquartered in Chongqing decried the "Gelaohui government" in Chengdu, and the new military governor of Yunnan, Cai E, sent troops to Sichuan to "deliver it from Gelaohui control." In a telegram addressed to the national government and the military governors of other provinces, the commander of the Yunnan troops in Sichuan accused Yin Changheng and Luo Lun of encouraging Gelaohui groups to harass and extort money from non-Sichuanese officials and merchants sojourning in the province.[66] Yin and Luo vehemently denied the charges, which they characterized as a pretext on the part of the Yunnan leaders to justify their attempt to profit from the disorder in their much wealthier neighbor to the north. Nevertheless, they must have felt pressured to squelch Gelaohui activity in Chengdu to keep the Yunnanese forces at a distance.[67] Yang Wei immediately moved to disband the Chengdu lodges.

In "Haorenjia," Li Jieren writes that the lodges were quickly shut down. He suggests, however, that the brief period of open Gelaohui activity had lasting effects on city life. The main character of the story, a wealthy landowner residing in Chengdu, is so traumatized by the experience of being forcibly elected to Gelaohui leadership in the wild first few months of 1912 that he withdraws into his well-fortified compound and refuses to concern himself in public affairs.[68] For others in Chengdu, however, participation in the Gelaohui opened new paths to local influence in the Republican era. The identification of Gelaohui armies as the heroes of the 1911 Revolution contributed to the legitimacy of the organization among some of the militarists who subsequently dominated the province. With the exception of Yang Wei, top-level political leaders in Republican Sichuan were much more tolerant of the Gelaohui than late Qing governors-general had been. This, in combination with the growing weakness of the police organization, allowed the Gelaohui to expand significantly in Chengdu, despite the official ban. In 1921, a Protestant missionary observed that "the social fabric of the whole province is honey-combed with this cult."[69] In the 1930s and 1940s, observers estimated that 70–80 percent of men on the Chengdu plain were members.[70]

Evidence from memoirs indicates that, by the beginning of the 1930s, the gowned brothers had divided Chengdu into four zones, corresponding to the original four city gates (two more had been created in 1913 and 1914), each of which had its own lodge. There was also a citywide lodge, with its own chief.[71] No further information is as yet available to support detailed analysis of the structure of the organizations, clarify the nature of their relations to each other, and address such important questions as how leaders were chosen and disputes settled. The key thing the memoirs do show, however, is that these lodges were organized territorially. This corresponds to traditional Gelaohui patterns in market towns and villages.[72] Presumably, any man capable of impressing the leaders of the lodge in his zone could aspire to membership. A recent study asserts that up to 90 percent of the men in Chengdu were members of lodges in the 1930s.[73]

Former gowned brothers from Chongqing have described the famous Gelaohui leaders of that city as men who could protect the welfare of lodge members by manipulating and evading the legal system and by effectively mediating disputes among members and between members and outsiders. These leaders were seldom wealthy or well educated, but their ability to inspire lodge members to work for the group suggests that they commanded a certain moral authority as well as the means to bolster this authority by violence or the threat of violence. Successful leadership of a community of gowned brothers required the construction and maintenance of a strong network of personal loyalties.[74] Gelaohui chieftains thus had to be excellent local politicians, rather than top-down administrators after the manner of Zhou Shanpei.

The local and political character of the Gelaohui leaders of Chengdu might explain why reports about the activities of street headmen appeared much more frequently in local newspapers in the Republican era than they did in the days of the New Policies reform.[75] In the Qing police organization, street headmen were theoretically important as the link between the police and the community, but in practice it is not clear that police authorities paid much attention to the headmen, and they were rarely called on to take an active role in community life. After the revolution, the relative importance of constables and street headmen in neighborhood affairs seems to have been reversed. Headmen probably helped organize and train the neighborhood militias that appeared periodically between 1912 and 1937.[76] There is little doubt that headmen had close relations with Gelaohui chiefs. Documentation of this is rare, but one report survives in the records of the Sichuan Provincial Social Affairs Bureau. According to this report, a Gelaohui-affiliated street headman in a Chengdu neighborhood organized 300 local children into a Young Heroes Association and used them to supervise and regulate life on his street.[77]

Social Order and Cultural Change During the Early Republic

The growth of the Gelaohui encouraged the development of a new spatial organization of life in Chengdu. As control over administrative matters such as public security and social regulation shifted from the centralized urban institutions of the New Policies era to the local Gelaohui chieftains, the city itself dissolved, in a sense, and became a group of smaller communities loosely tied into a network of Gelaohui organizations extending across the Chengdu plain and beyond.

This dissolution of Chengdu mirrored the carving up of Sichuan into garrison areas for the various militarists, but the city's Gelaohui leaders were more successful than the provincial militarists at coming to terms with each other: gang warfare and feuding do not seem to have been common in Chengdu in the Republican period.[78] This may well have been due to the strength of the defensive, self-protective aspects of the Gelaohui tradition. It is also possible that the citywide lodge mentioned in the memoirs constituted a sort of central mediation board to manage friction between Gelaohui lodges in the region.

What was the nature of the relationship between Gelaohui leaders and the masses of urban residents? Just as the provincial militarists used their control over the economy to co-opt assemblymen, journalists, and civil administrators, so the local Gelaohui leaders brought into their organizations people who occupied key positions in Chengdu's neighborhoods, such as the street headmen. By the 1920s, most constables, too, were gowned brothers.[79] As a result, the police force lost the reputation for impartiality that Zhou Shanpei had devoted so much effort to establish. According to one history of the Chengdu police, Republican-era constables were widely thought to accept bribes and the officers were thought to protect Gelaohui brothers.[80] The police probably also assisted lodge leaders, as yamen runners had in the old days, by supplying them with information about matters that might affect their sections of the city, such as the ins and outs of militarist politics as well as the movements of powerful or wealthy strangers.[81]

Merchants joined Gelaohui lodges for self-protection and supplied the funds to support lodge activities, including the periodic meetings at which lodge business was conducted and new members were inducted amid much ceremony. Merchants may have occupied positions of prestige within many of the lodges.[82] As for the laborers, craftsmen, and peddlers who made up the bulk of the male population of the city, their feelings about the Gelaohui organizations probably varied depending on their personal relationships to the leadership. The extent to which Gelaohui leaders had the capacity and will to control the economy of Chengdu—and exploit laborers and consumers for the benefit of themselves and their lodge brothers—is not at all clear. Because most sectors of the economy were dominated by myriad small-scale enterprises, however, it is unlikely that Gelaohui leaders were able to do much more than levy protection fees on businesses and collect membership fees from all the men in their districts.[83]

Given the influence that Gelaohui chiefs exerted over Chengdu's neighborhoods, it was in the interests of the militarists, who moved in and out of Chengdu with some frequency, to cultivate good relations with them. In the early Republican period, the militarists were largely occupied with the problems of building and sustaining armies, creating alliances with other militarists and bandits, and tapping into the easiest sources of money: the salt wells of Ziliujing and the port of Chongqing, which was the main entrepôt for the opium trade.[84] Thus, they were usually quite satisfied to leave Chengdu's administration in the hands of the gowned brothers and what remained of the police force. That began to change in the mid-1920s, however, as we shall see when we consider the career of Yang Sen in the next chapter.

The new centrality of the Gelaohui in Sichuan probably gave the average male citizen of Chengdu more say in neighborhood affairs than Zhou Shanpei had been willing to grant under his centralized, disciplinary regime. It would be interesting to learn whether the inhabitants of Chengdu believed Gelaohui authorities to be more "just" than Qing officials, but that question awaits further research. It is clear, however, that many aspects of city culture changed significantly after the fall of the Qing and that some of these changes were quite welcome to parts of the community. Since Qing times, Gelaohui lodges had capitalized on the considerable enthusiasm throughout Sichuan for such illegal or officially disreputable activities as prostitution, gambling, and opium consumption. Under Zhou Shanpei, Chengdu's police force had been committed to controlling such activities, with the stated goal of eventually eradicating them absolutely. Certainly, this had not been achieved by 1912. During the Republican era, though, opium dens and brothels proliferated, and many restaurants and teahouses hosted gambling and other sorts of gatherings.[85] Those gowned brothers who reveled in the excitement of a good gambling session and a diverse marketplace for narcotics and sexual services were no doubt pleased, although elites in the city bewailed these developments in the local newspapers, and others certainly suffered from them in ways difficult for historians to document but easy enough to imagine.[86]

In a development that was much less welcome to many of the gowned brothers, the republican rhetoric of the 1911 Revolution was seized upon by some, such as Yang Wei, to argue that women should be accorded new freedoms in Chengdu's public life. This issue created more cultural tension in Chengdu than the florescence of commerce in drugs and sex. Gelaohui lore produced by Sichuan authors in the 1930s asserts that the tradition of the gowned brothers demanded respect for virtues such as loyalty and filial piety. Despite the growth of the New Culture movement, which attacked many aspects of traditional culture, Gelaohui leaders felt no antagonism toward orthodox or conventional Chinese norms in the areas of gender and family relations. The young leaders of the New Culture movement and the Gelaohui chiefs shared no common conception of "public life" itself: there was too great a gap between formally educated youth, who published reformist newspapers and supported open elections, and Gelaohui leaders, whose organizations appealed to a wide range of men in part because of the clubbishness and clandestine excitement associated with them. As young female students in the city started bobbing their hair and attending schools in the late 1910s and 1920s, New Culture advocates such as Chengdu native and novelist Ba Jin praised them for taking their first brave steps toward emancipation. Gelaohui figures such as Liu Shiliang, on the other hand, satirized and condemned them for being frivolous and obsessed with fashion, ignoring their obligations to their families, and flirting with militarists.[87] Violence against female students and anyone suspected of corrupting girls was one of the things for which Gelaohui-dominated Chengdu was best known among eastern Chinese intellectuals in the 1920s and 1930s.[88]

The Five Elders and Seven Sages and the Evolution of the Urban Reform Community

While the Gelaohui expanded into the regions of neighborhood life left open to it by the decline of formal administration after the revolution, Chengdu's elite community was torn apart and reconstituted in new ways by the ascendancy of the militarists and the advent of the New Culture movement. The reform community that had rallied around Zhou Shanpei did not collapse entirely after the fall of the Qing, but it broke up into a number of different groups with different political priorities. Those that managed to acquire the most influence on city affairs were culturally, and often socially, conservative. Chengdu did produce some famous New Culture intellectuals, including Wu Yu and Ba Jin, but, compared to Shanghai or Beijing, the city tended to suffocate radicals. The careers of Wu Yu and Ba Jin illustrate this point; the former spent many hours of his days in Chengdu corresponding with acquaintances in eastern China and complaining to his diary about the oppressiveness of the city, and the latter, like the hero of his novel *Family*, escaped to Shanghai while a young man.[89]

Some Chengdu activists of the early Republican years, such as Yang Wei, considered social and political egalitarianism central to the concept of a "republic," but few in Chengdu were prepared to follow them. The *Citizen's Gazette* assigned to its humor column a story of a student who appeared before a county magistrate in 1912 to present a petition. When he addressed the magistrate as "mister" (*xiansheng*) instead of "your honor" (*daren*), the magistrate had him severely beaten, exclaiming that he would never accept a form of address used in the past to refer to fortune-tellers.[90] Chengdu people were "shocked" when the Ministry of Justice in Beijing rejected a local court decision sentencing a man to life in prison for killing his father, noting that the man was known to be mentally ill and could not be held responsible for the patricide—which the new law codes merely called "murder."[91] The most famous challenge to old ways of thinking in Chengdu in the first decades of the twentieth century was Wu Yu's attack on his father for squandering the family's wealth on a concubine.[92] Although Wu Yu won all the legal judgments relative to his dispute with his father, he was shunned by many who considered his public criticism of his father outrageous. Wu Yu's anger at this treatment by the Chengdu elite community contributed to the urgency of his critique of Confucian culture, which he articulated in several famous essays in *New Youth* magazine. It did not, however, make him a popular figure in Chengdu, except among a relatively small circle of radical youth. But he also had friends among a somewhat larger group of literati who appreciated his poetry much more than his views on morality and the Confucian tradition.[93]

When some of the less conservative militarists occupied Chengdu in the early 1920s, political radicals such as Wu Yuzhang got a chance to play a role in the city's politics, but they were not much interested in local issues. Wu Yuzhang devoted most of his energies to organizing a movement for Sichuanese autonomy and the creation of a new Chinese federation, which he hoped would bring about the overthrow of the Beiyang government based in Beijing. Although he also introduced Chengdu to Marxism in 1921 and 1922, through public lectures and essays in the local papers, there is little evidence to suggest that anyone in the city was inspired to political action because of this.[94]

Chengdu's elite community was weakened and divided for reasons besides the lack of a common and compelling political agenda. Militarist oppression and economic anxieties effectively splintered the community. The republican system of government initially allowed for the free formation of political parties, and several quickly formed in Chengdu in 1912, much to the disgust of conservatives such as Xu Zixiu, for whom the Chinese word for "party" (*dang*) conjured up images of petty factionalism in support of private interests. Other Chengdu elites, however, such as the Railroad Protection movement leader Zhang Lan, involved themselves in party politics. The parties suffered a serious blow in 1914, though, when Yuan Shikai banned the Nationalist party and Sichuan's military governor Hu Jingyi publicly resigned his membership in another party. Between 1917 and 1935, most Sichuan militarists did what they could to keep the political parties that formed in eastern China, such as the Nationalists and Communists, from building bases in Sichuan.[95] Instead, they established their own personal party-like organizations, which usually imitated the forms and ideology of the Gelaohui tradition.[96]

With the formal political parties disbanded and more and more power concentrated in the hands of army commanders, activists who wanted to remain in Chengdu came under strong pressure to serve the militarists. Some of those who had military or police training, like Yang Wei, became army commanders themselves, although by the 1920s most of these men had retired to comfortable lives in Chengdu. Then, as Yang Wei's experience suggests, they contributed to a modest revival of Buddhist and Daoist studies.[97] For men who aspired to be civil administrators or professionals, the years between 1911 and 1937 were very trying. The dramatic exodus of non-Sichuanese late in 1911 and the establishment of an entirely new provincial administration resulted in simultaneous scrambling for jobs and surging cynicism about the process of political appointment among Chengdu's elites. Wu Yu's diary is preoccupied in the early years of the Republic with observing personnel changes in the provincial government and assessing the prospects of positions for himself and his friends and relatives. Political appointment became an obsession.[98] Wu Yu, himself, eventually dropped out of the contest for jobs and turned to teaching and writing to supplement his landed income.

Education, the traditional vocation of the Chengdu elite, also felt the effects of militarist manipulation and financial strain, however. Guo Moruo describes how the city's schools, established in the New Policies era, were gutted by turmoil in 1912. The most accomplished and ambitious teachers abandoned their classrooms and threw themselves into the frenzied contest for political office.[99] Throughout the Republican period, most schools were starved for funds, with the result that teachers were often forced to take two or more jobs to try to get by, leaving them in no position to take a broad and active interest in local affairs. Except for brief bursts of nationalist protest in 1919–20 and 1925–26—inspired by the May Fourth incident and the May Thirtieth and Wanxian incidents,[100] respectively—most of the political activism of Chengdu teachers and students was aimed at securing steady funding for education. While a visiting professor at the provincial teachers college in Chengdu in 1924, the educator Shu Xincheng commented on the demoralization he saw among his colleagues there, particularly when the college was forced to end the semester two months early for lack of funds to pay the staff. He remarked on the fact that, unlike in eastern China, teachers in Chengdu still clung to the former status markers of the profession, wearing long gowns and refusing to travel about town except in sedan chairs. But, he reflected ironically, the latter was probably due as much to their need to get from one part-time job to another quickly as to their waning sense of social superiority.[101]

Shu Xincheng blamed the demoralization of Sichuan's teachers on the suffocating interference of militarists in educational affairs. This phenomenon, according to Shu, was more severe in Sichuan than in any other place he had visited in China. Already in 1912, Sichuan's military leaders had ignored the instructions of the Ministry of Education and insisted on the power to appoint principals and academic supervisors for public schools, something that, Wu Yu noted, had never occurred under the Qing.[102] By 1924, Shu Xincheng wrote, the militarist Yang Sen claimed the authority to assign his own political advisers to positions in public and private schools.[103]

Yet there were two educational communities in Chengdu in the Republican period that stood somewhat beyond the reach of militarist politics, took an interest in Chengdu's public affairs, and attempted to speak on behalf of the city as a whole, especially when the actions of the militarists appeared to threaten it. Although neither group was interested in or capable of mounting a serious and direct challenge to the militarists' claims to dominate city affairs, each had its own reform agenda for Chengdu's public life. Their ability to realize their visions for the city arose from the particular conditions of urban life in the militarist era, which gave them special roles in Chengdu politics. The next few pages briefly describe these two elite communities: that which the local people called the Five Elders and Seven Sages and that clustered around Chengdu's foreign establishment, which included the YMCA and West China Union University. Chapter 7 discusses how and to what extent these groups were able to promote and implement their plans for the city.

The term "five elders and seven sages" referred not to any particular twelve men but to a group of prominent Chengdu literati who took it upon themselves to speak on behalf of the city. The term first gained currency in 1917, when these literati collectively appealed to the militarist Liu Cunhou to settle his disputes with the Yunnan and Guizhou armies without harming the city. As we have seen, the appeal did not have the desired effect, and Chengdu was ravaged in the ensuing battle. Nevertheless, the Elders and Sages accepted the invitation of Liu Cunhou and subsequent militarist authorities in Chengdu to serve as more or less informal advisers, representing the interests of the urban community. For two decades, these men met periodically with the titular leaders of the provincial administration, giving them advice and accepting responsibility for certain public matters, primarily in the areas of education and welfare.[104] All the members of this group had earned degrees in the Qing examination system, and many were also prominent educators. Xu Zixiu, Chengdu's most famous teacher in the early twentieth century, and Fang Xu, who had been educational commissioner for Sichuan in the Qing, are good examples.

Throughout most of the Republican period, the Elders and Sages were the most visible community spokesmen and protectors of the public welfare in Chengdu. Their prestige came from the fact that Sichuan's militarists, and many Chengdu people as well, considered them to be exemplars of moral cultivation and, perhaps, symbols of a more orderly, if not harmonious, age. The stalwart neo-Confucian Xu Zixiu, in particular, was viewed as a paragon of wisdom by a broad swath of the Chengdu community.[105] Their influence also derived from their relations with the militarists, many of whom had studied under one or more of the Elders and Sages before the revolution. The claimants to provincial leadership wanted to demonstrate their own moral character by publicly seeking the advice of their teachers in matters concerning local administration. The Elders and Sages were thus useful to the militarists as a source of legitimacy.

And, finally, the Elders and Sages had few rivals as public community leaders: Gelaohui chieftains, as I have suggested, were not interested in the sort of publicity that came from newspaper coverage or formal meetings with militarists. As for the militarists and their staffs, they certainly did not object to favorable newspaper coverage, and even established their own papers in order to assure themselves of it. But the exigencies of provincial politics and the transitory nature of their rule in Chengdu worked against any attempt on their part to identify themselves as protectors of the city, as we shall see when we consider the strange career of Yang Sen in the next chapter.

The only real rivals to the Elders and Sages as public champions of the city were the men and women associated with the foreign-run and foreign-inspired institutions. Like the Elders and Sages, the foreign establishment, particularly the YMCA and West China Union University, wanted to be seen by the public at large as a positive force in Chengdu. The foreigners and their Chinese colleagues also commanded resources that gave them some influence over the militarists, such as connections to outside authorities and some outside funding. The people of Chengdu received some of this largesse directly, when, in the words of the British consul general Meyrick Hewlett, the "discriminating and intelligent generosity of the British-American Tobacco Company" allowed him to make "a very lavish distribution of 100,000 cigarettes" during the Chinese New Year celebration in 1917.[106]

Property owned by or associated with people from the United States and Europe was never harmed by the Chengdu militarists in the early Republican era, and the same was true for Japanese property, until 1936.[107] For the most part, the people of Chengdu also tolerated, if not welcomed, the foreign presence in the city. As elsewhere in China, tensions between Chinese and foreigners were greatest in the mid-1920s, when nationalist and anti-Christian feelings grew into widespread protests after the May Thirtieth incident in Shanghai in 1925. In Chongqing, the suburban villas of British residents were looted that year, but nothing of the sort happened in Chengdu.[108] A female British missionary was murdered in broad daylight on a busy Chengdu street in 1926, and, although all agreed the perpetrator was a madman, the missionaries did blame nationalist agitation by Chengdu students for creating a hostile atmosphere that encouraged the attack.[109]

As in other parts of China, foreigners in Chengdu became involved in the civil wars, as various militarists sought them out for personal protection or mediation with other factions. Many an embattled commander checked himself and his family into the French hospital or accepted the hospitality of the Union University when humiliating defeat seemed imminent.[110] To nationalistic students, the protection that foreigners extended to militarists and their families constituted imperialistic interference in China's affairs, and they accused the foreigners of prolonging China's internal strife for their own benefit. There was no firm consensus on this point among the residents of Chengdu, however. Meyrick Hewlett, who lived in Chengdu from 1916 to 1922, rhapsodizes in his memoirs about the friendliness of the people of Chengdu toward him, due in part to his mediation of the 1917 fighting, and even claims to have received "more than one act of valuable assistance" from Chengdu's gowned brothers.[111]

Part of the explanation for the tolerance for foreigners in Chengdu during the early Republic lies in its distance from the centers of foreign power in China. The British and French stationed consul generals there throughout the Republican period, and the Germans and Japanese had consuls or consular agents for part of the time. But foreign gunboats never threatened Chengdu, as they did Chongqing and other port cities. Another factor, particularly after Chiang Kai-shek's Nationalist government took power in eastern China in 1927, was the strong provincialist or localist feeling among the militarists and Gelaohui leaders that made internal Chinese threats seem more pressing than foreign threats.[112] Also important, however, is the fact that by the early Republican period the foreign establishment in Chengdu had attracted the interest of many city people, for reasons beyond the free cigarettes.

From its inauguration in 1910 and the success of its technology exhibition that same year, the YMCA was popular in Chengdu. Early in 1912 it presented a series of lectures on the American system of government, which was enthusiastically received by a large audience interested in knowing more about the meaning of a "republic." That same year, Yin Changheng's administration and the Chamber of Commerce granted the YMCA a large piece of land in the heart of the city, next to the Qing provincial judge's yamen and near the commercial arcade.[113] There, a YMCA compound was built. By the mid-1920s, the compound contained an outdoor track and a meeting hall with a movie theater. Theoretically, the YMCA facilities were open to all young men, but its organizers focused primarily on attracting the support of the wealthy, educated, and powerful, even if they had to overlook a possible patron's dubious character. Guo Moruo recalled going to the YMCA auditorium in 1912 to hear Yin Changheng explain why he was a fit leader for Sichuan in a speech called "Heroes and the Sex Drive." Guo summarized the speech as follows: "Throughout history, heroes have had strong sex drives. I like sex. Therefore, I am a hero."[114]

Compared to the YMCA, West China Union University was not as generous with its resources, and at times in the 1920s there was tension over the question of whether the Chengdu public had the right to walk around the campus and enjoy its beautiful grounds. University officials, both Chinese and foreign, were skillful at defusing these disputes, however. The university was wounded, but not mortally, when most of its students withdrew in the wake of the Wanxian incident of 1926. The servants employed by the university's foreign staff also left their employers that year, but returned after a short strike. New students were recruited to replace those who refused to re-enroll.[115] Union University's relations with the neighboring community were eased by the fact that Liu Yubo, one of the Elders and Sages, taught Chinese literature there.

The YMCA, and the foreigners in general, cultivated the Elders and Sages as well as the militarists. In the spring of 1918, a meeting was called at YMCA headquarters to promote the study of the Chinese Classics.[116] In 1920, YMCA and missionary doctors cooperated with the Police Bureau in devising a strategy to end the cholera epidemic that killed some 4,000 city residents that year.[117] British consul-general Hewlett called Yin Changling, one of the most influential of the Elders and Sages and a cousin of Yin Changheng, "one of the truest friends I ever had in China." In the 1920s and 1930s, Yin Changling headed what became the most important philanthropic institution in Chengdu, the Cihuitang (Hall of Benevolence).

The YMCA and other foreign innovations, if not the foreigners themselves, seem to have been widely popular among the elite community, even among self-proclaimed radicals. Wu Yu sent his daughters to an American-run mission school, even though they were made to pray, because he was impressed that the school had the girls do chores. He invited the teachers to dinner, and they brought a record player, which he praised for its ability to "make people happy."[118] His daughters wrote essays admitting that although at first they hated to be in school with "low-class people" (*xialiuren*), their thinking about class distinctions gradually changed. His second daughter vowed to establish a school for poor children when she finished her own schooling. In the meantime, she formed a prayer group.[119] Wu Yu did not oppose this; Confucianism is rotten, he wrote, but people need religion, and they should be free to choose which to follow.[120]

Wu Yu's openness to new ideas was rather unusual in Chengdu during the Republican period. The fact that he was able to criticize Confucianism openly and still live a comfortable life in the city, however, highlights the extent of political change in Sichuan after 1911. When the Qing government was still in place, Wu Yu's disgust at its official ideology put his life in danger. He did not witness the Railroad Protection movement in 1911 because he had fled to the countryside to escape an arrest warrant issued by the governor-general. In the early Republican era, in the absence of a strong central authority, adherence to neo-Confucian orthodoxy was not a key political issue. Chengdu's politics came to revolve around militarist rivalries, sometimes marked by provincialist sentiment, and were imbued with the culturally conservative localism that Gelaohui ideology sanctioned and supported.[121]

City management was not central to Chengdu politics between 1911 and 1924. In many ways, the city that had been gathered together and disciplined by Zhou Shanpei and the New Policies institutions he cultivated dispersed again in the early Republic. But the image of urban civilization that underlay Zhou's reforms was preserved in some quarters, particularly among the Elders and Sages. The YMCA and people associated with it, on the other hand, helped introduce Chengdu to a new reform program: the city administration movement of the 1920s.

7 THE CITY ADMINISTRATION MOVEMENT OF THE 1920S

When General Yang Sen marched into Chengdu in February 1924, the residents were no doubt grateful that Sichuan's contentious militarists had transferred control of the city without a repetition of the street fighting of April and July 1917, when retreating Yunnan and Guizhou troops had set many neighborhoods ablaze.[1] In the first few days of his occupation, Yang Sen took firm command of Chengdu's streets. In what may have been a tribute to the police methods Yang Wei used in 1912, Yang Sen made personal inspection tours through the city and ordered his subordinates to display severed human heads—identified as those of looters—at all the major intersections.[2] The warlord era had taught Chengdu's inhabitants to expect official violence, but they could hardly have been prepared for the very different sort of devastation visited on many of their neighborhoods during the sixteen months between Yang Sen's arrival and his hasty departure as his rivals temporarily united against him. Not since the New Policies era had anyone been so determined to remake Chengdu, culturally as well as physically. And, by the summer of 1925, most residents of Chengdu were happy to see Yang Sen gather his troops, abandon his plans for the city, and leave.

Heian—dark—is the adjective most often paired with "Sichuan" in commentaries on the province published in the periodicals of eastern China during the 1920s. The story of Yang Sen's administration of

Chengdu reveals that this apparent darkness was partly the effect of a sort of one-way glass between the "advanced" cities of the coast and the cities of the interior. News from below the Yangzi's Three Gorges made its way fairly freely into Sichuan; Yang Sen and his assistants, like most Sichuan leaders in the 1920s and 1930s, knew quite a bit about contemporary political and cultural movements in cities on the eastern coast and were anxious to bring these changes to Sichuan's cities. But no one in the Republican era looked to Sichuan for answers to the dilemmas of the day, and most of the news that made its way down the Yangzi—other than stories about warfare, opium, and harsh taxation—concerned problems stirred up as Yang Sen and his rivals fought with one another to control the province. Sichuan natives who sojourned in eastern China helped consolidate the province's sorry reputation by founding numerous "reform Sichuan" societies that loudly proclaimed it a disaster area.[3] When Wu Yu, whose anti-Confucian essays in the influential magazine *New Youth* earned him a teaching job at Peking University in the early 1920s, received an empty envelope in the mail from the Association of Western Sichuan Scholars in Beijing, he remarked caustically in his diary that it "sufficiently revealed the incompetence" of the people of the Chengdu area.[4] Publicly and privately, Chengdu was pegged as hopelessly backward.

But in the early 1920s Chengdu experienced a brief cultural revolution of sorts. During those years, Lu Xun's iconoclastic short story "Diary of a Madman" gained an audience in Chengdu—earlier than in many eastern Chinese communities—because his admirer Wu Yu praised it in print shortly after it appeared.[5] Wu Yuzhang, the president of the higher normal school in the years before Yang Sen's arrival, formed a socialist study association and published articles on the topic in the *Citizen's Gazette* in 1923. In the spring of 1924, Chengdu marked the death of Lenin with a mass meeting in a public park, presided over by Yang Sen's chief of police.[6] But not everyone in Chengdu in the 1920s was a proponent of "progress." Indeed, many were actively hostile. Two months before the ceremony for Lenin, the Dacheng Association, a society dedicated to the study and propagation of Confucianism that counted among its members most of

Chengdu's Elders and Sages, sought and received the provincial government's promise that the city's Confucian Temple would be preserved from land-hungry officials so that the society could carry out the time-honored Confucian rituals. One of the leaders of the Dacheng Association, Xu Zixiu, refused appointment as a teacher at Chengdu University in 1926 because, it is said, he could not bear to serve on the same faculty as Wu Yu.[7]

Chengdu in the 1920s could not be called a pluralistic seedbed for cultural experimentation; nor, however, was it completely isolated in the immutable grip of tradition and warlord terror. Innovation was possible, and new visions of urban organization and culture developing in eastern China found supporters among a younger generation of Chengdu elites. Many of these young men briefly looked to Yang Sen as their champion. During his time in Chengdu, Yang Sen supported people who thought of themselves as progressive reformers, in touch with the currents that were leading China toward the future. Unfortunately for these ambitious young progressives, Yang Sen's approach to urban reform, unlike that of Zhou Shanpei and his late Qing reform colleagues, took little account of local politics. The history of Yang's attempt to remake Chengdu demonstrates that, even in the face of an outraged populace, a determined man at the head of an army could turn parts of a city into a monument to his "virtuous administration." Along with his new streets and parks, Yang Sen's reforms created tremendous tension in the city—tension that was expressed in behavior that could be and was interpreted simply as cultural reaction.

After Yang was forced out of the city, however, many of his initiatives were quietly sustained by a new coalition forged between some of his young advisers and older men who had been part of the New Policies reform community. Yang Sen's career in Chengdu shows Republican-era city administration at its most authoritarian and personal, but in its wake it is possible to see a revival of late Qing reform ideas, as they were recast under the influence of the social concerns of the 1920s. Ultimately, this revival led to a greater institutionalization of urban administration in Chengdu.

Yang Sen's Chengdu Labors

When Yang Sen (Fig. 7.1) led his army into Chengdu through its East Gate in February 1924, he already had some acquaintance with the city. Although he had grown up in a Sichuanese village a considerable distance to the east, he first lived in the provincial capital at the height of the New Policies period, between 1905 and 1912.[8] In his early twenties at the time, he attended the Accelerated Officers Training School, established in Chengdu in order to staff Sichuan's New Army brigades. From that vantage point, he had a clear view of the first great wave of urban reform in Chengdu, spearheaded by Zhou Shanpei and his associates.

Yang was serving as a low-ranking officer in Chengdu during the Railroad Protection movement and witnessed the collapse of Zhao Erfeng's administration in November 1911. He was among the troops that restored order in the city after the riots that toppled Pu Dianjun and propelled Yin Changheng to power. Yang Sen then left Chengdu early in 1912 to seek his fortune elsewhere in those tumultuous times, ended up on the losing side of the Second Revolution that attempted to overthrow Yuan Shikai in 1913, and sought shelter in Yunnan. When Cai E's Yunnan forces marched into Sichuan in 1916, he returned with them and quickly became a dominant figure in the crowded field of Sichuan militarists. Between 1916 and 1924, he visited Chengdu periodically to attend the military conferences at which Sichuan's generals fruitlessly attempted to negotiate a lasting peace and recruited aides and junior officers from among the city's educated youth.

Although he had never exercised authority over a city of Chengdu's size and political significance, Yang Sen had already established a name for himself as an urban innovator during his occupation of Luzhou, a small city on the Yangzi west of Chongqing. There, he had assembled a group of energetic young assistants, many of them graduates of Peking University, who helped Yang develop a new vision of himself as an urban reformer, destined to create new cities for Sichuan. It was with this image of himself that he arrived in Chengdu, ready to act.

Fig. 7.1 Yang Sen. (*Chengdushi shizheng nianjian* 1928.)

One of Yang Sen's first gestures in Chengdu, however, was entirely in keeping with the city's political traditions: he presided over
the opening of Chengdu's annual flower festival. As noted in Chapter 4, the flower festival had acquired a new role in the late Qing reform era when provincial officials tried to turn it into a commercial
and industrial-promotion exposition by requiring all counties to display their agricultural and industrial products. In 1920 the exposition,
which had declined following the revolution, was revived with much
fanfare, as May Fourth activists promoted economic nationalism and
boycotted Japanese goods. Throughout the 1920s, successful staging
of the exposition became a mark of good administration for Sichuan's
militarists.[9] As a young military student in Chengdu, Yang Sen must

have attended the late Qing industrial expositions. The two he pre-sided over in 1924 and 1925 could not rival their predecessors as provincewide events, given the political fragmentation of Sichuan at the time. Still, the 1925 fair attracted exhibits from 40 to 50 of the province's 144 counties.[10]

As the 1924 fair was winding down, Yang Sen gave a major finan-cial boost to a more novel event: a citywide campaign to promote lit-eracy. The Chengdu branch of the National Association for the Ad-vancement of Mass Education (Zhonghua pingmin jiaoyu cujinhui) began its work in the spring of 1924, with a budget of some 7,000 yuan, 3,000 of which came from Yang Sen and the city government office (shizheng gongsuo) supervised by Yang's elementary school classmate Wang Zuanxu. Well-known educational leaders in the city led twelve teams that vowed to recruit 1,000 volunteers to hold night classes for Chengdu's tens of thousands of shop clerks and laborers, using the "thousand character" textbooks published by James Yen's national movement. In September 1924, Yang Sen attended a meet-ing of the association and congratulated it for setting up 297 teaching stations where 10,267 students were learning to read. Citing an article in Shanghai's Shenbao that pointed out the ephemeral quality of much literacy training, the general encouraged the association to maintain its enthusiasm and carry on.[11]

Even more important to Yang Sen than the mass literacy cam-paign was the promotion of physical exercise among the citizenry. To this end, he expanded Chengdu's Shaocheng Park and turned part of it into a public exercise ground. After its creation in 1910, Shaocheng Park had quickly become the focal point of Chengdu civic culture. In 1913, an obelisk was erected there in memory of the Chengdu martyrs who had died in the course of the Railroad Protection struggle of two years earlier, and many public ceremonies and demonstrations were held beneath it.[12] Before Yang Sen built a running track, however, the park was used on a day-to-day basis primarily by the patrons of its many teahouses and restaurants. In the spring of 1925, Yang Sen presided over an ostensibly provincewide athletic meet—the first, he claimed, since the late Qing.[13] He urged Chengdu's residents to exer-cise regularly and launched attacks on footbinding, long fingernails (unsanitary and a sign of sloth), card games (they make strong men weak, whereas ball games make weak men strong), men who failed to wear shirts in public (uncivilized), and men who wore traditional long gowns (they waste cloth, and short jackets promote martial spirit by allowing freer movement).[14]

Another addition to Shaocheng Park during Yang Sen's administration was the Popular Education Institute (Tongsu jiaoyuguan).[15] The director was Lu Zuofu, who had set up a similar institution in Luzhou when Yang Sen had occupied that town. Lu and his staff designed a museum with exhibits on natural history, history, agriculture, industry, sanitation, education, and military technology. There were also a zoo, a library, a concert hall, and classrooms.[16] The museum displayed products from around the province, obtained at the 1924 industrial exposition. In addition to providing general education, the institute, which visiting scholar Shu Xincheng declared the best in China,[17] served as the site of a rationalistic attack on folk beliefs.[18] When Yang Sen gave the foreign operators of a school for the blind an old temple to use as a classroom, institute staff salvaged the religious statuary for display in the museum.[19] Another weapon in Yang Sen's attack on *mixin*—superstition—was the dreaded "Seven Kills" stela, the relic of rebel leader Zhang Xianzhong's devastation of Sichuan in the mid-seventeenth century (see Chapter 1). Local lore maintained that disaster would follow if the stela were allowed to see the light of day, and so it had been kept covered up in the offices of the Chengdu county magistrate. When the Popular Education Institute was set up, Yang Sen ordered the stela moved into the museum.[20] The institute also hosted performances by school groups of new-style plays, to "reform Chengdu's traditional customs."[21]

Shaocheng was not the only park favored by Yang Sen. He also devoted funds to the construction of Central Park, at the site of the headquarters of the Qing provincial commander, which after Yang Sen's time would be renamed in Sun Yat-sen's honor (see Map 3, p. 196). Nearer his own residence in the former headquarters of the Manchu general, Yang appropriated the grounds of a temple and turned them into a park. This park was unusual for being completely wooded and, in the absence of the otherwise ubiquitous teahouses, remarkably uncrowded and peaceful. Yang Sen also put Arbor Day, first brought to China by Yuan Shikai, back on Chengdu's calendar and presided over a ceremonial planting of trees on the Qingming holiday, when the dead are traditionally honored.[22]

The development of the southern end of the Shaocheng, the former Banner garrison, into an elite quarter made it an obvious target for Yang Sen's most dramatic—and disruptive—plan for remaking Chengdu. He had the road between his office-residence and Shaocheng Park macadamized to introduce this new paving technique to Chengdu. Yang Sen's street-widening and paving project, launched within weeks of his arrival and continued right up to his departure, is what he is most remembered for in Chengdu today. A team of engineers from the city government office drew up a list of the city's streets, divided them into grades, and designated a required width for each, allowing space for sidewalks. The group decided to begin at the most congested spot: Chengdu's main commercial district, along Great East Street, which stretched from the middle of town to the East Gate, along which most traffic to Chongqing and the rest of eastern Sichuan passed (see Map 3). Plans were published in the newspapers, and the street headmen for the affected neighborhoods were summoned to a meeting and informed that they would be in charge of raising the money needed for the new streets from owners and tenants of all adjacent properties.[23] The results were quite dramatic, as can be seen in before (Fig. 7.2) and after (Fig. 7.3) photographs of Fuxing Street, near the late Qing commercial arcade, which was one of the central commercial streets designated for widening.

In addition to paving existing streets, Yang Sen built a new one—Chunxi Road—that he hoped would become the symbol of his administration of Chengdu. This road was constructed on the site of the Qing provincial judge's yamen, a sprawling compound that extended between Great East Street and the commercial arcade built at the end of the Qing. Because it was bordered by the two busiest commercial centers in the city, the old judicial yamen was an obvious choice for the model modern street that Yang Sen wanted to build (see Map 3). In January 1925, the new road was completed and a commemorative plaque installed. The elderly scholar Yang Sen invited to choose a name for the new road selected "Chunxi" (spring brilliance), an allusion to a verse in chapter 20 of the *Daodejing* that speaks of the pleasures of the common people.[24] The opening of Chunxi Road inaugurated a new era in Chengdu's transportation history; it was the first street within the walled city that could easily accommodate rickshaws. Several dozen were operating in the city before Yang Sen left, and soon they outnumbered the old-style sedan chairs that had hitherto been the primary means of transportation for those who chose, and could afford, not to walk.[25] Figure 7.4 shows a Chengdu street that has not yet been widened but is filled with rickshaws and lined with electrical poles.

Yang Sen's road-building energies extended outside the city as well, and his engineers were instructed to map out a route for a road to span the 55 kilometers between Chengdu and Guanxian, site of the Dujiangyan waterworks that irrigated the Chengdu Plain. Twice before, in 1915 and 1922, plans had been laid for the construction of such a road, but each effort had been halted by fighting. Yang Sen, too, was unable to oversee the completion of the road during his time in Chengdu. Because he had given the rights to operate the road to a prominent Chengdu merchant, however, the construction continued even after its political sponsor left, and the first automobile in the province traveled along the packed-earth Guan-Cheng Road early in 1926.[26]

In addition to his cultural and construction projects, Yang Sen brought a third type of innovation to Chengdu: a political style that might be characterized as "authoritarian populism." He tried to craft for himself an image as a direct, plain-speaking, simple man, who appeared in the public park in shirtsleeves and opened his office every day for two hours to receive anyone who desired to meet with him. He reopened a public lecture hall from the early years of the Republic and gave the ceremonial first lecture standing on a table in front of a huge crowd. A local newspaper reported that because Yang Sen wore simple street clothes and a straw hat when he entered the hall, those

Fig. 7.2 View of Fuxing Street before widening. (*Chengdushi shizheng nianjian* 1928.)

in attendance failed to recognize him and no one stood up. His speech on that occasion explained that he had revived the custom of holding public lectures, in decline since 1911, because he desired to ascertain the thoughts of the people and address them directly as he carried out his administrative plans.

On the street I travel about in a sedan chair, and you certainly can't speak to me. If I want to accomplish something, and I say it's a good thing, but you say it's bad, how can we discuss the matter together? The number-one reason why this model public lecture site has been established is just so that any person, no matter who, can come give a talk and express his opinions and criticize me.[27]

Zhou Shanpei's 1906 speeches to Chengdu residents on the value of the police force may have been Yang Sen's inspiration, but the content of Yang's exhortatory speeches was quite different from Zhou's. As we saw in Chapter 3, Zhou Shanpei's speeches, at least in their published versions, emphasized the rationality and utility of the

Fig. 7.3 View of Fuxing Street after widening. (*Chengdushi shizheng nian-jian* 1928.)

police. Yang Sen, on the other hand, focused on his own merits as a caring and innovative leader.

Yang's emphasis on accessibility and folksiness was paired with a decidedly disciplinarian manner, which he developed well before coming to Chengdu in the mid-1920s. As ruler of Luzhou in the early 1920s, Yang Sen invited boys from a local elementary school into his office one day and gave them candy and little copper plaques engraved with "Will not marry a girl with bound feet." He insisted that they immediately pin the plaques to their uniforms.[28] During an athletic meet in Luzhou, he rounded up more than a hundred female spectators with bound feet and ordered a youth corps to lead them to his office. There, he gave them a lecture and ordered them to take off the binding strips, which he burned.[29] In Chengdu, he nailed signs to the lampposts and walls, with a series of "Yang Sen says: . . . ." instructions for appropriate behavior based on his own cultural reform program. "Yang Sen says: By wearing short jackets, you not only save

Fig. 7.4 Scene typical of a major street not long before widening of roads began in Chengdu. Rickshaws and electrical poles are already in evidence
among the sedan chairs and long-gowned pedestrians. (The United Church of Canada/Victoria University Archives, Toronto: catalog no. 98.083P/25N.)

cloth, but also promote martial spirit!" is one example. In a recent biography of Yang Sen published in Chengdu, local historians assert that the general regarded these instructions as something more than helpful suggestions—they claim that he instructed teams of inspectors to shear off the bottoms of men's long robes and beat any man found in a public place without a shirt.[30] A contemporary observer noted that the police forced all city residents to donate money for Yang Sen's Arbor Day ceremony and ordered them to appear at the tree-planting site, although only several dozen ordinary citizens actually joined the students, who were forced to go.[31] Yang Sen himself boasted of taking a whip to gamblers he spotted while riding by Shaocheng Park. When the police ignored his orders to clear the streets of residents' pigs, he recalled that he beat the police chief in front of a crowd, despite the man's cries that "he should not be struck, since he was a *xiucai*" (imperial degree holder).[32]

The Sources of Yang-Senism

Although his memoirs—written on Taiwan when he was 90—imply otherwise, Yang Sen's program for Chengdu did not spring full-grown from his own head. Zhou Shanpei's New Policies program had been a broad but fairly well defined package of institutions and procedures mandated by the central authorities and assigned to provincial officials to implement. Yang Sen's policies, which he tended to combine under the rubric "city administration" (*shizheng*), contained elements from several discrete reform currents. With his ersatz populist style and his enthusiasm for novel schemes that could be presented as "new" (*xin*), Yang Sen attracted many enthusiasts of social and political movements. The director of the memorial ceremony held on his death in 1977 observed that Wu Yuzhang and other Communists had even had hopes of convincing Yang Sen to become "China's Lenin"[33]—which helps explain why two months after Yang Sen arrived in Chengdu, a thousand people were permitted to gather in Shaocheng Park to honor the deceased Soviet leader.

Yang Sen's choice of the term "city administration" to encompass his reform program reflects its growing currency in Republican Chinese cities in the early 1920s, after the establishment of an office for city administration in Beijing in 1914 and the promulgation by the Beiyang government in 1919 of national regulations for city organization.[34] Sun Yat-sen's son, Sun Fo, designed a rival city organizational plan for Guangzhou, headquarters of the Nationalist movement, in 1921,[35] and the example set by the Beijing and Guangzhou city governments was quickly followed by political leaders in other cities. Looking back in 1928, at the height of what might be called the city administration movement, one observer noted that "over the past ten years the cities and towns of every province have been affected by the current of the times and have begun some sort of construction. . . . City government offices in each region have sprung up like bamboo shoots after a rain."[36]

New governmental institutions were not the only sign of a burst of interest in city administration. Chinese who had been attracted to the field of urban planning and related subjects while studying abroad returned to China in the early 1920s and set up academic programs at colleges in Beijing and Shanghai. Articles on city administration appeared in many different publications in the 1920s, including the Beijing and Guangzhou city government gazettes, which provided readers with accounts of urban administration in other countries, in addition to reports on work in their own cities.

In the early 1920s, Sichuan was being wooed by both "national" governments, the Beiyang government of the north and the Nationalist government of the south, and received government publications from both capitals. Chengdu's officials seem to have placed great importance on at least nominal adherence to central regulations. In 1921, Liu Xiang, then the supreme power in Chengdu, opened a new, Beijing-style city government office (*shizheng gongsuo*) in the city. As in Beijing, one of the first projects the city government undertook was planning a central park, plans that Yang Sen inherited. A road-widening project was also in the works under Liu Xiang, but little was accomplished except for a ring road outside a length of the city wall, which was quickly destroyed by heavy carts. To fund the park and road projects, the city government instituted a popular monthly "city administration public benefit" lottery (*shizheng gongyijuan*).

Most of the proceeds of the lottery went to military uses, but Yang Sen later used it to fund some of his projects.[37]

Other, more robust examples of city administration were occasion-- ally cited in the city's newspapers. In 1922 a Chengdu newspaper reporter traveled to Nanchong, in eastern Sichuan near Yang Sen's old home, to investigate the urban reforms undertaken by Zhang Lan, Yang Sen's childhood teacher. Zhang Lan had recently returned to his hometown from a sojourn in Beijing, bringing with him new concepts in city administration and planning. The reporter found Nanchong to be orderly, with newspaper reading rooms, a library, a dye factory, and an educational society. Although Nanchong could not compete with Nantong, the Jiangsu base of industrialist Zhang Jian, he explained, in terms of development it surpassed any city in Sichuan. However, he added, if one were to talk of "city admin- istration," it "simply cannot be counted as that."[38] What did this reporter mean by "city administration"? What was lacking in Nan- chong? His article supplies a list of goals that could not be accom- plished because of a shortage of funds: knocking down the city wall and building roads around the city, constructing a "model street" in the city center, and refurbishing the markets. All are public construc- tion projects.[39]

Many of the men who advised Yang Sen during his administration of Luzhou, Chongqing, and then Chengdu, shared this infrastruc- ture-oriented view of the most pressing tasks facing city govern- ments. The emphasis on public construction can be traced in large part to the influence of the National Road-Building Association of China (Zhonghua quanguo daolu jianshe xiehui). This association was founded in Shanghai in 1921 and may have served originally as a sort of employment agency for civil engineers.[40] By the mid-1920s, it claimed more than 80,000 members and supported both scholarship and advocacy in the area of public construction, transportation, and urban planning.[41] In 1928 and 1930, the association published two huge volumes—*The Complete Book of City Administration* (*Shi- zheng quanshu*) and *The Complete Book of Roads* (*Daolu quan- shu*)—that encapsulated its members' expertise and plans for the development of China's cities.[42]

The association's approach to city administration, as revealed in the volume on that subject, emphasized the construction of roads within and around the city and between cities. A comprehensive network of finely engineered roads was most definitely an early twentieth century hallmark of modern urbanism. In pointing out the "backward" state of the early Greek city-states, the standard American text on ancient history in the years after World War I cited their "narrow, wandering streets, which we should call alleys," along with their "dingy sun-dried brick houses," to create a visual image of listless antiquity.[43] In Europe, Le Corbusier criticized the "corridor streets" of the cities of the past, clogged with city people and commerce, and urged that they be replaced by "an abstract gridded green plane dedicated to the movement of cars, while buildings . . . and pedestrians are lifted from the ground."[44] An added incentive in China was that bridge building and road building had long been considered ideal philanthropic activities for elites interested in displaying their virtue. The expression "build bridges and repair roads" (*xiuqiao bulu*) came to be a common metaphor for accomplishing a good deed with long-lasting effects.[45] In addition to the symbolic attractions of road-building projects, both new and old, the economic benefits of such projects were touted by no less an authority than Sun Yat-sen, the Father of the Republic, in his *Fundamentals of National Reconstruction*. The relationship between improved transportation and local prosperity was quite clear in eastern China, where the road-building activities of such men as Zhang Jian had strongly influenced the fortunes of towns in the Yangzi delta.[46]

The Road-Building Association did not confine its urban-reform advocacy to roads. Wu Shan, the executive director of the association and a native of Sichuan, argued in the city administration volume that human capital for the cities of the future could best be developed in Soviet-style model nurseries, run by specialists trained in scientific child rearing.[47] Other articles cited the health advantages of the "garden city" model of urban planning developed in England and the importance to the human spirit of the beautification of cities. While the ideas and proposals encompassed in the Road-Building Association's vision of city administration are quite rich, the experts represented in the *Complete Book of City Administration* have relatively little to say on the topics of urban social welfare and popular participation in city government. To them, city administration seems to have been primarily a matter of training specialists to design, build, and properly manage the physical infrastructure of the modern city.

The "city administration" advocates of the early 1920s may have been technocrats, but they were also enthusiasts. Dong Xiujia, who had studied urban economics at the University of Michigan and city administration at the University of California, celebrated the rise of the city as China's best hope for the future. In what was very likely a conscious rebuttal of traditional Confucian and contemporary Chinese romantic views on the moral superiority of simple country living, Dong argued that city culture was a progressive culture of cooperation, which could reform the selfish and isolationist culture of China's rural areas. Proximity forced city dwellers to accommodate to one another, and successful city administration promoted human harmony. Humanity would be elevated by urbanization, if it could develop a proper understanding of city administration.[48]

Chengdu first learned of the Road-Building Association from Chen Weixin, a friend of Wu Shan, in the spring of 1924. Chen, a native of Chengdu, had been sent by the city's YMCA to receive training as a YMCA organizer in Shanghai. During World War I, he joined James Yen's YMCA mission among the Chinese laborers in France. After the war, back in Shanghai, he became involved in the Road-Building Association and helped set up branches in Henan and Wuchang. In 1923 he returned to Chengdu as the Commercial Press's agent in the city and as a missionary of urban reform. Because of his experience with the YMCA, however, his understanding of the proper goals of urban administrators differed somewhat from that of many of his colleagues in the Road-Building Association.[49]

In Chengdu, Chen Weixin threw himself into many projects. He organized a Chengdu branch of the Road-Building Association, which worked closely with Yang Sen. He was also on the board of directors of the Mass Education movement. In the spring of 1924,

Chen Weixin's name appeared in Chengdu newspapers more frequently than that of any other local personage except for Yang Sen and Wang Zuanxu, director of the city government office.

In April 1924 and then again in May, Chen Weixin published long articles setting out what he saw as the most urgent tasks facing Chengdu's administrators. In the first, he listed eight priorities:

1. Remove parts of shops and houses that encroach on the streets;
2. Fix the city's sewer system;
3. Construct new tree-lined streets, with benches along them;
4. Open new public toilets with attendants to collect fees and provide toilet paper (women's toilets were to be free, however, since only poor women would use them);
5. Establish official farmers' markets to get stalls out of intersections and raise revenues;
6. Turn temple grounds throughout the city into small public parks so children are not obliged to play in the streets;
7. Encourage public lectures so that the people will understand the intentions of the government; and
8. Set up a rickshaw company with 2,000 to 3,000 rickshaws.[50]

In this conception of the requirements of city administration, the influence of the Road-Building Association is quite apparent, although Chengdu residents who remembered the New Policies reforms would not have considered any of these proposals novel, with the exception of the shaded benches that were to line the streets. Over the next year and a half, Yang Sen and his administrators implemented all of them, to some extent.

Chen Weixin's next series of suggestions, published in May, shifted the emphasis from construction to other types of reform. It began with a call for wider participation in city affairs:

As to the nation, whose nation is it? Of course, it is the Chinese people's nation. What about city administration? It is the city administration of the residents of Chengdu. If we want to reform the country, it cannot be done by a small group of government officials. If city administration is bad and we want to renew it, how can two or three people in power achieve that?

Then Chen listed eight more tasks:

1. Regulate prostitution;
2. Regulate the poor people employed in funerals and other public events;
3. Reorganize and regulate the sedan chair business;
4. Institutionalize beggars;
5. Prohibit the impressment of laborers;
6. Prohibit opium dens;
7. Develop a "garden city"; and
8. Reopen the city gates (several had been closed in early 1924, due to nearby fighting).

If these eight issues were addressed, Chen argued, the people of Chengdu would be imbued with a new, energetic spirit, which would save them from the fate of such people as the Koreans, whose weakness led to their becoming subjects of a foreign power.[51]

In this new list it is still possible to see influences from the city administration movement—the call for the creation of a "garden city" and the concern for transportation and communication implied in the eighth point. The linking of urban reform, civic participation, and national strength also featured in the arguments of the Road-Building Association. But mixed with these is a concern for social conditions in the city, such as the prevalence of opium smoking and prostitution, which owes much more to Chen's YMCA background than to the city administration experts. Shirley Garrett's summary of the philosophy of the Chinese YMCA seems almost a restatement of Chen Weixin's ideas on urban priorities: "If large numbers of people could learn to read, if laborers would stop gambling and brush their teeth, if beggars could be trained to useful occupations, if people as a whole could hear lectures on the importance of health and good citizenship, China might yet pull itself up by its bootstraps."[52] It is important to note, however, that New Policies activists had also been concerned about opium consumption, regulation of prostitution, and institutionalization of beggars.

Like Fu Qiaocun, the author of the 1909 *Comprehensive Guide to Chengdu*, Yang Sen was also concerned with infusing Chengdu's citizens with a new, energetic spirit. One of the city's Muslim residents recalled that when Yang Sen, out of curiosity, visited a mosque during a prayer service, he was so impressed with the orderliness and gravity of the worshippers that he exclaimed, "A people like this could never be defeated!"[53] But, like Chiang Kai-shek with his New Life movement a decade later, Yang Sen believed that a new spirit of discipline and energy could be achieved in Chengdu entirely through personal physical cultivation and clean living on the part of the masses, who would be rigorously and severely guided in their efforts by dedicated political leaders such as himself.[54] He had little interest in religious, social, or economic issues. One missionary resident in Chengdu reported that Yang Sen's grasp of social conditions in the city seemed superficial: "Governor Yang was at our home one evening and I asked him if the government had any information or any department investigating industry from the human standpoint. He said there were fourteen factories in Chongqing employing in all several thousand women, but he knew nothing of Chengdu. He switched on to a short dissertation on wet nurses and their lucrative opportunities."[55] Yang Sen's justification of his road-building campaign did not even touch on economic development. His speech at the first meeting of the Chengdu branch of the Road-Building Association included this statement: "Warfare has been going on in Sichuan for many years, and the people have suffered much. It is all due to the poor state of our roads. If we can complete the roads quickly, then we can concentrate the armies and transport military supplies very conveniently. War won't continue long after that." After the roads are built, he concluded, rival general Liu Xiang and he would not fall into any more misunderstandings, which were entirely due to the difficulties of communicating with each other.[56]

Although Chen Weixin and the Road-Building Association had a great impact on Yang Sen, parts of his reform program are attributable to the predilections of his Luzhou advisers. Most important of these was Lu Zuofu, who attained fame later in his life as the founder of the Minsheng Shipping Company. Lu Zuofu was powerfully influenced by the events and ideas associated with the May Fourth movement. At the time of the May Fourth incident in 1919, he was an editor and reporter for an upstart newspaper in Chengdu that had been sympathetic to the nationalistic student protests. Its Beijing correspondent, Wang Guangqi, telegraphed reports on the Beijing demonstrations and helped found the Young China Study Society. Lu Zuofu and his newspaper colleagues, Sun Shaojing and Li Jieren, set up a Chengdu branch of the society. The Popular Education Institute he helped build in Chengdu reflects Lu Zuofu's commitment to the Young China Study Society's reform program, particularly the call for a more broadly based educational system.[57] Sun Shaojing, on the other hand, became one of the leaders of the Road-Building Association brand of city administration after he returned to Chengdu from study in Japan and Germany. He served as manager of Chengdu's city government office from 1924 until his assassination in 1927 and was instrumental in carrying forward Yang Sen's policies after the general's abrupt departure.

The most striking characteristic of Yang Sen's administration of Chengdu, his political style coupling a superficial populism with a harsh disciplinarianism, is a fit subject for psychoanalysis, were such a thing possible posthumously. Some of the elements of his background that may have fed into it include his early exposure to intensely emotional Gelaohui ritual,[58] with its emphasis on loyalty, righteousness, and the use of violence in the name of such principles; his military training, which he loved for its physical challenges; his rapid rise to prominence, caused by and cause for his extraordinary self-confidence; and the disorderly flood of revolutionary ideas entering Sichuan throughout the early Republican era.

Yang Sen in the Eyes of Chengdu Elites

As is clear by now, parts of Yang Sen's urban development and reform agenda had strong advocates in Chengdu before he arrived there. Despite the lackluster record of the city government office between 1921 and 1924, proposals for "city administration" initiatives appeared with some regularity in the local papers throughout those years. A few days after Yang Sen established himself in the city, six people placed an appeal in a local paper identifying "city administration" as the "foundation of civil government, which all countries with the rule of law try energetically to establish." They complimented Yang Sen on what he had accomplished in Luzhou and asked that he make it a top priority to investigate the budgets of previous Chengdu city administrators to discover how they had diverted funds from the city development lottery to military and other uses, and to prevent any such practices in the future.[59]

The courtship was a two-sided affair. Yang Sen's philosophy for managing young Sichuanese who had been educated abroad or in Beijing and Shanghai was to invite them to join his administration or often, if they were female, his household.[60] One of the very few hold-outs among this group of "new people" in Chengdu was the writer Li Jieren, who antagonized his fellow returned students by refusing to attend the banquets Yang Sen lavished on their group and by openly criticizing them as political opportunists (*zhengke*).[61]

Also absent from Yang Sen's banquet table, although not by their own choice, were Chengdu's more traditional elite. The most prominent of these, the Elders and Sages introduced in Chapter 6, had long considered themselves mediators between the people of the city and their various overlords. The Elders and Sages were by no means ideologically opposed to all of Yang Sen's urban reform agenda. Most of them had been quite supportive of Chengdu's New Policies reforms, which had also included public construction and emphasized the value of discipline and productivity. As the standard bearers for "Confucian values" in the city, they did not support Yang Sen's encouragement of co-education in the public schools. Rather than openly fight it, however, they chose to concentrate on running their own school, attached to the Dacheng Association.[62] Principal Xu Zixiu's response to the growing prestige and significance of the military, which began in earnest in Chengdu around the time Yang Sen arrived in the city for officer training in 1905, was to compile a collection of accounts of valorous and virtuous military heroes in Chinese history.[63] Whether or not Yang Sen read Xu Zixiu's book, he clearly did not model himself on

Confucian warriors of the past, however, and neither did he appeal explicitly to any Chinese tradition in his speeches to the residents of Chengdu. The YMCA leader Chen Weixin often cited the Chinese classics in his calls to action; nothing of the sort may be found in Yang Sen's speeches and writings.

Although Yang Sen's fascination with "newness" and lack of respect for the classical tradition may have rankled Xu Zixiu, who held up Yan Xishan as a model of the modern-day Confucian warrior-administrator, what infuriated the Elders and Sages most during Yang's administration was the disrespect with which he treated them. Their open confrontation with Yang Sen occurred after the road-widening plan had been issued and worried merchants along Great East Street calculated that many of them were likely to lose more than half the area of their shops to the new road and its sidewalks. The merchants petitioned to reduce the planned width of the road. When their appeals were ignored, they approached the Elders and Sages to present their case to Yang Sen. According to one of Yang Sen's military attachés, Yang Sen received them politely and, while pointing out to them the advantages of improved transportation and sanitation that the wider streets would bring, secretly instructed his aides to order soldiers to proceed at full speed with the destruction of property within the planned road bed. When the Elders and Sages left their meeting with Yang Sen, they discovered that what they had hoped to prevent had already largely occurred.[64] Shortly afterward, adding to the insult, Yang Sen is said to have issued a proclamation stating that any further objections to the road-building project would be considered obstructions to urban progress and would be dealt with severely.[65]

Once Yang Sen had humiliated Chengdu's most prestigious city fathers, the merchant community seems to have swallowed its losses quietly. Harry Franck, an American adventurer passing through the city, assessed its mood as one of deep outrage, although he observed that Yang Sen "showed no more outward sign of resentment at their dislike than the merchants and shopkeepers, sitting among the scanty remainders of their marts and homes, did of the dejection and anger underneath their placid pale-yellow faces, though every one knew they would 'get' the reforming governor at the first opportunity."[66] Chengdu's merchants had no powerful organization of their own to lead a challenge to the general. The Chamber of Commerce established during the New Policies era had lost its ability to influence provincial authorities. Sichuan's militarists, including Yang Sen, had sources of income outside Chengdu, which rendered them relatively independent of the city's merchants.[67] Instead, they tried to co-opt the more affluent merchants, some of whom were willing to abandon merchant solidarity in exchange for the opportunities that collaboration with militarists could bring.

Within Chengdu's merchant community, Yang Sen worked most closely with a transplant from Shanghai, Yu Fenggang, who had come to Chengdu in 1916 as accountant for the local branch of the Commercial Press. Yu used his financial talents for the benefit of a series of Chengdu militarists, building up, in the meantime, enough personal capital to allow him to leave the Commercial Press and open several jewelry stores in the center of town. One of these stores was close to the commercial arcade, next to a pharmacy owned by a translator employed in the French consulate-general. The plans for the construction of Chunxi Road called for the leveling of the pharmacy, which put Yang Sen in a diplomatic bind. Yu Fenggang earned his gratitude by offering the site of his jewelry store as an alternative route. In exchange, Yang Sen gave him the right to buy as much of the new streetfront property as he wanted. Yu Fenggang, who envisioned Chunxi Road as Chengdu's equivalent of Shanghai's Nanjing Road, bought most of it and, over the next ten years, earned a fortune as Chunxi Road did indeed become Chengdu's premier location for upscale consumer items and entertainment.[68]

Yu Fenggang became head of the Chamber of Commerce in 1925, and subsequent efforts to oust him from that position succeeded only in dividing merchants into warring factions.[69] A letter to the editor published in a local newspaper in 1927 recommended changing the structure of the chamber, arguing that, as things stood, it was so expensive to buy the votes required to become head of it that merchants who did so were practically forced to oppress their weaker colleagues and conspire with the militarists.[70]

Maintaining Public Order in the Face of
Unpopular Urban Reform

Beyond the elite level of the community, Yang Sen's programs could be quite disruptive and painful. Although the destruction of buildings for the widening of Great East Street and other existing commercial areas affected primarily the wealthier merchants, peddlers who worked the streets were forced to abandon their customary territory during and after construction. The Chunxi Road site had been occupied by several schools, a marketplace, and an unknown number of families who rented buildings from the city government office; all these were forced to move, apparently with no compensation.[71] But no public demonstrations seem to have followed the actions of Yang Sen and his demolition teams. By 1924, Chengdu's students and educators were fully capable of mounting mass demonstrations to protest cuts in educational funding or imperialistic pressure on China,[72] but organized public protests by neighborhood groups over municipal issues such as street widening or public services did not occur. This was due partly to the severity and violence of Yang Sen's rule and partly to the fact that Chengdu's neighborhoods were, themselves, quite orderly places.

The disturbed state of the countryside had helped push the population of Chengdu from some 350,000 in the late Qing to over 400,000 in 1924.[73] Unlike the huge population increase during the years of war with Japan after 1937, Chengdu's new residents in the 1920s do not seem to have substantially strained the cohesion of the city's neighborhoods. In 1926, Western missionaries in the city published a guide to polite conduct in Chengdu in which they advised that the proper response to "the calls of the inevitable small boy" in the street, when they were particularly offensive, was to send one's Chinese teacher to the neighborhood in question to see the "local elder": "He will see the street official, relate the circumstances, and ask to have the children in that neighborhood exhorted to behave themselves, which means that several families of parents will hear of the matter: and in all probability there will be no more rudeness on that street for a year or two."[74] The "street official" referred to here is probably the street headman.[75]

Chengdu's gowned brothers also occupied themselves with managing city conflicts, most likely in cooperation with the street headmen and militias. Yang Sen himself was quite familiar with the Gelaohui. As a very young boy, he had been awestruck at the sight of a Gelaohui ceremony his father had taken him to.[76] He was coy, however, about discussing his own participation in the network of gowned brothers. No doubt he knew very well who was influential among the Chengdu lodges and did what he could to co-opt them as he had the wealthy merchant Yu Fenggang. It is not surprising, in this light, that the two items on Chen Weixin's reformist agenda that Yang Sen ignored were prostitution and opium dens, two customary sources of income for lodge leaders.[77]

With street headmen and Gelaohui leaders effectively regulating public conduct, Yang Sen did not have to fear the development of spontaneous resistance to his plans within the city's neighborhoods. Even had it occurred, the strength of Yang Sen's commitment to his own vision of Chengdu's development, so great that he dared to humiliate the Elders and Sages publicly, would have made him unresponsive to the protests of the common people. According to a Western observer, Yang Sen's soldiers were among the least disciplined in the province.[78] Insecurity about the arbitrary actions of soldiers, coupled with the certainty of suppression of any act of protest, did not make for an environment that welcomed public acts of resistance.

Resistance via Ridicule: Liu Shiliang's "Reactionary" Wit

Despite the vigilance with which Yang Sen and his fellow militarists surveyed their territories for potential rebellion, in Chengdu Yang quickly became a target of widespread ridicule in the teahouses and bathhouses frequented by most men. Evidence for this comes first from Yang Sen's own speeches, in which he often remarked on the rumors flying around the city, as if he were proud of having befuddled and affronted the ignorant masses. In September 1924, he told the

Mass Education Association that their efforts were being hampered by rumors that the real reason for gathering together uneducated people was to make it easier for his military to conscript laborers, or collect exorbitant fees, or pick out the pretty women.[79] After calling for free and open criticism of his urban reform projects in a speech at the model public lecture hall, he went on to attack those who had circulated malicious stories about him: for example, that he could not bear to see long hair coiled on women's heads and therefore cut it off with scissors, or that he had seen some female students eating snacks at a peddler's stand during the flower festival and had called them over and smacked their faces.[80] Older residents of Chengdu interviewed in 1991 shared a number of unverifiable stories about Yang Sen's wild conduct in the city in 1924. In order to promote exercise among women, Yang Sen is said to have ordered one of his wives to swim in the river and thrown her in when she hesitated. It was also said that he had his soldiers beat to death a student from the higher normal school who had become involved romantically with a fellow student, another one of Yang Sen's wives, whom Yang Sen also killed. In a collection of essays commemorating her deceased father, Yang's daughter Wanyun bewailed the fact that throughout his life her father had been suspected by many of having more wives than he could count and being unable to recognize his own children.[81] Chengdu residents, forced to bear Yang Sen's heavy-handed ways and destructive public works projects, got back at him by making fun of him.

Of all Yang Sen's critics, the most witty and audacious was Liu Shiliang, who grew up in Sichuan's salt-well district and came to Chengdu shortly after 1911 as a representative of salt merchants. He quickly became good friends with Fan Kongzhou, the publisher and head of the city's Chamber of Commerce, and set up his own business, a bathhouse, in the center of town. He was fond of satirical verses and composed a couplet every year on the anniversary of the founding of the Republic, pointing out by means of puns and other devices the huge gap between Republican ideals and militarist reality. He displayed these on the pillars of a prominent office building in the neighborhood of his bathhouse.[82] He wrote a particularly bitter couplet on the occasion of the assassination of Fan Kongzhou in 1917.[83]

In 1924, new sanitary regulations promulgated by Wang Zuanxu's city government office required Chengdu's bathhouses to substitute porcelain tubs for wooden ones. Liu, who could not afford to upgrade his equipment, closed his bathhouse and opened a teahouse. At the same time, many of his merchant friends lost their shops to the Chunxi Road construction. The upheaval prompted Liu to write a couplet that became the epitaph of Yang Sen's career in Chengdu:

> The road has already been leveled, when will the Duli [Yang
> Sen's title] roll?
> The people's homes have been torn down, we hope the General
> will drive soon.

The verse's superficially congratulatory message was a thin cover for the underlying hostility and scorn. The cleverness of the couplet lies in its pun on the character for "roll" (*gun*), which could refer either to the technical process of compressing a road surface with a stone or to the colloquial expression *gundan*—roll away like an egg or, in other words, get the hell out of here.[84] Liu's couplet was immediately popular in Chengdu and attached itself so tenaciously to Yang Sen that the director of his memorial ceremony in 1977 chose it as the title of his eulogy, regarding it as a fitting tribute to Yang Sen's steadfastness against those who would stand in the way of progress and development.[85] During the rest of Yang Sen's stay in Chengdu, Liu Shiliang lay low, protected, according to his biographer, by some of the Five Elders and Seven Sages, who found in his somewhat coarse wit a useful tool in their feud with the general.

Many of the rumors that surrounded Yang Sen concerned issues of proper conduct between men and women and acceptable behavior and dress, especially for women. Given the nature of Yang Sen's own household, this is not surprising. Yang Sen's family would have been an oddity in any city in China, at any period of its history. His collection of well-educated, short-haired, fashionably dressed wives appeared frequently in public, sometimes on bicycles.[86] A sarcastic observer quoted them as greeting the participants in a convention of Christian missionaries in the city in January 1925 with hearty cries of "Ham is really greasy!" (*huo tui you duo*, or "How do you do"). It was widely believed that the provincial higher normal school had only agreed in the fall of 1924 to admit female students because one of Yang Sen's wives wanted to attend.[87]

It is difficult to assess the extent to which the ridicule heaped on Yang Sen's unusual family hampered his efforts to reform what he considered Chengdu's indolent and frivolous culture and backward cityscape. His military defeat in the summer of 1925 ended his Chengdu experiment too soon to judge whether he could eventually have won over the populace to his program of construction and cultural change. In his sixteen months in Chengdu, Yang Sen did not achieve his aim of building an urban monument to his vision of a "new Sichuan." Even at the height of his efforts in 1925, a member of the Chengdu elite wrote a letter to a friend in Beijing that declared the "eight beautiful sights" of the city—"visible everywhere in the streets"—to be *qiuba* (slang for soldiers), thieves, opium, food and drink peddlers, toilets, vagrants, bound feet, and coffin shops.[88]

Yang Sen's authoritarian reformist style helped foster a cynical view of city administration and planning among a large sector of Chengdu society. By trying to force his ideas down the throats of the people of Chengdu, Yang stirred up tremendous resentment. Unable to protest in any other way, Chengdu's people responded with scorn and laughter, interpreted by Yang Sen and his supporters as a stubborn rejection of modern ways. Yang Sen's rule over Chengdu turned Liu Shiliang into a popular hero, enabling him to enjoy a successful career as a satirical poet and magazine publisher. By the time Chiang Kai-shek introduced the New Life movement to Chengdu in the mid-1930s, Liu Shiliang had had a decade of practice poking fun at such attempts at "cultural renewal," and he did not hesitate once more to display his skills.[89]

But, at the same time, Yang Sen did encourage those in the city who wanted to introduce some of the new ideas concerning urban administration then becoming popular along the coast. Many of his initiatives were continued by his successors, less flamboyantly but more successfully. In 1928 the city government noted with pride that the shopkeepers along one street in the city had requested that their street be widened before it was scheduled to be.[90]

The Urban Administration Consensus
in the Nationalist Era

The municipal government yearbook in which officials celebrated the enthusiasm of Chengdu merchants for continued road-building efforts makes it clear that the post–Yang Sen city administration had done what it could to involve the more conservative city elites in its work. A preface by Deng Xihou, one of the militarists who helped defeat Yang Sen, cites precedents for city government in the Chinese classics and ends with the statement, "We do not look to the aliens of the four directions for our models; our Chengdu long ago had a city head, and we are reviving this abandoned administrative position" (*xue buzai siyi; wu Chengdu jiu you shizhang, wu xiu feiguan yi*).[91] Each of the subsequent sections of the book begins with a title page inscribed by one of the Five Elders and Seven Sages.

In addition to placating the Elders and Sages, city officials in Chengdu took steps to give the institutions of the city government more visibility and prestige than they had enjoyed in Yang Sen's time, when the general had taken such a prominent personal role in city affairs. Much as Zhou Shanpei had done with his speeches at police stations, the city government publicized its goals and explained how it intended to achieve them. A weekly city government gazette was launched in July 1927. It reported on the regular meetings of city officials, with detailed accounts of deliberations over such issues as regulating public toilets and rickshaws and increasing popular awareness of the work of city administration. One suggestion adopted was to have city workers engaged in street repair wear uniforms identifying them as city workers, as was done in Shanghai.[92] The weekly also published letters from citizens with recommendations for civic improvement, including advice on such matters as keeping the trees that had recently been planted along the roadsides alive.[93] The grander schemes of the city government of the late 1920s, including a plan to build a comprehensive water system for the city, had to be shelved for lack of funds.[94] In the late 1920s and early 1930s, however, the city administration movement in Chengdu led to the revival of many of the administrative institutions and techniques established by Zhou Shanpei during the New Policies era.

This revival of the spirit of the New Policies reached its peak in 1934. The year before, General Liu Xiang had captured Chengdu and begun to accomplish what had long been the great ambition of all of Sichuan's militarists—the military unification of most of the province.[95] Once in command of Chengdu, he immediately gave one of his most experienced officers a substantial budget to reorganize Chengdu's police.[96] The officer, Yu Yuan, was a native of Shehong county south of Chengdu. He had become a soldier as a young man in 1914 and worked his way up through the ranks, for the most part in Yang Sen's army. A few years after Yang Sen's decisive defeat at the hands of Liu Wenhui and his allies in 1925, Yang and Yu parted ways, and Yu eventually joined forces with Liu Wenhui's nephew— and military rival—Liu Xiang. As Liu Xiang's subordinate, Yu was appointed head of the Chengdu police early in 1934.[97] Within a year, Yu Yuan had presided over the most comprehensive overhaul of Chengdu policing since 1907. He re-established police training schools, ordered the newly trained and outfitted constables to conduct a thorough census, and published a detailed report on the work of the revivified Police Bureau, renamed the Public Security Bureau (Gonganju), in line with Nationalist government regulations.[98]

The apparent ease with which Yu Yuan rebuilt the dilapidated Chengdu force lends support to the argument that the New Policies police reform is one of the most significant political events in twentieth-century Chinese history.[99] Without the firm institutional foundation laid by Zhou Shanpei between 1903 and 1907, it is doubtful that Chengdu would have proven so receptive to Yu Yuan's efforts. As it was, the city's Elders and Sages supported Yu Yuan, contributing graceful and enthusiastic endorsements to the 1934 report on the work of the Public Security Bureau.[100] Among Yu's administrative staff there must have been some old-timers who remembered Zhou Shanpei's reforms of thirty years before. A fairly comprehensive history of the New Policies police program found its way into the 1934 report, as well as into a textbook on Chengdu geography and society written in 1936 especially for the revived constable training institute.

Many of the policing techniques described in the 1934 report resemble those that Zhou Shanpei first introduced to Chengdu, including training chants much like those used at the school for constables set up by Zhou in 1906.[101] Yu Yuan himself was probably not acquainted with Zhou Shanpei, but many of his colleagues in Liu Xiang's service had met Zhou during sojourns in eastern China. In the years between 1912 and 1937, Zhou lived in Tianjin and Shanghai and encouraged young Sichuan natives to visit him. Through them, he kept his hand in Sichuan politics until his death in 1958.[102]

Zhou Shanpei and Yang Sen implemented urban reform with very different motives and with very different approaches. Each of the waves of reform in which these two men played central roles was brought to an end by political shifts that were essentially external to the city-level reforms: Zhou was driven from Chengdu by the national constitutional crisis, and Yang was forced out by his defeat in the fight to control the province. But the legacies of their divergent styles and goals shaped the context of reform in the 1930s. Zhou saw urban administration as a new arena in which to practice the arts of traditional statecraft, and he gained the support of community elites for new institutions and even for new ideals as he established a role for city administration in Chengdu within the existing sociopolitical system. The New Policies reforms began as an attempt to reconstruct the provincial capital as a prototype of a new model of Chinese administration and society and had the unintended result that the city itself became an important geopolitical entity apart from its hinterlands for the first time. Zhou's work and network laid a lasting foundation for the shape of this new entity, and the palpable improvements brought about by reforms in this era created the possibility for further reform by winning acceptance for change in an essentially conservative urban society. Although his reforms shook up the city and sometimes provoked opposition, he won support for both reform and city administration by appealing to the traditions of Chinese statecraft in the execution of his new projects.

In contrast, Yang Sen simply wanted to make visible and dramatic changes to the city that would create an image of himself as a modern man of action and power, and he embraced the city administration movement as the means to this end. By 1924, advocates of city planning and development in eastern China had articulated an alluring vision that made well-regulated cities the key to a powerful Chinese nation. Their city boosterism, with its emphasis on public construction, could easily be extended to cities in which industrial development had not yet occurred. Far beyond the city experts' own bases in Shanghai and other coastal cities, their enthusiasm for paved streets and parks and planned development in general caught the imagination of people, like Yang Sen and his young colleagues, who wanted to be doing great things. The city had by then become emblematic of national strength as well as a stage for pretenders to provincial power. In pursuit of these prizes, Yang Sen alienated the community with his relentless and impolitic push for rapid modernization. He flouted local political traditions and the political process, the elites hated his style, and the trauma and resentment engendered by some of his projects undermined support for the very idea of reform.

The combined legacy of Zhou and Yang created a curious situation after both waves of rapid reform had subsided. The glitter of reform had been seriously tarnished by Yang's approach to urban change, but the challenges of maintaining order in the city remained. For older residents of Chengdu, elements of the city administration movement recalled the New Policies reform programs of their youth, and people began to recall the first reform era as a sort of golden age. Once the impetuous and authoritarian Yang Sen was out of the way, Chengdu's more traditional elites joined hands with the city experts Yang had hired. They forged a new urban administration consensus that looked to the New Policies for inspiration and gradually incorporated later innovations that did not pose radical threats to the social order. Together, they ensured that new concepts of proper city planning and administration continued to have an important place in the local political discourse, long after the most ardent early supporter of "city administration" in Chengdu had fled the city.

8 LEGACY OF THE NEW POLICIES: CONTINUITY AND CHANGE IN CHENGDU IN COMPARATIVE PERSPECTIVE

Beginning in 1937, the work of Chengdu's administrators was exposed to the critical gaze of a multitude of outsiders as thousands of refugees fleeing the Japanese occupation of eastern China arrived in Chengdu and other southwestern cities. In 1938, the Nationalist government itself moved to Chongqing, Sichuan, and several prominent universities from eastern China established temporary campuses in Chengdu. To people who had known life in Shanghai, Chengdu seemed backward. By 1937, many eastern cities had built streetcar and sewer systems and were experimenting with new styles of housing, including large apartment blocks.[1] The two-story shops along Shanghai's Nanjing Road, the inspiration for Chengdu's Chunxi Road, had been replaced with large, brilliantly lit department stores. Railroad lines connected all the major eastern cities in a new urban network.[2] Isolated Chengdu, still hundreds of miles from the nearest railroad track, appeared at a superficial level to be a nineteenth- rather than a twentieth-century Chinese city. But in fact, much had changed in Chengdu over four decades.

The Dynamics of Change

The two waves of urban-centered reform that swept through Chengdu between 1895 and 1937 changed Chengdu in significant ways, although urban reform did not at all proceed in a linear progression in these decades of revolution and civil war. Change was driven by the ebb and flow of both external political developments and internal reform movements. The accomplishment of each administration's reform goals was often blunted by abrupt transitions of power, policy, and personnel. The periodically redirected efforts to reshape the city and its functions turned their force upon the inertia of established patterns in the daily life of the populace with varied results.

The motivations and models for remaking the city underwent a series of transformations as the city's relationship to the central power and the interests of successive urban authorities changed. From a Qing government interested primarily in the maintenance of order within the city arose a movement that embraced institutional and cultural change as a means to national strength, directed by officials who saw the techniques of city management as useful tools through which to demonstrate their statecraft skills. In the absence of an effective central government after the 1911 Revolution, local rulers once more became concerned primarily with maintaining control over the city. They encouraged the growth of Gelaohui influence and sought public legitimacy from their ties to local notables such as the Elders and Sages. In the 1920s, city administration became a recognized professional specialty, and militarists such as Yang Sen found it an attractive way to promote their own claims as revolutionary leaders.

The transformation of Chengdu was accomplished both by and despite the warlords, technocrats, and practitioners of statecraft, who led reforms by variously intimidating or negotiating with the elites, commercial interests, and new and old organizations with sufficient influence to be taken into account. The complex dynamic that played itself out during these tumultuous times cannot easily be summarized or labeled. Autocracy and democratic innovations contended throughout the period: each sometimes deployed for and sometimes against social and institutional change. The street headmen recruited by Zhou Shanpei, for example, helped mediate between the interests of Chengdu neighborhoods and those of police authorities in the late Qing and, particularly during the strike of 1911, protected the community from what might have been a harsh intervention at the hands of the state. In the militarized 1920s, however, street headmen dared not openly resist Yang Sen's army as it imposed a new pattern on Chengdu's streets. Instead, many involved themselves with the underground Gelaohui groups that regulated economic and social life in the fragmented city. Rather than bridging the gap between neighborhoods and the formal government in the Republican era, street headmen became part of the shadow administration of the Gelaohui, which operated quite independently of the formal government appointed by the militarists and with a different agenda.

The reaction of the residents to the initiatives of city administrators depended on the way they were implemented: style as well as substance affected the popular view of reform. Despite resistance to particular policies of Zhou Shanpei, his early reforms created a readiness to accept reform in general and forged new models for institutions and new expectations for urban administration. The backlash against the chaos of revolutionary Chengdu that began as early as 1912 and continued into the 1920s extinguished much of the ardor for reform that had been kindled by the successes of the New Policies. The people of Chengdu became conservative, and many of the more reform-minded leaders were driven out of the city during this period. Yang Sen's highhanded actions in 1924 and 1925 created resentment and stiffened distrust of reform.

Although Chengdu's citizens did not meekly accept every new dictum from the city authorities, there is only limited evidence of the development of what has come to be called a civil society.[3] Public involvement in community affairs was not institutionalized, but new avenues for political influence developed during each of the reform movements. Political pressure was often brought to bear by interested groups against new policies, sometimes successfully and sometimes not. There were occasional small-scale gestures of protest or resistance, frustrations were vented through satire, and public feeling now and again poured out in large demonstrations. Still, an authoritarian element remained strong in the imposition of social change from above. Both Qing and Republican administrators recruited small groups of local elites to finance and carry out their projects. Elected bodies, particularly the city councils, and executive officers tended to maintain separate spheres of policy interest, thus avoiding conflict with each other and leading to continuance of an essentially top-down mode of city administration.

The Extent of Change

By 1937, the nature of city administration, the scope of state authority, and the physical infrastructure in Chengdu had been significantly altered. All these changes reflected, to varying degrees, the lasting legacy of the Qing New Policies reforms.

City administration underwent a number of transformations through the decades, but remained essentially a top-down process, with variations in the constitution of the groups at the top. Initially undertaken as a branch of the bureaucracy very much in the mold of conventional imperial administration, city administration soon came to involve a somewhat broader community leadership as bureaucrats crafted compromises between the newly developed reform community and the more conservative existing elites. Further broadening of the city leadership through the introduction of proto-democratic institutions such as the city assembly proved ephemeral. Instead, the 1920s saw a swing back toward autocracy, and city administration was executed by outside experts imposed on the community by the militarists in control of the city. During this period, the de facto devolution of authority over social systems and public order at the street level to the Gelaohui divorced the city administration from neighborhood dynamics. The city government restricted itself to showy projects such as remaking the city streets. However, by the 1930s city administration was again carried out via a sort of condominium of elites, similar to the late Qing pattern of cooperation in which the formal administrators consulted with local elites to implement changes at a gradual pace and minimize disruption. The critical contribution of the New Policies was the establishment of a new concept of city administration. This part of the New Policies legacy was an unintended outgrowth of the programs in Chengdu, rather than a goal of their enactors or implementers. Although trampled underfoot by the Revolution and ensuing disorder, the idea was strong enough to be resurrected despite the strife surrounding its return to Chengdu under Yang Sen.

Zhou Shanpei and his colleagues energetically expanded the scope of the state's authority during the New Policies period. Some of the areas of city life that Zhou brought under the purview of government did not remain there, but most of the institutions set up during this time survived the fall of the Qing, and the role of government was indelibly altered. The late Qing police administration launched programs to manage many urban problems that had formerly been left to charitable societies (such as burying unclaimed bodies) or handled informally (such as street disputes). It also became active in a new effort to regulate activities that were suspect in the popular morality (prostitution, pawnshops, and gambling) or promoted the newer ideals of an orderly city (public health administration and police patrols). Other undertakings launched during this period were the new police force, street cleaning, street lights, fire control, and flood relief. The government directly took on the mission of creating and maintaining a safe and regulated public space.

Another groundbreaking innovation was state involvement in social improvements such as sheltering and retraining the most unfortunate residents: beggars, prostitutes, orphans, and the elderly destitute. The workhouses, reformatories, orphanages, and sanitariums established under this initiative made a visible difference in city life. However, efforts in support of other social changes, such as opera reform and modest changes in the place of women in public society, development of civic culture, and regulation of dress and behavior were far less successful. Zhou Shanpei made a concerted effort to make opera more respectable and open it to women spectators, but could not sustain this effort in the face of strong local opposition.

Most of the attempts to alter the public behavior and habits of the city residents amounted to little more than public relations campaigns, and even Yang Sen's idiosyncratic attempts to enforce dress codes on the street had limited impact. Modifying public attitudes was far more difficult for the reformers than remaking public spaces, but in transforming the city streets they did define a new role for government that gave substance to the developing idea of city administration.

Economic development was a major aim of the New Policies, but despite the innovations and, especially later, the drastic changes in the city infrastructure that were advanced with this goal in mind, the economy was not as much affected by the reforms as was the concept and scope of city government. The New Policies emphasized institutional change, and physical alteration of the city space, such as the street lamps and clean open streets, was mostly secondary to the creation of new and important institutions such as the police force and the numerous schools established to train people for new roles in the new order. During the second wave of reform in the 1920s, infrastructural development became the primary focus of government activity, and the city was altered dramatically by the building and widening of roads and the creation of new civic spaces such as parks. During the New Policies era, Chengdu's economy was reshaped somewhat by the new trade organizations and large-scale educational reorganization. During the 1920s, the cityscape was significantly changed by the road projects, the establishment of the parks and commercial arcade, and the erection of electrical and telephone networks. Still, in both periods, the response of the economy fell far short of the late Qing aspirations to a vibrant and powerful economic revitalization such as had been achieved in Japan. It is difficult to cast this as a policy failure given the tremendous upheaval during the years following implementation. The fact remains that the New Policies legacy took the form of reorganized city spaces, refocused city government, and renewed city administration ideals, and not of substantial changes in the economic and social order of the city.

Just as important, although this new model of urban government was accepted by the citizens of Chengdu, representative government never took hold. Rejecting revolutionary upheaval, the citizenry preferred that administrators maintain order and leave them otherwise alone. City government found a more prominent role in city life and carved out areas of responsibility in regulating sanitation, providing police and fire services, promoting commercial growth, and pioneering social change. Although the emphases of the programs directed by the city government in these areas changed and although the notion of a city government itself took firm root, residents' attitudes toward government did not change nearly as much. Yet despite the conservatism that the warlord period inculcated in residents of Chengdu, the development of a distinctive urban entity as a community and administrative unit is a lasting legacy of these decades.

Chengdu in Comparative Perspective

All major Chinese cities experienced the waves of reform produced first by the New Policies of the 1900s and then by the city administration movement of the early Republic. The nature and relative strength of the two waves varied significantly, however, in cities across China. The contrasts are clear when an interior city such as Chengdu is compared to the national capital, Beijing, and coastal cities such as Shanghai and Guangzhou. Three sets of phenomena that had little or no influence in Chengdu operated with much greater effect in these cities: the presence of foreign-administered districts, industrialization and related population growth, and the rise of the Nationalist party. As a result, urban development and administration had come to mean something quite different in eastern Chinese cities by the mid-1930s than it meant in Chengdu.

In Beijing, there was much more continuity between the New Policies era and the early Republic. Yuan Shikai, one of the most successful of the New Policies governors, assumed the office of president of the Republic and established his capital in Beijing. In 1914 he authorized the establishment of a municipal council, which took over many of the functions of the late Qing police bureau. Inspired by new urban technologies being introduced in the foreign diplomatic

quarters in the city, the Beijing municipal council threw itself energetically into the task of building up public amenities such as asphalt
roads, electricity, sewer and water systems, and streetcars, as historian
Mingzheng Shi has shown.[4] Periodic military unrest and low levels of
funding hampered the expansion of city services, but, compared with
Chengdu, Beijing welcomed technological change. At the same time,
Republican era Beijing witnessed the development of a modern "mass
politics," through which city groups tried to publicize and promote
their causes, a phenomenon analyzed by David Strand.[5] As Strand's
account of Beijing rickshaw pullers' attacks on streetcars suggests, the
relative success of the Beijing modernizers produced a stronger reaction to urban initiatives among groups in Beijing than existed in Republican Chengdu. Beijing's residents, like their Chengdu counterparts, still had little direct influence on city planners and the formal
government, but they did assert themselves in civic affairs to a much
greater extent. In the very contentiousness of Beijing politics of the
1920s, we can see a city much more actively engaged in weighing the
value of urban innovation.

In many coastal cities of wealthy eastern China, less dominated by
officialdom than Chengdu and Beijing, the administrative reforms of
the New Policies had less effect on social life than did other changes
that were occurring simultaneously: industrialization, rapid population growth, technological change, the rise in the influence of busi-
nessmen and financiers, the birth of a middle class of "petty urbanites," and the development of a sophisticated, urban, consumer
culture associated with the new middle class.[6] These socioeconomic
trends did not end abruptly with the fall of the Qing dynasty. Economic development continued at a steady, and even faster, pace in
the years after 1911.

In the modernizing cities of eastern China, the 1920s city administration movement was closely associated with the Nationalist party.
Guangzhou, the early Nationalist base, was the seedbed of the
movement in the early 1920s, thanks to the support of Sun Fo, Sun
Yat-sen's son. Under Mayor Sun Fo, the Nationalist administration
of Guangzhou introduced elements of "scientific" planning, including

the collection of a wide range of data about social conditions, in order to regulate urban life more thoroughly. Ultimately, Nationalist administrators aimed, in the words of Michael Tsin, to produce "disciplined members for the body politic."[7] Thus, unlike the situation in Chengdu and Beijing, reform in Guangzhou was an integral part of a highly organized and ambitious political movement. Social and cultural change was emphasized as much as technological change in the early Nationalist vision of city administration.

After the Nationalist government was established in Nanjing in 1927, it issued a comprehensive series of laws on the organization of cities, designed to centralize control over urban resources as much as to promote social change. Most of these laws were never implemented effectively in the new national capital, however, because, as in Chengdu in the mid-1920s, the city administration did not reach into the urban neighborhoods of Nanjing.[8] Shanghai, however, provided more fertile ground for urban planners. As Bryna Goodman has shown, the problems associated with governing late Qing Shanghai's rapidly growing and diverse population proved too complex for Qing officials to handle by themselves. Thus, they turned many matters of urban administration over to civic groups such as the native-place associations formed by immigrants from different parts of China.[9] Strongly influenced by the urban institutions set up in the city's foreign-run areas, Shanghai's merchant community took the lead in organizing city services and building roads in the Chinese sectors of the city. In 1905, a municipal council was formally appointed to govern the Chinese city. Many of its members had long been active in urban affairs. The council's duties included supervision of the police and merchant militia, management of public schools for children and adults, and improvement of the city's infrastructure.[10] In Shanghai, the New Policies institutions thus grew out of nineteenth-century innovations. The new institutions of Shanghai were neither as dominated by officialdom nor as strikingly new to the local people as were Zhou Shanpei's New Policies initiatives in Chengdu.

Shanghai's urban institutions suffered from the political chaos surrounding the 1911 Revolution, as did those of Chengdu. The city of Shanghai itself continued to grow rapidly, however, attracting substantial foreign and domestic investment in modern industries. The demand for labor pushed total population in all zones of the city up from around one million in 1910 to almost three million in 1930.[11] Given the rapid influx of strangers and the radical transformation of social life during the early Republic, the New Policies era did not stand out as particularly formative in the history of Shanghai, as it did in Chengdu. Among local elites, the New Policies experiments in local self-government, brought to an end by Yuan Shikai in 1914, were the era's most notable feature.[12]

In the foreign concessions, urban construction continued unabated during the early Republic. When Shanghai's universities began offering courses on urban administration in the 1920s, students could see the planning concepts outlined in their textbooks being implemented in the foreign zones of their city. After the Nationalist government gained control in 1927, the city's economy supported a large municipal administration. Because they wanted to prove themselves capable of taking over the foreign settlements, Shanghai's Chinese administrators cared much more about matching the urban developments there than they did about reviving the late Qing urban legacy. Christian Henriot has shown that they were surprisingly successful in their efforts to improve Shanghai's sanitation and public welfare.[13]

In contrast to the relatively steady development of Shanghai, the first twenty years of the Republic were wrenching for the people of Chengdu. The incessant and costly warfare, the loss of prominence in the national and provincial political order, the rise of the Gelaohui— all these helped produce a certain nostalgia for the glory days of the New Policies era in Chengdu. The disorder of civil war that convulsed the city for so long created a divide between Chengdu and the coastal cities that was as significant to attitudes about urban governance as the geographical distance that separated them. Chengdu emerged from the long years of military conflict with a conception of city government that emphasized maintaining an orderly society far more than fostering commercial growth or promoting cultural change. Before 1911, Chengdu had been considered progressive in its implementation of urban reforms; by the late 1920s it had turned back to the progressive ideals of that previous generation for the security that had been so scarce in the intervening years.

Thus, after Yang Sen's regime resurrected the idea that city administration was important, Chengdu's Elders and Sages stepped forward to remind the city what it had been like in the last few years of the Qing era. To many, the New Policies urban vision developed by Zhou Shanpei and the late Qing reformers represented an attractive alternative to what they saw with their own eyes in the late 1920s and early 1930s. The community had been sobered by twenty years of strife, however, and few dared hope, as Zhou Shanpei had, to be able to "civilize" the city. Nevertheless, Zhou's conception of *wenming*—social harmony, productivity, and respect for the cultural tradition within a clean, orderly, and technologically advanced urban environment regulated by elite consensus—survived into the 1930s as a guide for city leaders in Chengdu. In the post-Mao era, as China again enters a period of rapid urban-centered change, Zhou Shanpei's New Policies achievements are once more celebrated in local histories, and the refurbished commercial arcade proudly stands in the heart of the city at the head of a revitalized Chunxi Road.

REFERENCE MATTER

NOTES

For complete author names, titles, and publication data for works cited here in short form, see the Works Cited list, pp. 305–26.

Chapter 1

1. The Shu kingdom, which surrendered the area to the Qin in 316 B.C.E., had probably built a city on the site of Chengdu before the Qin did in 310, but little is known about the area in this early period. On the history of construction in and around what is now Chengdu, see Sichuansheng wenshiguan 1987.

2. On Sichuan's population in the Qing, see Skinner 1987. For a survey of Sichuan's social history during the Qing, see Wang Di 1993.

3. A foreign resident of the city stated that a well-executed survey conducted in 1903 showed 350,000 people living inside the walls and another 100,000 in the suburbs (Legendre 1906, 483). Another, who had lived in the city longer and could read Chinese, reported the total figure from the same survey as 306,000, although in 1907 he himself reckoned the city's population at 350,000 (Vale 1904, 85; Vale 1907, pt. 1, 8).

4. I have borrowed this delightful phrase from Sennett 1994.

5. Much has been written on the morphology, architecture, institutions, and social organization of premodern Chinese cities. In English, Skinner 1977 and Rowe 1984 and 1989 provide excellent introductions to scholarly work on the subject.

6. A. F. Wright 1977, 46–50.

7. Hubbard 1923, 120.

8. The provincial government was forced to repair a stretch of wall extending over 1,000 feet that collapsed in the 1880s (Zhou Xun 1986, 263).

9. Mote 1977, 102–4.

10. Legendre 1906, 155; Kemp 1909, 171.

11. Legendre 1906, chap. 17, provides by far the most detailed description of Chengdu's layout and architecture during the late Qing among those known to me. Hubbard 1923 describes many of the same phenomena twenty years later. Ba Jin's (Pa Chin's) *Family* describes life in a *gongguan* in Chengdu's wealthy northeastern corner in the decade after the 1911 Revolution.

12. Zhou Xun 1987, 7.

13. Sichuansheng wenshiguan 1987, 457; Fu Chongju 1987, 1: 275–76.

14. Legendre (1906, 171) describes the barriers and watchmen in some detail but says nothing about the income of the watchmen. Perhaps, as a foreigner and a medical doctor, he was exempt from fees.

15. Many of these are described in Sichuansheng wenshiguan 1987. See also Fu Chongju 1987 and Zhou Xun 1987. Shanxi banks were institutions run by firms from that province that served merchants primarily by transferring funds.

16. Fu Chongju 1987, 1: 34.

17. Sichuansheng wenshiguan 1987, 379–82. Actually, this book notes, Xue Tao's well was on the other side of town, but its symbolic site was shifted east during the Song dynasty.

18. The grandfather of Communist general Chen Yi bought and sold slave girls for a living in late Qing Chengdu (Benton 1992, 36).

19. Fu Chongju 1987, 1: 74.

20. "Blocks" here is a translation of the Chinese term *jie*, usually translated "street." In Chengdu, no *jie* extended a greater distance than the typical city block in the United States, with the single exception of Dong Da Jie (Great East Street).

21. Many of these associations were called *qingjiaohui* (Zhou Xun 1987, 63). This sort of organization, as it existed in cities in Taiwan during the Qing era, is analyzed in Feuchtwang 1977, 596–600. Adam Grainger (1918, 5), who represented the China Inland Mission in Chengdu and elsewhere in western Sichuan for thirty years beginning in 1889, states that the associations had several different names, including *tudihui*, or "Society of the God of the Precinct" as he renders it.

22. Vale 1904, 58–59. The English frankpledge system is discussed in Bayley 1985, chap. 2.

23. The terms used for various levels of the *baojia* system varied from place to place and at different times. The Chengdu county gazetteer of 1873 indicates that the county was divided into six large *jia* and thirty-four smaller units called either *bao* or *tuan* (*Chongxiu Chengduxian zhi* 1971, 166). On the system in general, see Wen Juntian 1935 and Hsiao Kung-chuan 1960.

24. An excellent example of official thinking in regard to *baojia* is Huang Liu-hung's *A Complete Book Concerning Happiness and Benevolence*, written in the late seventeenth century and reprinted for the guidance of local officials throughout the Qing period. For a recent English translation, see Huang Liu-hung 1984.

25. Legendre 1906, 409–16.

26. Hosie 1897, 84–85.

27. Vale 1907, pt. 1, 9–11.

28. Goodman 1995 presents a detailed study of such associations as they existed in Shanghai between 1853 and 1937. Chengdu's native-place associations are described in Zhou Xun 1987, 15–16, and Fu Chongju 1987, 1: 43–44.

29. Zhou Xun 1987, 47–48.

30. Fu Chongju 1987, 1: 74.

31. Guo Moruo 1929, 48.

32. On Chinese cities that were strongly influenced by their locations at the borders of Han influence, see Gaubatz 1996.

33. Hutson 1915, 22. The Dujiangyan system and irrigation on the Chengdu plain has been described recently in Van Slyke 1988.

34. "Granary of heaven" is George Hartwell's (1939) apt translation for Sichuan's poetic nickname *tianfu zhi guo*. Sichuan's and Chengdu's geography and natural history are discussed in Wang Di 1993, chap. 1, and in Hubbard 1923.

35. See Wang Di 1993, 21–35, for data on the frequency of flooding and drought in Sichuan during the Qing period.

36. Legendre 1906, 484.

37. Sichuansheng wenshiguan 1987, 72; Fu Chongju 1987, 1: 16.

38. Sichuansheng wenshiguan 1987, 88–91.

39. Wang Di 1993, 68.

40. Fu Chongju 1987, 1: 564. Zhou Xun 1986, 213–14. See Chapter 7 in this book for more on this stela.

41. Entenmann 1982; Wang Di 1993, chap. 2.

42. Fu Chongju 1987, 1: 16.

43. Hosie 1922; Wang Di 1993, chap. 4.

44. Hutson 1915, 10.

45. Fu Chongju 1987, 1: 109–10.

46. Treudley 1971 describes a village near Chengdu that in the 1940s still consisted entirely of the families of the male descendants of early eighteenth-century immigrants to Sichuan. Han Suyin (1965, 28–33) states that in the case of her own family, Hakka immigrants from Guangdong who arrived in Sichuan in the 1690s, visits back to the ancestral village were made regularly until the middle of the nineteenth century, when the connection was broken due to warfare and social upheaval.

47. Fu Chongju 1987, 1: 34.

48. *Xuantong yuannian Shengcheng jingqu diyici diaocha hukou yilanbiao* (1909).

49. Geil 1911, 305.

50. The history and organization of Chengdu's Banner garrison is described in Liu Xianzhi 1983 and Zhou Xun 1986, 50–51. On this Qing institution in general, see Crossley 1990.

51. Hosie 1897, 86–87.

52. Legendre 1906, 163.

53. Liu Xianzhi 1984. Liu also notes that a contingent of Chengdu Bannermen traveled to Xi'an in 1900 to rally around the imperial court, driven from Beijing by the foreign invasion in the wake of the Boxer uprising.

54. Liu Xianzhi 1984.

55. Chengdu's array of official yamen is described in Sichuansheng wenshiguan 1987.

56. The Manchu general was ordered to share equally with the governor-general in the task of supervising relations between Christian converts and their non-Christian neighbors in the 1860s, but in 1872 the Manchu general complained that few reports on such matters were sent to him. See Sichuansheng dang'anguan 1985, 303.

57. A detailed description of the Qing civil and military bureaucracies in Sichuan may be found in Zhou Xun 1986.

58. Reed 1995 describes the organization and work of yamen functionaries in Qing-era Baxian, the county in which Chongqing was situated.

59. On late Qing Chongqing, see Wyman 1993.

60. Legendre 1906, 171.

61. Zhou Xun 1987, 19–20.

62. Lu Zijian 1984, 432.

63. Zhou Xun 1986, 42–53.

64. Zhou Kaiqing 1976, 305; Legendre 1906, 157.

65. Fu Chongju 1987, 2: 381–455 gives detailed accounts of the various land and water routes from Chengdu to other cities. The telegraph system is discussed in the same work (1: 85).

66. Vale 1902, 7.

67. Wu Yu's diary (*Wu Yu riji* 1984) records the regular visits of his tenants with rice and rent money in the years right after the 1911 Revolution, although he does not indicate how long they spent in the city and how they occupied themselves while there.

68. See especially Li's novel *Sishui weilan*, translated into English as *Ripples Across Stagnant Water*.

69. Beijing's mid-Qing administration is described in Dray-Novey 1981.

70. Rowe 1984 and Goodman 1995 show this clearly for Hankou and Shanghai, respectively. See also Rankin 1986.

71. In his study of late Qing Canton, Rhoads (1975, 24–25) saw little political activism among the merchants. For another view, see Tsin 1990. On Shandong's provincial city, Ji'nan, see Buck 1978.

72. Zhou Xun 1987, 15–16.

73. Legendre 1906, 176.

74. Wang Di 1993, 354.

75. Zhou Xun 1986, 74.

76. Zhou Xun (1986, 204–32) states that many of Sichuan's lower-level official positions, including most of the county magistrate spots, had been automatically awarded to expectant officials assigned to Sichuan based on their place on a seniority list for most of the Qing period. Ding Baozhen, governor-general in the 1870s, received imperial approval to amend this system, however, so that governors-general could choose the most qualified expectants for office. According to Zhou, who served many of Sichuan's late Qing governors-general, most of them did appoint officials based on accomplishment, with the exception of Liu Bingzhang, who was susceptible to bribery.

77. Official recognition of this sort may be found in the gazetteers of Chengdu and Huayang counties. For the former, a gazetteer was compiled early in the nineteenth century and reissued in an updated edition in 1873. Huayang county issued a gazetteer in 1816 and another in 1934.

78. Rowe 1989, 297–306, discusses this phenomenon in Hankou. Its existence in Chongqing in the late nineteenth century is evidenced in a report by a *zong jianzheng*, or chief supervisory head, who was given the responsibility for safeguarding Christian properties in the city in the 1890s and reported formally to the Baxian magistrate. See Sichuansheng dang'anguan

1985, 490. Zhou Xun (1986, 214) reports that officials ordered *jiebao*, or street *bao* heads, to drive prostitutes out of Luzhou, just west of Chongqing, in the Guangxu era.

79. *Chongxiu Chengduxian zhi* 1971, 166–76.

80. This conclusion is necessarily tentative, since not much evidence on this point has yet surfaced. Nevertheless, Zhou Xun, who was a keen and detailed analyst of Chengdu's administrative structure, says nothing about the role of *baojia* personnel in any of his works, except in a brief section on the late Qing Baojia Bureau discussed below. Many references to the actions of *baozheng* (*bao* heads) appear in late Qing newspaper accounts of areas outside Chengdu. I have found one reference to a *yuebao* active in Chengdu itself in the late nineteenth century. This man was sent to suppress a violent demonstration at a Catholic church during the Chengdu anti-Christian activities of 1895 and reported to the Baojia Bureau and the Huayang magistrate. See *Jiaowu jiao'an dang* 1974, 5, pt. 3: 1674.

81. Zhou Xun 1986, 32–36; Zhou Xun 1987, 17.

82. Sichuansheng dang'anguan 1985, 47.

83. Hosie 1897, 85.

84. A sociological analysis of the position of yamen underlings in Qing administration may be found in Ch'ü T'ung-tsu 1962. See also Watt 1972, chap. 10. Reed 1995 offers a more detailed historical account of these men in the Chongqing area. A rigorous and illuminating study of "customary fees" in late Qing Sichuan may be found in Hickey 1990, chap. 5. See also Hickey 1991.

85. A cogent analysis of subcounty administration and the "entrepreneurial state brokers" who carried it out in the Qing period may be found in Duara 1988, chap. 2.

86. Zhou Xun 1986, 244–45.

87. Rankin 1986, 58–59; Rowe 1989, 306.

88. Zhou Xun gives no date for the founding of this bureau, although he states that it existed in the beginning of the Guangxu reign (1875). Because it is not mentioned in the 1873 Chengdu county gazetteer, I am inclined to think that it had not been established at that time. Some Sichuan bureaus set up during the Guangxu reign (1875–1908) in areas other than Chengdu appear to have been dominated by local elites, rather than officials. On these institutions, see Niimura 1983, Yamamoto 1994, and Reed 1995.

89. Zhou Xun 1986, 133; Zhou Xun 1987, 17. Zhou uses the term *juding*; the term *juyong* is used in official reports concerning the 1895 anti-Christian activities in Chengdu (*Jiaowu jiao'an dang* 1974, 5, pt. 3: 1673–74).

90. Zhou Xun 1986, 254–55.

91. Reed 1995 shows that competition and strife among runners and between runners and other sorts of security personnel was quite common in Chongqing. It is likely to have been so in Chengdu as well, but the detailed county-level records available for Baxian do not survive in the case of Chengdu and Huayang counties.

92. Qing legal penalties are described in grim detail in Kuhn 1990.

93. Legendre (1906, 192–93) wrote that he never witnessed a fistfight or heard of any violent crime during his stay in Chengdu in 1902 and 1903, and noted that, even during festivals, Chengdu people were very peaceable and calm.

94. Zhou Xun 1986, 214–15.

95. The men who did much of the corrupting could certainly be oppressive in their own ways, however. Zhou Xun (1987, 18) certainly saw them that way; he considered Chengdu's "gowned brothers" rapacious bullies. For more on the brothers, who were members of illegal, semi-secret brotherhoods, see Chapter 6 in this book.

96. Zhou Xun 1986, 255.

97. The Chinese legal tradition is penetratingly analyzed in Huang 1996.

98. Hartwell 1921, 8–9 (romanization altered).

99. The historical development of *fengshui* is discussed in A. F. Wright 1977, 54–55.

100. F. W. Mote (1977, 117) argues that "no Chinese building was obviously datable in terms of period styles. No traditional Chinese city ever had a Romanesque or a Gothic past to be overlaid in a burst of classical renascence, or a Victorian nightmare to be scorned in an age of aggressive functionalism."

101. Hartwell 1921, 10–12 (romanization altered).

102. Whether these were *baojia*-type leaders equipped with official seals and responsibilities or simply prominent men of the neighborhood is unclear from Hartwell's account.

Chapter 2

1. In his book on this reform period, Douglas Reynolds (1993, 14) prefers not to translate *xinzheng* but suggests that "new systems" captures the Chinese meaning more closely than "new policies." He has a point, but the latter term has become standard in the historical literature and may actually do a better job of reflecting the great range of the reform proposals adopted in

this period. *Xinzheng* came to stand in Chinese writings for the innovative era of Qing rule between 1901 and 1912 as a whole more than for the particular administrative innovations themselves.

2. Qing rulers had not always rejected major administrative reform initiatives. Zelin 1984 describes an ambitious early eighteenth-century fiscal reform program. Even in the nineteenth century, large-scale innovations such as the new provincial armies built up by governors Zeng Guofan and Li Hongzhang were possible. These, however, were designed so as to avoid challenging the old bureaucratic structure.

3. This edict appears in English translation in Reynolds 1993, 201–4. The Chinese text for his translation is from *Guangxu chao Donghua lu*, 4: 135–36.

4. The best published summaries in English of the New Policies from the viewpoints of the central government and the most prominent reform theorists are M. C. Wright 1968, Ichiko 1980, and Cameron 1931. A comprehensive unpublished survey is Morrison 1959.

5. M. C. Wright 1968, 1–23.

6. This interpretation of the New Policies has been common in Chinese accounts of late Qing history. Examples are cited in Bays 1978, 128–30; and Reynolds 1993, 3–4.

7. Duara 1988, 59.

8. Ibid., 73–85.

9. Stapleton 1997.

10. Works that help illuminate the intellectual antecedents of the New Policies programs include Hsiao 1975, Kuhn 1975, Bays 1978, and Kamachi 1981.

11. Han Suyin 1965, 82. Han has her uncle put this event in early 1894, although later the correct year is given. Her account of Chengdu and her family's history is fascinating, but frustratingly inaccurate at times. She has constructed the story from a rich variety of historical and fictional sources, without clearly indicating when she is relying on which.

12. The Chengdu anti-Christian activities of 1895 are described from the missionaries' point of view in Cunningham 1895 and analyzed in Hyatt 1964. The events are also discussed in Wei Yingtao 1990, 170–72. Some of the reports on the case made by Sichuan's governor-general Liu Bingzhang and other Chinese officials are available in *Jiaowu jiao'an dang* 1974, vol. 5, pt. III: 1645–778 and vol. 6, pt. II.: 1189–226.

13. It was the Duanwu festival, often celebrated with dragon-boat racing in China. In Chengdu it had become the custom for people to gather at the East Parade Ground on this day and toss plums at each other. It is possible

that this custom was banned as a result of the events of 1895. Fu Chongju (1987, 1: 204) does not list "plum-throwing on the East Parade Ground" among the ways of celebrating the Duanwu festival in his 1909–10 guide to Chengdu.

14. Hyatt 1964, 35.

15. *Jiaowu jiao'an dang* 1974, vol. 5, pt. III: 1659. In Changsha, according to Joseph Esherick (1976, 123–42), masons and carpenters upset that foreigners were bringing artisans in from Hankou to construct their houses constituted an important force in the antiforeign riots that broke out in 1910.

16. Ibid., vol. 6, pt. II: 1191–205.

17. Ibid., vol. 5, pt. III: 1745–46.

18. Ibid., vol. 6, pt. II: 1191–205.

19. As cited in Hyatt 1964, 44. I have yet to see a Chinese source that discusses in any detail the local events in the aftermath of the destruction of the mission properties.

20. Hyatt 1964, 40–45.

21. J. Ch'en 1972, 29.

22. Bays 1978, 19.

23. Kwong 1984; H. Chang 1980.

24. Wang Tao's writings are analyzed in Cohen 1974; Huang Zunxian's in Kamachi 1981. On the Japanese influence in general in this period, see Reynolds 1993 and Jansen 1975, chap. 5.

25. H. Chang 1980, 280–81. The development of Kang Youwei's political philosophy is examined in Hsiao 1975.

26. Kamachi 1981, 211–30; Esherick 1976, 13–19. Daniel Bays's study of Zhang Zhidong highlights the strands of thought from the Chinese tradition that could make Huang Zunxian's Japanese-inspired innovations acceptable to the classically trained Zhang (Bays 1978, 20–28). Other analyses of the receptivity of Chinese ideology to new ideas in this period may be found in Cohen 1974 and Schwartz 1964.

27. For an historical survey of the 1890s reform movements, see H. Chang 1980. In his discussion of the politics of the Qing court between 1895 and 1898, Luke Kwong (1984) argues that the reform proposals of that period should be considered an extension of the self-strengthening program, rather than a break with it, and that the Empress Dowager and many others at the court were not opposed to major administrative change at that time.

28. Adshead 1984, 26–28.

29. Xu Pu 1986, 185; Kwong 1984, 87; Hsiao 1975.

30. Wei Yingtao 1990, 311.

31. Ibid., 318.

32. Wang Lüping and Cheng Qi 1993, 2–3.

33. The history of the Zunjing Academy and reaction to the 1898 reform movement in Sichuan are discussed in more detail in Wei Yingtao 1990, chap. 5.

34. Hu Lisan 1985, 77.

35. For Xu's comments to his class, see Tao Liangsheng n.d.

36. Reynolds 1993, 13.

37. The polarizing effects of the Boxer fiasco and the concurrent Zilihui uprising are described in detail in Esherick 1976 and Bays 1978, chap. 5.

38. E. Wilson 1991, 18–25.

39. A. F. Wright 1977, 34.

40. Lees 1985, 9.

41. Gluck 1985, 26–28.

42. Rowe 1984, 343.

43. See Chapter 7.

44. Hsiao 1975, 265. Similar arguments were presented by Feng Guifen, in essays written in the 1860s that received imperial patronage and wide circulation in 1898. On Feng's theories, see Kuhn 1975, 265–68.

45. The issue of systemic corruption was a major concern of the Sichuan scholars who contributed to Song Yuren's publications in the late 1890s (Wei Yingtao 1990, 313–14).

46. H. Chang 1980, 280.

47. This English translation of Kang's title is proposed in Dikötter 1992.

48. Hsiao 1975, 463.

49. H. Chang 1971, 268.

50. Bays 1978, 29.

51. Ibid., 45.

52. Ibid., 110.

53. Ibid., 101.

54. The final line of the epigram commented that Cen Chunxuan, who brought the New Policies to Sichuan, "does not study and lacks skills (*buxue wushu*)" (Zhou Xun 1987, 96).

55. An excellent example of the wide divergence of provincial approaches to the New Policies may be found in Roger Thompson's (1995) account of Zhao Erxun's and Yuan Shikai's ideas about broadening political participation.

56. The new administrative codes (*guanzhi*) were drafted as a result of the court's decision to prepare a new constitution with a place for delibera-

tive assemblies. Documents concerning the new codes may be found in *Qingmo choubei lixian dang'an shiliao* 1979, 1: 367–601. See also Bays 1978, 201–4; and Thompson 1995, chap. 4.

57. On the influence of *Beiyang guanbao*, see Thompson 1995, 40–42.

58. For a fairly recent statement of that judgment, see MacKinnon 1980, chap. 4. Zhang Zhidong did not neglect military reform. His "Self-strengthening Army," with its German advisers, was founded in 1895, but was much smaller than Yuan's New Army. See Powell 1955, 60–71.

59. Powell 1955, 13–14. On the organization of the Green Standards, see also Luo Ergang 1945.

60. MacKinnon 1980, 39–45.

61. Kamachi 1981, 220.

62. Ibid., 223. In his study of late Qing police reform, Wang Jiajian (1984, 22) states that Huang Zunxian was most concerned with the corruption common among *baojia* leaders and garrison guards.

63. Lin Nengshi 1970, 70–73. Huang Zunxian himself became Hunan's first police director.

64. Bays 1978, 77.

65. Lai Shuqing 1989, 36.

66. MacKinnon 1980, 152. The history of Yuan's Tianjin police is analyzed in Yoshizawa 1990.

67. MacKinnon 1980, 152–55.

68. Thompson 1995, 20.

69. Ibid., 37–39.

70. Ibid., chap. 6.

71. Fincher 1968, 190.

72. Meribeth Cameron (1931, 160–61) quotes a letter from "An Old China Hand" published in the *North China Herald* in 1909, which constitutes a forceful expression of this judgment.

73. Buck 1978, 28–29 (romanization altered).

74. Thompson 1995, 144.

75. Ibid., chap. 3.

76. Ibid., 142–44.

77. Kenneth Pomeranz (1993) makes the case that the self-strengthening efforts of the late nineteenth century had already profoundly affected the political economy of North China, enriching some areas and making "hinterlands" out of others. Pomeranz's approach is a regional analysis, and he has little to say about the changes in the relationships between cities and rural areas within the region he studied.

78. I have discussed this point in regard to police reform in Sichuan in Stapleton 1997.

79. MacKinnon 1980, 146.

80. Ibid., 157.

81. Ibid., 160.

82. This phrase is used, for example, in the 1903 Sichuan police regulations, which were to be applied initially only in Chengdu. In modern Chinese-English dictionaries, such as that of Liang Shiqiu, the phrase is translated as "national capital."

83. Bays 1978, 114–16.

84. A list of schools located in Chengdu in 1910 may be found in Fu Chongju 1987, 1: 54–58. For a detailed discussion of education in late Qing Sichuan, see Wang Di 1993, chap. 7.

85. For a detailed history of the New Policies concerning education, see Bastid 1988.

86. Esherick 1976, 110.

87. Ibid., 66–69. David Buck also emphasizes the nationalistic and defensive aspect of the New Policies. See Buck 1978, chap. 3.

88. Judith Wyman (1993, 208–14) discusses this concern as it manifested itself in late Qing Chongqing.

89. James Cole (1986, pt. II) has described the history of the phenomenon of the Shaoxing secretary. Zhou Zhen was a native of one of Shaoxing's peripheral counties, Zhuji.

90. Zhou Xun (1987, 29) helped conduct the next comprehensive audit of the provincial treasury in 1902 and expressed his admiration of the 1890 accounts.

91. Biographies of Zhou Shanpei include Huang Suisheng 1964, Shi Tiyuan 1981, Qiao Shaoxin 1984, and Jin Han 1986. Interviews with his children, Anne Chou and Chou Ch'eng-ch'ing, in Taiwan in September 1992 have also informed this account, as have his own writings.

92. Qiao Shaoxin 1984, 70. See also Huang Suisheng 1964, 187.

93. Cohen 1974, 268.

94. Wang Jiajian 1984, 19–20.

95. Link 1981, chaps. 3 and 4.

96. Even without the foreign enclaves, however, the wealthy Jiangnan region had long fostered cultural creativity, as Philip Kuhn (1990, 70–72) notes when discussing the Qianlong emperor's suspicion of the "extravagant customs" of this "decadent" area.

97. Y. Zhang 1996, 18. Zhang notes, however, that for many of the intellectuals this moment was brief, to be followed by disillusioned bitterness about the promise of the city, a mood which pervaded literature of the 1920s.

98. Liu Ts'un-yan 1984, 24. "Petty urbanite" is Perry Link's (1981, 189) translation of "*xiao shimin.*"

99. On the nostalgia of such late Meiji writers as Nagai Kafū, see Seidensticker 1983. Perry Link (1981, 137) notes that late Qing publishers and authors had scant interest in contemporary Japanese literature, preferring instead to translate Japanese translations of Western works.

100. Link 1981, 133–34.

101. Y. Zhang 1996, 9–11.

102. Orderliness created at least the appearance of the community harmony that was so important to Confucian political theorists. On the Qing statecraft tradition, see Will 1990 and Ocko 1983.

103. The foreign occupying force had demolished the city walls (Thompson 1995, 40).

104. Unless otherwise noted, my account of Zhou's life before 1903 is based on Huang Suisheng's article, the most convincing I have seen. On *fubang* status and other Qing civil degrees, see Ho 1962, 29.

105. Qiao Cheng, n.d.

106. Chou Ch'eng-ch'ing interview, Taipei, September 1992.

107. Zhou Shanpei 1960.

108. Seidensticker 1983, 20.

109. Westney 1987.

110. Gluck 1985, 178–86.

111. Jansen 1975, chap. 5. See also Reynolds 1993, chap. 3.

112. Huang Suisheng 1964, 188; Zhou Shanpei 1960.

113. Hartwell 1921, 23; Reynolds 1993, 74. Huang Suisheng (1964, 188), corroborates the Nakajima account. Fu Chongju (1987, 1: 58) mentions this school in his 1910 guidebook to the city, listing it in his "very effective but already disbanded" category. He notes that the provincial educational commissioner had memorialized the throne for its approval of the venture.

114. For a recent assessment of this student movement, see Reynolds 1993, chap. 4.

115. Zhou Shanpei 1960.

116. Interview with Chou Ch'eng-ch'ing, Taipei, September 1992. An article about Zhou published recently by a Sichuan native who was a student when Zhou was an official in Chengdu (Chen Yan 1977, 50) claims that

Zhou bought his official rank with the financial backing of several overseas Chinese. Whatever the truth of the matter, the account suggests that people in Chengdu may have believed it when Zhou returned in 1905. It is conceivable that Zhou himself spread this rumor in the hopes that it would give him more clout in provincial politics.

117. All of these initiatives are publicized in issues of *Sichuan guanbao* from the years 1907 to 1911.

Chapter 3

1. He Yili 1987. Female Boxer groups called Red-Lantern-Shining (*hongdengzhao*) in eastern China are discussed in Esherick 1987, 297–98. Documents on Sichuan's 1902 uprisings, in which officials express concern over the "infiltration of the evil remnants of the fist bandits [Boxers]," are collected in Sichuansheng dang'anguan 1985. See also Adshead 1984, 33–36.

2. This incident is reminiscent of the 1813 attack on Beijing described in Naquin 1976. Kuijun's report on the incident to the Foreign Affairs Ministry, which claims there were only 21 rebels, may be found in *Xinhai gemingqian shinianjian minbian dang'an shiliao* 1985, 2: 742–43. The event appears in fictionalized form in Li Jieren 1956, pt. I, chap. 4.

3. This account is given by Zhou Xun (1986, 221), who worked for the judge a year later when he was serving as acting governor-general. Legendre (1906, 193), however, reports that French consul-general Bons d'Anty told him that twelve Boxers roamed the city freely for several hours, while all residents cowered in their homes, until Bons d'Anty persuaded a military officer to venture out of his compound and chase them out of the city.

4. *Xinhai gemingqian shinianjian minbian dang'an shiliao* 1985, 2: 733–42.

5. Cen's reports on his suppression campaign are in ibid., 2: 744–51. The provincial execution ground was moved from the North Parade Ground inside the walls to a spot outside the north wall when the former site became the headquarters of Sichuan's New Army (Zhou Xun 1987, 55–56).

6. *Xinhai gemingqian shinianjian minbian dang'an shiliao* 1985, 2: 751.

7. Adshead 1984, 37–42, surveys Cen's administration.

8. Orders in regard to militia organization, as well as records of the attempts to follow them in the Chongqing area, are found in Sichuansheng dang'anguan 1985, 725–56. Cen's announcement of the reorganization of the Baojia Bureau appears on pp. 751–52.

9. Dray-Novey 1993.

10. Thompson 1995.

11. Chen Yan 1977, 7–13.

12. *Sichuan tongsheng jingcha zhangcheng* 1903.

13. Ibid.

14. Stapleton 1997.

15. It is not clear how bureau officials determined the boundaries of police precincts; the subprecincts may have corresponded to earlier *baojia* divisions, or they may have been created at this time. The original police regulations from 1903 note that the bureau could adjust precinct boundaries as it deemed necessary. The names of the temples and other buildings where the six precinct and forty subprecinct offices were located are listed in Fu Chongju 1987, 1: 50–52.

16. All these plans are described in considerable detail in *Sichuan tongsheng jingcha zhangcheng* 1903. See Stapleton 1993, chap. 3, for a fuller discussion of this document.

17. Xiao Denghui 1989.

18. A copy of this document (*Sichuan tongsheng jingcha zhangcheng*) may be found in the Qing Police Ministry materials in the First Historical Archives. This copy was probably sent to Beijing when the Police Ministry was founded in 1905. Joshua Vale (1904) summarizes it in English.

19. On the importance of historical context for the development of the style of policing practiced by a force, see Miller 1973 and J. Q. Wilson 1968.

20. Most of these restrictions on constable conduct appear in chap. 6 of the *Sichuan tongsheng jingcha zhangcheng* 1903. Uniforms are described in chap. 5.

21. Ibid., chap. 5.

22. *Shubao*, July 14, 1903.

23. Strand 1989, 95.

24. Steve MacKinnon's (1975, 82–99) interpretation of Yuan Shikai's police reform in Zhili suggests that Yuan thought of constables primarily as instruments with which to secure order, much like yamen runners. According to David Strand's (1989, 73–91) description, however, the style of policing cultivated in Beijing in the 1920s bears some resemblance to Zhou Shanpei's earlier paternalistic conception of Chengdu's police.

25. Provisions for police rewards and punishments are set out in *Sichuan tongsheng jingcha zhangcheng* 1903, chap. 6.

26. Ibid., chap. 5.

27. Xiliang's career in Sichuan is discussed in Adshead 1984, chap. 3, and Des Forges 1973.

28. Lary 1985, 51.

29. These funds were advertised in *Chengdu ribao*. See, for example, the issues of Jan. 7 and 9, 1910.

30. Ibid., June 23, 1911. The extent of the expectant problem is discussed in more detail in Vale 1902; Stapleton 1993, 129–32; and Wang Di 1993, 384.

31. *Chengdu ribao*, June 23, 1911. The rule is referred to in this issue of the paper; it is not clear when it was adopted.

32. Zhou Xun 1986, 131–44.

33. Fu Chongju 1987, 1: 140–56. This figure is for graduates of academic programs in police studies. It does not include those who, like Zhou Shanpei, studied police on their own in Japan.

34. Several petitions from such returned students to Governor-General Zhao Erxun may be found in file no. 493 of the Zhao Erxun materials in the First Historical Archives in Beijing.

35. Report by French consul-general Bons d'Anty, cited in Des Forges 1973, 47. The uniforms of the Chengdu force probably changed over time, but evidence on this is lacking. A photograph over the caption "Officers of the Chinese Police Force, as first introduced on European lines in West China" appears in Little 1910, 165. It shows two fierce-looking men in turbans and Chinese-style jackets with dragons embroidered on their sleeves, shod in what appear to be cloth shoes, and holding sabers. This outfit corresponds neither to the regulations on uniforms in *Sichuan tongsheng jingcha zhangcheng* 1903, chap. 5, nor to the depictions of police officers in Fu Chongju's *Tongsu huabao* of 1912. I suspect that the subjects in the photograph are actually soldiers in the provincial army (*xunfangjun*), since their outfits do correspond to Guo Moruo's (1929) description of these soldiers as they appeared in 1911.

36. *Sichuan Chengdu disanci shangye quangonghui diaochabiao* 1908.

37. Fu Chongju 1987, 1: 114–16.

38. "Sichuan jingcha geyuan gongguobiao."

39. See, for example, Zhou Shanpei's lengthy report on the work of the bureau, published in several issues of the *Sichuan guanbao* in mid-1906. The other occasion for considerable disciplining of police officers occurred shortly after Zhou Zhaoxiang took over the bureau. See reports in the *Chengdu ribao* of Sept. 19 and 20, 1910.

40. "Sichuan jingcha geyuan gongguobiao."

41. Xiliang reported to the throne that, after serving for a time on the Chengdu force, the graduates of the third class of the Police Academy had been sent out to establish police in county seats (*Xiliang yigao* 1959, 1: 566).

42. Lu Guangzhong's résumé may be found in the First Historical Archives, Interior Ministry, file no. 286, along with those of other Sichuan police officers. For more information on career patterns of Chengdu officers, see Stapleton 1993, appendix 3.

43. *Shubao*, July 14, 1903.

44. *Sichuan guanbao* 1910, no. 33.

45. *Sichuan guanbao* 1906, no. 19.

46. "Sichuan jingcha geyuan gongguobiao."

47. *Sichuan jingwu guanbao*, no. 2 (1911).

48. *Sichuan guanbao* 1908, no. 5.

49. *Chengdu ribao*, Oct. 2, 1909.

50. *Sichuan jingwu guanbao*, no. 1 (1911). See also Grace Service's (1989, 57) account of an incident in which an irate servant attacked her husband outside their Chengdu home in 1910. A crowd summoned the corner constable, who watched as Bob Service grappled with the man by himself for some time. When the latter had finally been subdued, the constable stepped in and led him away.

51. Letters and documents on this incident are held in the First Historical Archives, Zhao Erxun material, file no. 480.

52. Guo Moruo 1929, 18.

53. Li Jieren (1956, 317–42) includes an account of the field day incident in his novel *Baofengyuqian* (Before the storm).

54. "Sichuan jingcha geyuan gongguobiao."

55. The proposal was published in *Sichuan guanbao* 1908, no. 21. Police Bureau reports to Beijing at that time were too detailed not to have mentioned such a plan, if there had been any thought of implementing it.

56. *Xuantong yuannian Shengcheng jingqu diyici diaocha hukou yilanbiao* 1909.

57. Zhou Shanpei 1957, 24. *Xiangyue* and *dibao* were terms used, along with *baozheng* (*baojia* head), to designate people outside the official bureaucracy who worked with officials to maintain order in communities.

58. See Chapter 6 in this book for a discussion of street headmen in Chengdu after 1911.

59. *Sichuan jingwu wendu huibian*, first year of Xuantong (1909–10), booklet no. 4.

60. *Sichuan jingwu guanbao*, no. 3 (1911). By this time, the police commissioners were called *quzheng*, since the term for precinct was changed from *ju* to *qu* in 1910, to comply with new regulations issued by the central government.

61. *Chengdu ribao*, Jan. 4, 1910.

62. Fu Chongju 1987, 1: 43.

63. Li Jieren 1980, pt. I, 458–60.

64. See, for example, the story "Shimin de ziwei" (Self-protection in the city) (Li Jieren 1947b).

65. Vale 1904, 126.

66. Davidson and Mason 1905, 48.

67. Li Jieren 1956, 59. The French doctor Legendre (1906, 192), however, observed that compared to the residents of most other large cities, those of Chengdu were very peaceable. He thought that the police had very little to do except arrest thieves and had only been set up "pour sacrificier à la mode européenne."

68. *West China Missionary News* 5, no. 11 (Nov. 1903): 177.

69. *Chengdu ribao*, Nov. 27, 1908.

70. "Sichuan jingcha geyuan gongguobiao."

71. *Sichuan guanbao* 1906, no. 18.

72. *Chengdu ribao*, Dec. 9 and 10, 1904. The names of the suspects were provided in a follow-up report in the paper on Dec. 13, 1904.

73. Xiliang's report on their work in this case is in *Xinhai gemingqian shinianjian minbian dang'an shiliao* 1985, 2: 766–68. He does not mention the involvement of revolutionaries, but see Zhou Kaiqing 1964, 29; and Wei Yingtao 1990, 552.

74. A report from a Beijing newspaper on the formation of the detective squad there in 1906 appeared in the *Sichuan guanbao* 1906, no. 11. The formation of the Chengdu squad was announced in the *Chengdu ribao*, Dec. 15, 1909.

75. *Firmiana* is the genus name of the *wuhua* tree after which Su Zilin styled himself, a Chinese member of the same family as the cocoa, cola, and coffee trees. According to Robert Paratley of the University of Kentucky Herbarium, *Firmiana* has flowers somewhat like those of the linden and is cultivated in Japan as a street tree. One member of the genus has been given the English name "Japanese varnish tree."

76. Documents on the Su Zilin case may be found in *Xinhai gemingqian shinianjian minbian dang'an shiliao* 1985, 2: 779–89. Some of the confessions of suspects captured early in 1909 are not included in this publication and may be found in the First Historical Archives, Zhou Erxun materials, file no. 346.

77. Chen Shaobo 1962; Huang Suisheng 1962; Xiong Kewu 1962.

78. *Xinhai gemingqian shinianjian minbian dang'an shiliao* 1985, 2: 744–45. See also Li Jieren's (1956, 223–72) account of this incident, in which the Chengdu magistrate, Wang Tan, is credited with uncovering and suppressing the plot.

79. *Chengdu ribao*, Aug. 14 and Sept. 22, 1909.

80. Ibid., Dec. 20, 1904.

81. Ibid., Jan. 10, 1910.

82. Ibid., Sept. 12, 1910.

83. Zhou Shanpei (ca. 1908) mentions some of these cases in his "Memo addressing charges of misconduct." He cites the case of the degree-holding legal meddler in his quarterly police report in *Sichuan guanbao* 1906, no. 17. The case of the thuggish nephew is reported in *Chengdu ribao*, Aug. 5, 1906. Zhou's own account of his arrest of Zhao Erfeng's chair bearer, which occurred when Zhao was Tibetan border commissioner, is recorded in Qiao Shaoxin 1984. On the Zhaojue monastery case, see Chapter 4 in this book.

84. Qiao Shaoxin 1984, 72.

85. Stapleton 1997.

86. *Chengdu ribao*, Aug. 8, 1906.

87. "Sichuan jingcha geyuan gongguobiao."

88. *West China Missionary News* 7, no. 12 (Dec. 1905): 258.

89. *Chengdu ribao*, Aug. 11, 1906.

90. Zhao Erxun forwarded a report on firefighting from Gao Zengjue to the Interior Ministry in 1910 (First Historical Archives, Zhao Erxun material, file no. 312).

91. *West China Missionary News* 9, no. 9 (Sept. 1907): 20.

92. *Shubao*, July 14, 1903.

93. *West China Missionary News* 7, no. 3 (Mar. 1905): 57–58.

94. It is not clear exactly when the police started collecting the lamp-oil tax. The first mention of it that I have seen is in documents on police work sent to the Interior Ministry in 1910.

95. I examine the question of police justice in Chapter 5, in the context of a discussion of late Qing legal reform and its impact on city affairs.

96. Guo Moruo 1929, 65.

97. According to Zhou Shanpei's son, Chen Yi told this story to Zhou Shanpei himself when they met after 1949 (interview with Chou Ch'eng-ch'ing, Taipei, Sept. 1992). Zhou Shanpei was widely known as Baldy Zhou, although accounts differ about the reason for the nickname. Some say it was because he had cut off his queue while in Japan, and others that his hair was naturally skimpy.

Chapter 4

1. On the Yoshiwara and its "decay" in the Meiji era, see Seidensticker 1983, 167–75.

2. Quoted in Wang Lüping and Cheng Qi 1993, 9. For more on Sichuan's pre-1901 reform community, see Wei Yingtao, 1990, 308–24.

3. Wang Di 1993, 568–81; Fu Chongju 1987, 1: 72.

4. The close-knit nature of Chengdu's elite community in the late Qing is evident in Zhou Shanpei's 1957 memoir of the 1911 Revolution, which he states began as a collaborative project between himself and Zhang Lan, a prominent Sichuan activist and politician in the late Qing and Republican eras.

5. Zhou Bangdao 1981. Among the Sichuan students who traveled to Belgium at this time was Han Suyin's father. See Han Suyin 1965 for his story.

6. Zhou Shanpei 1957. One, Yang Wei, re-established the Chengdu police force after the 1911 Revolution (see Chapter 6). Another was the elder brother of Huang Jilu, the Nationalist official.

7. Li Jieren 1986a.

8. These papers are described in Wang Lüping and Cheng Qi 1993, 4–7 and 21–23. See Chapter 5 for more on Chengdu's late Qing newspapers.

9. Gao Chengxiang 1990, 483–84.

10. Li Xiaoti 1992, 15–30.

11. *West China Missionary News* 4, no. 3 (Mar. 1902).

12. Li Jieren 1956, 156–57.

13. Fu Chongju 1987, 1: 199–200, 271–75.

14. Wei Yingtao 1991, 222–27.

15. The Sichuan Official Press Office (Sichuan guanbao shuju) sent this list to the Interior Ministry in Beijing, and it is preserved in file no. 783 in the Interior Ministry materials in the First Historical Archives. On the late Qing educational reforms in general, see Bastid 1988.

16. Kemp 1909, 169.

17. Simkin 1911.

18. Like Chiang Kai-shek and his Whampoa military academy graduates, Zhou Shanpei developed a coterie of disciples when he trained the officers of the Guangzhou New Army in 1904 and 1905. Among them was Cai E, the leader of the 1916 revolution against Yuan Shikai (see Huang Suisheng 1964).

19. This incident is discussed in Zhou Shanpei 1938b, 81–82. Zhou Shanpei objected to the account of this incident in the first edition of Li Jieren's novel *Dabo* (The great wave; Li Jieren 1980) and gave his own version.

20. Adshead (1984, 119) suggests that "the viceregal government implicitly abandoned Chengdu when it abolished the examination system." Chengdu elites, however, seem to have been quick to take advantage of changes in the civil service system by rushing into the new schools and professional academies. Judging from Li Jieren's (1986a) memoirs of his school days, the sons of families based in Chengdu dominated his middle school, which was attached to the provincial high school. Guo Moruo's 1929 memoirs of his aborted career at the same school also point to the power of Chengdu patronage.

21. *Shubao*, issues 2–4 (1910).

22. Adshead (1984, 119) suggests that the Chengdu elite feared that the Yangzi segment of the railroad would benefit Chongqing merchants at their expense. His own view is that "in the long run . . . the railway could hardly fail to make Chungking the Basle of the Upper Yangtze, Tzu-liu-ching its Zurich, with Chengtu merely its Berne." Although some in Sichuan strongly believed that the Chongqing to Chengdu segment of the railroad should be built before the Yichang (Hubei) to Chongqing segment, Adshead's argument may underestimate the flexibility of the Chengdu elite, who, because of their access to financial and political capital and advanced education, would probably have been able to benefit from the railroad just as much as the merchants of Chongqing.

23. Wei Yingtao 1990, 349–70. See also Prazniak 1981.

24. The lottery, begun in 1905, was heavily publicized in the local newspapers, including Fu Qiaocun's pictorial, which published an illustration of the crowds attending one of the drawings. Fu himself started a lottery agency to sell tickets, but the venture was a financial disaster for him. According to his detailed account, the official agents in charge of the lottery used it primarily to enrich themselves (Fu Chongju 1987, 2: 221–24).

25. *Chengdu ribao*, Aug. 17 and 19, 1906.

26. *Sichuan jingwu wendu huibian*, first year of Xuantong (1909–10), booklet no. 2.

27. Zhou Shanpei 1938b, 81. See also Chen Yan 1977, 52.

28. Hutson 1915, 25–26.

29. Kilborn 1920, 44–45.

30. This was not the case in other parts of Sichuan. Official reports, preserved in the Zhao Erxun materials in the First Historical Archives, on

the drive to conduct a census in order to prepare for elections to local assemblies in 1909 state that in many rural areas the census was rumored to be part of a foreign plot to subjugate Sichuan. See file no. 309.

31. Wyman 1997. See also Esherick 1987, chap. 3.

32. Wei Yingtao 1990, 318.

33. Simkin 1911, 6.

34. *Sichuan guanbao*, XT 2, no. 9 (1910).

35. Vale 1907, pt. 1: 9–11. The romanization has been changed.

36. Ibid., pt. 2: 7–8. Legendre 1906, 134, 189–90.

37. *Xiliang yigao* 1959, 1: 646.

38. Fu Chongju 1987, 2: 370.

39. *Xiliang yigao* 1959, 1: 646; Chen Daoxin 1987, 12.

40. Li Jieren (1947a, 235) claims the hairstyle enforced on workhouse inmates was known as the "shoe sole" cut. It is also described in Chen Yan 1977.

41. Simkin 1911. The inspiration for Zhou Shanpei's band may have been Robert Hart's Customs Service band (see Spence 1980, 118).

42. *Chengdu ribao*, Sept. 17, 1909.

43. Fu Chongju 1987, 1: 193.

44. On Meiji police surveillance, see Westney 1987, 94.

45. Zhou Shanpei ca. 1908.

46. *Sichuan guanbao*, GX 33, no. 14 (1907).

47. This may be an urban myth, but it shows up in the popular Chengdu histories of Zhou Shanpei. In Zhou's own memoirs, he recalls that some provincial officials tried to embarrass him by suggesting that he compose an inscription to be placed over the door of the police station at the entrance to the licensed zone. Zhou claims to have immediately written, in large characters, "To awaken our good people" (*jue wo liangmin*) (see Qiao Shaoxin 1984, 72).

48. Qiao Shunan et al. ca. 1908.

49. Fu Chongju 1987, 1: 194.

50. *Tongsu huabao*, Aug. 7, 1912.

51. *Xuantong yuannian Shengcheng jingqu diyici diaocha hukou yilanbiao* 1909.

52. *Sichuan jingwu wendu huibian*, first year of Xuantong (XT 1) (1909).

53. Cameron 1931, 136.

54. *Sichuan guanbao*, GX 33, nos. 17 and 19 (1907).

55. *Sichuan jingcha geyuan gongguobiao*.

56. Vale 1905, 55.

57. Qiao Shaoxin 1984, 72.

58. *Qingmo choubei lixian dang'an shiliao* 1979, 1: 51–52.

59. Statistics booklets survive for Chengdu's Banner garrison, which acquired its own police force staffed by Banner personnel in 1906. They are preserved in the First Historical Archives, Interior Ministry materials, file no. 312. I have not located the reports for the rest of the Chengdu police districts, but the information in them is reflected in part in Fu Chongju 1987.

60. *Chengdu ribao*, Oct. 30, 1909; First Historical Archives, Zhao Erxun materials, file no. 322.

61. *Chengdu ribao*, Sept. 1, 1909.

62. Christian missionaries were concerned about the effects of boarding-house life on young boys and set up a Christian hostel, where James Yen lived for a few years (Hayford 1990, 17).

63. Xiong Kewu 1962 and 1980.

64. Vale 1904, 86.

65. *Sichuan guanbao*, GX 32, no. 19 (1906).

66. Qi Ren 1913.

67. *West China Missionary News* 9, no. 1 (Oct. 1907): 1–2.

68. *Sichuan guanbao*, GX 33, no. 18 (1907); Fu Chongju 1987, 1: 193–94.

69. *Chengdu ribao*, Oct. 3, 1909.

70. *Sichuan guanbao*, XT 2, no. 31 (1910).

71. Fu Chongju 1987, 1: 561–63.

72. Li Jieren 1986a.

73. The private correspondence and official memoranda exchanged between the members of the education association and the governor-general is preserved in the First Historical Archives, Zhao Erxun material, file no. 480. Among the documents is a memo addressed to Zhao Erxun from his adviser, Zhou Zhaoxiang, recommending the appointment of Gao Zengjue to head the police.

74. Wei Yingtao 1991, 143–44.

75. "Chentu Notes," *West China Missionary News* 9, no. 6 (June 1907): 15. The first head of the Commercial Bureau awarded Fu Qiaocun a contract to supervise the construction of the rickshaws. Fu's guidebook (1987, 1: 306–7) notes that Song Yuren had first introduced rickshaws to Chengdu in 1898. In that year Song's *Shuxuebao* published essays debating the possible effects of rickshaws on the livelihood of the people.

76. *Chengdu shangbao*, no. 1 (May 1910).

77. Xie Fang 1987, 177–80. Zhou Shanpei's proclamation forbidding merchants in the commercial arcade from lowering their prices for special friends may be found in *Chengdu ribao*, Sept. 20, 1909. The first electric lighting system in Chengdu was set up in the mint in 1906 (He Yimin 1989, 606).

78. *Chengdu ribao*, Aug. 17, 1906, Aug. 9, 1909, and Oct. 30, 1909.

79. *Chengdu ribao*, Aug. 12, 1909.

80. Many of these reports may be found in the Zhao Erxun archives, file no. 463.

81. Dai Deyuan 1990, 39–40. On opera reform in general in the late Qing, see Li Xiaoti 1992, chap. 5.

82. Wheatley 1971.

83. *Sichuan jingwu wendu huibian*, XT 1 (1909), booklet no. 2.

84. Yang Bingde 1993, 341.

85. *West China Missionary News* 9, no. 5 (May 1907): 1–5.

86. Ibid., 7, no. 2 (Feb. 1905): 27.

87. Yang Bingde 1993, 343.

88. Fu Chongju 1987, 1: 277.

89. Xie Fang 1987, 179.

90. *Chengdu ribao*, Jan. 7, 1910.

91. First Historical Archives, Interior Ministry material, file no. 323.

92. Liu Xianzhi 1983. Han Bannerman were descendants of Han families that had been incorporated into the Manchu system before the conquest of the Ming in 1644.

93. Yukun 1980, 206.

94. *Chengdu ribao*, Sept. 20, 1909.

95. Such was the case with the new courthouse built in 1909. Officials offered landholders a "fair price" for their property and told them not to protest, because the sale was in the public interest (*Chengdu ribao*, Sept. 20, 1909).

96. Hosie 1914, 2: 3.

97. Sichuansheng wenshiguan 1987.

Chapter 5

1. Kemp 1909, 161; romanization altered. A similar assessment may be found in Ross 1912, 303–4.

2. Hutson 1915: 25.

3. Zhou Shanpei 1938a, 87.

4. Min Tu-ki 1989, 138–47.

5. On Liang Qichao's political thought, see H. Chang 1971; on the *Shibao*, see Judge 1996. Many of the *Shibao*'s editorials were reprinted in Sichuan's official gazette, the *Sichuan guanbao*. The fourteenth issue in GX 33 (1907–8), for example, carried a *Shibao* editorial on legal reform.

6. *Sichuan tongsheng jingcha zhangcheng* 1903. The police rules in this document are summarized in English in Stapleton 1993, appendix 2.

7. *Shubao*, no. 1 (1903).

8. Vale 1904, 106.

9. *Sichuan guanbao*, GX 33, no. 11 (1907). English translations of these police directives appear in Stapleton 1993, appendix 6. Chen Yan (1977) claims that Zhou's police directives were the only official announcements in the late Qing period to which most people in Chengdu paid attention, because they were simple and direct, unlike the flowery proclamations of other officials.

10. The degree of central control over the New Policies reforms varied. On the new central ministries, see Cameron 1931. On the great variation in provincial police administrations in the late Qing era, see Lai Shuqing 1989, 89–90.

11. Meijer 1950, 33.

12. *Qingmo choubei lixian dang'an shiliao* 1979, 2: 807.

13. *Sichuan guanbao*, GX 34, no. 32 (1908). On the commercial code, see Kirby 1995.

14. *Sichuan guanbao*, XT 3, no. 22 (1911).

15. The text of the police law may be found in Dai Hongying 1985, 15–27.

16. See Stapleton 1993, 184–94, for descriptions of some of the cases handled in Chengdu police courts.

17. Gao Zengjue report dated XT 2.3.25 (May 4, 1910), in the First Historical Archives, Interior Ministry material, file no. 312.

18. First Historical Archives, Zhao Erxun material, file no. 306.

19. Report in response to charges from the provincial assembly. n.d. (ca. 1910). First Historical Archives, Zhao Erxun material, file no. 343.

20. *Sichuan jingwu wendu huibian*, XT 2 (1910–11) second period, booklet no. 2.

21. Wei Yingtao 1990, 357–63; Thompson 1995, chap. 3.

22. *Sichuan jingwu wendu huibian*, XT 2 (1910–11) second period, booklet no. 2.

23. *Chengdu ribao*, Oct. 15, 1909. Zhao's speech also appears in Wei Yingtao and Zhao Qing 1981, 1: 2–7.

24. Wei Yingtao and Zhao Qing 1981, 1: 9–12.

25. Ibid., 1: 15–110. For more detailed discussion of the work of the provincial assembly, see Wei Yingtao 1991, 355–67.

26. Stapleton 1997.

27. Wei Yingtao and Zhao Qing 1981, 1: 29–37, 60–64.

28. *Chengdu ribao*, Sept. 15, 1910. The regulations of the city council were published in the first issue of the provincial assembly's gazette, *Shubao* (1910).

29. *Chengdu ribao*, Aug. 22 and Sept. 12, 1910.

30. Ibid., Sept. 10, 1910.

31. *Sichuansheng gexian difang zizhi shiye yu jingji zhuangkuang fenqi baogao* 1917.

32. *Sichuan guanbao*, Oct. 31, 1911. Because the uprising of the Comrades' Armies was in full swing by this date, Zhao Erfeng's agreement to consider the city council's proposal may already have seemed moot to many in Chengdu.

33. *Sichuan guanbao*, GX 34, no. 21 (1908).

34. Thompson 1995, 131–33. Thompson interprets the city council's position on terminology as illustrative of the disdain felt by urban elites toward rural leaders. The city council's proposal to the provincial assembly may be found in *Shubao*, issue 7, as well as in the Qing Interior Ministry archives, where Thompson found it, and the Interior Ministry's response to the proposal, which was to state that the matter would be considered in due time, may be found in *Sichuan guanbao*, Apr. 29, 1911.

35. Wei Yingtao, 1990, 368–70.

36. Chang P'eng-yüan 1968, 160–75. Deng Xiaoke's 1911 activism is examined in Adshead 1984 and Hedtke 1968. Twelve issues of *Shubao* appeared in 1910 and 1911 before it ceased publication.

37. For a description of these papers, see Judge 1996, chap. 1.

38. Wei Yingtao and Zhao Qing 1981, 1: 191.

39. *Shubao*'s report of the charges is included in ibid., 1: 154–58.

40. First Historical Archives, Zhao Erxun material, file no. 343.

41. See Stapleton 1997 for a discussion of Zhou Zhaoxiang's centralizing approach to provincial police reform and his distrust of "evil gentry."

42. *Shubao*, no. 8 (1911).

43. The memorial requesting permission for Zhou Zhaoxiang's trip to Manchuria is in the First Historical Archives, Zhao Erxun materials, file no. 289 (Wang Renwen 1911).

44. This issue as it concerns the new assemblies is examined by Roger Thompson (1995). Joan Judge (1996) analyzes the role of newspapers in national politics in the New Policies era.

45. S. C. Yang 1933/1934, 64–65.

46. First Historical Archives, Zhao Erxun materials, file no. 324.

47. Guo Moruo 1929.

48. Zhou Shanpei 1957.

49. Descriptions and analyses of the Railroad Protection movement may be found in Adshead 1984, Hedtke 1968, and Wei Yingtao 1990. Documents related to the movement and memoirs of participants and witnesses are collected in Dai Zhili 1959, Zhou Kaiqing 1964, Wei Yingtao and Zhao Qing 1981, and Guoshiguan shiliaochu 1981. For stimulating discussions of gentry interest in provincial autonomy, see Ichiko 1968 and Fincher 1968.

50. Wei Yingtao 1990, 618; Zhou Shanpei 1957, 10; Guo Moruo 1929.

51. The day-to-day events of the Railroad Protection movement in Chengdu are described in Wei Yingtao 1990, chap. 9; S. C. Yang 1933/1934; and "Events in Szchwan," in *West China Missionary News* 14, no. 1–2 (Jan.–Feb. 1912): 11–17. They are depicted with more detail and color in Guo Moruo 1929; and in Li Jieren's novel *The Great Wave*, which Li wrote in the 1930s based on his own memories of the events, as well as considerable research in documents collected at the time. Zhou Shanpei's critique of the first edition of *The Great Wave* is in Zhou 1938b. Li revised the novel, taking account of some of Zhou's objections, twenty years later. The fourth volume of the revised version was not complete when Li died in 1962, but the unfinished revised version of the novel was included in Li's *Complete Works*, published in the 1980s.

52. See the discussion of the march in Wei Yingtao 1990, 608–9; and Guo Moruo 1929.

53. Jin Huihai 1988, 160.

54. On this newspaper, see Wang Lüping and Cheng Qi 1993, 28–30. Many excerpts from it are included in the first volume of Wei Yingtao and Zhao Qing 1981. The announcement of the founding of the female association appears on pp. 240–42. The Muslim branches, and even a Banner branch, are mentioned in a memoir by Yang Kaijia in the same book (p. 385). See also Wei Yingtao 1990, 612–20.

55. Wei Yingtao 1990, 624–25.

56. Li Jieren has a detailed description of life in Chengdu during the strike in his novel *The Great Wave* (1980, pt. I, chap. 10), including a scene

in which a crowd tries to force sedan chair bearers to join the strike (a constable steps in to allow the bearers to continue on their way).

57. Guo Moruo 1929. See also Li Jieren, 1980, 380–83; and S. C. Yang 1933/1934, 71.

58. Wei Yingtao and Zhao Qing 1981, 365–75.

59. Zhou Shanpei 1957, 24–25.

60. The organization of relief agencies and special security patrols was announced in issues of *Chengdu ribao* and *Sichuan guanbao* throughout the late summer and fall of 1911.

61. Reproductions of several such cartoons that appeared in Fu Qiaocun's *Tongsu huabao* may be found in S. C. Yang 1933/1934.

62. Wei Yingtao 1990, 649–50; Guo Moruo 1929.

63. Li Jieren 1980, 559–62. Zhou Shanpei 1957, 38.

64. Wei Yingtao 1990, 650–63.

65. Ibid., 699–700.

66. Ibid., 706–9. Zhou Shanpei was instrumental in bringing about Zhao Erfeng's resignation. See Zhou 1938a, which gives a detailed account of the negotiations. Chengdu's flag-bedecked streets of this period are depicted in Li Jieren 1980, 1458.

67. Liu Xianzhi 1983, 37–38.

68. Li Jieren 1980, 1462–63; Guo Moruo 1929; *Wu Yu riji* 1: 22–23.

69. S. C. Yang 1933/1934, 82–83.

70. S. C. Yang 1933/1934; Guo Moruo 1929; Zhou Shanpei 1938a, 108.

71. Liu Xianzhi 1983, 38.

72. A Zhao Erfeng loyalist fired a shot at Yin from a shop on the Great East Street, but hit one of Yin's attendants. Yin is said to have rewarded the loyalist for his bravery and hired him as an adviser (Guo Moruo 1929).

Chapter 6

1. Adshead 1984, 103; Li Jieren 1980, 1482–86; *Wu Yu riji* 1984, 1: 12–19.

2. Wei Yingtao 1990, 714.

3. Stapleton 1993, 315. Adshead 1984, 110–11, cites Chongqing customs reports that large numbers of Shanxi banks closed in the wake of the revolution and that commercial investment from other provinces declined.

4. On the origins of the "warlord era" in China, see McCord 1993. Kapp 1973 surveys Sichuan's warlord politics.

5. An excellent account of the impact of militarism on Beijing may be found in Strand 1989, esp. chap. 9. Perhaps because of its status as the long-

time national capital, Beijing was spared the sort of street warfare that terrorized Chengdu several times between 1916 and 1937.

6. See Hewlett 1943, 125–28, on the treatment of defeated Yunnan troops in Chengdu in 1920, for example.

7. This theory would be difficult to document, but I think glimpses of such an emotional response to Chengdu's loss of political and economic centrality may be found in Wu Yu's diary, in which he occasionally refers condescendingly to moneygrubbing Chongqing.

8. On Chongqing's rise to provincial prominence, see McIsaac 1994.

9. Jin Huihai 1987, 98–99.

10. Guo Moruo 1929.

11. Jin Huihai 1987, 99.

12. S. C. Yang 1933/1934; Wu Guangjun 1985, 71.

13. Guo Moruo 1929. Guo also describes Yang Wei's attempts to discipline his boss, Yin Changheng, who was fond of drunken revelry and dallying with actors.

14. *Tongsu huabao*, Aug. 3, 1912.

15. Wei Yingtao 1990, 749–751.

16. Jin Huihai 1987. A telegram from Yang Wei in Beijing to Hu Jingyi thanking Hu for helping secure his release appears in the first issue of the provincial gazette established by Hu (*Sichuan zhengbao*, Nov. 20, 1913). This may represent an attempt by Hu to distance himself from Yang's attackers and testifies to Yang's positive reputation in Chengdu.

17. Jin Huihai 1987.

18. On the 1917 fighting, see *Sichuan junfa shiliao* 1981–88, 1: 103–51; *Wu Yu riji* 1984, 1: 301–6, 323–34; and Hewlett 1943, 94–110. The ins and outs of provincial politics may also be traced in Zhou Kaiqing 1974 and Kapp 1973.

19. Kapp 1973, 10.

20. Jin Huihai 1987.

21. *Guomin gongbao*, Apr. 28 and May 7, 1918.

22. One concrete sign that Zhang planned to refurbish the image of the police was his decision in the fall of 1919 to purchase 1,400 new winter uniforms (*Guomin gongbao*, Nov. 9, 1919).

23. Xiong Zhuoyun 1965, 106. Information on the city's population between 1916 and 1937 is scanty, but the official *Chengdushi shizheng nianjian* 1928 gives a figure of slightly more than 400,000 for the year 1924, which means that the population had increased by around 20 percent between 1911 and the mid-1920s.

24. *Sichuansheng neiwu tongji baogaoshu* 1920.

25. Pang Xiaoyi and Dai Wending 1988, 49–52.

26. *Sichuan dudufu zhengbao*, Aug. 25, 1912.

27. *Sichuan zhengbao*, Jan. 20, 1914.

28. Wei Yingtao 1990, 805; *Sichuan junfa shiliao* 1981–88, 1: 140.

29. *Minshi ribao*, June 21, 1922. On the background, training, and behavior of soldiers employed in warlord armies, see Lary 1985.

30. *Sichuansheng gexian difang zizhi shiye yu jingji zhuangkuang fenqi baogao* 1917, Chengdu county report.

31. Kapp 1973, chap. 3. On Sichuan's economy in the warlord era, see Gunde 1976, Myers 1967, and essays in each volume of the collection *Sichuan junfa shiliao* 1981–88.

32. Many newspapers were shut down in Chengdu by various militarists at various times. Li Jieren was arrested during one such incident. See Su Facheng 1985. On the relationship between Sichuan militarists and the newspaper industry in general, see Xiang Chunwu 1988.

33. An example of a set of very complicated regulations for the exchange of paper currency and copper coins, which constables were asked to enforce, may be found in *Sichuan zhengbao*, Nov. 20, 1913.

34. Gan Diankui 1983.

35. Shao Ying 1986, 55–59.

36. *Guomin gongbao*, Dec. 1919.

37. Very little information is available on the Chengdu Chamber of Commerce and merchant world in the period 1919–37. See, however, the discussion of Yu Fenggang's relationship with the militarist Yang Sen in the next chapter. My understanding of the Chengdu merchant community has benefited from discussions and correspondence with Mr. Jiang Mengbi, one of the compilers of an as-yet unpublished chronology of Chengdu's commercial history, a project of the Chengdu political consultative committee (Zhengxie).

38. Li Jieren 1986b, 112.

39. *West China Missionary News* 28, no. 3 (Mar. 1926): 16.

40. "Chengdu shangyechang" 1991, 23.

41. On Chongqing finance and trade, see *Liu Hangchen xiansheng fangwen jilu* 1990, chaps. 3 and 15.

42. Zhou Kaiqing 1974, 23.

43. The anti-Confucian scholar Wu Yu was one of the people who jumped at the opportunity to buy land in Chengdu, where real estate prices had been steadily climbing, as a result of New Policies construction. For a

fairly detailed description of how such land purchases were negotiated, see *Wu Yu riji* 1984, 1: 26–34.

44. Yang Bingde 1993, 344–48.

45. Li Jieren 1986b, 100.

46. Sichuansheng wenshiguan 1987, 421.

47. Beech 1933. On the history of mission architecture in China, see Cody 1996.

48. J. Ch'en 1979, 126*n*.

49. Street militia are mentioned frequently in *Guomin gongbao* and Wu Yu's diary; in the latter, see, for example, *Wu Yu riji* 1984, 1: 74; 2: 292. For a short story on street militia in the mid-1920s, see Li Jieren 1947b.

50. For a survey of scholarly studies of the Gelaohui, see Stapleton 1996.

51. The proclamations issued by Governor-General Ding Baozhen during his campaign against the Gelaohui in the 1870s may be found in Hou Shaoxuan and Yan Qiu 1981.

52. Cited in Wyman 1993, 99. On this point, see also Wyman 1997.

53. Zhong Maoxuan 1984, chap. 1.

54. The same was true in Guo Moruo's childhood village of Shawan, but Shawan, according to Guo (1929), was sharply divided into factions of "Sichuan natives" and relatively recent immigrant families. Possibly there were two or more Gelaohui organizations in many villages and towns.

55. Wang Di 1993, 548.

56. Zhou Xun 1987, 18.

57. Li Jieren 1947a, 8–9.

58. Li Mingxin 1981, 57–59.

59. One of the main characters of Li Jieren's novel *Sishui weilan* (Ripples across stagnant water), a Gelaohui activist in a town to the north of Chengdu, tells a story about how a Chengdu Gelaohui leader induced a prison guard to help a murderer escape (see pp. 74–79). Between the time Li Jieren wrote "Haorenjia" (1924) and the time he wrote *Sishui weilan* (the early 1930s) Li learned a lot about the Gelaohui. His four-year-old son was kidnapped by Gelaohui figures in 1931 and only returned to him after he had paid a substantial ransom and agreed to let the childless leader consider the boy his adopted son. Li's daughter recalls that this man often came to their house and told them about Gelaohui exploits (Li Mei 1990, 19–20).

60. Zhao Qing 1990, chaps. 6–8.

61. Shi Tiyuan 1981, 49.

62. Stapleton 1996.

63. Chen Zuwu n.d., 73.

64. S. C. Yang 1933/1934, 84 (romanization altered). The last line of this passage—"now quite familiar to the people"—is further evidence that the Gelaohui was not a significant factor in Chengdu community life before 1911.

65. Qin Nan, *Shu xin* (Bitter Sichuan), cited in Zhao Qing 1990, 62.

66. Zhao Qing 1990, 67–68. Documents produced during this episode may be found in Dai Zhili 1959, 525–31.

67. Stapleton 1996, 38.

68. Li Jieren 1947a, 10.

69. Hutson 1921.

70. Stapleton 1996, 29.

71. Shao Yun 1988, 62. The names of the lodges and their respective leaders are given in this article.

72. Skinner 1964/65.

73. Shao Yun 1988, 62.

74. Tang Shaowu et al. 1989.

75. This judgment is based on extensive reading of *Chengdu ribao* (1904–11), *Guomin gongbao* (1912–37), and *Minshi ribao* (1921–29).

76. Local newspapers such as the *Guomin gongbao* and the *Minshi ribao* frequently reported on the activities of street militia in the 1920s. A relatively detailed account published in the latter on Dec. 20, 1927, indicates that, at that time at any rate, street militia heads received their appointments from a provincial Militia Affairs Bureau, which exercised some supervision over them. The *Minshi ribao* launched an editorial campaign that year to try to persuade authorities not to allow street militia to collect fees from residents of their districts in order to buy guns and other equipment. The paper referred to militia heads insultingly as *tuanfa*—militia lords—a play on the term *junfa* (warlord). See *Minshi ribao*, Dec. 22, 1927.

77. Cited in Zheng Ping 1992, 24. Zheng does not give the date of this document, but the Social Affairs Bureau documents in the provincial archives date from the 1930s and 1940s, and the great majority of the records available in the archives are from the period between 1935 and 1949.

78. Studies of the Gelaohui in the Republican period have little to say about disputes among the gowned brothers. See Zhao Qing 1990, for example. But this is clearly a topic that awaits careful research.

79. For accounts of the Gelaohui's role in the post-1911 Chengdu police, see Xiong Zhuoyun 1965 and Pang Xiaoyi and Dai Wending 1988.

80. Pang Xiaoyi and Dai Wending 1988, 49–52.

81. Xiong Zhuoyun 1984.

82. Zhao Qing 1990 and Treudley 1971 discuss the finances and activities of Gelaohui lodges, but neither these nor any other studies of the Gelaohui available are able to provide much detail on these points. The account in Zhong Maoxuan 1984 of the life of Liu Shiliang suggests that Chengdu merchants were active lodge members; see esp. chap. 5.

83. For an initial comparison of the economic clout of Chengdu's Gelaohui to that of Shanghai's Green Gang, see Stapleton 1996. There were periodic strikes among silk weavers and other workers in the years between 1911 and 1937, but Chengdu's labor history has not yet been extensively explored. For a detailed and fascinating history of the political activism of Beijing rickshaw pullers, see Strand 1989.

84. *Liu Hangchen xiansheng fangwen jilu* 1990, 133–40.

85. Xiong Zhuoyun 1965; Zhong Qiming 1990.

86. For interesting discussions of class issues and their relation to urban culture, as well as the difficulties inherent in historical and cross-cultural study of prostitution, see Taylor 1991, pt. IV; and Hershatter 1997.

87. Chengdu in the 1920s is represented in fiction from the point of view of New Culture activists in Ba Jin's (Pa Chin's) *Family* and Mao Dun's *Rainbow*. On Liu Shiliang, see Stapleton 1995.

88. This reputation was largely the result of publicity over the Shu Xincheng case (see Stapleton 1998), but also owed something to the writings of Wu Yu and the novels by Ba Jin and Mao Dun mentioned in the previous note.

89. Another example is Hu Shi's friend, Ren Hongjuan, a Sichuan native who contemplated establishing a business in Sichuan in the early 1920s, but was forced to return to Shanghai, partly because the outspokenness of his wife, Chen Hengzhe, did not please local notables in Chongqing and Chengdu. Chen had made some public comments about the backwardness of Sichuan and the "barbaric civil wars" fomented by the men she called Sichuan's "robber-barons." See *Hu Shi laiwang shuxin xuan* 1983, 1: 147–66.

90. *Guomin gongbao*, Apr. 22, 1912.

91. *Wu Yu riji* 1984, 1: 66.

92. Wu Yu made the case public in 1910 when he was editor of *Shubao*, and both his father and he himself appealed for judgment to many provincial authorities between 1910 and 1912, including the leaders of the Comrades' Armies. Wu Yu's father died in 1912, effectively settling the case, but without resolving the question of the justice of Wu Yu's position, which is still a sensitive matter in Chengdu. See *Wu Yu riji* 1984 and Tao Liangsheng, n.d., for two sides of the debate. Li Jieren's *Dabo* treats the case very

diplomatically, in characteristic Li Jieren fashion, but is much more sympathetic to Wu Yu than the account written by Tao Liangsheng, who was Li's contemporary. Li Jieren was a friend and colleague of Wu Yu, and Tao Liangsheng was Xu Zixiu's student (and Han Suyin's uncle by marriage).

93. See *Wu Yu riji* 1984.

94. Wu Yuzhang 1985. Wu was more influential as a Communist labor organizer in Chongqing later in the 1920s and in the 1930s. After 1949, he became the first president of People's University in Beijing.

95. Kapp 1973.

96. Stapleton 1996.

97. Kapp 1973 (pp. 11–21) calls these men the "first generation of republican militarists." Men such as Liu Xiang and Yang Sen, who came to prominence in the 1920s and whom Kapp argues were much more focused on provincial rather than national affairs, are the second generation. Yin Changheng was among the many prominent members of the first generation who turned to Buddhist devotions and patronized temples in Chengdu.

98. *Wu Yu riji* 1984, vol. 1.

99. Guo Moruo 1929.

100. The May Fourth incident occurred in Beijing in 1919, when protests erupted over the decision of Versailles peace negotiators to award Germany's interests in Chinese territory to Japan. In the May Thirtieth incident of 1925, police in the foreign-run International Settlement shot demonstrators protesting the treatment of workers in a Japanese-owned factory in the city. On September 5, 1926, a British gunboat fired on the Sichuan city of Wanxian after forces headquartered there prevented foreign vessels from leaving port because their sister ship was accused of capsizing native boats. All three incidents inspired antiforeign demonstrations in cities throughout China.

101. Shu Xincheng 1934, 134–35.

102. *Wu Yu riji* 1984 1: 24.

103. Shu Xincheng 1934, 157–58.

104. See Chapter 7 for more on the philanthropic activities of the Elders and Sages.

105. Xu Zixiu's status as a symbol of traditional learning helped make him the main target of cultural radicals in the city, such as Wu Yu, whose diary is full of passionate comments about "that hypocrite" Xu Zixiu. Wu Yu also had a personal reason for disliking Xu, since Xu had been the leader of the movement to condemn Wu Yu for his "unfilial" treatment of his father. In spite of his rejection of neo-Confucianism, however, Wu Yu and

other New Culture advocates in the city had considerable respect for some of the Elders and Sages. One, Liu Yubo, was a close relative of Wu Yu and had tried his best to mediate between Wu Yu and his father, whom many Chengdu elites privately acknowledged to be irresponsible and unbalanced. The best source on the Elders and Sages is a manuscript by Tao Liangsheng, but scattered information on them may be found in almost all works that touch on Chengdu society in the Republican period. For a detailed, but semi-fictionalized, account of them, see Zhong Maoxuan 1984.

106. Hewlett 1943, 96.

107. The agent for Standard Oil was arrested and held in prison for several weeks in 1918, but released after Consul General Hewlett negotiated on his behalf, at the request of the United States consul in Chongqing (Hewlett 1943, 118–20). On the Japanese in Chengdu in general, see Hewlett 1943, 138, and for more details on the 1936 "Great Sichuan Hotel incident," in which two Japanese journalists were killed, see Coble 1991, 316–19.

108. *West China Missionary News* 27, nos. 8–9 (Aug.–Sept. 1925): 32.

109. *West China Missionary News* 28 (1926).

110. On relations between militarists and the foreigners in Chengdu, see Hewlett 1943, Bodard 1975, Service 1989 (esp. chap. 28), and *West China Missionary News* 28, no. 12 (Dec. 1926): 11–15. Hewlett puts himself at the very center of the action when he describes how he mediated between the Yunnan and Sichuan armies during the 1917 fighting, explaining how all the Yunnan authorities "poured their hearts out" to him in order to seek emotional relief and followed his advice on how to settle the fighting (pp. 94–109).

111. Hewlett 1943, 91, 122–23, 136–38.

112. Kapp 1973 and Hewlett 1943.

113. The early history of the Chengdu YMCA is described in the memoirs of Grace Service, wife of one of its founding secretaries. See Service 1989.

114. Guo Moruo 1929.

115. West China Union University's 1926 troubles may be followed in issues of *Guomin gongbao* from that year, as well as in *West China Missionary News* 28, no. 12 (Dec. 1926): 11–15. Shu Xincheng (1934, 165–68) discusses the question of public access to the campus.

116. *Guomin gongbao*, Apr. 9, 1918.

117. *West China Missionary News* 22, no. 8 (Aug. 1920): 39.

118. *Wu Yu riji* 1984, 1: 83, 88.

119. Ibid., 1: 162–64.

120. Ibid., 1: 246. Wu Yu also turned to the missionaries for help in sending money to Shanghai safely during the fighting in 1917 (see ibid., 1: 280).

121. On this issue, see Stapleton 1998.

Chapter 7

1. For a chronology of Republican Sichuan's complicated military history, see Zhou Kaiqing 1972a and 1974 and Kapp 1973.

2. A dramatic account of Yang Sen's arrival in Chengdu is found in "Shengcheng bimen wuri ji" (Record of five days when the provincial capital gates were closed), *Guomin gongbao*, Feb. 12, 1924.

3. Some of these groups published periodicals. An example is *Xin Sichuan* (New Sichuan), published in Nanjing by the propaganda department of the Comrades' Association of Nationalist Party Sichuanese Sojourning in the Capital (Zhongguo Guomindang Sichuan lüjing tongzhihui). This publication is replete with detailed accounts of the brutality and treachery of all Sichuanese holders of power.

4. *Wu Yu riji* 1984, 2: 232.

5. Fan Puzhai 1985, 486.

6. *Guomin gongbao*, May 3, 1924.

7. Tao Liangsheng n.d.

8. For biographical details, see Ma Xuanwei and Xiao Bo 1989 and "Yang Sen xiansheng fangwen jilu" 1963.

9. *Guomin gongbao*, Jan. 1, and Feb. 28, 1920. Coverage of each subsequent year's fair generally included speeches delivered by provincial authorities, remarking on the importance of the event.

10. Shu Xincheng 1934, 223.

11. *Guomin gongbao*, Apr. 14, May 2, and Sept. 16, 1924; *West China Missionary News* 26, no. 9 (Oct. 1924): 31–32. On James Yen and his literacy movement, see Hayford 1990.

12. Gu Yuanzhong 1989.

13. Han Lei 1985, 32.

14. Ma Xuanwei and Xiao Bo 1989, 41.

15. As noted in Chapter 5, the late Qing provincial assembly had proposed establishing an institution called a *tongsu jiaoyushe*, and so it seems clear that Lu Zuofu's institute had a Chengdu precedent. As far as I know, though, the *jiaoyushe* never existed.

16. Lu Guoji 1984, 47–52.

17. Shu Xincheng 1934, 174.

18. On elite attitudes toward folk religion in the Republican period, see Duara 1991. The number of those who, like Lu Zuofu and Yang Sen, defied and attacked "superstition" in Chengdu seems to have been relatively small, perhaps due to the strength of Gelaohui organizations.

19. *West China Missionary News* 27, no. 6 (June 1925): 36.

20. "Yang Sen xiansheng fangwen jilu" 1963, interview no. 8. Meyrick Hewlett, British consul general in Chengdu from 1916 to 1922, claims that the stela placed in the museum by Yang Sen was a fake. Hewlett himself may have given Yang Sen's coterie the idea to display the stela. In his memoirs, Hewlett (1943, 116–18) notes that in 1918 he had tried to persuade one of Yang Sen's predecessors to give him the real stela so that he could donate it to the British Museum.

21. *Minshi ribao*, Oct. 17, 1924.

22. Shu Xincheng 1934, 169–73 and 219–21.

23. Both *Guomin gongbao* and *Minshi ribao* reported extensively on the plans for the road-building campaign in April and May 1924.

24. Jiang Mengbi 1991.

25. Wu Yu, teaching in Beijing, learned about the new rickshaws in Chengdu from a friend's letter. See *Wu Yu riji* 1984, 2: 232.

26. Xian Ning 1980, 5–6.

27. *Guomin gongbao*, Apr. 15 and 16, 1924.

28. Luo Cairong 1979, 436.

29. "Yang Sen xiansheng fangwen jilu" 1963, interview no. 6.

30. Ma Xuanwei and Xiao Bo 1989, 41. A list of "Yang Sen says" proclamations may also be found on this page. See also Yang Sen 1979, 107.

31. Shu Xincheng 1934, 220.

32. "Yang Sen xiansheng fangwen jilu" 1963, interview no. 8.

33. Luo Cairong 1979, 439.

34. This institution and its activities are described in M. Shi 1993.

35. See Tsin 1999.

36. Lu Danlin, "Xu" (Preface), in Lu Danlin 1928.

37. This summary of the record of accomplishments of Chengdu's new-style city managers was published in *Guomin gongbao* on Nov. 18, 1923, well before Yang Sen arrived in the city. The work of the city government office is also described in an article in *Minshi ribao* on July 9, 1922.

38. *Minshi ribao*, July 19, 1922.

39. Zhang Jian's Nantong, which was an important model of urban administration for older conservative elites in the late 1910s and early 1920s, is described in Köll 1997 and Q. Shao 1994.

40. On the influence of American engineers and planners in establishing these professions in Republican China, see Cody 1996.

41. *Guomin gongbao*, Mar. 1, 1924.

42. Lu Danlin 1928 and 1930.

43. Breasted 1935. This statement is echoed in an American observer's comment on changes in Chinese cities in the 1930s: "Wide streets take the place of narrow, ill-smelling crooked alleys. . . . All the mechanical gadgets of our civilization have been taken over and put to work . . . the Chinese are able successfully to function as a modern corporate society" (Frank B. Lenz, "Take a Look at China," in *Brooklyn Central* [New York: YMCA, n.d.], cited in Garrett 1974, 213).

44. Agrest 1996, 58–59.

45. Q. Shao 1994, 161–62.

46. Ibid., 55–62.

47. On Wu Shan, see the brief biography by Lu Danlin (1967), the chief editor of the *Complete Book of City Administration*. According to this account, Wu Shan was trained in law and administration in Japan in the early Republican era and then joined Sun Yat-sen's staff in Guangzhou. Although he had no expertise in engineering or public works, he was recruited by C. T. Wang (Wang Zhengting), Chinese founder of the Road-Building Association and leader of the Chinese YMCA, to replace the foreigners directing the Road-Building Association in 1921. In 1928–29, he oversaw road construction in Henan and areas of the northwest and was criticized for destroying historic structures when he had a road built through the Hangu Pass.

48. Dong Xiujia 1927, 1–4. For a survey and analysis of a range of ideas about cities among Chinese of this era that gives prominence to antagonistic views, see Mann 1984, 86–107.

49. My knowledge of the career of Chen Weixin is based on his speeches, recorded in the *Guomin gongbao*, and interviews with Ren Zili, former director of the Chengdu YMCA, in Chengdu in 1991.

50. *Guomin gongbao*, Apr. 2–10, 1924.

51. *Guomin gongbao*, May 25, 1924.

52. Garrett 1974, 231–32.

53. Ma Yanhu 1989.

NOTES TO PAGES 236–40 301

54. Yang Sen's emphasis on clean living could be selective. Opium addiction among Chengdu residents, which probably contributed substantially to his income, was not something he brought up in his public lectures. This may have been due to his dependence on Gelaohui leaders to maintain order in Chengdu.

55. "Women Who Work," in *West China Missionary News* 27, no. 5 (May 1925): 7–13 (romanization altered).

56. *Guomin gongbao*, Mar. 3, 1924.

57. The Chengdu city government yearbook from 1928 (the only one published in the Republican era) cites the May Fourth movement as the inspiration for many patriotic demonstrations, but states that the only way to establish real national strength is to spread literacy, to make citizens out of the masses of people (*Chengdushi shizheng nianjian* 1928, 357).

58. "Yang Sen xiansheng fangwen jilu" 1963, interview no. 2.

59. *Guomin gongbao*, Feb. 14, 1924.

60. Ma Xuanwei and Xiao Bo (1989, 35) cite, for example, the case of Hu Lanjia, a teacher from Luzhou with leftist leanings. When Yang Sen's fourth wife was sent to invite her to join the family, she replied that the daughters of prominent leaders of the Gelaohui did not become people's concubines. The prominent and promiscuous warlord in Mao Dun's novel *Rainbow* is clearly modeled on Yang Sen in his Luzhou days. Mei, the novel's central character, may resemble Hu Lanjia, but Mei was a native of Chengdu. She seems to have borrowed many of her personality traits from Qin and Juehui, the elite young heroine and hero, respectively, of Ba Jin's (Pa Chin's) *Family*.

61. Shu Xincheng 1934, 149–53. Li Jieren studied literature in France and, like Sun Shaojing, returned to Chengdu in 1924. Unlike Sun, however, he kept out of all city administration projects until he became vice-mayor of Chengdu in the 1950s. In the late 1920s he edited newspapers and helped set up a paper factory south of Chengdu. In the 1930s he worked in some of Lu Zuofu's enterprises.

62. On the Dacheng Association, see the *Dachenghui conglu*.

63. Ibid., no. 3 (July 1923).

64. Wang Liankui 1979, 441. See also Ma Xuanwei and Xiao Bo 1989, 38–39.

65. Jiang Mengbi 1991.

66. Franck 1925, 547. Franck spent a month in Chengdu and met with Yang Sen several times.

67. Sichuan's industry was still primarily small-scale. The money that supported Sichuan's armies came primarily from the land tax, often levied years in advance, taxes on the salt produced in the Ziliujing area, sales of opium, and control over shipping on the Yangzi and commerce in Chongqing. See Kapp 1973, 40–43; and Zhou Kaiqing 1972b.

68. Jiang Mengbi 1991; Stapleton 1998.

69. Tang Juecong 1991.

70. Letter from Ye Maoru, *Minshi ribao*, Mar. 17, 1927. Ye recommended that a committee structure be adopted with 20 or 30 representatives, each selected by groups of two or three guilds. He cited Sun Yat-sen as the proponent of this sort of arrangement.

71. Jiang Mengbi 1991, 6. The YMCA also gave up a section of its property but was reimbursed.

72. Such activities in Chengdu are the focus of Ba Jin's autobiographical novel *Family*.

73. *Chengdushi shizheng nianjian* 1928.

74. "Chinese Forms of Politeness," *West China Missionary News* 28, no. 3 (Mar. 1926): 33.

75. In 1923 the city government office drew up regulations that set out guidelines for what it hoped would be a close relationship between street headmen and the city officials; see *Chengdushi shizheng nianjian* 1928, 5. Because of the frequent regime changes, which affected city recordkeeping as well as city institutions, it is difficult to assess the effectiveness of these regulations.

76. "Yang Sen xiansheng fangwen jilu" 1963, interview no. 2.

77. On the involvement of Gelaohui lodges in Chengdu with the commerce in opium, see Shao Yun 1988, 61. Their involvement in prostitution in Chengdu is not discussed in any published accounts, but seems likely. Organized gambling was another major source of income for lodges, according to Shao Yun. Yang Sen's attacks on gambling seem to have been limited to that done in public.

78. United States Archives, Chongqing Consular correspondence, letter from John R. Muir to United States Consul-General in Chongqing, May 22, 1924.

79. *Guomin gongbao*, Sept. 16, 1924.

80. Ibid., Apr. 16, 1924.

81. Yang Wanyun 1979, 421. Yang Sen was close to all of his 28 children, she emphatically declared, noting that the children were the offspring of

eight wives. Like Yang Sen himself, though, she avoided the question of exactly how many wives he had had in his life.

82. The life of Liu Shiliang is described in Zhong Maoxuan 1984. Many of Liu's verses may be found in Lin Kongyi 1982.

83. Zhong Maoxuan 1984, 33–34.

84. Ibid., 89.

85. Luo Cairong 1979.

86. Lu Guoji 1984, 35; Franck 1925, 558.

87. Shu Xincheng 1934, 131–32.

88. *Wu Yu riji* 1984, 2: 240.

89. Lin Kongyi 1982, 106.

90. *Chengdushi shizheng nianjian* 1928, 7.

91. Ibid., 5. The use of the name "Chengdu" in this text may have grated on the aesthetic sensibilities of the Elders and Sages, since the city was usually referred to as "Furongcheng" (Hibiscus City) or the poetic abbreviation "Rong" in writings in classical Chinese.

92. *Chengdushi shizheng zhoukan*, no. 4 (Aug. 6, 1927). Even in Yang Sen's time, the desirability of openness in administration was recognized by some. Several of Yang Sen's advisers, including Sun Shaojing and Lu Zuofu, joined with newspaper reporters to form a "Friday inspection team" (*xingqiwu canguantuan*) that announced its intention to make regular visits to governmental and nongovernmental institutions and report on what it saw, while making suggestions for improvement (*Guomin gongbao*, Apr. 27, 1924).

93. *Chengdushi shizheng zhoukan*, no. 1 (July 16, 1927).

94. An essay on Chengdu's need for a water supply system urged the city to learn from the failures of Tianjin, Beijing, and Guangzhou and set out regulations for a committee that would oversee preparations; a new system was not set up until 1946, however. See *Chengdushi shizheng zhoukan*, no. 4 (Aug. 6, 1927).

95. Kapp 1973.

96. On administration of the Chengdu police in Liu Xiang's time, see *Sichuan shenghui gonganju gongzuo baogao* 1934.

97. Wang Zongli 1986. Wang claims that Yu personally directed the attack on a British gunboat during the 1926 Wanxian incident, which destroyed whatever reputation for good government Yang Sen may have had before then among British diplomats such as Meyrick Hewlett.

98. *Sichuan shenghui gonganju gongzuo baogao* 1934.

99. Wakeman 1991, 93. See also MacKinnon 1983.

100. Wang Zongli (1986) claims that Yu Yuan joined the Communist party in 1927, but also that he was introduced to Liu Xiang's employ by Zhang Lan, who was well acquainted with Chengdu's Elders and Sages, because he was the vice chairman of the Railroad Stockholders Association in 1911 and president of Chengdu University in 1926. Zhang Lan was a friend to some of the early Communists in Sichuan, such as Wu Yuzhang, but he was also close to a wide range of other Sichuan elites, including Zhou Shanpei. In the early years of the New Policies era, before he came to Chengdu, he was director of the elementary school Yang Sen attended.

101. See Chapter 3.

102. Interview with Anne Chou, Zuoying, Sept. 1992.

Chapter 8

1. The most comprehensive source on Shanghai's modernization is Zhang Zhongli 1990. On Beijing, see M. Shi 1993; on Ji'nan, Buck 1978; on Tianjin, Rogaski 1999.

2. Sheehan 1999.

3. The debate over the development of "civil society" in China is the topic of a special issue of *Modern China* (19, no. 2 [1993]).

4. M. Shi 1993, 396–400.

5. Strand 1989, chaps. 8, 11.

6. Within the regions surrounding such cities as Shanghai and Guangzhou, however, change occurred at many different rates, as R. Keith Schoppa (1982) has shown.

7. Tsin 1999.

8. Coleman 1984, 110.

9. Goodman 1995.

10. Elvin 1974.

11. Wakeman 1995, 9.

12. An extensive collection of documents on Shanghai's experience with local self-government was published in 1915. Elvin 1974 makes use of this collection to analyze the history of Shanghai's first city council.

13. Henriot 1993, chaps. 7–9.

WORKS CITED

Adshead, S. A. M. 1984. *Province and Politics in Late Imperial China: Vice-regal Government in Szechwan, 1898–1911*. London: Curzon Press.

Agrest, Diana. 1996. "The Return of the Repressed: Nature." In *The Sex of Architecture*, ed. Diana Agrest, Patricia Conway, and Leslie Kanes Weisman, 49–68. New York: Harry N. Abrams.

Bastid, Marianne. 1988. *Educational Reform in Early Twentieth-Century China*. Trans. Paul J. Bailey. Ann Arbor: Center for Chinese Studies, University of Michigan.

Bayley, David H. 1985. *Patterns of Policing: A Comparative International Analysis*. New Brunswick, N.J.: Rutgers University Press.

Bays, Daniel H. 1978. *China Enters the Twentieth Century*. Ann Arbor: University of Michigan Press.

Beech, J. 1933. "University Beginnings: A Story of the West China Union University." *Journal of the West China Border Research Society* 6: 91–104.

Benton, Gregor. 1992. *Mountain Fires: The Red Army's Three-Year War in South China, 1934–1938*. Berkeley: University of California Press.

Bodard, Lucien. 1975. *Le Fils du Consul*. Paris: B. Grasset.

Breasted, James Henry. 1935. *Ancient Times: A History of the Early World*. 2nd ed. Boston: Ginn.

Buck, David D. 1978. *Urban Change in China: Politics and Development in Tsinan, Shantung, 1890–1949*. Madison: University of Wisconsin Press.

Cameron, Meribeth E. 1931. *The Reform Movement in China, 1898–1912*. Stanford: Stanford University Press.

Chang, Hao. 1971. *Liang Ch'i-ch'ao and Intellectual Transition in China, 1890–1907*. Cambridge, Mass.: Harvard University Press.

————. 1980. "Intellectual Change and the Reform Movement, 1890–8." In *The Cambridge History of China*, vol. II, *Late Ch'ing, 1800–1911*, pt. II, ed. John K. Fairbank and Kwang-ching Liu, 274–338. Cambridge, Eng.: Cambridge University Press.

Chang P'eng-yüan. 1968. "The Constitutionalists." In *China in Revolution: The First Phase, 1900–1913*, ed. Mary Clabaugh Wright, 143–83. New Haven: Yale University Press.

Chen Daoxin. 1987. "WanQing Chengdu jingcha shilue" (A brief history of Chengdu's police in the late Qing). *Chengduzhi tongxun*, no. 4: 7–14.

Ch'en, Jerome. 1972. *Yuan Shih-k'ai.* 2nd ed. Stanford: Stanford University Press.

————. 1979. *China and the West: Society and Culture, 1815–1937.* Bloomington: Indiana University Press.

Chen Shaobo. 1962. "Tongmenghui zai Sichuan de jici wuzhuang qiyi" (Several armed uprisings of the Revolutionary Alliance in Sichuan). In *Xinhai geming huiyilu* (Memoirs of the 1911 Revolution), ed. Zhongguo renmin xieshang huiyi, 3: 117–24. Beijing: Zhonghua shuju.

Chen Yan. 1977. "Zhou Shanpei yu Zhou Zhaoxiang" (Zhou Shanpei and Zhou Zhaoxiang). *Zhongwai zazhi* 21, no. 2: 50–55.

Chen Zuwu. n.d. "Xuanhe yishi de fengyun renwu Yin Changheng" (Yin Changheng: one-time notorious man-of-the-hour). *Wenshi ziliao xuanji* 77: 59–76.

Chengdu ribao (Chengdu daily). Published by the Sichuan Official Gazette Bureau from the fall of 1904 to the fall of 1911. Nonoverlapping runs of this paper are preserved in the Sichuan Provincial Library, the Shanghai Municipal Library, and the Tōyō Bunko in Tokyo.

Chengdu shangbao (Chengdu commercial news). Published by the Chengdu Chamber of Commerce in 1910 and 1911.

"Chengdu shangyechang" (Chengdu's commercial arcade). 1991. *Jinjiang wenshi ziliao* 1: 14–26.

Chengdushi shizheng nianjian (Yearbook of Chengdu city government). 1928. Chengdu: Chengdu shizheng gongsuo.

Chengdushi shizheng zhoukan (Chengdu city government weekly). 1927–28. Chengdu: Chengdu shizheng gongsuo. In 1928, the name was changed to *Chengdushi shizheng gongbao* (Chengdu city government gazette), and it became a monthly.

Ch'ien Tuan-sheng. 1950. *The Government and Politics of China.* Cambridge, Mass.: Harvard University Press.

Chongqing Prefect. Ca. 1909. Report on the charges against the Dazu county magistrate. First Historical Archives, Zhao Erxun materials, file no. 335.

Chongxiu Chengduxian zhi (Revised gazetteer of Chengdu county). 1971. Reprinted—Taibei: Taiwan xuesheng shuju. Originally published in Chengdu in 1873.

Ch'ü T'ung-tsu. 1962. *Local Government in China Under the Ch'ing.* Cambridge, Mass.: Harvard University Press.

Coble, Parks M. 1991. *Facing Japan: Chinese Politics and Japanese Imperialism, 1931–1937.* Cambridge, Mass.: Council on East Asian Studies, Harvard University.

Cody, Jeffrey W. 1996. "Striking a Harmonious Chord: Foreign Missionaries and Chinese-Style Buildings, 1911–1949." *Architectronic* 5, no. 3 (December). http://www.saed.kent.edu/Architronic/

Cohen, Paul A. 1974. *Between Tradition and Modernity: Wang T'ao and Reform in Late Ch'ing China.* Cambridge, Mass.: Harvard University Press.

Cole, James H. 1986. *Shaohsing: Competition and Cooperation in Nineteenth-Century China.* Tucson: University of Arizona Press for the Association for Asian Studies.

Coleman, Maryruth. 1984. "Municipal Politics in Nationalist China: Nanjing, 1927–1937." Ph.D. diss., Harvard University.

Crossley, Pamela Kyle. 1990. *Orphan Warriors: Three Manchu Generations and the End of the Qing World.* Princeton: Princeton University Press.

Cunningham, Alfred. 1895. *A History of the Szechuen Riots (May–June, 1895).* Shanghai: "Shanghai Mercury" Office.

Dachenghui conglu (Dacheng Association recorder). 1922–25. Chengdu.

Dai Deyuan. 1990. "Xiqu gailiang yu Sanqinghui" (Opera reform and the Sanqing society). *Sichuan xiju*, no. 5: 39–42.

Dai Hongying. 1985. *Jiu Zhongguo zhian fagui xuanbian* (Selected public security laws and regulations from Old China). Beijing: Qunzhong chubanshe.

Dai Zhili. 1959. *Sichuan baolu yundong shiliao* (Historical materials on Sichuan's Railroad Protection movement). Beijing: Kexue chubanshe.

Davidson, Robert J., and Isaac Mason. 1905. *Life in West China.* London: Headley Brothers.

Des Forges, Roger V. 1973. *Hsi-liang and the Chinese National Revolution.* New Haven: Yale University Press.

Dikötter, Frank. 1992. *The Discourse of Race in Modern China.* Stanford: Stanford University Press.

Dong Xiujia. 1927. *Shizhengxue gangyao* (Outline of the study of city administration). Shanghai: Shangwu yinshuguan.

Dray-Novey, Alison. 1981. "Policing Imperial Peking: The Ch'ing Gendarmerie, 1650–1850." Ph.D. diss., Harvard University.

———. 1993. "Spatial Order and Police in Imperial Beijing." *Journal of Asian Studies* 52, no. 4 (Nov.): 885–922.

Duara, Prasenjit. 1988. *Culture, Power, and the State: Rural North China, 1900–1942*. Stanford: Stanford University Press.

———. 1991. "Knowledge and Power in the Discourse of Modernity: The Campaigns Against Popular Religion in Early Twentieth-Century China." *Journal of Asian Studies* 50, no. 1 (Feb.): 67–83.

Elvin, Mark. 1974. "The Administration of Shanghai." In *The Chinese City Between Two Worlds*, ed. Mark Elvin and G. William Skinner, 239–62. Stanford: Stanford University Press.

Entenmann, Robert Eric. 1982. "Migration and Settlement in Sichuan, 1644–1769." Ph.D. diss., Harvard University.

Esherick, Joseph W. 1976. *Reform and Revolution in China: The 1911 Revolution in Hunan and Hubei*. Berkeley: University of California Press.

———. 1987. *The Origins of the Boxer Uprising*. Berkeley: University of California Press.

Fan Puzhai. 1985. "Wu Youling xiansheng shilue" (Brief account of Mr. Wu Youling). In *Wu Yu ji* (Wu Yu's collected works), ed. Zhao Qing and Zheng Cheng, 483–88. Chengdu: Sichuan renmin chubanshe.

Feuchtwang, Stephan. 1977. "School-Temple and City God." In *The City in Late Imperial China*, ed. G. William Skinner, 581–608. Stanford: Stanford University Press.

Fincher, John. 1968. "Political Provincialism and the National Revolution." In *China in Revolution: The First Phase, 1900–1913*, ed. Mary Clabaugh Wright, 185–226. New Haven: Yale University Press.

Franck, Harry A. 1925. *Roving Through Southern China*. New York: Century.

Fu Chongju (Qiaocun). 1987. *Chengdu tonglan* (A comprehensive guide to Chengdu). 2 vols. Chengdu: Bashu chubanshe. Originally published in Chengdu in eight volumes, 1909–11.

Gan Diankui. 1983. "Qingmo zhi Minguo junfa geju shiqi Sichuan jinrong wenluan qingkuang" (Sichuan's chaotic monetary system from the late Qing to the warlord-partition era during the Republic). *Sichuan junfa shiliao* (Materials on Sichuan warlords) 2: 501–20.

Gao Chengxiang. 1990. "Fu Qiaocun." In *Sichuan jinxiandai renwu zhuan* (Biographies from modern and contemporary Sichuan), ed. Ren Yimin, 6: 483–86. Chengdu: Sichuan daxue chubanshe.

Gao Zengjue. 1910. Report of the Sichuan police superintendent on accomplishments made from the time he took office in GX34.10 to XT2.2. Dated XT2.3.25. First Historical Archives, Interior Ministry materials, file no. 312.

Garrett, Shirley S. 1974. "The Chambers of Commerce and the YMCA." In *The Chinese City Between Two Worlds*, ed. Mark Elvin and G. William Skinner, 213–38. Stanford: Stanford University Press.

Gaubatz, Piper Rae. 1996. *Beyond the Great Wall: Urban Form and Transformation on the Chinese Frontiers*. Stanford: Stanford University Press.

Geil, William Edgar. 1911. *Eighteen Capitals of China*. London: Constable.

Gluck, Carol. 1985. *Japan's Modern Myths: Ideology in the Late Meiji Period*. Princeton: Princeton University Press.

Goodman, Bryna. 1995. *Native Place, City, and Nation: Regional Networks and Identities in Shanghai, 1853–1937*. Berkeley: University of California Press.

Grainger, A. 1918. "Street-Preaching, etc." *West China Missionary News* 20, no. 3 (Mar.): 5–13.

Gu Yuanzhong. 1989. "Chengdu gongyuan shihua" (History of Chengdu's public parks). *Sichuan wenwu*, no. 2: 73–75.

Gunde, Richard. 1976. "Land Tax and Social Change in Sichuan, 1925–1935." *Modern China* 2, no. 1: 23–48.

Guo Moruo. 1929. *Fanzheng qianhou* (Before and after the revolution). Shanghai: Xiandai shuju.

Guomin gongbao (Citizen's gazette). 1912–35. Chengdu.

Guoshiguan shiliaochu, ed. 1981. *Xinhainian Sichuan baolu yundong shiliao huibian* (Collected historical materials on the 1911 Sichuan Railroad Protection movement). 2 vols. Taibei: Guoshiguan.

Han Lei. 1985. "Jindai tiyu zai Chengdu de chuqi chuanbo" (The early period in the spread of modern physical education to Chengdu). *Chengduzhi tongxun*, no. 5: 28–33.

Han Suyin. 1965. *The Crippled Tree*. New York: G. P. Putnam's Sons.

Hartwell, George E. 1921. "Reminiscences of Chengtu." *West China Missionary News* 23, nos. 8–9 (Aug.–Sept.): 5–27.

————. 1939. *Granary of Heaven.* Toronto: United Church of Canada, Committee on Missionary Education, and United Church of Canada, Woman's Missionary Society, Literature Department.

Hayford, Charles W. 1990. *To the People: James Yen and Village China.* New York: Columbia University Press.

He Yili. 1987. "Liao Guanyin, Zeng Ayi." In *Sichuan jinxiandai renwu zhuan* (Biographies from modern and contemporary Sichuan), ed. Ren Yimin, 4: 47–52. Chengdu: Sichuan daxue chubanshe.

He Yimin. 1989. "Lun Qingdai Chengdu de chongjian yu jindaihua" (On the rebuilding and modernization of Chengdu during the Qing dynasty). In *Chengdu chengshi yanjiu* (Research on urban Chengdu), ed. Guo Furen et al., 591–610. Chengdu: Sichuan daxue chubanshe.

Hedtke, Charles. 1968. "Reluctant Revolutionaries: Szechwan and the Ch'ing Collapse, 1898–1911." Ph.D. diss., University of California, Berkeley.

Henriot, Christian. 1993. *Shanghai, 1927–1937: Municipal Power, Locality, and Modernization.* Trans. Noël Castelino. Berkeley: University of California Press.

Hershatter, Gail. 1997. *Dangerous Pleasures: Prostitution and Modernity in Twentieth-Century Shanghai.* Berkeley: University of California Press.

Hewlett, Meyrick. 1943. *Forty Years in China.* London: Macmillan.

Hickey, Paul C. 1990. "Bureaucratic Centralization and Public Finance in Late Qing China, 1900–1911." Ph.D. diss., Harvard University.

————. 1991. "Fee-Taking, Salary Reform, and the Structure of State Power in Late Qing China, 1909–1911." *Modern China* 17, no. 3 (July): 389–417.

Ho Ping-ti. 1962. *The Ladder of Success in Imperial China.* New York: Columbia University Press.

Hosie, Alexander. 1897. *Three Years in Western China.* 2nd ed. London: George Philip & Son.

————. 1914. *On the Trail of the Opium Poppy.* 2 vols. London: George Philip & Son.

————. 1922. *Szechwan: Its Products, Industries, and Resources.* London: George Philip & Son.

Hou Shaoxuan and Yan Qiu. 1981. "Gelaohui de yuanqi yu Qing wangchao dui ta de zhenya" (Reasons for the rise of the Gelaohui and the attempts of the Qing dynasty to suppress it). In *Sichuan baolu fengyun lu* (A record of the Railroad Protection storm in Sichuan), ed. Zhengxie Sichuansheng wenshi ziliao yanjiu weiyuanhui and Sichuansheng renmin zhengfu wenshi yanjiuguan. Chengdu: Sichuan renmin chubanshe.

Hsiao, Kung-chuan. 1960. *Rural China: Imperial Control in Nineteenth Century China*. Seattle: University of Washington Press.

———. 1975. *A Modern China and a New World: K'ang Yu-wei, Reformer and Utopian, 1858–1927*. Seattle: University of Washington Press.

Hu Lisan. 1985. "Yang Rui." In *Sichuan jinxiandai renwu zhuan* (Biographies from modern and contemporary Sichuan), ed. Ren Yimin, 1: 75–80. Chengdu: Sichuansheng shehuikexue chubanshe.

Hu Shi laiwang shuxin xuan (Selected letters to and from Hu Shi), vol. 1. 1983. Ed. Zhongguo shehui kexueyuan. Hong Kong: Zhonghua shuju.

Huang Liu-hung. 1984. *A Complete Book Concerning Happiness and Benevolence*. Trans. and ed. Djang Chu. Tucson: University of Arizona Press for the Association for Asian Studies.

Huang, Philip C. C. 1996. *Civil Justice in China: Representation and Practice in the Qing*. Stanford: Stanford University Press.

Huang Suisheng. 1962. "Tongmenghui zai Sichuan de huodong" (The activities of the Revolutionary Alliance in Sichuan). In *Xinhai geming huiyilu* (Memoirs of the 1911 Revolution), ed. Zhongguo renmin xieshang huiyi, 3: 129–44. Beijing: Zhonghua shuju.

———. 1964. "Zhou Shanpei de yi sheng" (The life of Zhou Shanpei). *Sichuan wenshi ziliao xuanji* 13: 187–95.

Hubbard, George D. 1923. "The Geographical Setting of Chengtu." *Bulletin of the Geographical Society of Philadelphia* 21, no. 4 (Oct.): 109–39.

Hutson, James. 1915. *Mythical and Practical in Szechwan*. Shanghai: National Review Office for the China Inland Mission.

———. 1921. "The Present Environment of the Chinese Church." *West China Missionary News* 23, no. 10 (Oct.): 16–21.

Hyatt, Irwin. 1964. "The Chengtu Riots (1895): Myths and Politics." *Papers on China* 18: 26–54.

Ichiko, Chūzō. 1968. "The Role of the Gentry, an Hypothesis." In *China in Revolution: The First Phase, 1900–1913*, ed. Mary Clabaugh Wright, 297–318. New Haven: Yale University Press.

———. 1980. "Political and Institutional Reform, 1901–11." In *The Cambridge History of China*, vol. 11, *Late Ch'ing, 1800–1911*, pt. II, ed. John K. Fairbank and Kwang-ching Liu, 375–415. Cambridge, Eng.: Cambridge University Press.

Jansen, Marius B. 1975. *Japan and China: From War to Peace, 1894–1972*. Chicago: Rand McNally.

Jiang Mengbi. 1991. "Chunxi lu de youlai yu fazhan" (Chunxi Road's genesis and development). *Jinjiang wenshi ziliao* 1: 5–13.

Jiaowu jiao'an dang (Documents on anti-Christian incidents), vols. 5–6. 1974. Taibei: Zhongyang yanjiuyuan jindaishi yanjiusuo.

Jin Han (pseud.). 1986. "Qingmo nengyuan Zhou Xiaohuai [Shanpei]" (Zhou Xiaohuai, an able official of the late Qing era). *Longmenzhen* 6, no. 5 (May): 40–61.

Jin Huihai. 1987. "Yang Wei." In *Sichuan jinxiandai renwu zhuan* (Biographies from modern and contemporary Sichuan), ed. Ren Yimin, 3: 98–102. Chengdu: Sichuan daxue chubanshe.

———. 1988. "Huang Jilu." In *Sichuan jinxiandai renwu zhuan* (Biographies from modern and contemporary Sichuan), ed. Ren Yimin, 5: 160–64. Chengdu: Sichuan daxue chubanshe.

Judge, Joan. 1996. *Print and Politics: 'Shibao' and the Culture of Reform in Late Qing China*. Stanford: Stanford University Press.

Kamachi, Noriko. 1981. *Reform in China: Huang Tsun-hsien and the Japanese Model*. Cambridge, Mass.: Council on East Asian Studies, Harvard University.

Kapp, Robert A. 1973. *Szechwan and the Chinese Republic*. New Haven: Yale University Press.

Kemp, E. G. 1909. *The Face of China*. London: Chatto & Windus.

Kilborn, O. L. 1920. "Historical Sketch." In *Our West China Mission*, 29–58. Toronto: Missionary Society of the Methodist Church.

Kirby, William C. 1995. "China Unincorporated: Company Law and Business Enterprise in Twentieth-Century China." *Journal of Asian Studies* 54, no. 1 (Feb.): 43–63.

Köll, Elisabeth. 1997. "Regional Enterprise in Modern China: The Da Sheng Cotton Mills in Nantong, 1895–1926." Ph.D. diss., Oxford University.

Kuhn, Philip A. 1975. "Local Self-Government Under the Republic: Problems of Control, Autonomy, and Mobilization." In *Conflict and Control in Late Imperial China*, ed. Frederic Wakeman, Jr., and Carolyn Grant, 257–98. Berkeley: University of California Press.

———. 1990. *Soulstealers: The Chinese Sorcery Scare of 1768*. Cambridge, Mass.: Harvard University Press.

Kwong, Luke S. K. 1984. *A Mosaic of the Hundred Days: Personalities, Politics, and Ideas of 1898*. Cambridge, Mass.: Council on East Asian Studies, Harvard University.

Lai Shuqing. 1989. *Qingmo jingcha zhidu de changshe yu shiban* (The establishment and trial of the late Qing police system). Taibei: Jingshi shuju.

Lary, Diana. 1985. *Warlord Soldiers: Chinese Common Soldiers, 1911–1937.* Cambridge, Eng.: Cambridge University Press.

Lees, Andrew. 1985. *Cities Perceived: Urban Society in European and American Thought, 1820–1940.* New York: Columbia University Press.

Legendre, A.-F. 1906. *Deux années au Setchouen.* Paris: Plon-Nourit.

Li Jieren. 1947a. "Haorenjia" (Good guy). Originally written in 1924 and published in a periodical in Chengdu. Revised by the author and made the title story in a collection of his short stories published in Shanghai by Zhonghua shuju in 1947. My notes refer to the page numbers in this edition, which was photographically reprinted in Hong Kong by Daxue shenghuoshe.

——. 1947b. "Shimin de ziwei" (Self-protection in the city). In *Haorenjia*, by Li Jieren, 124–35. Shanghai: Zhonghua shuju.

——. 1956. *Baofengyuqian* (Before the storm). Beijing: Zuojia chubanshe.

——. 1980. *Dabo* (The great wave). 4 parts. In vol. 2 of *Li Jieren xuanji* (Selected works). Chengdu: Sichuan renmin chubanshe.

——. 1986a. "Zhuinian Liu Shizhi xiansheng" (In memory of Mr. Liu Shizhi). Originally published in *Fengtu shizhi* 1, no. 6 (1946). Reprinted in vol. 5 of *Li Jieren xuanji* (Selected works), 49–81. Chengdu: Sichuan renmin chubanshe.

——. 1986b. "Weicheng zhuiyi" (Memoirs of an endangered city). Originally published in *Xin Zhonghua* 5, nos. 1–6 (1937). Reprinted in vol. 5 of *Li Jieren xuanji* (Selected works), 96–148. Chengdu: Sichuan renmin chubanshe.

——. 1987. *Sishui weilan* (Ripples across stagnant water). Originally published in Shanghai by Zhonghua shuju in 1936. Revised by the author and republished by Zuojia chubanshe in 1955. My notes refer to the page numbers in a critical edition (*huijiaoben*) published in Chengdu by the Sichuan wenyi chubanshe in 1987.

Li Mei. 1990. "My Father Li Jieren." In Li Jieren, *Ripples Across Stagnant Water* (English trans. of Li Jieren 1987), 13–25. Beijing: Chinese Literature Press.

Li Mingxin. 1981. "Lixianpai yu shibing yundong he Gelao wuzhuang" (The constitutionalist faction and the officers movement, and arming the Elder Brothers). In *Sichuan baolu fengyun lu* (A record of the Railroad Protection storm in Sichuan), ed. Zhengxie Sichuansheng wenshi ziliao yanjiu weiyuanhui and Sichuansheng renmin zhengfu wenshi yanjiuguan. Chengdu: Sichuan renmin chubanshe.

Li Xiaoti. 1992. *Qingmo de xiaceng shehui qimeng yundong, 1901–1911* (Lower-class enlightenment in the late Qing period). Taipei: Zhongyang yenjiu yuan, Jindaishi yanjiu suo.

Lin Baoqun. Petitions to the Interior Ministry. 1912. Second Historical Archives, Beiyang Interior Ministry materials, file no. 1001/2550.

Lin Dianxiang. Ca. 1908. Investigation of fourteen counties in the East Sichuan circuit. First Historical Archives, Zhao Erxun materials, file no. 492.

Lin Kongyi, ed. 1982. *Chengdu zhuzhici* (Chengdu bamboo-branch poetry). Chengdu: Sichuan renmin chubanshe.

Lin Nengshi. 1970. "Qingji Hunan de xinzheng yundong (1894–1898)" (The late Qing New Policies movement in Hunan). Master's thesis, National Taiwan University.

Link, E. Perry. 1981. *Mandarin Ducks and Butterflies: Popular Fiction in Early Twentieth-Century Chinese Cities*. Berkeley: University of California Press.

Little, Archibald. 1910. *Gleanings from 50 Years in China*. London: Sampson, Low, Marston.

Liu Hangchen xiansheng fangwen jilu (The reminiscences of Mr. Liu Hangchen). 1990. Taipei: Zhongyang yanjiu yuan, Jindaishi yanjiu suo.

Liu Ts'un-yan. 1984. "Introduction: 'Middlebrow' in Perspective." In *Chinese Middlebrow Fiction: From the Ch'ing and Early Republican Eras*, ed. Liu Ts'un-yan, 1–40. Hong Kong: Chinese University Press.

Liu Xianzhi. 1983. *Chengdu Man-Mengzu shilue* (Outline history of Chengdu's Manchus and Mongols). Chengdu: Chengdu Man-Meng renmin xuexi weiyuanhui.

———. 1984. "Chengdu Man-Mengzu shihua" (Historical talk on Chengdu's Manchus and Mongols). Unpublished manuscript.

Lu Danlin. 1967. "Wu Shan de shengping" (The life of Wu Shan). *Sichuan wenxian*, no. 59: 11.

Lu Danlin, ed. 1928. *Shizheng quanshu* (A complete book of city administration). Shanghai: Zhonghua quanguo daolu xiehui.

———. 1930. *Daolu quanshu* (A complete book of roads). Shanghai: Zhonghua quanguo daolu xiehui.

Lu Guoji. 1984. *Wode fuqin Lu Zuofu* (My father, Lu Zuofu). Chongqing: Chongqing chubanshe.

Lu Zijian. 1984. *Qingdai Sichuan caizheng shiliao* (Historical materials on Sichuan's finances during the Qing), vol. 1. Chengdu: Sichuansheng shehui kexue yuan chubanshe.

Luo Cairong. 1979. "'Wang jiangjun zaori <kaiche>': Jinian Yang Sen jiangjun" ("Hoping the general starts his car soon": In memory of General Yang Sen). In *Yang Sen jiangjun jinian ji* (Collected writings in memory of General Yang Sen), 434–40. Taibei: Yang Sen jiangjun jinian ji bianji xiaozu.

Luo Ergang. 1945. *Lüying bingzhi* (The Army of the Green Standard). Chongqing: Shangwu yinshuguan.

Ma Xuanwei and Xiao Bo. 1989. *Yang Sen.* Chengdu: Sichuan renmin chubanshe.

Ma Yanhu. 1989. "Yiju hua" (One sentence). *Chengdushi Yisilanjiao xiehui hexun*, no. 9 (July): 40.

MacKinnon, Stephen R. 1975. "Police Reform in Late Ch'ing Chihli." *Ch'ing-shih Wen-t'i* 3, no. 4 (Dec.): 82–99.

———. 1980. *Power and Politics in Late Imperial China: Yuan Shi-kai in Beijing and Tianjin, 1901–1908.* Berkeley: University of California Press.

———. 1983. "A Late Qing-GMD-PRC Connection: Police as an Arm of the Modern Chinese State." *Selected Papers in Asian Studies* (Western Conference of the Association for Asian Studies), n.s. 14.

Mann, Susan. 1984. "Urbanization and Historical Change in China." *Modern China* 10, no. 1 (Jan.): 79–113.

Mao Dun. 1992. *Rainbow.* Trans. Madeleine Zelin. Berkeley: University of California Press.

McCord, Edward A. 1993. *The Power of the Gun: The Emergence of Modern Chinese Warlordism.* Berkeley: University of California Press.

McIsaac, Mary Lee. 1994. "The Limits of Chinese Nationalism: Workers in Wartime Chongqing, 1937–1945." Ph.D. diss., Yale University.

Meijer, Marinus J. 1950. *The Introduction of Modern Criminal Law in China.* Batavia: De Unie.

Miller, Wilbur R. 1973. *Cops and Bobbies: Police Authority in New York and London, 1830–1870.* Chicago: University of Chicago Press.

Min Tu-ki. 1989. *National Polity and Local Power: The Transformation of Late Imperial China.* Ed. Philip A. Kuhn and Timothy Brook. Cambridge, Mass.: Council on East Asian Studies, Harvard University.

Minshi ribao (Gaze of the people daily). 1921–29. Chengdu.

Morrison, Esther. 1959. "The Modernization of the Confucian Bureaucracy: A Historical Study of Public Administration." Ph.D. diss., Radcliffe College.

Mote, F. W. 1977. "The Transformation of Nanking, 1350–1400." In *The City in Late Imperial China*, ed. G. William Skinner, 101–53. Stanford: Stanford University Press.

Myers, Ramon H. 1967. "The Usefulness of Local Gazeteers [*sic*] for the Study of Modern Chinese Economic History: Szechuan Province during the Ch'ing and Republican Periods." *Tsing Hua Journal of Chinese Studies* n.s. 6, no. 1/2 (Dec.): 72–102.

Naquin, Susan. *Millenarian Rebellion in China: The Eight Trigrams of 1813*. New Haven: Yale University Press, 1976.

Niimura Yōko. 1983. "Shinmatsu Shisenshō ni okeru kyokushi no rekishiteki seikaku" (The historical character of bureau managers in late Qing Sichuan). *Tōyōgakuhō* 64, no. 3–4 (Mar.): 103–34.

Ocko, Jonathan. 1983. *Bureaucratic Reform in Provincial China: Ting Jih-ch'ang in Restoration Kiangsu, 1867–1870*. Cambridge, Mass.: Council on East Asian Studies, Harvard University.

Pa Chin (Ba Jin). 1989. *Family*. Prospect Heights, Ill.: Waveland Press.

Pang Xiaoyi and Dai Wending. 1988. "Sichuan shenghui jingchaju shimo" (An account of the Sichuan provincial capital police bureau). In *Shaocheng wenshi ziliao xuanji* 1: 43–56.

Pomeranz, Kenneth. 1993. *The Making of a Hinterland: State, Society, and Economy in Inland North China, 1853–1937*. Berkeley: University of California Press.

Powell, Ralph. 1955. *The Rise of Chinese Military Power, 1895–1912*. Princeton: Princeton University Press.

Prazniak, Roxann. 1981. "Community and Protest in Rural China: Tax Resistance and County-Village Politics on the Eve of the 1911 Revolution." Ph.D. diss., University of California, Davis.

Qi Ren (pseud.). 1913. "Sichuan jingcha yange ji" (A record of the development of Sichuan's police). *Sichuan shenghui jingcha yuebao*, nos. 1–2.

Qiao Cheng. n.d. "Zhou Xiaohuai [Shanpei] tan 'Wu Xu weixin' zhong de Liu Guangdi" (Zhou Xiaohuai discusses Liu Guangdi's actions during the 1898 reforms). Clipping in the author's possession from *Wenshi zazhi*, a publication of the Sichuansheng wenshiguan.

Qiao Shaoxin. 1984. "Zhou Xiaohuai [Shanpei] zishu wangshi ji" (Zhou Xiaohuai discusses events of the past). *Chengdu wenshi ziliao xuanji* 6: 72–75.

Qiao Shunan et al. n.d. (ca. 1908). Private letter in regard to prostitution in Chengdu. First Historical Archives, Zhao Erxun materials, file no. 322.

Qingmo choubei lixian dang'an shiliao. 1979. (Archival and historical materials on the late Qing constitutional preparations). 2 vols. Ed. Gugong bowuyuan, Ming-Qing dang'anbu. Beijing: Zhonghua shuju.

Rankin, Mary Backus. 1986. *Elite Activism and Political Transformation in China, Zhejiang Province, 1865–1911.* Stanford: Stanford University Press.

Reed, Bradly W. 1995. "Money and Justice: Clerks, Runners, and the Magistrate's Court in Late Imperial Sichuan." *Modern China* 21, no. 3 (July): 345–82.

Report in response to charges from the provincial assembly. n.d. (ca. 1910). First Historical Archives, Zhao Erxun materials, file no. 343. This document is written from the perspective of Zhou Zhaoxiang, although it may have been written for Zhou by a supporter within the provincial government.

Résumés of Sichuan police officers. n.d. (ca. 1909). First Historical Archives, Interior Ministry materials, file no. 286.

Reynolds, Douglas R. 1993. *China, 1898–1912: The Xinzheng Revolution and Japan.* Cambridge, Mass.: Council on East Asian Studies, Harvard University.

Rhoads, Edward J. M. 1975. *China's Republican Revolution: The Case of Kwangtung, 1895–1913.* Cambridge, Mass.: Harvard University Press.

Rogaski, Ruth. 1999. "Hygienic Modernity in Tianjin." In *Remaking the Chinese City: Modernity and National Identity, 1900–1950,* ed. Joseph W. Esherick, 30–46. Honolulu: University of Hawaii Press.

Ross, Edward A. 1912. *The Changing Chinese: The Conflict of Oriental and Western Cultures in China.* New York: Century.

Rowe, William T. 1984. *Hankow: Commerce and Society in a Chinese City, 1796–1889.* Stanford: Stanford University Press.

———. 1989. *Hankow: Conflict and Community in a Chinese City, 1796–1895.* Stanford: Stanford University Press.

Schoppa, R. Keith. 1982. *Chinese Elites and Political Change: Zhejiang Province in the Early Twentieth Century.* Cambridge, Mass.: Harvard University Press.

Schwartz, Benjamin. 1964. *In Search of Wealth and Power: Yen Fu and the West.* Cambridge, Mass.: Harvard University Press.

Seidensticker, Edward. 1983. *Low City, High City: Tokyo from Edo to the Earthquake.* New York: Alfred A. Knopf.

Sennett, Richard. 1994. *Flesh and Stone: The Body and the City in Western Civilization.* New York: W. W. Norton.

Service, John S., ed. 1989. *Golden Inches: The China Memoir of Grace Service.* Berkeley: University of California Press.

Shao, Qin. 1994. "Making Political Culture: The Case of Nantong, 1894–1930." Ph.D. diss., Michigan State University.

Shao Ying. 1986. "Chubanjia Fan Kongzhou" (The publisher Fan Kongzhou). *Chengdu zhi tongxun* 10, no. 3: 55–59.

Shao Yun. 1988. "Chengdu 'Paoge' Shilue" (A rough history of Chengdu's "gowned brothers"). *Chengdu zhi tongxun* 16, no. 1: 55–65.

Sheehan, Brett. 1999. "Urban Identity and Urban Networks in Cosmopolitan Cities: Banks and Bankers in Tianjin, 1900–1937." In *Remaking the Chinese City: Modernity and National Identity, 1900–1950,* ed. Joseph W. Esherick, 47–64. Honolulu: University of Hawaii Press.

Shi, Mingzheng. 1993. "Beijing Transforms: Urban Infrastructure, Public Works, and Social Change in the Chinese Capital, 1900–1928." Ph.D. diss., Columbia Univerity.

Shi Tiyuan. 1981. "Zhou Shanpei congzheng suoji" (A glimpse of Zhou Shanpei's official career). *Chongqing wenshi ziliao xuanji* 12: 152–64.

Shu Xincheng. 1934. *Shuyou xinying* (Heartfelt reflections on a trip to Sichuan). Shanghai: Zhonghua shuju.

Shubao (Sichuan news). Chengdu. Published by members of the Sichuan provincial assembly from 1910 to 1911. Twelve issues. Only the inaugural issue (July 14, 1903) is extant in the Sichuan Provincial Library.

Shuxuebao (Sichuan study news). 1898. Thirteen issues.

Sichuan Chengdu disanci shangye quangonghui diaochabiao (Investigative report on the third commercial industrial fair held in Chengdu, Sichuan). 1908. Compiled by the Sichuan Commercial Bureau (Shangwuju). Copy in the Shanghai Municipal Library.

Sichuan dudufu zhengbao (Sichuan military government gazette). Chengdu. 1912.

Sichuan guanbao (Sichuan official gazette). Chengdu. Published by the Sichuan Official Gazette Bureau from the fall of 1904 to the fall of 1911. There were three issues per month until 1911, when six issues per month were published.

Sichuan jingcha geyuan gongguobiao (Evaluations of all Sichuan police officers). First Historical Archives, Police Ministry materials, file no. 71. Quarterly reports from Spring 1903 to Summer 1906 (missing Spring

1906). First Historical Archives, Interior Ministry materials, file no. 312. Quarterly reports from Fall 1906 to Fall 1908.

Sichuan jingwu guanbao (Sichuan police gazette). Chengdu. Published by the Sichuan Police Bureau. 1911. Three issues.

Sichuan jingwu wendu huibian (Compendium of documents concerning Sichuan police matters). Compiled once in the first year of Xuantong (XT1) and twice in the second year (XT2). Six booklets were produced for the year XT1, two for the first half of XT2, and four for the second half of XT2. File no. 312 of the Interior Ministry materials in the First Historical Archives contains two of the booklets from XT1 (no. 2 and no. 4) and three of the booklets from the second half of XT2 (no. 2–4). The Sichuan Provincial Library has the first booklet for XT1 and the second booklet for the first half of XT2.

Sichuan junfa shiliao (Historical materials on Sichuan warlords). 1981–88. 5 vols. Comp. Sichuansheng wenshi yanjiuguan. Chengdu: Sichuan renmin chubanshe.

Sichuansheng dang'anguan, ed. 1985. *Sichuan jiao'an yu yihequan dang'an* (Documents on Sichuan anti-missionary cases and the Boxers). Chengdu: Sichuan renmin chubanshe.

Sichuansheng gexian difang zizhi shiye yu jingji zhuangkuang fenqi baogao (Reports by period on local self-government initiatives and economic conditions from each county in Sichuan province). 1917. Reports from 40 counties are in this collection. Second Historical Archives, Beiyang Government Interior Ministry materials, file no. 977.

Sichuan shenghui gonganju gongzuo baogao (Work report from the Sichuan provincial capital public security bureau). 1934.

Sichuansheng neiwu tongji baogaoshu (Statistical report on the internal affairs of Sichuan province). 1920. The statistics in this report were collected in 1916. A copy of the report is in the Chongqing Library.

Sichuansheng wenshiguan, ed. 1987. *Chengdu chengfang guji kao* (A study of the old walls and neighborhoods of Chengdu). Chengdu: Sichuan renmin chubanshe.

Sichuan tongsheng jingcha zhangcheng (Regulations of the Sichuan province-wide police). 1903. First Historical Archives, Police Ministry materials, file no. 179.

Sichuan zhengbao (Sichuan political gazette). Chengdu. Published by the office of the Sichuan governor. 1913–14. Wu Yu was editor for a time.

Simkin, Robert L. 1911. "The Formal Opening of the Chengtu Y.M.C.A." *West China Missionary News* 13, no. 1 (Jan.): 4–7.

Skinner, G. William. 1964/65. "Marketing and Social Structure in Rural China." *Journal of Asian Studies* 24, no. 1: 3–43; no. 2: 195–228; and no. 3: 363–99.

———. 1987. "Sichuan's Population in the Nineteenth Century: Lessons from Disaggregated Data." *Late Imperial China* 8, no. 1 (June): 1–79.

Skinner, G. William, ed. 1977. *The City in Late Imperial China*. Stanford: Stanford University Press.

Spence, Jonathan. 1980. *To Change China: Western Advisers in China, 1620–1960*. New York: Penguin Books.

Stapleton, Kristin E. 1993. "Police Reform in a Late-Imperial Chinese City: Chengdu, 1902–1911." Ph.D. diss., Harvard University.

———. 1995. "Thick-Black Studies and Bamboo-Branch Poetry in Republican-Era Chengdu." Unpublished paper presented at the annual meeting of the Association for Asian Studies, Apr. 1995.

———. 1996. "Urban Politics in an Age of 'Secret Societies': The Cases of Shanghai and Chengdu." *Republican China* 22, no. 1 (Nov.): 23–63.

———. 1997. "County Administration in Late-Qing Sichuan: Conflicting Models of Rural Policing." *Late Imperial China* 18, no. 1 (June): 100–132.

———. 1998. "The Meanings of Chunxi Road: Street Culture in Republican Chengdu." Unpublished paper presented at the annual meeting of the Association for Asian Studies, Mar. 1998.

Strand, David. 1989. *Rickshaw Beijing: City People and Politics in the 1920s*. Berkeley: University of California Press.

Su Facheng. 1985. "Guanyu 'Xinchuanbao' de yixie qingkuang" (Concerning some circumstances surrounding *New Sichuan News*). *Chengdu baokan shiliao zhuanji* 1: 33–35.

Tang Juecong. 1991. "Wang Jianming yu Chengdu shanghui" (Wang Jianming and the Chengdu Chamber of Commerce). *Jinjiang wenshi ziliao*, no. 1: 135–44.

Tang Shaowu, Li Zhusan, and Jiang Xiangchen. 1989. "Jiefang qian Chongqing de paoge" (Chongqing's Gowned Brothers before the Liberation). *Chongqing wenshi ziliao* 31: 131.

Tao Liangsheng. n.d. (ca. 1978). "WanQing zhi Minguo zhi mo Wulao Qixian qinling ji" (A personal account of the Five Elders and Seven Sages from the late Qing to the end of the Republic). Unpublished manuscript.

Taylor, William R., ed. 1991. *Inventing Times Square: Commerce and Culture at the Crossroads of the World*. New York: Russell Sage Foundation.

Thompson, Roger R. 1995. *China's Local Councils in the Age of Constitutional Reform, 1898–1911*. Cambridge, Mass.: Council on East Asian Studies, Harvard University.

Tō-A dōbunkai. 1917. *Shina shōbetsu zenshi*, vol. 6, *Sichuan*. Tokyo: Tō-A dōbunkai.

Tongsu huabao (Colloquial pictorial news). 1909–12. Chengdu.

Treudley, Mary Bosworth. 1971. *The Men and Women of Chung Ho Ch'ang*. Taibei: Orient Cultural Service.

Tsin, Michael Tsang-woon. 1990. "The Cradle of Revolution: Politics and Society in Canton, 1900–1927." Ph.D. diss., Columbia University.

———. 1999. "Canton Remapped." In *Remaking the Chinese City: Modernity and National Identity, 1900–1950*, ed. Joseph W. Esherick, 19–29. Honolulu: University of Hawaii Press.

Vale, J. 1902. "Expectants." *West China Missionary News* 4, no. 1 (Jan.): 6–10.

———. 1904. "The Sz-Chuan Police Force." *West China Missionary News* 6, nos. 3–6 (Mar.–June): 56–59, 82–86, 106–11, and 125–27.

———. 1905. "The Chinese Census: The Method of Taking It." *West China Missionary News* 7, nos. 1–3 (Jan.-Mar.): 6–7, 38–39, and 54–55.

———. 1907. "Beggar Life in Chentu [*sic*]." *West China Missionary News* 9, no. 4 (Apr.): 8–11; no. 7 (July): 7–10.

Van Slyke, Lyman. 1988. *Yangtze: Nature, History, and the River*. Reading, Mass.: Addison-Wesley.

Wakeman, Frederic Jr. 1991. "Models of Historical Change: The Chinese State and Society, 1839–1989." In *Perspectives on Modern China: Four Anniversaries*, ed. Kenneth Lieberthal et al., 68–102. Armonk, N.Y.: M. E. Sharpe.

———. 1995. *Policing Shanghai, 1927–1937*. Berkeley: University of California Press.

Wang Di. 1993. *Kuachu fengbi de shijie: Changjiang shangyou quyu shehui yanjiu, 1644–1911* (Out of a closed world: research on society in the upper Yangtze macroregion). Beijing: Zhonghua shuju.

Wang Jiajian. 1984. *Qingmo Minchu woguo jingcha zhidu xiandaihua de licheng (1901–1928)* (The progress of the modernization of Chinese police organization in the late Qing and early Republican eras). Taibei: Taiwan shangwu yinshuguan.

Wang Liankui. 1979. "Zhuisui Huigong wushiba nian" (Fifty-eight years of following Yang Sen). In *Yang Sen jiangjun jinian ji* (Collected writings in memory of General Yang Sen), 449–46. Taibei: Yang Sen jiangjun jinian ji bianji xiaozu.

Wang Lüping and Cheng Qi. 1993. *Sichuan baokan jilan* (Guide to Sichuanese newspapers and periodicals), vol. 1, *1897–1930*. Chengdu: Chengdu keji daxue chubanshe.

Wang Renwen. 1911. Memorial asking permission for Police Superintendent Zhou Zhaoxiang to inspect rural police in Manchuria. Dated XT3.6.5. First Historical Archives, Interior Ministry materials, file no. 289.

Wang Zongli. 1986. "Aiguo aimin de lao yingxiong Yu Yuan lieshi" (The martyr Yu Yuan, patriotic and loving old hero). *Chengdu wenshi ziliao xuanji* 14: 70–79.

Watt, John R. 1972. *The District Magistrate in Late Imperial China.* New York: Columbia University Press.

Wei Yingtao, ed. 1990. *Sichuan jindaishi gao* (A draft history of Sichuan in modern times). Chengdu: Sichuan renmin chubanshe.

———. 1991. *Xinhai geming yu Sichuan shehui* (The 1911 Revolution and Sichuan society). Chengdu: Chengdu chubanshe.

Wei Yingtao and Zhao Qing, eds. 1981. *Sichuan xinhai geming shiliao* (Historical materials concerning the 1911* Revolution in Sichuan). 2 vols. Chengdu: Sichuan renmin chubanshe.

Wen Juntian. 1935. *Zhongguo baojia zhidu* (The Chinese *baojia* system). Shanghai: Shangwu yinshuguan.

West China Missionary News. 1899–1937. Chongqing and Chengdu.

Westney, D. Eleanor. 1987. *Imitation and Innovation: The Transfer of Western Organizational Patterns to Meiji Japan.* Cambridge, Mass.: Harvard University Press.

Wheatley, Paul. 1971. *The Pivot of the Four Quarters: A Preliminary Enquiry into the Origins and Character of the Ancient Chinese City.* Chicago: Aldine.

Will, Pierre-Etienne. 1990. *Bureaucracy and Famine in Eighteenth-Century China.* Trans. Elbord Forster. Stanford: Stanford University Press.

Wilson, Elizabeth. 1991. *The Sphinx in the City: Urban Life, the Control of Disorder, and Women.* London: Virago Press.

Wilson, James Q. 1968. *Varieties of Police Behavior.* Cambridge, Mass.: Harvard University Press.

Wright, Arthur F. 1977. "The Cosmology of the Chinese City." In *The City in Late Imperial China,* ed. G. William Skinner, 33–73. Stanford: Stanford University Press.

Wright, Mary Clabaugh. 1968. "Introduction: The Rising Tide of Change." In *China in Revolution: The First Phase, 1900–1913,* ed. Mary Clabaugh Wright, 1–63. New Haven: Yale University Press.

Wu Guangjun. 1985. "Xinhai geming hou de Sichuan junshi xunjing zong-
jian—Yang Wei" (Sichuan's chief of military police after the 1911 Revolution—Yang Wei). *Sichuan wenshi ziliao* 35: 69–74.

Wu Yu riji (Wu Yu's Diary). 1984. 2 vols. Chengdu: Sichuan renmin chubanshe.

Wu Yuzhang. 1985. "Liyong 'zizhi' jiangtai zuo xuanchuan gongzuo" (Using
the 'self-government' speakers' platform to do propaganda work). In *Sichuan junfa shiliao* (Historical materials on Sichuan warlords), ed. Sichuansheng wenshiguan, 3: 1–4. Chengdu: Sichuan renmin chubanshe.

Wyman, Judith. 1993. "Social Change, Anti-Foreignism and Revolution in
China: Chongqing Prefecture, 1870s to 1911." Ph.D. diss., University of
Michigan.

———. 1997. "The Ambiguities of Chinese Antiforeignism: Chongqing,
1870–1900." *Late Imperial China* 18, no. 2 (Dec.): 86–122.

Xian Ning. 1980. "Sichuan zuizao de gonglu he changtu qiche" (Sichuan's
earliest highway and long-distance bus service). *Lishi zhishi*, no. 3: 5–6.

Xiang Chunwu. 1988. "Sichuan junfa dui xinwen shiye de kongzhi he cui-
can" (Sichuan warlords' control over and devastation of the newspaper
industry). *Sichuan junfa shiliao* (Materials on Sichuan warlords) 5: 161–84.

Xiao Denghui. 1989. "WanQing Minguo Sichuan jingcha jiaoyu yu xunlian"
(Police education and training in late Qing and Republican Sichuan).
Gongan zhi shiliao, no. 1: 8–13.

Xie Fang. 1987. "Fan Kongzhou." In *Sichuan jinxiandai renwu zhuan* (Biographies from modern and contemporary Sichuan), ed. Ren Yimin, 4: 177–
82. Chengdu: Sichuan daxue chubanshe.

Xiliang yigao (The papers of Xiliang). 1959. 2 vols. Ed. Zhongguo kexueyuan
lishi yanjiusuo. Beijing: Zhonghua shuju.

Xinhai gemingqian shinianjian minbian dang'an shiliao (Archival historical
materials on popular uprisings in the ten years before the 1911 Revolution). 1985. Ed. Diyi lishi dang'anguan. Beijing: Zhonghua shuju.

Xiong Kewu. 1962. "Xinhaiqian wo canjia de Sichuan jici wuzhuang qiyi"
(Several armed uprisings I participated in in Sichuan before 1911). In *Xinhai geming huiyilu* (Memoirs of the 1911 Revolution), ed. Zhongguo renmin xieshang huiyi, vol. 3: 1–25. Beijing: Zhonghua shuju.

———. 1980. "Shudang shigao" (Draft history of the Sichuan party). *Xinhai
geming shi congkan* 2: 167–82.

Xiong Zhuoyun. 1965. "Fandong tongzhi shiqi de Chengdu jingcha"
(Chengdu's police during the era of reactionary authority). *Sichuan wenshi ziliao xuanji* 16: 101–20.

————. 1984. "Yijiusanliunian 'Chengdu Dachuan fandian shijian' neimu" (The inside story of the 1936 "Chengdu Great Sichuan hotel incident"). *Chengdu wenshi ziliao xuanji* 7 (Dec.): 82–92.

Xu Pu. 1986. "Song Yuren." In *Sichuan jinxiandai renwu zhuan* (Biographies from modern and contemporary Sichuan), ed. Ren Yimin, 2: 185–90. Chengdu: Sichuansheng shehuikexue chubanshe.

Xuantong yuannian Shengcheng jingqu diyici diaocha hukou yilanbiao (Chart of the first statistical report of the first year of Xuantong on the population of the police districts in the provincial capital). n.d. (1909). First Historical Archives, Zhao Erxun materials, file no. 308.

Yamamoto Susumu. 1994. "Shindai kōki Shisen ni okeru zaisei kaikaku to kōkyoku" (The financial reformation and public bureaus in Sichuan during the Qing period). *Shigaku zasshi* 53, no. 7 (July): 59–78.

Yang Bingde, ed. 1993. *Zhongguo jindai chengshi yu jianzhu, 1840–1949* (China's modern cities and architecture). Beijing: Zhongguo jianzhu gongye chubanshe.

Yang, S. C. 1933/34. "The Revolution in Szechwan, 1911–1912." *Journal of the West China Border Research Society* 1: 64–90.

Yang Sen. 1979. "Jiushi yiwang" (Recalling the past at age 90). In *Yang Sen jiangjun jinian ji* (Collected writings in memory of General Yang Sen), 79–124. Taibei: Yang Sen jiangjun jinian ji bianji xiaozu.

Yang Sen jiangjun jinian ji (Collected writings in memory of General Yang Sen). Taibei: Yang Sen jiangjun jinian ji bianji xiaozu.

"Yang Sen xiansheng fangwen jilu." 1963. Transcript of oral history interview with Yang Sen, in the archives of the Modern History Institute, Academia Sinica, Taiwan.

Yang Wanyun. 1979. "Daonian fuqin" (In memory of my father). In *Yang Sen jiangjun jinian ji* (Collected writings in memory of General Yang Sen), 421–23. Taibei: Yang Sen jiangjun jinian ji bianji xiaozu.

Yoshizawa Seiichirō. 1990. "Kōsho matsu Tenshin ni okeru junkei sōsetsu to minshū" (The establishment of police and the people in late Guangxu Tianjin). Master's thesis, Tokyo University.

Yukun. 1980. "Rongcheng jiashu" (Letters home from Hibiscus City [Chengdu]). In *Xinhai gemingshi congkan* (Materials on the history of the 1911 Revolution), ed. Qin Quanzheng and Du Chunhe, vol 1: 203–15. Beijing: Zhonghua shuju.

Zelin, Madeleine. 1984. *The Magistrate's Tael: Rationalizing Fiscal Reform in Eighteenth-Century Ch'ing China*. Berkeley: University of California Press.

Zhang, Yingjin. 1996. *The City in Modern Chinese Literature and Film: Configurations of Space, Time, and Gender*. Stanford: Stanford University Press.

Zhang Zhongli, ed. 1990. *Jindai Shanghai chengshi yanjiu* (Research on Modern Shanghai). Shanghai: Shanghai renmin chubanshe.

Zhao Qing. 1990. *Paoge yu tufei* (Gowned brothers and local bandits). Tianjin: Tianjin renmin chubanshe.

Zheng Ping. 1992. "Minguo shiqi Sichuan Gelaohui de manyan yu yingxiang" (The spread and influence of Sichuan's Gelaohui in the Republican period). Master's thesis, Nanjing University.

Zhengzhi guanbao (Political gazette). Beijing. 1907–11.

Zhong Maoxuan. 1984. *Liu Shiliang waizhuan* (Unofficial biography of Liu Shiliang). Chengdu: Sichuan renmin chubanshe.

Zhong Qiming. 1990. "Manhua 'liusan' jinyanjie" (Speaking of the 'June 3rd' anti-opium day). *Shaocheng wenshi ziliao* 3 (Dec.): 123–28.

Zhou Bangdao. 1981. Biography of Xu Zixiu, in Zhou Bangdao, *Jindai jiaoyu xianjin zhuanlue* (Biographies of pioneers in modern education), 242–44. Taibei: Zhonghua wenhua daxue chubanbu.

Zhou Kaiqing. 1964. *Sichuan yu Xinhai geming* (Sichuan and the 1911 Revolution). Taibei: Sichuan wenxian yanjiushe.

——. 1972a and 1974. *Minguo Chuanshi jiyao* (Chronicle of Sichuan events during the Republic). 2 vols. Taibei: Sichuan wenxianshe.

——. 1972b. *Sichuan jingji zhi* (Sichuan economic annals). Taibei: Taiwan shangwu yinshuguan.

——. 1976. *Shushi congtan* (Collected talk about Sichuan matters). Taibei: Sichuan wenxian zazhishe.

Zhou Shanpei. n.d. (ca. 1908). Untitled memo addressing charges of misconduct. First Historical Archives, Zhao Erxun materials, file no. 309. There is no signature or seal on this document, but the content indicates its author clearly.

——. 1938a. "Xinhai Sichuan shibian zhi wo" (My role in the events of 1911 in Sichuan). Reprinted in *Jindai Zhongguo shiliao congkan* (Collected sources of modern Chinese history), ed. Shen Yunlong, vol. 251: 1–79. Taibei: Wenhai.

——. 1938b. "Zheng *Dabo* zhi wu" (Correcting the mistakes in *The Great Wave*). Reprinted in *Jindai Zhongguo shiliao congkan* (Collected sources of modern Chinese history), ed. Shen Yunlong, vol. 251: 81–108. Taibei: Wenhai.

————. 1957. *Xinhai Sichuan zhenglu qinliji* (An eyewitness account of the struggle over the railroad in Sichuan). Chongqing: Chongqing renmin chubanshe.

————. 1960. "Tan Liang Rengong" (On Liang Qichao). *Wenshi ziliao xuanji* 3: 133–45.

Zhou Xun. 1986. *Shuhai congtan* (Collected talk about Sichuan). Chengdu: Bashu chubanshe.

————. 1987. *Furong huajiu lu* (A record of talking of Chengdu's past). Chengdu: Sichuan renmin chubanshe.

CHARACTER LIST

The entries in this list are ordered strictly letter by letter, ignoring word and syllable breaks.

anmin gongsuo 安民公所

bainian daji 百年大計
bao 保
baoan 保安
baojia 保甲
Baolu tongzhihui 保路同志會
baozheng 保正
Beiyang guanbao 北洋官報
buxue wushu 不學無術

Cai E 蔡鍔
Cen Chunxuan 岑春煊
chang 唱
changji 娼妓
changliaohu 娼遼戶
Chen Baozhen 陳寶箴
Chengdu ribao 成都日報
Chengdu tonglan 成都通覽
Cheng-Hua cheng yishihui 成華
　城議事會
Chen Weixin 陳維新

Chunxi 春熙
Cihuitang 慈惠堂
congliang 從良
cong zhengye 從正業

Dacheng 大成
Da Han gong 大漢公
daigu ren hu 代僱人戶
Da lu gong 大路公
dang 黨
Daolu quanshu 道路全書
daren 大人
Datongshu 大同書
Deng Xiaoke 鄧孝可
Deng Xihou 鄧錫侯
dengyoujuan 燈油捐
dianshi 典史
diaochachu 調查處
dibao (baojia functionary) 地保
Dibao (Capital gazette) 邸報
difang fenting 地方分廳
difang zizhi 地方自治

dongfang 冬防
dongshihui 董事會
Dongwen 東文
Dong Xiujia 董修甲
Duanfang 端方
Duanwu 端午
Dujiangyan 都江堰
duli 督理

Erlang 二郎

fading tuanti 法定團體
Fan Chongshi 范崇實
fangjuan 房捐
fangshenghui 放生會
Fang Xu 方旭
Fan Kongzhou 樊孔周
fatuan 法團
fengshui 風水
fubang 副榜
Fu Qiaocun (Chongju)
   傅樵村(崇矩)
Furongcheng 芙蓉城
fuwei 副委
Fuxing 福興

gaodeng xuetang 高等學堂
Gao Zengjue 高增爵
Gelaohui 哥老會
gonganju 公安局
gongde xin 公德心
gongguan 公館
gongkou 公口
gongsuo 公所
gongtui 公推
guafen 瓜分
guanzhi 官制
gundan 滾蛋
Guolu 嘓嚕

Guomin gongbao 國民公報
Guo Moruo 郭沫若
Guoshiguan 國史館

Haishanghua liezhuan 海上花
   列傳
Haorenjia 好人家
heian 黑暗
He Yuqing 何玉卿
Hongdenghui 紅燈會
Huang Jilu 黃季陸
Huang Zunxian 黃遵憲
Huayang 華陽
huidang 會黨
Hu Jingyi 胡景伊
Hu Lanjia 胡蘭畦
hunshui 渾水
hutong 胡同
huo tui you duo 火腿油多

jia 甲
jianghuhui 江湖會
jiangli gongsuo 講理公所
jiansheng 監生
jianshihu 監視戶
jiaoyu zonghui 教育總會
jiebao 街保
jieyan zongju 戒煙總局
jiezheng 街正
jiliangsuo 濟良所
jimaodian 雞毛店
Jin Bangping 金邦平
jingcha 警察
jingcha zhuyi 警察主義
jingwu xuetang 警務學堂
Jinjiang 錦江
jisushe 寄宿舍
juding 局丁
jue wo liangmin 覺我良民

junfa 軍閥
junyongpiao 軍用票
juren 舉人
juyong 局勇
juzheng 局正

kai fengqi 開風氣
Kang Youwei 康有爲
kuchai 苦差
Kuijun 奎俊

Liang Qichao 梁啓超
Liang Shuming 梁漱溟
Liao Guanyin 廖觀音
Liao Ping 廖平
Li Bing 李冰
Li Hongzhang 李鴻章
Li Jieren 李劼人
liquan 利權
Liu Cunhou 劉存厚
Liu Guangdi 劉光第
Liu Kunyi 劉坤一
Liu Shiliang 劉師亮
Liu Wenhui 劉文輝
Liu Xiang 劉湘
Liu Yubo 劉豫波
Li Yuanhong 黎元洪
lougui 陋規
Lu Guangzhong 路廣鐘
Luo Lun 羅綸
Lu Zuofu 盧作孚

maiguo 賣國
matou 碼頭
mixin 迷信
mingju 名舉
Minsheng 民生

nonghui 農會

nügong xiyisuo 女工習藝所

pai 牌
pangdao 旁道
paoge 袍哥
pingli 評理
Pu Dianjun 蒲殿俊

qi 氣
qigai gongchang 乞丐工廠
Qimeng tongsu bao 啓蒙通俗報
qingjiaohui 清醮會
qingshui 清水
Qingyang 青羊
qiuba 丘八
quangongju 勸工局
quanyechang 勸業場
quanyedao 勸業道
quzheng 區正

renmin yingyou heli zhi liyi 人民
    應有合理之利益
Rongcheng 蓉城

Shaanxijie 陝西街
shakai mondai 社會問題
shangwu caipansuo 商務裁判所
shangwuju 商務局
shangye jiangxisuo 商業講習所
shangye quangonghui 商業
    勸工會
shanren laoye, guoba shengfan
    善人老爺鍋巴賸飯
Shaocheng 少城
Shawan 沙灣
shen 紳
Shenbao 申報
Sheng Xuanhuai 盛宣懷
Shen Jiaben 沈家本

shenshi 紳士
Shengcheng 省城
Shengcheng baojiaju 省城保甲局
Shibao 時報
shique 實缺
shiye jiuguo 實業救國
shizheng gongsuo 市政公所
shizheng gongyijuan 市政公益捐
Shizheng quanshu 市政全書
shoushan zhi qu 首善之區
shoushi 首事
Shubao 蜀報
shuru wenming 輸入文明
Shu Xincheng 舒新城
Shuxuebao 蜀學報
Shuxuehui 蜀學會
Sichuan baolu tongzhihui baogao
　四川保路同志會報告
Sichuan guanbao 四川官報
Sichuan guanbao shuju
　四川官報書局
Sichuan huiguan 四川會館
Sichuan tongsheng jingcha zhangcheng
　四川通省警察章程
siheyuan 四合院
Sishengci 四聖祠
Song Yuren 宋育仁
Sun Fo 孫科
Sun Shaojing 孫少荆
suowei ren panzi 所謂人叛子
Su Zilin 蘇子林

Tao Liangsheng 陶亮生
tianfu zhi guo 天府之國
tixueshi 提學使
tongjichu 統計處
Tongmenghui 同盟會
Tongsu huabao 通俗畫報
Tongsu jiaoyuguan 通俗教育館

tongsu jiaoyushe 通俗教育舍
Tongsu ribao 通俗日報
tongzhijun 同志軍
tuan 團
tuanfa 團閥
tuanlian 團練
Tuanlian baojia zongju 團練
　保甲總局
tudihui 土地會
tudimiao 土地廟

wangguo 亡國
Wang Guangqi 王光祈
Wang Renwen 王人文
Wang Tao 王韜
Wang Zhengting 王正廷
Wang Zuanxu 王纘緒
weijinglü 違警律
weisheng 衛生
weixin 維新
weiyuan 委員
wenming 文明
wenming zhi meiming
　文明之美名
Wenshu 文殊
wuhuawang 梧花王
wulao qixian 五老七賢
Wu Shan 吳山
wuxue youshu 無學有術
Wu Yu 吳虞
Wu Yuzhang 吳玉章

xialiuren 下流人
xialiu shehui 下流社會
xiangyue 鄉約
xiansheng 先生
xiaoyihui 孝義會
Xiliang 錫良
xin 新

xingqiwu canguantuan
  星期五參觀團
Xinhua jie 新化街
xinzheng 新政
Xiong Kewu 熊克武
xiucai 秀才
xiuqiao bulu 修橋補路
xue buzai siyi; wu Chengdu jiu you
  shizhang, wu xiu feiguan yi
  學不在四夷吾成都舊有市長
  吾修廢官矣
xunfangjun 巡防軍
xunjingdao 巡警道
xunjing yubeiying 巡警預備營
Xu Zixiu 徐子休

yamen 衙門
Yang Rui 楊銳
Yang Sen 楊森
Yang Shukan 楊庶堪
Yang Wanyun 楊萬運
Yang Wei 楊維
Yin Changheng 尹昌衡
Yin Changling 尹昌齡
youxue wushu 有學無術
yuebao 約保
Yuelai 悅來
Yu Fenggang 俞風崗
Yu Yuan 于淵

zayuan 雜院
Zhang Jian 張謇
Zhang Lan 張瀾
Zhang Qun 張群
Zhang Zhidong 張之洞

Zhao Erfeng 趙爾豐
Zhao Erxun 趙爾巽
Zhaojuesi 昭覺寺
zhao liangmin yilü kandai
  照良民一律看待
Zhao Xi 趙熙
zhengdao 正道
zhengke 政客
zhengsu 正俗
zhengwei 正委
Zhengwuchu 政務處
zhili zhou 直隸州
zhiyingju 支應局
zhongdeng shehui 中等社會
Zhongguo Guomindang Sichuan
  lüjing tongzhihui 中國國民黨
  四川旅京同志會
Zhonghua pingmin jiaoyu
  cujinhui 中華平民教育
  促進會
Zhonghua quanguo daolu jianshe
  xiehui 中華全國道路建設
  協會
Zhongwai ribao 中外日報
Zhou Shanpei 周善培
Zhou Xun 周詢
Zhou Zhaoxiang 周肇祥
Zhou Zhen 周振
Zhu Shan 朱山
"Ziqiang weishengxue" 自強
  衛生學
zongban 總辦
zong jianshihu 總監視戶
zong jianzheng 總監正
Zunjing 尊經

INDEX

Harvard East Asian Monographs
(* out-of-print)

DATE DUE

ILL (PSV)		
41326925		
4/30/08		